Exploring College Writing

Frameworks for Writing
Series Editor: Martha C. Pennington, Georgia Southern University

The *Frameworks for Writing* series offers books focused on writing and the teaching and learning of writing in educational and real-life contexts. The hallmark of the series is the application of approaches and techniques to writing and the teaching of writing that go beyond those of English literature to draw on and integrate writing with other disciplines, areas of knowledge, and contexts of everyday life. The series entertains proposals for textbooks as well as books for teachers, teacher educators, parents, and the general public. The list includes teacher reference books and student textbooks focused on innovative pedagogy aiming to prepare teachers and students for the challenges of the 21st century.

Published:
The College Writing Toolkit
Tried and Tested Ideas for Teaching College Writing
Edited by Martha C. Pennington and Pauline Burton

The "Backwards" Research Guide for Writers
Using Your Life for Reflection, Connection, and Inspiration
Sonya Huber

Writing Poetry through the Eyes of Science
A Teacher's Guide to Scientific Literacy and Poetic Response
Nancy Gorrell with Erin Colfax

Forthcoming:
Tend Your Garden
Nurturing Motivation in Young Adolescent Writers
Mary Anna Kruch

Becoming a Teacher Who Writes
Let Teaching be Your Writing Muse
Nancy Gorrell

Writing from the Inside
The Power of Reflective Writing in the Classroom
Olivia Archibald and Maureen Hall

Arting, Writing, and Culture
Teaching to the 4th Power
Anna Sumida, Meleanna Meyer, and Miki Maeshiro

Seriously Creative Writing
Stylistic Strategies in Non-Fictional Writing
Sky Marsen

Reflective Writing for English Language Teachers
Thomas S. C. Farrell

Exploring College Writing

Reading, Writing, and Researching across the Curriculum

Dan Melzer

SHEFFIELD OAKVILLE

Published by Equinox Publishing Ltd.

UK: Unit S3, Kelham House, 3 Lancaster Street, Sheffield, South Yorkshire S3 8AF

USA: DBBC, 28 Main Street, Oakville, CT 06779

www.equinoxpub.com

First published 2011

British Library Cataloguing-in-Publication Data

A catalogue record for this book is available from the British Library.

ISBN   978 1 84553 780 7   (hardback)
                978 1 84553 779 1   (paperback)

Library of Congress Cataloging-in-Publication Data

Melzer, Dan.
  Exploring college writing : reading, writing, and researching across
the curriculum / Dan Melzer.
      p. cm.
  Includes bibliographical references and index.
  ISBN 978-1-84553-780-7 -- ISBN 978-1-84553-779-1 (pb)
  1. English language--Rhetoric--Study and teaching. 2. Report
writing--Study and teaching. I. Title.
  PE1404.M45 2011
  808'.06--dc22
                            2011005956

Typeset by Steve Barganski, Sheffield
Printed and bound in Great Britain by Lightning Source UK Ltd, Milton Keynes

Contents

Editor's Preface   xv

Acknowledgments   xvii

To the Reader   1

A "Learn-by-Doing" Approach to Academic Literacies   1
Outstanding Features   3
Content and Organization   4
Writing Activities and Projects   6

Part I: An Introduction to College Writing

1: Expectations for College-Level Writing   11

What is College-Level Writing?   12
    Five Myths about College Writing   14
    Making the Transition to College Writing   16
    Examples of College Writing Assignments   19
    How Do Writing Researchers Define Academic Writing?   21
    College Writing Guides and Rubrics   23
What is "First-Year Writing"?   28
    Five Myths about First-Year Writing   30
Student Writing Case Study: First-Year Writing   34
Examples of Student Writing from First-Year Writing Courses   53
Review of Key Ideas in Chapter 1   54

2: College Writing Situations   55

The Rhetorical Situation and College Writing   56
    Purpose   59
    Audience   59
    Persona   59

Text   60

Context   60

Sample Student Essay: Matt Miles, "Personal Appearance
    and its Implications of Sexuality"   61

Genres as Responses to Rhetorical Situations   68

Sample Student Essay: Feras Sleiman, "Review of *Dying
    to Win: The Strategic Logic of Suicide Terrorism*"   71

Sample Student Essay: David Winchell, "Review:
    The Revolution Will Not Be Televised"   74

Tips for Writing in Academic Genres   76

Common College Rhetorical Strategies   78

Summarizing   78

Synthesizing   81

Analyzing   83

Evaluating   87

Arguing   89

Contrastive Rhetoric: Language Diversity and College Writing   93

Review of Key Ideas in Chapter 2   104

Writing Projects for Part I   106

Writing Project I.1: Literacy History Narrative   106

Writing Project I.2: Writing Inventory   108

Writing Project I.3: Academic Writing Rhetorical Analysis   110

Part II: Exploring Academic Reading, Writing,
    and Researching Processes

3: Academic Writing Processes   115

Exploring Academic Writing Processes   116

Five Myths about College Writing Processes   117

Understanding your Professors' Writing Assignments   120

Finding Topics   125

Drafting and Revising   128

Editing and Proofreading   133

Timed Writing   136

Getting Feedback   139
   Peer Response   139
   Writing Groups   141
   Writing Centers   142
Creating a Writing Portfolio   145
   What is a Writing Portfolio?   145
   Why Do Professors Use Portfolio Evaluation?   146
   What is a Portfolio Cover Letter?   146
Collaborating: Group Writing Projects   147
   Strategies for Group Writing   148
Document Design   150
   Some General Visual Design Principles   153
   Strategies for Creating Effective Web Sites   155
   Integrating Visuals   159
   Common Types of Visuals   160
Review of Key Ideas in Chapter 3   165

4: Academic Reading Processes   **167**

Expectations for College-Level Reading   169
   Contrasting High School and College-Level Reading   169
   Features of College Reading   174
College Reading is Critical Reading   176
Reading and Writing Connections   179
Exploring Academic Reading Processes   181
   Five Myths about College Reading Processes   182
   Prereading Strategies   184
   Reading Difficult Texts   186
   Active Reading Strategies   188
Common College Reading Purposes   197
   Summarizing   197
   Comparing   197
   Evaluating   198
   Analyzing   198
   Responding   198
Reading Visual Images   202

Examples of Visual Images   202
Strategies for Reading Visual Images   204
Review of Key Ideas in Chapter 4   205

5: Academic Researching Processes   207

Expectations for College-Level Research   209
    Sample Student Essay: Lydia Tolman,
      "The Rise of Starbucks"   209
Differences between High School and College Research   214
Academic Research as Inquiry   216
    The Nature of College Research   217
    Examples of College Research Assignments   218
Exploring Academic Researching Processes   221
    Five Myths about College Researching Processes   221
    Strategies for Finding a Research Question   224
    Locating Sources   228
    Scholarly Sources vs. Non-Scholarly Sources:
      What are the Differences?   230
    Types of Textual Research Sources   231
    Primary Research Sources: Interviews and Surveys   236
    Evaluating Sources   239
    Integrating and Responding to Sources   242
Understanding and Avoiding Plagiarism   249
    The Need to Cite Sources   249
    Common Questions about Citing Sources   250
    What you Need to Know about Plagiarism   252
Review of Key Ideas in Chapter 5   254

Writing Projects for Part II   256

Writing Project II.1: Reading, Writing, and Researching
    Processes Self-Survey   256
Writing Project II.2: Reading, Writing, and Researching
    Advice for Future College Students   260
Writing Project II.3: Researched Academic Argument Portfolio   262

Part III: Exploring Reading, Writing, and Researching across the Curriculum

6: Introduction to Writing across the Curriculum   269

Disciplines and Discourse Communities   270
Reading, Writing, and Researching in General Education Courses 272
   Examples of General Education Mission Statements   273
   Differences between the First-Year Writing Course
     and Writing in General Education Courses   276
Reading, Writing, and Researching in the Major   278
   Sample Writing Rubrics and Assignments in the Major   278
   Common Expectations for Writing in the Major   285
Reading, Writing, and Researching across the Curriculum   288
   Five Myths about Reading, Writing, and Researching
     across the Curriculum   289
   Sample Student Essay in Physical Sciences: Katrina Outland,
     "The Blob that Attacked Waikiki:
     The Box Jellyfish Invasion of Hawaii"   292
   Sample Student Essay in Social Sciences: Dana Driscoll,
     "The Ubercool Morphology of Internet Gamers:
     A Linguistic Analysis"   296
   Sample Student Essay in Arts and Humanities:
     Stephanie LeBlanc, "Blurred by our Cultural Lens:
     Issues with Oral Literature and the American School System"   306
   Reading, Writing, and Researching in the Natural Sciences   313
   Reading, Writing, and Researching in the Social Sciences   313
   Reading, Writing, and Researching in the Arts and Humanities   314
Review of Key Ideas in Chapter 6   315

7: Reading, Writing, and Researching in the Natural Sciences   316

Writing and Critical Thinking in the Natural Sciences   317
   Sample Natural Sciences Writing Assignments   318
   Examples of Writing in the Natural Sciences   323
   Exploring Genre in the Natural Sciences: The Lab Report   325

Sample Lab Report: "The Optimal Foraging Theory:
  Food Selection in Beavers Based on Tree Species,
  Size, and Distance"   327
Expanding the Conventions of Science Writing:
  A Student Gets Creative   333
Reading in the Natural Sciences   334
  Sample Annotation of a Science Text   335
  Sample Natural Sciences Reading: John L. Gittleman,
    "Carnivore Group Living: Comparative Trends"   336
Researching in the Natural Sciences   341
  The Nature of Inquiry and Research in the Natural Sciences   342
  What Counts as Evidence in the Natural Sciences?   343
  Natural Science Reference Books and Databases   344
  Citing Sources in the Natural Sciences: CSE Style   345
Student Writing Case Study: Geology   349
Examples of Student Writing in the Natural Sciences   366
Review of Key Ideas in Chapter 7   366

8: Reading, Writing, and Researching
    in the Social Sciences   368

Writing and Critical Thinking in the Social Sciences   369
  Examples of Writing in the Social Sciences   372
  Exploring Genre in the Social Sciences: Ethnography   376
  Sample Ethnography: Napoleon Chagnon, excerpt
    from *Yanomamö: The Fierce People*   382
Reading in the Social Sciences   385
  Sample Double-Entry Journal for a Social Sciences Text   386
  Sample Social Sciences Reading: Annette Lareau, excerpt from
    Unequal Childhoods: Class, Race, and Family Life   388
Researching in the Social Sciences   394
  The Nature of Inquiry and Research in the Social Sciences   394
  What Counts as Evidence in the Social Sciences?   395
  Social Science Reference Books and Databases   398
  Citing Sources in the Social Sciences: APA Style   401
Student Writing Case Study: Sociology   404

Examples of Student Writing in the Social Sciences   432
Review of Key Ideas in Chapter 8   432

9: Reading, Writing, and Researching
in the Arts and Humanities   434

Writing and Critical Thinking in the Arts and Humanities   436
   Writing in a Philosophy Department: Oregon State University   436
   Examples of Writing in the Arts and Humanities   441
Exploring Genre in the Arts and Humanities: The Performance Review   444
   Examples of Performance Review Assignments   445
   Sample Film Review: Pat Dowell and John Fried, "Pulp Friction:
     Two Shots at Quentin Tarantino's *Pulp Fiction*"   448
Reading in the Arts and Humanities   453
Researching in the Arts and Humanities   458
   The Nature of Inquiry and Research in the Arts and Humanities   459
   What Counts as Evidence in the Arts and Humanities?   465
   Arts and Humanities Reference Books and Databases   467
   Citing Sources in the Arts and Humanities: MLA Style   470
Student Writing Case Study: Literature   473
Examples of Student Writing in the Arts and Humanities   485
Review of Key Ideas in Chapter 9   485

Writing Projects for Part III   487

Writing Project III.1: Writing Assignments across the Curriculum   487
Writing Project III.2: Interview with a College Professor   488
Writing Project III.3: Academic Discourse Community
   Mini-Ethnography   490

References   493

Author Index   501

Subject Index   503

Editor's Preface

Dan Melzer's *Exploring College Writing: Reading, Writing, and Researching across the Curriculum* is a textbook designed for first-year and sophomore composition courses that incorporates the desirable features of a range of theoretically supported and popular approaches to teaching writing within a larger context that includes reading and research processes in different fields of study. Dan Melzer is uniquely qualified to have written this book. His background includes degrees in English studies, literature, creative writing, and rhetoric and composition, and he is an associate professor and director of reading and writing at a large state university campus in the United States, California State University at Sacramento. Dr. Melzer thus combines a sophisticated knowledge of the field of writing with an ideal vantage point from which to view the writing needs of students attending American colleges and universities.

Exploring College Writing is unique in combining the best features of ethnographic and social constructionist educational orientations with discipline-based (WID) and writing-across-the-curriculum (WAC) pedagogy that incorporates rhetorical, genre-centered instruction as well. Melzer has designed a college writing textbook that speaks very directly to students as apprentices within a higher-education academic environment where they need to learn about the expectations of professors in both their general education (core curriculum) classes and in their major fields of study. The progression of the book is from general features of academic reading, writing, and researching to more specialized forms of reading, writing, and researching in physical sciences, social sciences, and arts and humanities. The discussion of general university academic culture and the more specialized areas is "scaffolded" on knowledge that students bring with them from high school and on field research which students carry out on academic contexts. This they do in an approach that includes exploratory Writing to Learn and Learn by Doing activities, in addition to extended writing projects in which students analyze writing assignments and reflect on their own processes and histories of reading, writing, and researching.

Using readings and other texts such as advertisements and charts as rhetorical models, students explore writing across the curriculum at their campus. Texts from both student and professional writers provide models for writing in first-year and more specialized courses in different disciplines. The range and specific selection of readings will be appealing to both college students and their teachers, including such topics as personal appearance, television, terrorism, internet gaming, the Big Bang, a mystery jellyfish invasion in Hawaii, and the cult film *Pulp Fiction*. Melzer has designed the book to connect the rhetoric, readings, and writing projects in ways that ensure their relevance for students and also help initiate students step by step into academic discourse.

Exploring College Writing is a highly readable, "user-friendly" book which talks directly to college students and includes anecdotes from the author's own experiences as a student and teacher as well as a variety of student and faculty voices from different fields speaking through their written work, writing assignments, and reflections on writing and college experiences more generally. It is an engaging composition book that sets college writing, reading, and researching within the overall experience of transitioning from high school to college and learning about general academic and specialized disciplinary cultures. It is a substantial book yet not in any way intimidating or out of reach of the typical university student. The author's experience and that of the others whose experience and written work he showcases makes *Exploring College Writing* an especially rich treatment of college composition that I expect students and their teachers will find both worthwhile to work through and enjoyable to read.

Martha C. Pennington
Series Editor, Frameworks for Writing

Acknowledgments

Chapter 1
Government assignment reprinted by kind permission of the author Professor Brian Dille. Physics assignment reprinted by kind permission of the author Professor Al Cordes. Social work assignment reprinted by kind permission of the author Professor Kia Bentley. Excerpt from the *University of Maryland Writing Guide* reprinted by kind permission of the author Professor Cynthia Whitesel. Excerpt from the *University of Chicago Writing Guide* reprinted by kind permission of the author Professor Lawrence McEnerney.

Matt Miles, "Personal Appearance and its Implications of Sexuality" from *E-Vision* Fall/Spring 2004, James Madison University Writing Program. Reprinted by kind permission of the author and *E-Vision*. © 2004.

Additional thanks to Andrea Ryncarz, Melissa Bratt, and Professor Tina Royer for quotes, interviews, and essays.

Chapter 2
Feras Sleiman, "Review of *Dying to Win: The Strategic Logic of Suicide Terrorism*" from *University of Michigan Journal of Political Science*, 2006. Reprinted by kind permission of the author and *University of Michigan Journal of Political Science*. © 2006.

David Winchell, "Review: *The Revolution Will Not Be Televised*" from *Res: A Journal of Undergraduate Research and Writing*, 2006. Reprinted by kind permission of the author.

Chapter 3
History assignment reprinted by kind permission of the author Professor Debra Salata.

Faustino P. Estoy III, "The New American Epidemic" from *Our Own Words*, 2006–2007. © First-Year Writing Program, Florida State University 2006. Reprinted by kind permission of the author and the First-Year Writing Program, Florida State University.

Chapter 4
History assignment reprinted by kind permission of the author Professor Stanley Schultz. Classics assignment reprinted by kind permission of the author Professor

Edward Capps. Psychology reading log assignment reprinted by kind permission of the author Professor Mona Ibrahim.

Additional thanks to Rodney Larsen for critical reading advice, Professor Sophia Isako Wong for active reading advice, and Laura Ceideburg for quotes.

Chapter 5
History research paper assignment reprinted by kind permission of the author Professor Donald Shaffer. Political science research paper assignment reprinted by kind permission of the author Professor Thomas Sowers. Psychology research paper assignment reprinted by kind permission of the author Professor Tom Shuell.

Lydia Tolman, "The Rise of Starbucks" from *The Printer's Devil*, 2004–2005. © Writing Program, Arizona State University 2005. Reprinted by kind permission of the author and the Writing Program, Arizona State University.

Chapter 6
Washington State GE mission statement reprinted by kind permission of Dr. Richard Law, GE Director. University of North Carolina, Asheville, GE mission statement reprinted by kind permission of Dr. Edward Katz, Dean of University Programs. Psychology department scoring sheet reprinted by kind permission of Professor Jim Sanford. Biology department scoring sheet reprinted by kind permission of Professor Larry Rockwood. Dance department scoring sheet reprinted by kind permission of Professor Elizabeth Price. School of Management criteria for competent writing reprinted by kind permission of Professor Beth Schneider.

Katrina Outland, "The Blob that Attacked Waikiki: The Box Jellyfish Invasion of Hawaii" from *The Journal of Young Investigators*, Volume 12, 2005. Reprinted by kind permission of the author and *The Journal of Young Investigators*. © 2005.

Dana Driscoll, "The Ubercool Morphology of Internet Gamers: A Linguistic Analysis" from *Undergraduate Research Journal for the Human Sciences*, 2002. Reprinted by kind permission of the Undergraduate Research Community of Kappa Omicron Nu. © 2002.

Stephanie LeBlanc, "Blurred by our Cultural Lens: Issues with Oral Literature and the American School System" from *E-Vision*, Fall/Spring 2009, James Madison University Writing Program. Reprinted by kind permission of the author and *E-Vision*. © 2009.

Chapter 7
Physics assignment reprinted by kind permission of the author Professor Hank Yochum. Biology assignment reprinted by kind permission of the author Professor

Lidia Kos. Chemistry assignment reprinted by kind permission of the author Professor Katherine Kantardjieff.

Additional thanks to Alfredo Cadenas and Professor Lisa Hammersley for interviews and essays.

Professor Miriam Ferzli, "The Optimal Foraging Theory: Food Selection in Beavers Based on Tree Species, Size and Distance." Reprinted by kind permission of the author.

Excerpt from John Gittleman, "Carnivore Group Living: Comparative Trends" from *Carnivore Behavior, Ecology and Evolution*, Volume I, John Gittleman (editor), Cornell University Press, 1989, pp. 183–187. © 1989 by Cornell University. Used by permission of the publisher, Cornell University Press.

Chapter 8
Ethnographic analysis assignment reprinted by kind permission of the author Professor Melissa Johnson.

Additional thanks to Professor Todd Miggliaccio, Bethany Coston, and Professor Scott Melzer for interviews, essays, and assignments.

Excerpt from Rebekah Nathan, *My Freshman Year: What a Professor Learned by Becoming a Student*, Cornell University Press, 2005, pp. 50–51. © 2005 by Rebekah Nathan. Used by permission of the publisher, Cornell University Press.

Excerpt from Napoleon Chagnon, *Yanomamö: The Fierce People*, Third edition, Wadsworth, 1983, pp. 114–116. © 1983 Wadsworth, a part of Cengage Learning, Inc. Reproduced by permission. www.cengage.com/permissions.

Excerpt from Annette Lareau, *Unequal Childhoods: Class, Race and Family Life*, University of California Press, 2003, pp. 91–96. © 2003 by the Regents of the University of California. Published by the University of California Press.

Chapter 9
Philosophy writing assignments reprinted by kind permission of the authors Professor William Uzgalis and Professor David Scott Arnold. Theater review assignment reprinted by kind permission of the author Professor Steve Gilliam. Film review assignment reprinted by kind permission of the author Professor Jyotsna Kapur. Dance review assignment reprinted by kind permission of the author Professor Artemis Preeshl. Religious studies research paper assignment reprinted by kind permission of the author Professor Phillip Jenkins. Women's studies research paper assignment reprinted by kind permission of the author Professor Holly Hassel. Humanities

research paper assignment reprinted by kind permission of the author Professor Ed Reber.

Additional thanks to Professor Brad Buchanan and Antonio Javier for interviews, essays, and assignments.

Pat Dowell and John Fried, 'Pulp Friction: Two Shots at Quentin Tarantino's *Pulp Fiction*' from *Cineaste* 21(3), July 2005, pp. 4–5. Used by permission of *Cineaste*.

Illustrations
Obsession for Men Spoof Ad and Obsession for Women Spoof Ad. Reproduced courtesy of Adbusters Media Foundation www.adbusters.org.

To the Reader

A "Learn-by-Doing" Approach to Academic Literacies

The goal of *Exploring College Writing* is to introduce students to academic literacies by asking them to explore, analyze, and practice academic reading, writing, and researching across disciplines. I wrote *Exploring College Writing* with some premises in mind about the most useful ways to introduce students to academic literacies – premises which I derived from my own experiences as a professor of composition and as a researcher and practitioner of writing across the curriculum. As a composition professor, my writing courses focus on academic literacies, and my primary goal is to introduce students to reading, writing, and researching in college as well as to make them aware of the ways that different academic discourse communities make meaning. As a researcher, I've always been interested in the similarities and differences in what instructors in different disciplines value. My major research project, a national study of college writing assignments across the curriculum (Melzer, 2009), has informed both the content and the activities of *Exploring College Writing*. The work of Writing Across the Curriculum scholars and researchers such as Chris Thaiss, David Russell, Patricia Bizzell, Mike Rose, Lucille McCarthy, and Marilyn Sternglass also inform my textbook, and you will find quotes from these scholars throughout the book. For a decade I have worked as a Writing Center and Writing Across the Curriculum Coordinator, and *Exploring College Writing* is an extension of the work I've done as a WAC practitioner. The premises of the book reflect a balance of theory, research, and practitioner knowledge.

Premise #1. A primary goal of composition courses is to introduce students to academic literacies and ask them to analyze and critically reflect on these literacies in the context of their own literacy histories.

Exploring College Writing gives students a broad introduction to college literacies by comparing high school and college writing, discussing the importance of first-year writing, and introducing students to reading, writing, and researching in the disci-plines. In each chapter, students connect college writing to their own literary histories and reflect on their own experiences as college writers.

Premise #2. An effective way to introduce students to academic literacies is to ask them to explore and analyze college writing using an ethnographic, fieldwork approach.

Exploring College Writing places students in the role of investigators, collecting and analyzing evidence of academic literacies in their institution by interviewing professors, collecting writing assignments and rubrics, observing academic discourse communities, and reflecting on their literacy experiences in the college courses they've taken. This "learn-by-doing" approach includes asking students to rhetoric-ally analyze a variety of authentic disciplinary texts as well as to practice writing in a variety of academic genres.

Premise #3. To introduce students to academic literacies, it's helpful to ask them to read and analyze authentic disciplinary texts, including student texts, and not just expository essays.

Exploring College Writing presents students with actual writing assignments, grading rubrics, and student essays from courses across disciplines, as well as examples of academic and professional writing from a variety of fields and in a variety of genres: scholarly book reviews, lab reports, ethnographies, case studies, textbook chapters, popular books, literature reviews, and others. Some of these texts are written for a popular audience; some are written for a general educated audience; and many are written for a disciplinary audience. These texts include writing from students in a variety of courses: first-year writing, geology, sociology, linguistics, chemistry, child development, history, biology, and literature.

Premise #4. There are some general qualities of academic writing that students should be aware of, but students should also be aware that different disciplines have their own genres, each with its own conventions and ways of knowing.

Exploring College Writing begins by discussing some general features of academic writing and some general strategies for college reading, writing, and researching in Parts I and II. The assumption is that every discipline asks students to develop and support arguments, to think critically, to engage with difficult texts, and to use research to make knowledge. Yet every discipline (and even different professors in the same discipline) asks students to do these things in different ways. After students explore general features of academic writing in Parts I and II, in Part III they're introduced to the genres, conventions, and ways of knowing for writing within different disciplines. The goal is not to try to make students experts in every discipline, but to give them rhetorical strategies for reading and composing in college and the awareness that each college course they take will present them with different ways of writing and making meaning.

Premise #5. No matter what discipline students are writing in, every rhetorical situation has features of purpose, audience, genre, persona, and context that students need to be aware of.

Students will be more successful academic writers if they have tools for approaching any rhetorical situation, no matter what the discipline. *Exploring College Writing* helps students understand factors in rhetorical situations and asks students to think about these factors by conducting rhetorical analyses of a variety of genres from a variety of disciplines.

Outstanding Features

Exploring College Writing has a number of features that make it unique and especially useful for introducing students to academic literacies.

- **An ethnographic, fieldwork approach**

Students "learn by doing" through interviewing professors, observing academic discourse communities, analyzing college writing assignments, practicing a variety of academic genres, and other kinds of activities.

- **A focus on what academic disciplines have in common before focusing on how they differ**

Rather than jumping right into difficult disciplinary texts and research methods, *Exploring College Writing* begins by asking students to reflect on their literacy histories and explore general features of academic writing and general strategies for reading, writing, and researching in college. It's only after this scaffolding that students are asked to investigate the genres, conventions, and research methods of writing in the disciplines.

- **A variety of real disciplinary genres and not only expository essays**

The examples and readings introduce students to authentic academic discourse from a variety of disciplines: abstracts, scholarly book reviews, critical analysis essays, lab reports, research reports, ethnographies, and case studies.

- **Integration of reading, writing, and researching**

Academic literacy is broadly conceived as not just composing, but also reading and researching. The emphasis is on the ways that reading, writing, and researching processes are connected in an academic environment.

- **Examples of student writing from different disciplines in each chapter**

Many of the examples and readings are from authentic undergraduate student writing from across the disciplines that have appeared in undergraduate writing journals published at a variety of institutions.

- **Case studies of student writing that include drafts and interviews with the students and professors**

Each case study includes a course syllabus, assignment descriptions, student rough and final drafts, professor response, and information from interviews with the students and their professors.

- **Informal writing activities ("Writing to Learn" and "Learn by Doing") as well as more formal, extended writing projects**

A variety of writing prompts and projects, including both individual and collaborative activities, encourage students to reflect, analyze, synthesize, and practice academic writing and researching.

- **Voices of professors and students from across the curriculum**

Each chapter includes quotes about academic reading, writing, and researching from students and professors in writing and across disciplines. All of the names of students and professors are their real names and are used with permission.

Content and Organization

Introducing students to academic literacies can feel like an overwhelming task. Professors can become overwhelmed by the variety of genres and conventions that make up writing across the curriculum, and students can feel overwhelmed if they're asked to start reading lab reports, ethnographies, and academic journal articles without any preparation. *Exploring College Writing* is organized in a sequence that provides preparation and scaffolding before students begin to closely investigate writing in the disciplines.

- **In Part I, students explore the question, "What is college-level writing?"**

Students begin by reflecting on their own literacy histories and their strengths and weaknesses as writers, and think about the ways high school writing might be similar to and different from college writing. Before students explore writing in the disciplines, they think about some features of academic literacy that all disciplines share: summary and analysis of difficult texts, active and critical reading, and argument supported by evidence. In these early chapters, students are also introduced to features that are part of any rhetorical situation, such as purpose, audience, and genre. The student writing case study in Chapter 1 provides a concrete example of a student drafting and revising in a composition course.

- **In Part II, students are introduced to strategies for college reading, writing, and researching processes.**

Students explore the features and processes of academic literacy and think about strategies for reading, writing, and researching that can be useful in any discipline. Reading, writing, and researching are presented as complex, interrelated, and context-bound processes.

- **In Part III, students explore writing across the curriculum.**

Once students have reflected on their own literacy history, have investigated academic writing broadly conceived, and have considered general strategies for college reading, writing, and researching, they're ready to explore writing across the curriculum in Part III. Part III begins with a discussion of discourse communities and a general introduction to writing beyond first-year composition, and then moves into a more detailed exploration of writing in the natural sciences, the social sciences, and the arts and humanities. A student case study is included at the end of each chapter in Part III: a case study of a student writing in a geology course (Chapter 7), a case study of a student writing in a sociology course (Chapter 8), and a case study of a student writing in a literature course (Chapter 9). Each case study begins with a syllabus providing an overview of the course goals and assignments. Assignment descriptions, information from interviews with the professors, and professor response to student writing provide detailed information about professor and disciplinary expectations. Some case studies focus in detail on a single student work as the primary writing assignment for the course, while other case studies include multiple kinds of student writing as illustrations for courses which require a variety of writing assignments.

Each case study includes rough and final drafts along with student commentary on their writing and researching processes, as well as analysis of the student's writing. The case studies were obtained from my colleagues across disciplines at California State University, Sacramento and other colleges. All of the case study students agreed to the use of their final and non-final drafts and their real names. All of their professors agreed to have their materials used but preferred to remain anonymous.

Writing Activities and Projects

Each chapter of *Exploring College Writing* presents a variety of kinds of focused reading, writing, and researching prompts and activities that I and other writing professors have found useful in teaching academic writing.

"Writing to Learn" Activities

The "Writing to Learn" activities are informal and exploratory, and they often ask for small-group discussion. The "Writing to Learn" prompts ask students to make personal connections, synthesize ideas and readings, reflect on what they already know or think about a topic, practice rhetorical analysis, and think critically about what they're reading.

"Learn by Doing" Activities

The "Learn by Doing" activities ask students to investigate and practice academic literacies by interviewing professors, collecting and analyzing academic writing, creating writing rubrics, practicing composing in academic genres, and other kinds of activities. Both the "Writing to Learn" and "Learn by Doing" activities are meant to be informal, low-stakes kinds of writing.

"Writing Projects"

More formal and extensive writing activities are offered at the end of Parts I, II, and III in added "Writing Projects" sections. Each of these writing projects is focused on asking students to reflect on, analyze, and practice academic literacies. Students might write a literacy history narrative, create an academic writing guide for future students, or conduct a mini-ethnography of an academic discourse community, as well as other activities. Projects can be done individually or in groups.

With its "learn by doing," fieldwork approach to academic literacies and its inclusion of authentic disciplinary writing from student and professional authors, *Exploring College Writing* will help students gain confidence as college writers and develop the rhetorical awareness they need to read, write, and research across the curriculum. I hope you find *Exploring College Writing*, which is the result of many years of research and practice in college writing, to be useful and enjoyable to work through, and I look forward to hearing from you about your experience. Please feel free to email me with your thoughts or questions.

Dan Melzer
California State University, Sacramento
melzer@csus.edu

Part I

An Introduction to College Writing

1   Expectations for College-Level Writing

College-level writing is a dynamic term that means a number of things. Mastering materials and research methods, engaging the readings, grappling with increasingly sophisticated grammar, and synthesizing disparate sources are all part of becoming a college-level writer...
>   —Kimberly Nelson, a student at the University of Iowa (Nelson, 2006: 295)

Writing assignments in college generally call for high levels of critical literacy, typically requiring skills in researching, reading complex texts, understanding of key disciplinary concepts, and strategies for synthesizing, analyzing, and responding critically to new information.
>   —Professor Lee Ann Carroll, Humanities and Teacher Education Division,
>   Pepperdine University (Carroll, 2002: 9)

I think college-level writing is writing that asks students to analyze materials – to make connections between texts (written and unwritten) and to explore those connections. I also think college-level writing is writing that asks students to join in a dialogue with other academics and allows (even encourages) students to challenge the texts they analyze rather than simply accept them.

—Professor Tina Royer, English Department, Sierra Community College
(interview)

1.1: Writing to Learn – What Do You Know about College Writing?

Throughout *Exploring College Writing*, you'll find Writing to Learn activities that ask you to use writing as a tool for thinking and learning. Most of these Writing to Learn activities are informal and exploratory. The focus is on exploring what you think and generating ideas and questions, not on finely tuned organization and perfect grammar.

The purpose of this Writing to Learn activity is to tap into what you already think about college writing before you read Chapter 1. Make a list of what you believe are the qualities of college-level writing (e.g. "College writing needs to have a lot of analysis"). This list could be based on writing assignments you've already experienced in your college classes or what your high school teachers told you about college writing. Being aware of how you already define college writing will help you make connections and re-examine your beliefs as you read this chapter.

What is College-Level Writing?

Making the adjustment from high school writing to college writing isn't easy – even for someone who wound up writing a textbook about college writing. In my first semester of college, I had a tough time understanding my professors' expectations for writing. Much of the writing I did in high school was for short quizzes or essay exams – because of the heavy teaching load, my high school teachers couldn't assign as much writing as they wanted to. Most of my high school teachers had five or six different classes and 150 students or more, with no teaching assistants to help them respond to writing. Standardized tests were also a factor in why many of my high school writing assignments were not as lengthy and complex as my college writing assignments. In high school, every year we had to take a standardized test with a one-hour timed writing exam. A big part of the writing I did in high school was preparing for these timed, standardized writing tests, and I learned some formulas for writing an essay under pressure. For example, one of these formulas was the "five-paragraph theme," comprising an introduction with a one-sentence thesis, three support paragraphs with a clear topic sentence at the beginning of each paragraph, and a conclusion that restated each of the main points. By the end of my senior year, I could crank out a five-paragraph theme in my sleep. This formula might have worked fine when I took the SAT (Scholastic Aptitude Test), but in my first semester at the University of Florida, the five-paragraph formula didn't work for me. When my college professors asked me to write a lab report, a book review, or a research essay exploring different psychologists' theories about nature vs. nurture, the five-paragraph theme wasn't much help.

Luckily, I had some high school teachers who challenged students to go beyond formulaic writing. There was the history teacher who assigned research papers that asked us to integrate ideas from outside sources and who forced us to think for ourselves and write complex arguments. There was also the creative writing teacher who taught us how to repeatedly revise and revise our ideas and organization and not just write one draft. Writing those history research papers in high school and getting feedback on them, and revising drafts of my stories for the creative writing course helped prepare me for college-level writing, but I still had a big learning curve that first semester. I thought I was a pretty good writer (I'd received good grades on most of my high school writing assignments), but at first I struggled with college-level writing. I'm a writing professor now, but that first semester I received plenty of "C" grades on my papers. If you're having some difficulty making the transition from high school to college writing, you're not alone – even the most successful high school writers might struggle as they adjust to the expectations of college writing. If you're a "non-traditional" student who is attending college after working or raising children, you'll probably also need to do some adjusting to college writing.

What I really needed to know that first semester at the University of Florida was: *What is college writing?* There's no simple answer to that question, and one thing you'll find out as you read this book and experience college courses is that each academic field of study (e.g. biology, history, psychology), and even each professor within the same field, will have different expectations for writing. One of the most difficult aspects of college writing for me was going from psychology, to chemistry, to history, and to literature courses all in the same semester, facing different kinds of writing assignments and different expectations for writing in each course. By the time

I was a senior in college, I also found that there were some general features of academic writing in any field that were helpful to know, such as the need to support assertions and join in conversation with what other scholars have said about a topic, or the ability to summarize, analyze, and synthesize complex texts. In this chapter, we'll focus on some general features of college writing and explore the question, *What is college-level writing?* After we've explored this question, you should feel more prepared for college writing.

Before we dive in and start exploring the question, *What is college-level writing?*, let's look at some common myths which some students have about college writing.

Five Myths about College Writing

Myth #1: An "A" paper in high school is pretty much the same as an "A" paper in college.

College writing builds on high school writing, but over four years of college you'll be challenged to go far beyond what you wrote in high school, and college professors' expectations for what counts as good writing will be higher than what you're used to. In college, a "C" usually translates to "average" and a "B" means "above average." That means an "A" is truly "excellent" or "exceptional" work. Later in this chapter we'll look at some writing rubrics that will give you an idea of the way some colleges define an "A" essay. The farther you go in college, as you take courses deeper and deeper into your major, the higher the bar will be set and the more you'll be expected to move from an "apprentice" academic writer to an "insider" within a specific discipline or field.

Myth #2: If you weren't successful as a high school writer, you won't be successful as a college writer.

Even though your college professors' expectations for writing will be high, this doesn't mean that if you struggled with writing in high school, you'll never be a good college writer. Scholars who study the way students learn to write in college have done research on students writing throughout college, from first year to senior year. These researchers have found that even students who were having a hard time making the transition from high school writing to college writing were successful by the time they were in their junior or senior year, if they persisted and sought help from professors, classmates, and their school's writing center. The researchers also found that many students take "two steps back" in their writing when they start college before they are able to take "two steps forward." *Exploring College Writing* can help you make the transition to college writing, but don't be shy about asking for feedback and help on your writing from classmates, your professor, and any tutoring resources available at your institution.

Myth #3: College writing is just a game of trying to get an "A" by giving your professors what you think they want.

I'll be honest, when I was an undergraduate at the University of Florida, a few of my professors just wanted me to repeat their opinions on an issue or the ideas they gave in a lecture when I wrote a paper for them. For some of my courses, college writing did just feel like a game of trying to give the professor what he or she wanted in order to get an "A." However, most college professors want you – and expect you – to think for yourself. Most college writing assignments ask you to give your perspective on an issue or your solution to a problem or your research results, and not just a single "right" answer. Even though some kinds of college writing, such as a lab report or an annotated bibliography, have a fairly specific form and format, most professors don't have a template which they want you to follow in your writing. Most often in college writing, you'll need to decide what form and style best fits your purpose for writing.

Myth #4: College writing is all about using big words and sounding impressive.

When I wrote my first college essay, I looked up every other word in a thesaurus and tried to find bigger and more impressive sounding words for what I was trying to say. I was guilty of writing sentences like, "Since the dawn of time, mankind and womankind have philosophized about the true nature of art in relation to society as a whole." I was trying hard to sound "educated" or "academic" – or at least how I thought academic writing should sound. The problem was that my writing sounded pretentious and wordy, and I didn't really have control of the vocabulary and sentence structures I was using. It's great to stretch your vocabulary as you progress in college, and to try to write and think in more and more complex ways from your first semester to your last. Sometimes you'll need to use some specialized vocabulary that's connected to the academic field of the course you're writing for. Don't sacrifice clarity, though, just to try to sound impressive. Your college assignments will ask you to try new voices and styles, but you still want to communicate effectively to your readers and not try too hard to sound "academic."

Myth #5: You won't be doing much writing if you major in a field like engineering, biology, or computer science.

I have a friend who majored in engineering in college, and he used to tell me that he couldn't understand how I could stand to be an English major, because he hated to write. He thought that once he was finished with his general education (or core curriculum) requirements, he'd never have to write again. His first semester as an engineering major, he was shocked when he had to write three lab reports in one course, weekly summaries of engineering research in another course, and a twenty-page group proposal for a bridge-building project in yet another course. Now my friend is an engineer for the state of Florida, and he tells me that he does as much writing as he does engineering. He said that one of the reasons he was promoted in his job was because he was good at writing proposals for new contracts. I would be exaggerating if I said that every professor you have in college will assign writing, but I'm not exaggerating when I say that every academic field uses writing to create knowledge and communicate the results of research, that every kind of work has its own types of writing, and that most workplaces are looking for good writers as one aspect of good communication skills.

Making the Transition to College Writing

Writing professors Patrick Sullivan of Manchester Community College and Howard Tinberg of Bristol Community College have published an entire book about making the transition to college writing, titled *What is "College-Level" Writing?* Here are some quotes in the book from teachers about making the transition from high school to college writing:

> When students leave high school, they should be able to develop a specific idea in detail, supporting that idea with meaningful facts, illustrations, experiences, analogies, quotes, or whatever is needed to make the thesis or premise clear.
>
> —Teacher at Armuchee High School in Rome, Georgia

If I had to pick one thing that separates adult-level writing from adolescent-level writing, it is the ability to reflect the needs of the audience in your writing.

—Business professor

The difference with "high-school writing" seems to be…that the students tend to assume that there is one correct answer to each question and one correct way to write it down. What they want from me is the "formula" that they can use. What I am trying to teach them is to <u>find</u> their own voice: develop their own opinion as opposed to trying to figure out mine.

—Germanic studies professor
(quoted in Sullivan, 2006: 17)

It's difficult to make generalizations about the similarities and differences between high school and college writing. After all, each high school and each high school teacher is different. There's a good chance that some of the writing you do in college will be exactly like the writing you did in high school. If you're coming to college after working for many years or raising children (or both), your transition to college writing will involve a different set of challenges. Nevertheless, the statements from the teachers above can help you think about some general differences in the expectations for high school versus college writing.

- **College writing tends to focus on thinking for yourself rather than on reporting what someone else has said about a topic.**

I'm sure you had some high school writing assignments that asked you to think for yourself, but in college *most* writing assignments ask you to present your own argument or interpretation, and usually there's not a single, "correct" answer or format the professor is looking for. The goal of most college professors is to get students to think for themselves and, as part of thinking for themselves, to be able to evaluate and analyze ideas. Writing is one of the main ways to accomplish this goal.

- **College writing requires sophisticated organization of ideas and not just plugging ideas into a formula like the five-paragraph theme.**

There's a good chance that in high school you were sometimes asked to write using a simple formula such as the five-paragraph theme. This formula might have been helpful for timed writing tests like the SAT, but most college professors want students to move beyond formulaic writing so they can think through more complex ideas and more challenging kinds of writing tasks. If you need to write a film analysis for your history of cinema course or a field observation report for your sociology of gender course, the five-paragraph theme isn't going to do you much good. If you wrote more complex essays or research papers in high school that couldn't be composed using a formula, you got a taste of what college writing is like.

- **College writing requires specific and well-developed support for your arguments.**

High school teachers want you to support your ideas – even a five-paragraph essay requires some support in each paragraph – but you'll find that college professors expect you to support your arguments in more depth than your high school teachers might have. To encourage you to think deeply about a topic and persuade your audience, most college professors are looking for well-developed essays that provide plenty of support for arguments. Adding specific examples, information from reliable sources, your own thoughtful and coherent opinions, or relevant examples from personal experience are some of the ways that college professors will ask you to develop your ideas and support your arguments.

- **College writing requires a lot of revising and plenty of time to engage in writing processes.**

It's no secret that many high school students have pulled an "all-nighter" to finish a research paper that was due the next day. Although I hate to admit it, I wrote papers the night before they were due at least a few times in high school. Since college writing assignments are often more complex than high school writing assignments, trying to do all your writing at the last minute won't work. You need to give yourself time to revise your essay, get feedback, and find out what other writers have said about the topic through research (we'll talk more about this in Part II).

- **You'll do more writing in college than you did in high school.**

High school teachers typically teach more courses than college professors, and usually their class sizes are larger as well. It's not surprising, then, that high school teachers aren't able to assign (and respond to) as much writing as they would like to. Although not every college professor assigns writing, you can expect to do more writing in college than you did in high school, and most of the writing assignments will be longer because the topics and readings are more complex. This writing is much more than busywork: college professors use writing to help you think about the subject area and to learn the common types of writing used in their academic field.

1.2: Writing to Learn – Reflecting on High School Writing

The purpose of this Writing to Learn activity is for you to reflect on your experiences writing in high school by choosing your best and worst experience with writing. Think of the best experience you had with writing in high school and describe the experience. Do the same for your worst experience with writing in high school. Be prepared to share your experiences in small groups and/or with the class as a whole.

Examples of College Writing Assignments

A good starting place for exploring the question, "What is college-level writing?," is to look at some actual college writing assignments. Following are three college writing assignments: one from a government course, one from a physics course, and one from a social work course. To collect these assignments – and all of the materials from professors in *Exploring College Writing* – I searched the Internet for representative assignments and received permission from the professors to include their course materials in this book. As you read these three assignments, think about what kind of writing the professors are asking for and about the similarities and differences in the writing expectations of each professor.

Government Assignment from Professor Brian Dille, Odessa College

In California the Direct Democracy Center has proposed an amendment to the California constitution that would create a direct democracy in California. First, the proposal calls for the creation of an electronic network that would allow every citizen to vote from their homes in all elections. Citizens would also participate directly in all legislative decision making through the network by instructing their representatives in the state legislature how they (the citizens) want their representatives to vote on each issue before the legislature. The representative would then be bound by law to follow the majority vote that comes over this network.

Your job is to evaluate this proposal. Describe the advantages and disadvantages of such a proposal. Then take a position and add one to two paragraphs about/addressing the question of why California should or should not adopt this amendment.

Physics Assignment from Professor Al Cordes, Clinton Community College

Think of a lab report as a document that reports new findings to people that are not necessarily familiar with the concepts with which you are experimenting. It should be written as though you are reporting the results of a new scientific study. Each report should have the following sections:

(1) **Introduction** This section should be a description of the background information that is critical to the experiment, including an explanation as to why the experiment is significant and a statement of the hypothesis to be tested.

(2) **Methods and Materials** This section should include a detailed description of how the data was collected, and describe dependent and independent variables where applicable.

(3) **Results** Here you should present tables and graphs of data neatly labeled. Calculations are also included in this section. They should be clear and well-organized.

(4) **Discussion/Conclusion** Here you explain and interpret your results. Answer the question: what do these results show? Patterns and trends should be identified and you should conclude as to whether your results support or refute your hypothesis. Also in this section, describe sources of error and how they impacted your results.

Social Work Assignment from Professor Kia Bentley, Virginia Commonwealth University

Every student in the class will be asked to write a book review of one of the supplemental texts listed in the syllabus. Your five-page (maximum, double-spaced, perfectly APA formatted) review should include a rich but brief description of the book's content and style, a thorough review of its strengths and weaknesses from your perspective, an analytical discussion of its potential contributions to the field, and its specific impact on your thinking and your learning. Reviewing already published book reviews (found in most social work journals) has been helpful to other students in getting a "feel" for a book review's usual style. Be prepared to discuss your reviews with your classmates on the due date.

1.3: Learn by Doing – Analyzing Writing Assignments at Your College

In the Writing to Learn activities in *Exploring College Writing*, you'll be using writing to explore and reflect on your own experiences or on the materials presented in the book. In the Learn by Doing activities, you'll be asked to apply what we've been discussing by doing some of your own investigating. The purpose of this Learn by Doing activity is for you to gain a sense of college writing expectations by taking a close look at writing assignments from teachers at your school. You'll get into small groups of 3–5, and each group member will bring a copy of one writing assignment from one of the classes they're taking. This assignment could be a description from a course syllabus or a separate assignment sheet that the teacher has handed out to the class or posted to a class Web site. You'll share the assignments in the group and come up with a list of expectations for writing that you found in the assignments. Be prepared to share this list with the whole class.

How Do Writing Researchers Define Academic Writing?

In the last few decades, researchers who are interested in how students learn to write in college have studied college writing by interviewing students and professors, analyzing writing assignments and student writing, and observing college classrooms. To prepare for writing this book, I did some investigating and tried to find some of the most common statements that these researchers have made about the qualities that define college writing. Below are some examples of how these researchers define "academic writing."

In the book, *What is College-Level Writing?*, Patrick Sullivan, a writing professor at Manchester Community College, says a college-level essay should demonstrate:

- A willingness to evaluate ideas and issues carefully
- Some skills at analysis and higher-level thinking
- The ability to shape and organize material effectively
- The ability to integrate some of the material from the reading skillfully
- The ability to follow the standard rules of grammar, punctuation, and spelling

(Sullivan, 2006: 17)

Howard Tinberg, a writing professor at Bristol Community College and the coeditor of the book *What is College-Level Writing?*, offers this list of attributes for good college-level writing:

- A clear sense of purpose and audience
- Genre knowledge (knowing what form one is writing in and the conventions required by that form)
- Control over matters of grammar and mechanics to suit a particular rhetorical purpose and audience and genre
- A depth of reflection and capability of expressing the implications of one's subject

(Tinberg, quoted in Bauman, 2007: 8)

Lee Ann Carroll, a writing professor at Pepperdine University who studied a group of students from their freshman year until they graduated, says in her book *Rehearsing New Roles*:

Writing assignments in college generally call for high levels of critical literacy, typically requiring skills in researching, reading complex texts, understanding of key disciplinary concepts, and strategies for synthesizing, analyzing, and responding critically to new information.

(Carroll, 2002: 9)

Mike Rose, an education professor at UCLA (University of California at Los Angeles), conducted a study of writing assignments from professors across his institution. He found that most of the assignments required:

The ability to reflect on a broad range of complex material, to select and order information, and to see and re-see data and events in various contexts.

A special kind of argument…not a series of emotionally charged appeals…but a calculated marshalling of information, a sort of exposition aimed at persuading.

[Working] with large bodies of information garnered from lectures and readings.

(Rose, 1989: 111)

Doug Hesse, a writing professor at the University of Denver, defines college level-writing as:

The ability to contribute to ongoing debates or discussions in ways that reflect both the writer's understanding of others' perspectives (what has been before and

what is being said now) and of current rhetorical situations. It's the ability to adapt
to audiences and purposes.

(Hesse, quoted in Bauman, 2007: 8)

Writing researchers have acknowledged that each course students take in each
academic field will present them with different types of writing and different writing
expectations, as the passages above show. However, there are certain general expectations of academic writing that seem to be shared by most college professors. These
general features of academic writing include audience awareness, support for assertions, depth of thought and reflection, sophisticated organization appropriate to the
type of writing (the *genre* of writing) that's been assigned, and the ability to synthesize and analyze information.

College Writing Guides and Rubrics

For another perspective on the kinds of expectations for college writing that Patrick
Sullivan, Howard Tinberg, Lee Ann Carroll, Mike Rose, and Doug Hesse discuss in
their definitions of academic writing, let's take a look at some college writing guides.
The University of Maryland University College and the University of Chicago have
each created online writing guides for students, and these guides each has an entire
section describing college-level writing. Below are excerpts from the writing guides.

Examples of College Writing Guides

**Excerpt from the University of Maryland University College's *Online Guide to
Writing and Research*, by Cynthia Whitesel**

College courses demand many different kinds of writing that employ a variety of
strategies for different audiences. You may be required to write long essays or short
answers in response to examination questions. You may be asked to keep a journal,
write a lab report, and document the process you use to perform research. You may be
called upon to create a design document, write a business report or plan, and report on
the results of research. These are only some of the many types of writing you may
engage in throughout your college career.

College writing, also called academic writing, is assigned to teach you the critical
thinking and writing skills needed to communicate in classes and in the workplace. To
acquire and practice these skills, you are asked to write many different types of
assignments under different circumstances. Sometimes your teacher will assign a topic
and define the audience; sometimes you will be called on to define and limit the topic
and audience yourself. In any case, college writing teaches you about the series of

decisions you must make as you forge the link between your information and your audience.

For example, you must decide what sources of information you will use, how you will interpret this information, how you will organize your ideas, and what words and strategies you will use to explain your ideas. Your college writing experience will teach you about the writing process and about writing for particular disciplines, such as those in the liberal arts and business management specializations. College writing offers the opportunity for you to learn many different strategies for approaching writing tasks so that you may communicate how much you know and understand about a subject to a particular audience, usually your classmates or your teacher.

The expository nature of college writing, with its emphasis on the knowledge you gain in your college courses and through research, makes such writing different from your previous writing and perhaps more challenging. Teachers may expect your essays to contain more research, show more awareness of differing points of view, and even reflect more sophisticated expository techniques, such as argument and persuasion. The main source of the content of your college writing will be assigned textbook readings, library books and articles, your experience, and even field studies you may have designed. You will often use the skills you learn in college writing throughout your career. (Whitesel, 2010)

Excerpt from the University of Chicago's *Writing in College: A Short Guide to College Writing* by Joseph M. Williams and Lawrence McEnerney

Some students make very smooth transitions from writing in high school to writing in college, and we heartily wish all of you an easy passage. But other students are puzzled and frustrated by their experiences in writing for college classes. Only months earlier your writing was winning praise; now your instructors are dissatisfied, saying that the writing isn't quite "there" yet, saying that the writing is "lacking something." You haven't changed – your writing is still mechanically sound, your descriptions are accurate, you're saying smart things. But they're still not happy. Some of the criticism is easy to understand: it's easy to predict that standards at college are going to be higher than in high school. But it is not just a matter of higher standards: Often, what your instructors are asking of you is not just something _better_, but something _different_. If that's the case, then you won't succeed merely by being more intelligent or more skillful at doing what you did in high school. Instead, you'll need to direct your skills and your intelligence to a new task.

We should note here that a college is a big place and that you'll be asked to use writing to fulfill different tasks. You'll find occasions where you'll succeed by summarizing a reading accurately and showing that you understand it. There may be times when you're invited to use writing to react to a reading, speculate about it. Far more often – like every other week – you will be asked to <u>analyze</u> the reading, to make a worthwhile <u>claim</u> about it that is not obvious (<u>state a thesis</u> means almost the same thing), to support your claim with good reasons, all in four or five pages that are organized to present an <u>argument</u>. (If you did that in high school, write your teachers a letter of gratitude.)

Now by "argument" we do not mean a dispute over a loud stereo. In college, an argument is something less contentious and more systematic: It is a set of statements coherently arranged to offer three things that experienced readers expect in essays that they judge to be thoughtful:

- They expect to see a *claim* that would encourage them to say, "That's interesting. I'd like to know more."
- They expect to see *evidence*, *reasons* for your claim, evidence that would encourage them to agree with your claim, or at least to think it plausible.
- They expect to see that you've thought about *limits* and *objections* to your claim. Almost by definition, an interesting claim is one that can be reasonably challenged. Readers look for answers to questions like "But what about…?" and "Have you considered…?"

This kind of argument is less like disagreeable wrangling, more like an amiable and lively conversation with someone whom you respect and who respects you; someone who is interested in what you have to say, but will not agree with your claims just because you state them; someone who wants to hear your reasons for believing your claims and also wants to hear answers to their questions.

At this point, some students ask why they should be required to <u>convince</u> anyone of anything. "After all," they say, "we are all entitled to our opinions, so all we should have to do is express them clearly. Here's my opinion. Take it or leave it." This point of view both misunderstands the nature of argument and ignores its greatest value.

It is true that we are all entitled to our opinions and that we have no duty to defend them. But universities hold as their highest value not just the pursuit of new knowledge and better understanding, but the sharing of that knowledge. We write not only to state what we think but also to show why others might agree with it and why it matters. We also know that whatever it is we think, it is never the entire truth. Our conclusions are partial, incomplete, and always subject to challenge. So we write in a way that allows others to test our reasoning: we present our best thinking as a series of claims, reasons, and responses to imagined challenges, so that readers can see not only what we think, but whether they ought to agree.

And that's all an argument is – not wrangling, but a serious and focused conversation among people who are intensely interested in getting to the bottom of things *cooperatively.*

Those values are also an integral part of your education in college. For four years, you are asked to read, do research, gather data, analyze it, think about it, and then communicate it to readers in a form in which enables them to assess it and use it. You are asked to do this not because we expect you all to become professional scholars, but because in just about any profession you pursue, you will do research, think about what you find, make decisions about complex matters, and then explain those decisions – usually in writing – to others who have a stake in your decisions being sound ones. In an Age of Information, what most professionals do is research, think, and make arguments. (And part of the value of doing your own thinking and writing is that it makes you much better at evaluating the thinking and writing of others.) (Williams and McEnerney, 2008)

The University of Chicago's college writing guide makes the point that college writing will have higher (and different) standards than high school writing. One way to investigate these college-level writing standards is to look at how an "A" level essay is defined in college. To do this, we'll look at three university writing rubrics. A writing rubric is a statement of writing criteria for a specific assignment, course, department, or university. Below are the criteria for an "A" essay from the university writing rubrics at California State University Sacramento, Georgia State University, and Brandeis University. Before you take a look at the writing rubrics, think about your own criteria for what makes an "A" essay.

1.4: Writing to Learn – Qualities of an "A" Essay

The purpose of this Writing to Learn activity is for you to reflect on your own ideas about what is required for an "A" essay before you read the university writing rubrics that follow. Individually or in small groups, create a list of criteria for what you think makes an "A" essay (criteria are qualities that are used as standards of judgment). Be prepared to discuss your criteria for an "A" essay with the class.

Examples of College Writing Rubric Descriptions of an "A" Paper

From the California State University, Sacramento Writing Rubric

An "A" paper: A paper in this category

- Addresses the assignment thoughtfully and analytically, setting a challenging task.
- Shows evidence of significant revision.
- Displays awareness of and purpose in communicating to an audience.
- Establishes a clearly focused controlling idea.
- Demonstrates coherent and rhetorically sophisticated organization; makes effective connections between ideas.
- Provides clear generalizations with specific detail and compelling support and analysis.
- Cites relevant sources and evaluates their validity, effectively integrating them into the text when appropriate.
- Displays evidence of careful editing with superior control of grammar and mechanics appropriate to the assignment. (CSUS Reading and Writing Sub-committee, 2010)

From the Georgia State University Writing Standards

The A paper exhibits originality of thought in stating and developing a central idea. The ideas expressed are clear, logical, and thought provoking. The paper contains the positive qualities of good writing listed below: 1. The paper concentrates on a central idea and reveals a clear and sound over-all organizational plan. 2. Major points in the paper are developed logically and are supported with concrete, specific evidence or details that will arouse the reader's interest. 3. The paper reveals the writer's ability to select effective, appropriate words and phrases to make careful use of transitional devices; to maintain a confident, appropriate tone; and to be free from mechanical errors. (Georgia State University, 2010)

From the Brandeis University Writing Rubric

A – Essays that receive an A grade present a creative and original argument, are thoroughly analytical, stylistically interesting, and formally tight. The essay must be ambitious but manageable within assigned page limits. The topic should be clearly defined, and the ideas in the essay must build upon themselves in such a way that arguments offered at the beginning of the paper establish a foundation that will be necessary for the arguments which follow. The essay must not only possess logical coherence, but must <u>show</u> this logical coherence to its reader through the use of transitions, effective topic sentences, and meaningful references to earlier arguments.

In addition to offering a fresh and interesting thesis, an A essay will display a strong motive that provides context for its arguments and shows the reader (and the writer) why the ideas presented in the essay are meaningful. The essay should be meticulously proofread and show almost no errors of grammar, punctuation, usage, or typography. An A grade is reserved for <u>exceptional</u> essays. (Brandeis University, 2010)

Notice that even though mechanical errors are mentioned in the descriptions of the qualities of "A" essays in these university writing rubrics, the focus is on being interesting and original, being thoughtful and thought-provoking, supporting ideas with specific examples, considering audience and purpose, and creating sophisticated and not formulaic essays. In college writing, the content of your writing and the quality of your thinking are usually the most important criteria. However, the organization of ideas and the care in editing the text are also of importance in most cases.

It's important to keep in mind that even though there are some general qualities that most college-level writing assignments share, expectations for writing will be different for each academic field (e.g. sociology, biology, engineering). Even different teachers in the same field will have different expectations for writing. Right now we're focusing on some common qualities of college writing across academic fields, but we'll explore differences across academic fields in more detail when we look at writing across the curriculum in Part III.

1.5: Learn by Doing – Creating a Class Writing Rubric

Now that you've looked at some examples of rubrics, this Learn by Doing activity asks you to work with your teacher and classmates to create a class rubric for college writing. As a class, generate a list of criteria for college writing. You might define college writing at different grade levels (an "A" essay, a "B" essay, and so on) or create a bulleted list of the features of good writing in college. Once the class has generated a rubric, your teacher can distribute it to the class and you can use it as a guide to help you improve your essays and understand the feedback your teacher gives you on your writing.

What is "First-Year Writing"?

What college composition instructors wish to see in their students is this: a history of reading widely and well, of writing often and in many genres, and of analytical thinking that informs their reading and writing.

—Professor Steve Fox, Department of English, Indiana University-Purdue University Indianapolis (Budden, Nicolini, Fox, and Greene, 2002: 81)

Writing in ENC1101 is approached as a process, an action, rather than a collection of products or things. Of course the process produces pieces of writing, but the process can be just as important in the class as the products.

—from *Our Own Words: A Student's Guide to First Year Writing*, at Florida State University (Cook, 2006)

All first-year writing courses are designed to strengthen your already considerable skills as a writer while encouraging you to:

- Develop your sense of authority as a writer
- Participate in conversations about writing as process
- Engage in student-centered approaches to writing and responding
- Become a more adept reader of a variety of texts and rhetorical situations
- Develop a critical understanding of academic argument and analysis as rhetorical tools
- Emphasize analysis and the importance of building and supporting your viewpoints and ideas

—from "What to Expect When you Take a First-Year Writing Course" at Ohio State University (Ohio State First-Year Writing Program, 2010)

The course that most students take to help them make the transition from high school writing to college writing is first-year writing (or "freshman composition"). Most colleges require that students take at least one composition course, and there's a good reason for this. College writing can be more complex than high school writing, and first-year writing courses can help students make this transition. Even if you received "A" grades on all of your essays in high school, or even if you've been working for many years and you've done well at the writing needed in your job, you'll find that college writing is a new challenge. Most students find that a college composition course is helpful for learning the expectations of college-level writing. Because I got good grades in my English courses in high school and had a good score on the verbal part of the SAT, I didn't need to take a first-year composition course when I started college at the University of Florida; but I wish I had taken such a course. If I had taken first-year composition that first semester of college, I would've had an easier time making the transition from high school to college writing, and I would've been a much more confident college writer.

Before we explore the question, *What is first-year writing?*, and look at examples of student writing from a first-year writing course, let's think about what first-year writing is *not* by looking at five myths about first-year writing.

Five Myths about First-Year Writing

Myth #1: First-year writing won't really help prepare me for the writing I do in my other courses.

No single writing course can prepare you for all of the different kinds of writing you're going to encounter in courses in different academic fields. However, many of the writing and thinking skills you'll practice in first-year writing are transferable. That means they are skills that can apply in different situations. If you learn more about your own writing processes and become better at revising your own writing in a first-year writing course, you'll be able to apply those skills in other courses – even if your writing processes will be different for different assignments and different types of writing. If you practice analyzing the factors involved in any writing situation and in writing for different purposes and audiences, you'll be able to apply those skills to the writing situations you'll encounter in courses beyond first-year writing. First-year writing is also the course where you'll be most likely to receive a lot of feedback on your writing from your peers and your professor.

Myth #2: Once I've finished first-year writing, I'm "complete" as a college writer.

Even though the college writing practice you have in first-year writing will help you succeed in future courses, you won't be "complete" as a college writer once you're finished with first-year writing. It's impossible for one or two writing courses to prepare you for all of the different kinds of writing you'll do in college. The courses you take to satisfy general education requirements will present you with new kinds of writing situations and new types of writing for each academic field; and when you enter your major, there will be higher expectations and entirely new types of writing that will be closely connected to the specific ways of thinking in the academic field of your major. Even different professors in the same department will have different expectations for writing and will give different types of writing assignments.

Myth #3: First-year writing will be similar to high school writing courses, only with longer essays.

Although some of the kinds of writing you were assigned in high school English courses will be similar to what you're asked to do in first-year writing, your first-year writing course will challenge you to grow as an academic writer, reader, and researcher. You will encounter new kinds of writing (new *genres*) that will ask you to do more than simply tell a personal narrative or compose a five-paragraph theme. You will be asked to read challenging texts in ways that require more than just memorizing facts, and to integrate those texts into your own writing. These texts will include much more than just works of literature, and will require a different set of reading strategies than the ones you used to read novels and poems in your high school English classes. In both your reading and your writing, you will be asked to engage in an extensive process. This process will be collaborative and will involve talking about class readings in discussions and responding to your peers' drafts. You may have been asked to do some of these things in high school English classes, but in your first-year writing course it's likely that you will be immersed in all of these things: writing a variety of genres, integrating research, and engaging in extensive reading and writing processes.

Myth #4: First-year writing is an easy course.

At my college, California State University Sacramento, every student is required to take a first-year writing course. Some students come into my course with the idea that first-year composition won't be a lot of work because it's a requirement and because there aren't any quizzes, exams, or facts to memorize. Students who think my course will be easy are always surprised by how much work it is to write and revise (and re-revise, often multiple times) college-level essays. Writing complex essays, and taking essays through many drafts, is actually much more work than memorizing facts from a textbook for a final exam. Even though first-year writing is going to be more challenging than you might have expected, the good news is that you'll receive more help with your writing in your first-year writing course than in any other course you'll take in college. You'll receive lots of feedback on your writing from your classmates and your professor, and you'll be surprised how much you grow as a writer by the end of the course.

Myth #5: First-year writing is focused on learning correct grammar and mechanics.

So far we've found that college writing is much more than simply writing well-edited sentences. As we explore first-year writing in this chapter, you'll see that writing courses tend to focus on using writing to think and make meaning, on communicating ideas with a sense of purpose and audience, and on engaging in processes of drafting and revising. Editing sentences in order to communicate successfully to your audience is one part of college writing, but it's not the focus of college writing or the focus of first-year writing courses. To gain a better sense of what first-year writing courses tend to focus on – not just at your school but in general – let's look at some recommended goals for composition courses from the Council of Writing

Program Administrators (WPA). WPA is a professional group that creates guidelines for writing courses. The WPA outcomes statement for writing courses can help give you a better idea of the differences between high school and college writing.

Council of Writing Program Administrators Outcomes Statement for First-Year Composition

Rhetorical Knowledge

By the end of first year composition, students should

- Focus on a purpose
- Respond to the needs of different audiences
- Respond appropriately to different kinds of rhetorical situations
- Use conventions of format and structure appropriate to the rhetorical situation
- Adopt appropriate voice, tone, and level of formality
- Understand how genres shape reading and writing
- Write in several genres

Critical Thinking, Reading, and Writing

By the end of first year composition, students should

- Use writing and reading for inquiry, learning, thinking, and communicating
- Understand a writing assignment as a series of tasks, including finding, evaluating, analyzing, and synthesizing appropriate primary and secondary sources
- Integrate their own ideas with those of others
- Understand the relationships among language, knowledge, and power

Processes

By the end of first year composition, students should

- Be aware that it usually takes multiple drafts to create and complete a successful text
- Develop flexible strategies for generating, revising, editing, and proof-reading
- Understand writing as an open process that permits writers to use later invention and re-thinking to revise their work
- Understand the collaborative and social aspects of writing processes
- Learn to critique their own and others' works
- Learn to balance the advantages of relying on others with the responsibility of doing their part
- Use a variety of technologies to address a range of audiences

Knowledge of Conventions

By the end of first year composition, students should

- Learn common formats for different kinds of texts

- Develop knowledge of genre conventions ranging from structure and paragraphing to tone and mechanics
- Practice appropriate means of documenting their work
- Control such surface features as syntax, grammar, punctuation, and spelling.

Composing in Electronic Environments

As has become clear over the last twenty years, writing in the 21st-century involves the use of digital technologies for several purposes, from drafting to peer reviewing to editing. Therefore, although the <u>kinds</u> of composing processes and texts expected from students vary across programs and institutions, there are nonetheless common expectations.

By the end of first-year composition, students should:

- Use electronic environments for drafting, reviewing, revising, editing, and sharing texts
- Locate, evaluate, organize, and use research material collected from electronic sources, including scholarly library databases; other official databases (e.g. federal government databases); and informal electronic networks and internet sources
- Understand and exploit the differences in the rhetorical strategies and in the affordances available for both print and electronic composing processes and texts

Faculty in all programs and departments can build on this preparation by helping students learn

- How to engage in the electronic research and composing processes common in their fields
- How to disseminate texts in both print and electronic forms in their fields

(Council of Writing Program Administrators, 2000)

1.6: Writing to Learn – Comparing College Writing and High School Writing

The purpose of this Writing to Learn activity is to have you to think about the ways the WPA outcomes for student writing are similar to and different from your high school teachers' goals for student writing. Reread the WPA outcomes statement and underline any goals that match with your high school teachers' expectations and goals for your writing. Circle any goals that don't match with the writing you did in high school. Be prepared to discuss what you've underlined and circled in small groups and with the class as a whole.

Student Writing Case Study: First-Year Writing

Melissa Bratt as a freshman at Sierra College in Northern California

So far in this chapter we've been talking about college writing and first-year writing courses in a general way, but it will be helpful to get more concrete and specific by looking at an actual first-year writing student in an actual composition course. The rest of this chapter is a case study of a student writer, Melissa Bratt. A *case study* is a systematic analysis of one example – one *case* – of the subject you're studying. Our example of a student writer, Melissa, was a first-year student at Sierra College, a community college in Northern California. Since Melissa's first-year writing course required her to turn in a final portfolio with all of her rough drafts, final drafts, and reflection letters for each essay, we'll be able to take a look at everything she wrote for the semester. I also interviewed Melissa and her professor for the case study. Let's start this case study of a first-year writing student by looking at the course information sheet that Melissa's professor handed out on the first day of the course.

English 1A – College Composition

Course Description and Goals

The stated purpose of this class is twofold: 1) to introduce to you writing in an academic setting and 2) to prepare you for college-level writing across the disciplines. However, my most basic goal is to help you become a better writer, thinker, and student in general. To this end, I hope to create a sense of community in this class. This should be a place where you are free to take risks, share your ideas, hear others' ideas, and grow. Even more, though, I want you to learn to like writing, to understand it. This class should inspire in you an understanding of its importance and its relevance to your everyday life.

Since my goal is not merely to teach you how to pass this course but to teach you how to be a better writer, much of our focus will be on the writing process. I value good writing, of course, but I also value the work that goes in to good writing. As a result, the main portion of your grade will be based on your portfolio. Your portfolio will be a reflection of your growth as a writer and will demonstrate your strengths and willingness to take risks.

You have probably already figured out that there is no easy process to writing. It takes a lot of work to write, for everyone, no matter what level of writing they are at. Do you think that what you are reading right now was written this way the first time without any revisions? Everybody has to revise, no matter how good of a writer they may be. Revising is the process of writing. You will revise everything that you write in this class.

Course Requirements and Grading

20% – **Four 5–7 page formal essays**. These essays must be typed, double-spaced with 12 point font and 1" margins. I will not grade these essays, but I will comment on them to give you some suggestions for revision. You earn points for these essays by bringing them to class for peer review and for getting your drafts to me on time.

For each formal essay, you will write a 1st draft which will be reviewed by your peers. Then you will revise the essay based on your peers' comments and turn it into me for more comments. You will then revise the essay again based on my comments and put it in your portfolio.

30% – **15 Blackboard Posts**. These posts will be responses to assigned readings. These are informal in the sense that I will not comment on them, but they are not freewrites. That is, they should be proofread and carefully thought-out. In order to receive credit for a post, you must post your own and respond to at least two other students' posts. And simply *summarizing* the reading(s) will not earn you any credit. You must *respond* to the readings to earn points.

40% – **Portfolio**. A collection of your formal essays, collected week 16. This portfolio will be a representative body of your work this semester. It should demonstrate your growth as a writer and thinker as well as your willingness to take risks. Your portfolio will include:

1. All drafts of all four formal essays, including the drafts I commented on and the drafts your peers commented on. These drafts will establish proof of prewriting, revising, and participation during workshops.
2. A cover letter for each formal essay in which you spend some time reflecting on your struggles or successes with that particular essay. This cover letter should also discuss what aspects of the essay you think are strong and which you think need more work.
3. Two pages telling me what you think your strengths and weaknesses as a writer were at the beginning of the semester and what they are now. Do you think you have grown as a writer or thinker?
4. A table of contents in which you explain your portfolio's organization.

10% – **Peer Review and Participation**. You earn these points for attending class and for actively participating in peer reviews and other course activities.

Attendance and Participation

You will quickly come to find that participation in the class is not expected, it is required. <u>Every</u> student will give their opinions and feedback regarding the readings. <u>Every</u> student will "share" some of what they write to the class. <u>Every</u> student will participate and speak in front of the class. In short, you will be using your writing, reading, speaking and thinking skills to communicate in a more clearly defined manner.

I expect you to come to class and be prepared each day. You are allowed only 3 absences without penalty. *After 3 absences, I reserve the right to lower your grade one full letter grade. And after 5 absences, you may receive a failing grade in the course.*

Likewise, if you are unprepared or do not participate once or twice, there will be no penalty, but if I see a pattern of unpreparedness or nonparticipation, *I reserve the right to lower your grade up to one full letter grade.*

One of the most important reasons why participation is so important in this class is that you will be workshopping each others' papers. Each of you will read, analyze, and comment on the success and problems of each others' papers. Not only will this help the writer identify areas that need more work, but it will also help you to develop your own analytical thinking skills when revising your own writing. This will be a vital part of the class, and your participation in these workshops will be a crucial part of your overall success in the class. <u>If you miss a workshop day, it will count as 2 absences. No exceptions.</u>

Plagiarism and Late Papers

My policy on plagiarism and late papers is simple: I don't tolerate either. ALL ASSIGNMENTS ARE DUE AT OR BEFORE THE BEGINNNING OF CLASS ON THEIR DUE DATE. I don't accept late papers.

Plagiarism is using other people's words or ideas without giving them credit for it. Just don't do it. We'll spend time in this class clearly defining plagiarism and clearing up any questions you may have. <u>If you plagiarize, you will receive a zero for the assignment, and you may receive a failing grade for this course.</u>

1.7: Writing to Learn – Understanding Writing Assignments

Read over the course information sheet again and underline what you think are the key points which the professor is making. What do you think the professor values most in writing? What are the most important goals of the class? What policies would Melissa most need to be aware of? Discuss what you highlighted in small groups and/or with the whole class.

If you go back and take another look at the WPA Outcomes Statement for First-Year Writing, you'll see that Melissa's professor's goals match with the goals of the Council of Writing Program Administrators. Based on the course description, some of the most important goals of this composition course are:

- To introduce students to academic writing
- To help prepare students for writing across the curriculum
- To use writing to help improve thinking
- To use writing to take risks and grow
- To practice writing as a process
- To use writing to respond to reading

When I interviewed Melissa's professor and asked her for her definition of college writing, here's what she said:

> I think college-level writing is writing that asks students to analyze materials – to make connections between texts (written and unwritten) and to explore those connections. I also think college-level writing is writing that asks students to join in a dialogue with other academics and allows (even encourages) students to challenge the texts they analyze rather than simply accept them.

This definition of college writing is similar to the definitions of college writing we've been discussing throughout Chapter 1. Notice that Melissa's professor mentions analyzing, exploring, challenging texts, and joining in a dialogue with other experts. In our interview, Melissa's professor also emphasized using writing as discovery. She said, "Most of my colleagues and I ask students to write not to show what they know, but to discover what they don't know."

In the course description, Melissa's professor mentions that there will be four formal essays. The first essay Melissa was given asked students to come up with their own theory of education. Here's the first assignment:

English 1A
Writing Assignment #1

Theory of Education

Your task will be to come up with a theory of education. That is, you will look back over what we've read and your own experiences and create a theory of the best way(s) to educate people.

While each of your essays will be similar, you may choose to focus your essay on theories of educating children, theories of educating different types of learners, etc. Make this essay your own.

While you will be required to use some of the readings for this unit in your essay, DO NOT BRING IN ANY OUTSIDE RESEARCH. This is supposed to be YOUR theory.
Notes:
When you use the readings for this unit in your essay, you may use them to support your ideas, certainly. But don't be afraid to challenge them as well. If there is a writer you disagree with – bring it up and say so.

Some Important Definitions (from dictionary.com)

the·o·ry

1. A set of statements or principles devised to explain a group of facts or phenomena, especially one that has been repeatedly tested or is widely accepted and can be used to make predictions about natural phenomena.
2. The branch of a science or art consisting of its explanatory statements, accepted principles, and methods of analysis, as opposed to practice: *a fine musician who had never studied theory.*

3. A set of theorems that constitute a systematic view of a branch of mathematics.

4. Abstract reasoning; speculation: *a decision based on experience rather than theory.*

5. A belief or principle that guides action or assists comprehension or judgment: *staked out the house on the theory that criminals usually return to the scene of the crime.*

6. An assumption based on limited information or knowledge; a conjecture.

ed·u·ca·tion

1. The act or process of educating or being educated.

2. The knowledge or skill obtained or developed by a learning process.

3. A program of instruction of a specified kind or level: *driver education; a college education.*

4. The field of study that is concerned with the pedagogy of teaching and learning.

5. An instructive or enlightening experience: *Her work in the inner city was a real education.*

1.8: Writing to Learn – Analyzing Writing Assignments

Imagine that you've been given the writing assignment above and, individually or in small groups, think about what you would need to focus on as you begin to work on the assignment. What are the key things the professor is looking for? What is the purpose of the assignment? Who is the audience? In what ways does the teacher want students to integrate course readings?

According to the reflection letter Melissa included with her final draft of Essay #1 in her portfolio, this first essay was the hardest for her to write. Melissa said, "First of all, this was the first essay I had written since leaving high school, so I was a little rusty on how exactly to start writing. Secondly, I had no idea what I wanted my theory of education to be." Part of Melissa's challenge was the fact that her college writing gave her more freedom, which meant it was up to her to shape her own ideas. In my interview with her, Melissa said, "My teacher left it so open that I didn't know where to begin; I had never had that much freedom of decision before." Melissa said that her strategy for getting started was to go back to the assignment and think about it for a few days, and also go back to the course readings to find ideas.

Notice that in this first essay, the professor emphasizes that she wants students to "make this essay your own" and that "this is supposed to be YOUR theory." Melissa's professor wants Melissa to integrate some of the course readings, but she doesn't want Melissa to simply summarize other authors' theories of education. Melissa's professor even encourages her to disagree with the authors they're reading in the course. In the assignment description for Essay #1, Melissa's professor says about the course readings, "Don't be afraid to challenge them."

Essay #1 emphasizes critical thinking, arguing for your own theory of education, and challenging the authors students are reading in the course. Let's take a look at a paragraph from Melissa's final draft of Essay #1 to see how she does these things.

> There are many people who oppose my theory of education. Paulo Freire, author of *Pedagogy of the Oppressed*, feels that my ideas to educate people are no more than a "banking system." Freire explains the "banking" system as a system where teachers deposit information into students or, as Freire puts it, containers. Once deposited the students, without any thinking whatsoever, "patiently receive, memorize, and repeat" (Freire 58). While Freire makes valid points, I disagree with his interpretation of a student as a container and his idea that the student doesn't think about the information they are receiving. If a student doesn't think about the information they are given then no one would ever form an opinion on the topic. Freire goes on to say, "Those truly committed to liberation must reject the banking concept in its entirety" (66). But, I don't believe the banking concept should be rejected "in its entirety." The banking system does have problems such as the teacher having too much control over the students, but those who want liberation can't completely disregard the main concept. Control can be bad, it's true, but no control whatsoever would be nothing but chaos, and not even the best person can learn in the midst of chaos. Students and teachers may try to change the way they teach and learn, but neither can admit that eliminating the banking concept altogether is the best way to educate an individual. Obviously, if the banking system has endured as long as it has, then there must be something good about it.

In this paragraph, Melissa smoothly integrates one of the course readings, explaining the banking system of education and using a quote from Freire that captures his tone and language. Then Melissa does some critical thinking. She thinks about the ways she disagrees with Freire, and she develops her own reasons as to why she disagrees. In most academic writing, professors expect you to think critically about what you're reading and give your own opinions of the topic, supported by a well-developed argument.

In the second essay for the course, Melissa's professor asked for a literacy narrative. A *literacy narrative* tells a story or stories from someone's history with reading and writing. It's a common assignment in first-year writing courses because it helps the professor and peers get to know each other as writers, and it asks students to reflect on their experiences with writing before they encounter the new situation of college writing. Some literacy narratives talk about the writer's favorite books, and others focus on the writer's good (and bad) literacy experiences at school or in their community. Here's the literacy narrative assignment that Melissa was given:

Writing Assignment #2

Literacy Narrative

How did you end up here at Sierra College in English 1A? In your major? In community college in general? This essay asks you to tell the story of your literacy journey – not how you learned to read, but how you've been educated and why you've chosen education as opposed to or in addition to a profession. You may choose to discuss the people who have influenced you and/or helped you. You may want to discuss the challenges you've faced and overcome. You may also include a discussion of what has motivated you.

Certainly, you can use the readings we've done in class as models for your own narrative. But, you'll notice, **there is no one way to write a literacy narrative. All of them are different in tone, in style, and in content.**

1.9: Writing to Learn – Getting Started with Writing Assignments

Notice that in this literacy narrative assignment students have considerable freedom in terms of the style, content, and organization of the essay. If you were given this assignment, how would you begin the process? How would you figure out what forms a literacy narrative could take, since the teacher leaves the assignment so open-ended?

Sometimes in college writing you'll be given assignments that have strict guidelines about organization or about what kind of style or content to include, and sometimes you'll be given more open-ended assignments like this literacy narrative.

Melissa could go back and analyze some of the literacy narratives that were assigned as readings in the course to give her ideas about how to organize her own literacy narrative, but it's up to her to decide what to write about and what style to write in. In her portfolio reflection letter for Essay #2, Melissa said, "I had fun writing this essay because I was able to write down all the excitement of my interests and how all the things that interested me helped guide me to my major." When I asked Melissa about the importance of choosing a topic that interests the writer, she said that her advice for college students is to "explore your options and choose topics you find interesting. You may not think so at first, but you are actually interested in a lot more topics than you realize." Because Melissa wrote about something she was interested in – her goal of working for the National Security Agency – she was also able to grow as a writer and expand her voice in this essay. In her cover letter she says, "I feel that that the passion with which I wrote this essay gives it a unique voice I've never written with before. I think that voice is the strength of my essay." In college, professors will push you to grow as a writer and expand your style and voice. Sometimes this will mean writing in a very personal voice, and sometimes this will mean learning to write in the voices of your academic field in order to take on authority as, for instance, a scientist, a psychologist, a business person, or an engineer.

In her cover letter for Essay #2, Melissa mentions that she received a lot of feedback from her peers and her professor during the process of drafting and revising this essay. Like most college writing professors, Melissa's professor wants her students to practice writing as a process and to improve in their own writing processes. When I asked her why she puts so much emphasis on writing as a process, Melissa's professor said:

> One thing I try to make really clear to my students is that the writing process is not something that English teachers are trying to impose on them. Instead, the process is natural for most writers. That is, writers engage the process whether they know it or not. My goal is to make them aware of that process and, more specifically, their own process so that they can use it to their advantage.

Even though Melissa's professor is talking about "the process," she also emphasizes that there's no single writing process. In our interview she told me, "I tell my students that the writing process is different for everyone. Some students cannot write their essays until they've created complete outlines. Others just sit down and type." In Part II, we'll talk a lot more about college writing processes, and we'll explore the idea that each college writing assignment will require a different type of writing process.

Melissa's professor said that the most important aspect of a writing process is revision:

I make sure students understand that revision is "re-vision" – they need to look at their paper again and find ways to make it different. My goal is that students revise. Period. It has been my experience that revising, especially when that revision is based on comments from another, almost always makes the paper better.

Melissa closely followed her professor's advice about revising. From her first draft to her final draft, Melissa made some major changes to improve her literacy narrative. It's worthwhile to take a closer look at the revisions Melissa made, because they reflect the kind of revision process for college writing that we're going to talk more about in Part II. Below is Melissa's first draft of her literacy narrative. As you read the essay, think about what suggestions you would make to Melissa for improving her essay in the next draft.

Bound for the NSA: 1st Draft

My heart raced as I turned the page. All books generally get really good at the end, but this book had been nothing but suspenseful from the very beginning. As I read the last line and closed the book, I reflected on the setting and the subject. Dan Brown's *Digital Fortress* took place at the National Security Agency and the plot revolved around codes. I was interested by the simplicity and the complexity of the codes and I was intrigued by the National Security Agency, also known as the NSA. I found myself on the internet constantly looking up different codes and how to break them. Then I moved on to looking up information on a government agency that up until a few years ago only 3–4% of people in the U.S. knew about. I found that the National Security Agency is home to the world's largest number of mathematicians and cryptologists, also known as code breakers and the more I read, the more interested I became. In that moment I knew that that is what I wanted to do for the rest of my life; I wanted to be a cryptologist for the NSA.

Growing up, I never really showed any strength in any one subject. My grades had always been good and I wasn't a goof off kid, but I didn't have anything that I was really good at. When I went into junior high school not a whole lot changed, but I began showing some promise in math. The algebra class I was in came easier to me than any other subject and by the time I entered high school, I was one math class ahead of where I would normally have been.

Freshman year, everyone in my computer class had to look at different careers on this program we had and at that point I had come across marine biology. This career paid well and I loved the ocean not to mention the marine life, so from freshman year until I read *Digital Fortress* the summer before my senior year, I was going to be a marine biologist. I was good at science but because I was better in math, I began to dread the amount of science classes I would have to take, so for as many science classes as I was taking, I still continued to take math.

When I went into my junior year, I still had the same determination I started with to become a marine biologist. By this time I also knew that if I were to take calculus AB and BC by my senior year, I was going to have to take both trigonometry and precalculus back to back in the same year. I didn't really know why I was going to take calculus, all I knew is that I had two periods free and I didn't want to take any other classes. Decades started half way through my junior year. Decades was a huge part of your English and history class and consisted of tons of research about a decade from the 20's to the 80's, a research paper, and a hour and a half full of skits about important events from your decade to be presented in front of the class. This was a project, at my school, that you poured all of your free time into, so needless to say, I never got a chance to look into what college I was going to go to and unfortunately college application deadlines came and went. Since I had missed critical deadlines for college preparation, I had decided I would just go to Sierra College to get my general education out of the way at a cheaper cost and then I would transfer to a 4-year college.

Over the summer, I decided to finally read *The Da Vinci Code* by Dan Brown and I was blown away with how good it was and how he held my interest from page one. I saw Brown had written other books so I decided to read them all, but when I started *Digital Fortress*, I had no idea the change my dreams were going to experience. As quickly as I became interested in marine biology, the quicker it was that I knew it was not the right career for me and for those who knew me well would say my intrigue in cryptology and the NSA bordered on the verge of obsessive. However, their choice in words only fueled my desires even more to work at this kind of place, doing this kind of job. What others saw as obsessive, I saw as a passion; a passion I had never shown for anything else before. Cryptology involved math, numbers, logic, and patterns; all the types of things that I was good at. This was a job I was confident I could do because I could major in mathematics and be trained specifically for cryptology at the NSA.

I graduated high school and went on to Sierra College just this year. After taking the necessary assessment tests, I found that I was ready to move on in all my classes, so I enrolled in the next math class, Math 31, and the next English class, English 1A. I started school at Sierra College with a newfound excitement. I realized that everyday that I am at college, I know that I am working toward my future at the National Security Agency and every math problem I attempt, I know that I am that much closer to the codes I'll get to decipher.

1.10: Learn by Doing – Practicing Peer Response

In this Learn by Doing activity, you're going to practice peer response and think about the revising process. Imagine that you're giving Melissa feedback on this first draft of her literacy essay and the teacher has asked you to answer the following questions:

1. What did you like best about this draft, and why?
2. Did Melissa fully address the literacy narrative assignment?
3. What did you want to know more about?
4. Where were you confused about the Melissa's ideas or organization?
5. How effective was Melissa's style and voice?
6. What are two or three areas Melissa should focus on in the next draft?

Now that you've thought about what advice you would give Melissa for revising the first draft of her literacy narrative, let's take a look at Melissa's actual revisions. Melissa revised her literacy narrative after receiving feedback from her peer response group, and then revised it again after receiving feedback from the professor. Here's the final draft of Melissa's literacy narrative essay, which was part of her final portfolio for the class.

Bound for the NSA: Final Draft

My heart raced as I turned the page. All books generally get really good at the end, but this book had been nothing but suspenseful from the very beginning. As I read the last line and closed the book, I reflected on the setting and the subject. Dan Brown's *Digital Fortress* took place at the National Security Agency and the plot revolved around codes. I was interested by the simplicity and the complexity of the codes and I was intrigued by the National Security Agency, also known as the NSA. I found myself on the internet constantly looking up different codes and how to break them. Everything from ancient codes like the "Caesar Box" invented by Julius Caesar to Morse code and polyalphabetic substitutions; every bit of it fascinated me. Then I moved on to looking up information on a government agency that up until a few years ago only 3–4% of people in the U.S. knew about, the NSA. I found that the National Security Agency is home to the world's largest number of mathematicians and cryptologists, also known as code breakers, and the more I read, the more interested I became. In that moment I knew that that is what I wanted to do for the rest of my life; I wanted to be a cryptologist for the NSA.

Growing up, I never really showed any strength in any one subject. My grades had always been good and I wasn't a goof-off kid, but I didn't have anything that I was really good at. When I went into junior high school not a whole lot changed, but I began showing some promise in math. The algebra class I was in came easier to me than any other subject, and upon taking a test to see where you placed in Algebra 1A, I showed enough of a proficient ability that I was able to skip Algebra 1B. So, by the time I entered high school, I was one math class ahead of where I would normally have been. Where more freshmen in high school start in algebra class, I would be starting in a geometry class.

Freshman year started, and like everyone else, I had no idea what I wanted to major in when I went to college. But when everyone in my computer class had to look at different careers on this program we had, I had come across marine biology. This career paid well and I loved the ocean, not to mention marine life. I imagined living along the ocean with a lighthouse in the distance and the thought was exciting. As far as work, I imagined being around sea otters and dolphins or doing research on new species. I found myself wanting to go to the ocean so I could imagine my life there as a marine biologist. I went to the Monterey Bay Aquarium and saw, for the first time, the staff that took care of the marine life. From freshman year until I read *Digital Fortress* the summer before my senior year, I was going to be a marine biologist.

When I went into my junior year, I still had the same determination I started with to become a marine biologist. By this time I also knew that if I were to take calculus AB and BC by my senior year, I was going to have to take both trigonometry and pre-calculus back to back in the same year. I didn't really know why I was going to take calculus, all I knew is that I had two periods free and I didn't want to take any other classes. I had also never considered a time when I wouldn't be taking a math class because I've taken math classes as long as I could remember and not taking one just seemed wrong. Towards the end of the year application deadlines for college were creeping up and I didn't have any free time because of a massive project at my school called Decades. Decades was a huge part of my English and history class and consisted of hours of research about a decade from the 20's to the 80's, a research paper, and hour and a half full of skits about important events from your decade to be presented in front of the class. This was a project, at my school, that you poured all of your free time into, so needless to say, I never got a chance to look into what college I was going to go to and unfortunately college application deadlines came and went. Unlike a lot of other students, my stress level could only handle so much, and with Decades practically choosing my grade for English and History I felt that that is what I needed to spend the time working on. I knew there were other options for college and if I didn't go straight to a four year school, it wouldn't be the end of the world. So, since I had missed critical deadlines for college preparation, I had decided I would just go to Sierra College to get my general education out of the way at a cheaper cost and then I would transfer to a 4-year college.

My decision to go to Sierra College had other benefits too. First of all, I would be able to stay at home and continue to save money for a UC college, and going to Sierra would allow me to get a feel for college-like classes without actually being at a university. With that choice made and nothing much to do over the summer, I decided to finally read *The Da Vinci Code* by Dan Brown. This book had been highly recommended to me by others I knew and this was the first chance I had had to sit down and read it. I was blown away with how good it was and how Dan Brown was able to hold my interest from page one. I saw Brown had written other books so I decided to read them all, but when I started his first book, *Digital Fortress*, I had no idea the change my dreams were going to experience. As quickly as I became interested in marine biology, the quicker it was that I knew it was not the right career for me. I had already begun to question my capability to major in marine biology and the people who knew me didn't think I would really like doing it either. Up until a little while ago, I had only imagined all the good parts of being a marine biologist, but I never gave a thought as to all the work I would do that didn't involve one-on-one contact with the animals. I had become aware of the lab work involved and the research I would do while stationed on a boat somewhere on the ocean for weeks on end. On top of all these negative aspects of this career, I've never enjoyed lab research and I hated cold weather.

When I mentioned a career at the National Security Agency being a cryptologist, my friends and family reacted in a much more positive way. They would say things like, "Yeah, that sounds a lot more like you," or "That sounds like that would interest you a lot more than marine biology." My mathematical abilities greatly outnumbered my science abilities and I was much better at working on tedious puzzles than testing molecules and DNA under a microscope. Those who knew me well would say my intrigue in cryptology and the NSA bordered on the verge of obsessive. However, their choice in words only fueled my desires even more to work at this kind of place, doing this kind of job. What others saw as obsessive, I saw as a passion; a passion I had never shown for anything else before. Cryptology involved math, numbers, logic, and patterns; all the types of things that I was good at. This was a job I was confident I could do because I could major in mathematics and be trained specifically for cryptology at the NSA.

Of course, getting into the National Security Agency is next to impossible because of the high level of security needed, so I also checked into scholarships and internships that they offered. I figured that if I could find a way to get into the NSA without actually applying for a job yet, then maybe I would have a chance. I found a program called the Analysis Training Program, or ATP. This program would be available to students enrolled in a 4-year school with a 3.0 G.P.A. The benefits would include full college tuition while going to work at the NSA over the summer and receiving a yearly paycheck. For me, the biggest benefit would be having a job at the National Security Agency waiting for me when I graduate. I still have some checking on the program to do and even contacting the colleges that offer the program. But, what I figured is, while I'm getting my general education out of the way at Sierra College, I can compile a resume from the Analysis Training Program and get some of the other requirements out of the way, which also included a one page paper on why I would want to work as an intelligence specialist.

But, for now, I graduated high school and went on to Sierra College just this year. After taking the necessary assessment tests, I found that I was ready to move on in all my classes, so I enrolled in the next math class, Math 31, and the next English class, English 1A. I started school at Sierra College with a newfound excitement. I realized that every day that I am at college, I know that I am working toward my future at the National Security Agency, and every math problem I attempt, I know that I am that much closer to the codes I'll get to decipher.

1.11: Writing to Learn – Analyzing Revisions

Write about the ways Melissa revised her literacy narrative. In which parts did she expand on her ideas? Do you think she did an effective job of developing her thoughts? In what ways did the essay improve from the first draft to the final draft? How much did she focus on revising her content, and how much did she focus on editing her sentences? Be prepared to discuss your observations with the class as a whole.

Melissa's next essay assignment, Essay #3, was focused on defining "good" writing. Here's the assignment that the professor handed out to the students:

English 1A
Writing Assignment #3

What is Good Writing?

Throughout your education, no doubt others have told you what good writing is. Maybe you've been told good writing is organized or free of grammatical errors. Maybe teachers have told you that good writing is creative. Certainly, you've been taught a lot about writing. But the focus of this essay will be answering the question: What do **you think** good writing is?

Discuss what **you think** constitutes good writing. Are there certain characteristics a piece of writing should have in order to be classified as *good*? Why are these characteristics important to you? Do you agree with something one of the authors we've read for this unit mentioned in his or her essay? Then respond to it in your essay and tell why. Do you disagree with any assertions made in one or more of the readings? Tell why. You may also want to consider whether there are different standards for different types of writing.

Notes:
Make sure to include some discussion of at least 2 of the readings for this unit.

Since this essay focuses on the definition of good writing, instead of analyzing the writing assignment or talking about Melissa's writing process, let's look at what Melissa's definition of good writing is. Before we look at what Melissa thinks good writing is, though, think about your own definition of "good writing."

1.12: Writing to Learn – Your Definition of Good Writing

What is your definition of "good writing"? Explore this question, and then compare your answer to the ways Melissa defined good writing. Be prepared to share your definition with the whole class.

Here are some excerpts from Melissa's essay about how she defines good writing:

Good writing is captivating.

Good writing is the kind of writing that keeps you thinking and keeps you interested.

Good writing has no one characteristic for all types of writing and it has no set rules to follow.

Good writing relates to the reader.

I feel it is important to know who you are "talking" to in order to know how you need to write.

The sign of good writing comes when the author's words mean more than what is written on the page.

Mystery makes writing come alive.

Grammatically correct sentences are important, but correct grammar doesn't mean the writing will be interesting.

The final essay for the course was a researched argument. When I asked Melissa's professor about this researched argument assignment, she told me that she doesn't teach a research paper just to make students learn how to correctly cite sources or to create a perfect MLA style Works Cited page. She said that the most important aspect of research writing is learning how to join an academic conversation. In our interview, Melissa's professor told me, "Rather than teaching research, I teach dialog. All of the papers in my 1A course require that students engage in a dialog with a text other than their own." Here is the assignment for the researched argument essay:

English 1A
Writing Assignment #4

Argument

Come up with a subject you feel strongly about or that you would like to know more about. Then do some research on it. **Your job is to write an essay about a subject and to take a stand on that subject.** YOU CANNOT "RIDE THE FENCE" – meaning that you cannot say it is equally both good and bad. Of course, you should point out opposing views and acknowledge flaws in your own argument if you notice them. But you must take a stand.

This essay will include outside research. You must use at least 2 sources, and only one of them can be from the internet.

Look back over the models we've discussed in class. Notice that **this essay can be written in very different ways.**

This kind of argument essay gave Melissa a chance to practice one of the fundamental aspects of college writing: taking a stand and using research to support a position. Notice that Melissa's professor encourages students to choose a topic they feel strongly about or want to know more about. If Melissa simply chose a "generic" topic such as abortion or the death penalty because it was the first thing to come to mind or because she thought it would be easier to research, she probably wouldn't have written a very good essay. As Melissa mentioned in her interview with me, if the writer is passionate about the topic, the writing will be stronger and more interesting to readers. Melissa says in her portfolio reflection letter for Essay #4 that "the topic I chose for this paper was what made it so exciting to write." Melissa chose a research question that relates to her own personal interests: "Should science present their research as an absolute truth when new technological advances can disprove prior certainties?"

One of the challenges Melissa faced in writing a researched argument is balancing her own ideas and arguments with information from outside sources. In her opening paragraph, Melissa does a good job of giving her readers her main arguments in her own words:

> Mark Twain once said, "There is something fascinating about science. One gets such wholesome returns of conjecture out of such a trifling investment of fact." Over thousands of years, science has always captivated people from many different walks of life because there is just something about the mysteries of the world around us and wondering how it all works that makes science so exciting. But for thousands of years science has also been quick to take what it has discovered and present it as a fact when almost nothing in science can ever truly be a fact. Science has come a long way since the first discoveries were made and it is because of the ever changing technological advances available to us that leaves science open to constant modifications. These changes are what can be so detrimental to future studiers of science. Once science puts its findings in print for students and others to learn from, it becomes devastating if changes are made because suddenly everything students have been learning becomes obsolete or incorrect. Since the beginning of scientific research, which started with the geocentric model of the universe, to the Brontosaurus not being a real dinosaur to Pluto's recent demotion as the last planet in our solar system, science is constantly changing what it once submitted as a fact. Science should not present all of its research as absolute truth when new technological advances can disprove prior certainties.

To support her arguments about the geocentric model of the universe, the brontosaurus not being a real dinosaur, and Pluto's demotion, Melissa gathered evidence from newspapers, articles, Web sites, and lectures from her astronomy professor. Melissa started researching early in the process, and she told me that one piece of advice she has for students is not to wait until the last minute to do your research. Melissa said, "My advice for future composition students about the researching process is do not procrastinate!! Of all the essays to get a head start on, it's the research paper."

Once Melissa collected and read her sources, her next challenge was to integrate ideas and information from those sources with her own thoughts. Here's an example of a paragraph in which Melissa smoothly integrates information from her astronomy professor's lecture with her own ideas and language:

> Galileo was the first astronomer to provide evidence that the geocentric model was wrong, that the sun was actually at the center of the universe, which became known as the heliocentric model. Galileo had discovered that Venus exhibited phases like the moon and he saw that four moons were orbiting Jupiter, which contradicted that everything in the heavens revolved around the Earth. Upon publishing his findings in

Dialogue Concerning the Two Chief World Systems – Ptolemaic and Copernican, which was "such a masterpiece of exposition of the heliocentric model that readers ignored the ordained conclusion," Galileo was brought before the Inquisitions and forced to publicly renounce his work and he spent the last eight years of his life under house arrest (Anderson 17). Years later, after condemning Galileo, science ultimately adopted the heliocentric model because of the numerous amount of evidence that was submitted by other astronomers.

It's difficult to integrate information from outside sources with your own reflections and your own language, and there were times in her researched argument that Melissa had so much information and so many direct quotes from outside sources that her own argument got lost. Here's a paragraph from her researched argument where Melissa was probably relying too much on the voice of outside experts and not enough on her own reflections:

> Some may argue that the model of the universe and the Brontosaurus were scientific mistakes from hundreds of years ago, but if you've been watching the news recently you would have seen science's latest altercation. "Throw away the place mats. Redraw the classroom charts. Take a pair of scissors to the solar system mobile" because on Friday August 25, 2006, Pluto was downgraded from the ninth planet in our solar system to a "dwarf planet" (Overbye A13). This decision came after a "multiyear search for a scientific definition of the word 'planet'. The term never had an official meaning before" so science has been labeling important information without having all the facts or definitions (Inman 43). If they've just now given "planet" an official definition, then what criteria have they been labeling Mars, Earth or Saturn under? This slip-up "will force textbooks to be rewritten" and will make teachers change their curriculum (Inman 43). Moreover, "a previous proposal, unveiled last week, would have set the bar for planet hood considerably lower" (Inman 44). This proposal would have "increased the number of planets in the solar system to 12, retaining Pluto and adding Ceres, Xena and even Pluto's moon Charon" (Overbye A13). If Pluto hadn't been excluded now, it would have been in the years to come, so had the definition for a planet passed to include Pluto and the three other heavenly bodies, it would only have been changed in the future. Within a week, science could have made another devastating blunder, which probably would have needed to be altered in the coming years. Dr. Stern, of the Southwest Research Institute in Boulder, Colorado wrote in an e-mail message, "This is so scientifically sloppy and internally inconsistent, that it is embarrassing" (qtd. in Overbye A13).

In this paragraph, Melissa gets off to a good start. She makes an effective transition between the examples she'd been discussing to her final example of the controversy over whether or not Pluto should be classified as a planet. She also does a good job of capturing Overbye's distinct voice in her first quote. However, Melissa does so much quoting from Inman and Overbye that she looses ownership of her writing and her argument, and the language and voice seems to be taken over by her outside sources. It's easy to fall into this "overquoting" mode when you're writing a research paper, so keep this in mind in your own college research writing. Take the time to digest others' ideas and to make the writing your own.

In her final reflection letter, Melissa said that she has always struggled with writing. She also said she realizes that just like with any other kind of skill, practice is the key to improving. "The thing is," Melissa said, "every time I write anything, I'm getting better." Melissa felt that her college composition course gave her practice in reading, writing, and researching which helped prepare her for her college career. You might feel a little overwhelmed at first when you take a college writing course and you see how much writing and revising you're going to be asked to do. Remember that there's a reason most colleges require students to take at least one composition course. The key to improving as a writer is practice, practice, practice; and the best place to begin to practice college writing is a first-year writing course.

Examples of Student Writing from First-Year Writing Courses

For more examples of student writing from first-year writing courses, visit the following online student writing journals:

Booth Prize, Stanford University
http://www.stanford.edu/dept/undergrad/cgi-
bin/drupal_ual/AP_univ_req_PWR_Boothe.html

e-Vision, James Madison University
http://www.jmu.edu/evision/

Interpolations: A Journal of First-Year Writing, University of Maryland
http://www.english.umd.edu/interpolations/

Our Own Words, Florida State University
http://wr.english.fsu.edu/First-Year-Composition/Our-Own-Words-The-James-
M.-McCrimmon-Award

The Printer's Devil, Arizona State University
http://writing.asu.edu/?q=content/the-printer%E2%80%99s-devil-contest

---

1.13: Writing to Learn – Analyzing Your Writing Course

Compare the syllabus and writing assignments in Melissa's course to the syllabus and writing assignments in the writing course you're taking right now. What are the similarities between Melissa's course and your course? In what ways are your instructor's expectations and assignments different?

Review of Key Ideas in Chapter 1

- College writing requires critical thinking, which means more than simply memorizing information and regurgitating it on a test. Critical thinking means questioning assumptions, evaluating arguments, and analyzing and interpreting texts.

- College writing often requires research and integration of evidence from outside reading, extended argument and analysis, and sophisticated organization of ideas. Formulas for writing like the "five-paragraph theme" might be helpful for some types of timed essay exams, but most college professors expect you to grow beyond formulaic writing.

- First-year writing courses help you make the transition from high school writing to college writing by giving you practice in writing for a variety of situations, teaching you writing as a process that requires multiple drafts, and introducing you to the conventions of college-level writing.

- Even though there are some general features of college-level writing, and first-year writing courses will help introduce you to these features, each academic field has its own types of writing and thinking and its own conventions. Even different professors in the same field will have different expectations for writing.

1.14: Writing to Learn – Advice for College Writing

Imagine that you're writing a letter or email to a high school senior who's thinking about going to your college. Give the high school senior some advice about preparing for college writing, and describe the expectations for college writing at your school. If you still have friends in high school, you can even send them your response to this Writing to Learn activity in a letter or an email.

2　College Writing Situations

Successful writing requires the accurate assessment of and adaption to the demands of particular writing situations.

　　—Professor Lucille McCarthy, English Department, University of Maryland-
Baltimore County (McCarthy, 1987: 262)

Writers know how to analyze any given writing situation so that they can gain insight into what is expected of them and what is appropriate and inappropriate in that situation.

　　　　　—Marian College Department of English and Communication (2010)

We should be developing the sort of good writers who are versatile, who can adopt to a wide variety of writing tasks and situations…We must recognize that different writing situations require different types of writing; that what is good in a piece of academic literary criticism may not be good in a newspaper book review and will likely not be good in a brochure.
—Professor Richard Coe, Department of English, Simon Fraser University
(Coe, 2002: 200)

At the heart of every assignment is the rhetorical situation – someone writing to someone about something for some purpose.
—Professor Stephen Wilhoit, Learning Teaching Center, University of Dayton
(Wilhoit, 2002: 62)

2.1: Writing to Learn – Reflecting on College Writing Situations

Before we talk about college writing situations in this chapter, do some brainstorming and think about what you believe are the most important factors in college writing situations. Individually or in groups, make a list of important factors for any college writing situation (e.g. "audience" or "level of formality"). To help you consider aspects of college writing situations, you might think back to writing assignments you've been given this semester.

The Rhetorical Situation and College Writing

In Chapter 1, we explored the question, *What is college writing?*, and we looked at some general features of college writing. In this chapter, we're going to explore some features of any college writing situation – what writing specialists call the *rhetorical situation*. Each writing situation – each *rhetorical situation* – involves a writer communicating to an audience using some type of text. There are many factors you'll want to consider when you face rhetorical situations in college, including your purpose for writing, the audience you're writing to, the persona or voice you take on in your writing, the type of text you're writing, the context of the course, and the broader social context of the situation. In this chapter, we'll look at common college-writing situations and thinking strategies to provide you with some tools for college writing. We'll also explore one of the most important concepts for college writing:

genre. Understanding the concept of genre and how it applies to college writing will help you be more successful with your writing in all of your college courses, no matter what your major subject is.

2.2: Writing to Learn – Defining *Rhetoric*

The purpose of this Writing to Learn activity is to see what you already think about a key term in writing courses: *rhetoric.* Without putting any pressure on yourself to come up with a "correct" definition, write a definition (or definitions) of *rhetoric.* Be prepared to discuss your definition of rhetoric with the class as a whole.

You might have heard the media or politicians refer to rhetoric as something negative (for instance, "The Senator's speech was full of empty rhetoric"), but writing professors define rhetoric in a different way – not as a derogatory term for empty verbiage. Here's how some well-known rhetoricians have defined rhetoric:

Aristotle: "Rhetoric is the art of discovering the available means of persuasion."

(Aristotle, I.2)

Wayne Booth: "The entire range of resources that human beings share for producing effects on one another: effects ethical (including everything about character), practical (including political), emotional (including aesthetic) and intellectual (including every academic field)."

(Booth, 2004: xi)

Kenneth Burke: "The use of words by human agents to form attitudes or induce actions in other human agents."

(Burke, 1969: 41)

George Kennedy: "Rhetoric, in the most general sense, is the energy inherent in emotion and thought, transmitted through a system of signs, including language, to others to influence their decisions or actions."

(Kennedy, 1991: 7)

Sally Miller Gearhart: "The creation or co-creation of an atmosphere in which people or things, if and only if they have the internal basis for change, may change themselves."

(Gearhart, 1979: 198)

At the heart of all of these definitions of rhetoric is someone trying to effectively communicate something to someone else. The need to communicate effectively is an important part of all college courses, whether you're asked to communicate in words, images, music, or numbers. In that sense, rhetoric is fundamental to everything you do in your college courses. Rhetoric can be print, visual, digital, oral – the list goes on. All acts of composition, in print or other media, are rhetorical acts.

Writing scholars say that rhetoric is always *situated*. This means that every time you write in college, you write for a specific situation – for a specific purpose and audience, in a specific type of text, in a specific academic field, and for a specific course. This situation shapes what you say and how you say it. Writing scholars call this the *rhetorical situation*. Rhetorical situations are complex, and they include a variety of factors: the writer's purpose for writing, the persona or the voice the writer takes on in writing, the audience for the writing, the type of text, and the wider contexts that include the social backgrounds and personal beliefs of the writer and audience or the community of readers the writer is composing for. This community of readers is called the *discourse community*. We'll talk more about discourse communities in Part III, when we begin to explore writing across the curriculum.

2.3: Writing to Learn – A Rhetorical Situation outside of School

The purpose of this Writing to Learn activity is to start you thinking about the concept of the rhetorical situation by reflecting on writing you've done outside of school. Think back to the last time you wrote something outside of school (e.g. an email, a blog post, a diary entry, a letter, a story). Describe the purpose and audience for the rhetorical situation. Describe the role you took on as a writer – your attitude, tone, and style. What kind of voice did you compose in? What was the form and format of the text?

If you completed Writing to Learn Activity 2.3, you've thought about your own experiences with a recent rhetorical situation. Let's define some of the major components of a rhetorical situation.

Purpose

A writer's purpose could include the goals the writer has for the written work, the purpose that is set out for the writer in an assignment, and the influence of factors such as the audience the writer is addressing or the type of writing. In college writing, your purposes for writing are always complex, and they might include your career goals, your desire to obtain an "A" grade, your goal of improving as a writer, the purpose defined in the assignment, the goals of the course, and other purposes as well. College writing assignments are likely to have multiple purposes for both the writer and the reader.

Audience

In college you'll most often be writing to professors as your primary audience, but professors can play a variety of roles when they read and respond to your writing. Sometimes professors will play the role of interested reader and read your writing to find out what you're thinking or to get to know you better as a writer and a thinker. At other times, professors play the role of representative of their academic field and they'll respond to you as a biologist, an anthropologist, a literary critic, or other representative of a specific discipline. Sometimes professors play the role of examiner, testing you to see what you've learned about the subject. Professors might also role-play hypothetical audiences when they respond to your writing. For example, a professor might ask you to imagine that you are writing a memo to the board of directors of a company or a letter to a senator. You may even be asked to address wider audiences outside of the course – for example, you might be asked to write a letter to the editor of your college newspaper, or to help create a newsletter for a non-profit organization for a service learning project. Your audience will affect your purpose for writing, the persona or voice you take on, and the way you develop and organize your text.

Persona

A writer's persona is the way the writer presents herself or himself in writing. Persona can include the voice, stance, tone, and style a writer takes on in writing. Persona includes a writer's word choice, the writer's attitude towards the subject and the reader, and the writer's level of formality. The persona you take on in your writing will depend on your purpose for writing, the subject you're writing about, the audience you're writing to, the type of text (genre) you're writing, and the context for writing. Since much of the writing you do in college will be academic texts for audiences of scholars in the academic field, it will be common for you to take on a more formal persona in your college writing than you would in emails to friends or discussions at the dinner table with your family. However, not all academic writing is formal. Sometimes your college professors will ask you to write personal narrative essays or electronic discussion board posts to your peers, or they will ask you to do informal, in-class writing, like the Writing to Learn activities in this book. There's no single persona you'll take on in all of your college writing: each rhetorical situation will demand a different voice and style.

Text

Writing scholars used to think of texts as only the printed word, but more recently they have expanded the way they define texts. A *text* could mean a research paper or a lab report, but it could also mean a Web site, a blog, a PowerPoint presentation, a brochure, a poster, or other kinds of texts. Because communicating in college includes more than the written word, writing specialists have coined the term, *academic discourse*, to describe college communication. *Discourse* in this sense can include communicating with photos, graphs, Web sites, podcasts, or other means. There are some types of texts and writing assignments you could encounter in courses in different academic fields – for example, short-answer examinations, reader response journals, or book reviews. Other types of texts and assignments are more common in a specific academic field – for example, lab reports in the natural sciences or company profiles in business. Specific kinds of texts, like the lab report, which have purposes, audiences, and forms that have evolved over time as a common response to a recurring rhetorical situation, are called *genres*. The ability to recognize and understand the genre of what you're writing is crucial in college, and we'll be looking more closely at the concept of genre later in this chapter.

Context

The context of a rhetorical situation includes all of the broader social, cultural, and historical factors that can influence writing. This could include the writer's context and culture, such as her/his history as a writer, the experiences the writer has had in class and with the professor, the writer's level of success and confidence in previous writing assignments in the course or in college in general, the writer's cultural background, and other writer characteristics and experiences. Context could include aspects of audience such as their socioeconomic class, their level of expertise with the topic, their ethnic background, their personal beliefs, and other aspects of their characteristics and experience. Context could be related to the type of text you're writing – for example, in a timed essay test, factors such as how long you have to write and how broad or narrow the questions are will have a major effect on what you say and how you say it.

Sample Student Essay

To make these different features of rhetorical situations more concrete, let's look at a sample student essay. Matt Miles, a student in a first-year writing course at James Madison University, was faced with a common rhetorical situation in college writing: an argumentative essay supported by outside sources and written for an academic audience. Look at the assignment Matt was given.

Essay Assignment

Faigley, in his introduction to the readings on body language, tells us that body image is socially constructed; that is, society dictates how we read and interpret the body. Western notions of beauty, for example, are largely determined by cultural standards espoused by pop culture and the media. Interestingly, however, many of the readings we will discuss over the next two weeks suggest the body is often mobilized to construct its own meaning. Young adults involved in the Punk movement of the 1970s, for example, donned safety pins through their lips and noses as a means of revolting against what they perceived to be an oppressive system of cultural values, a system which privileged and rewarded conformity. Today, body piercings are commonplace and rarely carry the political connotations of the past. Why? In this cycle, we will examine how body images are constructed by both society and the individual. More importantly, we will explore the relation between the body and hegemony, the prevalent, but invisible, ideology that maintains status quo in our society.

Readings:
Rafferty, "Kate Winslet, Please Save Us!" p. 525
hooks, "Straightening Our Hair" p. 531
King, "The Other Body: Disability and Identity Politics" p. 544

For this assignment, you should write an essay in which you make and support a claim that is related to the topic of body image. You might consider how a cultural practice regarding the body serves to oppress a group, as hooks does in her essay. Similarly, you might consider how a particular group or community of people construct "acceptable" images of the body. For example, you might consider how the media portrays disability or beauty, or you might consider how advertisements construct bodies to be consumed. As you search for a focus for this essay, peruse the other readings in this section of the text for ideas.

Remember that your claim must be contestable and it should not be based solely on value judgments.

Requirements:

- Minimum of 1000 words
- Minimum of three scholarly sources, one of which must be non-electronic
- MLA format (APA and Chicago are also acceptable formats)

In Matt's case, the rhetorical situation involved making a claim about a specific topic his class had been reading about ("body image") and supporting his claim with evidence from what other writers have said on the topic. Matt was writing to a general academic audience, and because his essay was published in *e-Vision*, a journal of first-year writing at James Madison University, his audience included college students and professors. Below is the final draft of Matt's essay, as it appeared in *e-Vision*.

Personal Appearance and Its Implications of Sexuality
By Matt Miles (Miles, 2004)

With David Beckham (and the metrosexual movement he has become associated with) and shows like *Queer Eye for the Straight Guy*, sexuality and physical appearance have seemingly become linked. The implication is good personal hygiene and having a trendy sense of fashion is only for women and gay men. Conversely, a heterosexual male cannot cater to his personal appearance without his sexuality being questioned. Our culture would have one believe if someone does not fit into these norms of fashion, they must transcend the binaries of sexuality and be categorized in a new classification of "metrosexual" (seemingly less-than-heterosexual). As arbitrary as it may seem when one thinks about it, society has developed the perception that personal appearance is directly related to sexual preference.

Where is this perception coming from? The past several years the media has bombarded the public with this idea that sexuality has a direct correlation with level of attractiveness. In an article published by the *Journal of Homosexuality*, author Nancy Rudd makes the suggestion that marketers should target more "innovative" and "trendy" clothing towards gay men and more casual clothing such as jeans and T-shirts for straight men (109). This more than implies trendy fashion is strictly for homosexual and not heterosexual men, for she makes a direct link between sexual orientation and trendy fashion. This is because the media has built up the stereotype that a man's sexual preference for another man makes him a reliable authority on attractiveness and fashion. Shows like *Queer Eye for the Straight Guy* and its parody, *Straight Plan for the Gay Man*, further perpetuate this notion. *Queer Eye's* concept is a group of homosexuals takes a heterosexual male (who happens to have no sense of hygiene or fashion sense) and imparts their "natural" sense of style on him. The implication of this show is a homosexual male has some type of natural knack for being attractive whereas a heterosexual male is seemingly less attractive. The show is not titled *Fashionable Eye for the Unfashionable Guy*. Indeed, the creators of the show felt it necessary to link a show about improving appearance with sexuality. The public accepts this relationship without hesitation and, in fact, glorifies the bi-product of the relation between the fashionable homosexual and his heterosexual subject – the metrosexual.

The term "metrosexual" was coined in 1994 by English journalist Mark Simpson and is defined as, "a dandyish narcissist in love with not only himself, but his urban life-style; a straight man who is in touch with his feminine side," or as another article put it, "a straight man who styles his hair using three different products" ("Today's Metro-sexual" 45; Simpson). Since then, this term has been judged the, "most overused word" by Lake Superior State University's annual "List of Words Banished from Queen's English" (Penttila). Despite the fact most definitions of the term "metrosexual" deal primarily with aspects of appearance, the term has undoubtedly become linked with sexuality. The obvious indication is the root "sexual," which refers explicitly to sexu-ality and sexual preference. In an article about famed metrosexual David Beckham, questioning of the athlete's heterosexuality comes up quite often. Finally, the author professes, "(he) is not a heterosexual after all. No...the captain of the England football squad is actually a screaming, shrieking, flaming, freaking metrosexual" (Simpson). This quote perfectly illustrates how Beckham is thought to be less-than-heterosexual due to his appearance. The author actually states he cannot be a heterosexual because he is well dressed and manicured. In another interview posted on ESPN.com in which TV personality Mike Greenberg (self-described metrosexual) admits he owns and uses Vitamin C facial cleanser and Kiss My Face lotion, he responds, "Yes, I'm practically a woman. I'm as close to being a woman as you can possibly get" (Buckheit). Greenberg not only demotes his own sexuality but his gender, as well, based solely on several things he does for his own personal hygiene. Both these examples associate men's appearance with feminine or less-than-heterosexual male lifestyles. For both men, their sexual preference does not define their sexuality; their appearance does.

The stereotype is not based solely on a man's overall appearance. However, judg-ments on a man's sexuality are being made based on relatively minor things he might do for his appearance or hygiene. An example of this is the new popular trend of the "metrosexual quiz" that can be found in numerous forms throughout the World Wide Web. In these quizzes, the user answers questions such as, "Have you ever tweezed, waxed or trimmed your eyebrows?" The correct answer (for being a metrosexual) is listed as, "Yes, frequently. I firmly believe eyebrows should be two distinct entities," whereas the answer for being completely heterosexual (that is, unconcerned with physical appearance) is, "No, Never" ("Are You Metrosexual?"). According to this particular quiz, if a man is guilty of grooming his eyebrows, he loses some of his heterosexuality. Other common questions in this and similar quizzes cover everything from how much a guy spends on a hair cut to what type of underwear he wears and what type of soap and shampoo he uses. The user has a list of options to choose from and, after answering several of these questions, can be rated on his level of metrosexuality. The rating systems usually go from something along the lines of "manly man" (being the most heterosexual) to some sort of metrosexual (being fashionable and slightly straight), and in some cases, if the person is too into self-care, some level of homosexual. If a man prefers more expensive haircuts and soaps, he is either homosexual or metrosexual, but certainly not heterosexual. Quizzes like these make the claim that by judging a man through how many shoes he owns or how many types of hair gels he uses, they can dictate to the user what type of sexual preference he has.

These examples of the media's bias have an impact on people's perceptions. In an article published in *Psychology of Women Quarterly* about studies regarding personality traits of physically androgynous people and others' perceptions of their sexuality, Laura Madison concludes that people do, in fact, link physical appearance with aspects of a person's psychological characteristics. She goes on to state this link is especially strong between men with more feminine characteristics (manicured nails, well-styled hair) and homosexuality (149). In Marti Yarbrough's article, "The Metrosexual Male: What Sisters Really Think of Them," women, in reference to their opinions of metrosexual men, say "I may question his sexual preference," and "[t]hey dress nice, smell good and are usually good eye candy, but they present a lot of questions. Like, is he borderline gay or bisexual?" (Yarbrough 34, 36). For these women, questions of sexual orientation are immediately evoked by a man who is well-dressed and has a pleasant smell. These studies and interviews illustrate how people's perceptions of appearance and sexuality have become linked.

Society has developed a bias that directly links a man's appearance with his sexual preference. If a man uses self-care products and dresses fashionably, he is considered less heterosexual than a man who does not take care of either his physical appearance or personal hygiene. It has become socially acceptable to commit the fallacy of generalizing and stereotyping straight men as being less attractive than men who are homosexual. And if a straight man does happen to have some fashion sense and takes care of his body, the term "heterosexual" does not apply. Society has developed a new classification to fit this type of person, "metrosexual," to indicate his seemingly lower level of heterosexuality. The media has caused and perpetrates this stereotype through shows like *Queer Eye for the Straight Guy* and many other types of articles and internet sources. In the politically correct society we live in, usually making a personal judgment about someone's lifestyle based solely on his appearance is frowned upon. However, this is an example where it has become acceptable to make such a stereotype. Shamefully, we live in a society where a heterosexual male who takes care of his personal appearance is scrutinized by the public eye.[5]

Works Cited

"Are you Metrosexual?" *Sportsnation*. 12 Sept. 2004 <http://proxy.espn.go.com
/chat/sportsnation/quiz?event_id=418>.

Buckheit, Mary . "Are Mike and Mike Metrosexuals?" *ESPN Page 2*. 11 Nov. 2004.
12 Sept. 2004 <http://sports.espn.go.com/page2/s/030922Metrogreenygolic
.html>.

Madison, Laura . "Inferences Regarding the Personality Traits and Sexual Orientation of Physically Androgynous People." *Psychology of Women Quarterly* 24.2
(2000): 148–161.

Penttila, Chris. "In vain: what does the future hold for the once-hot metrosexual?"
Entrepreneur 32.7 (2004): 24. Expanded Academic ASAP. Carrier Library, James
Madison University. 12 Sept. 2004 < http://web2.infotrac.galegroup.com>.

Rudd, Nancy A. "Appearance and self-presentation research in gay consumer cultures: issues and impact." *Journal of Homosexuality* 31.1 (1996): 109–134.

Simpson, Mark. "Meet the Metrosexual." *Salon* 22 Jan. 2002. 12 Sept. 2004
<http://www.salon.com/ent/feature/2002/7/23/metrosexual>.

"Today's Metrosexual." *Global Cosmetic Industry* 172 (2004): 45.

Yarbrough, Marti . "The Metrosexual Male: What Sisters Really Thing of Them." *Jet*
105.8 (2004): 34–38.

Let's look more closely at aspects of the rhetorical situation Matt was faced with
and how he responded to the rhetorical situation.

Matt's Purpose

Each writing situation has purposes for both the writer and the reader. Matt's purpose
was to persuade: he needed to make a claim and support it. Since he knew his readers
were going to be college students and professors, he needed to make an argument that
was well reasoned and supported with evidence. Because Matt's topic is connected to
popular culture, some of his evidence is from popular culture sources, like ESPN; but
most of his evidence comes from academic journals. Matt's purpose is clearly to
persuade an academic audience, and this is reflected in his reasoning, his persona, and
the kinds of sources he uses. When you write for academic purposes, you need to be
aware of the key terms that scholars talk about when they discuss your subject, and
you need to let your audience know how you're defining those key terms. Notice how
Matt defines key terms like *metrosexual*, *sexuality*, and *gender*.

In college you'll have many purposes for writing: to persuade an audience, to
inform a non-expert about a topic, to demonstrate to your professor that you understand reading material, to take a position in a debate, and other purposes as well. Most
college assignments have more than one purpose. For example, in a summary/

response journal, you may be asked to summarize the main points of an article and respond to the ideas presented in the article. Sometimes your professor will give you a specific purpose or purposes for a writing assignment, and sometimes you'll be able to choose your own purpose for writing. Your purpose will affect the tone you take, the kind of language you use, the way you structure your writing, and the type of evidence you include to support your ideas.

Matt's Audience
Purpose is always connected to audience. You could argue that Matt's primary audience is his professor, but notice that in the assignment the professor doesn't present Matt with one particular way to write the essay. The professor is looking for a claim supported by evidence from other scholars, which is a common type of academic writing. In Matt's case, the professor is playing the role of a representative of the general academic discourse community. Since Matt knew that it was possible his essay could be nominated to be included in the James Madison University student writing journal, *e-Vision*, he also had to think about a possible audience of college students and professors from across his own college. As Matt was drafting and revising his essay, he needed to consider the types of arguments a skeptical college-level audience would make about his claim.

Often in college, professors will give assignments that pose a hypothetical audience: writing a business memo to a company, reporting on a science experiment to non-experts, making an argument to readers of a specific academic journal, or other imagined purposes and audiences. Even if you're writing only to your professor, it's important to keep in mind that most professors will (consciously or unconsciously) play the role of the community of scholars in their field when they respond to your paper. Most assignments will ask you to take a stance as a writer in relation to your audience. Sometimes you'll take the stance of a novice writing to a professor who's playing the role of the expert audience, but most often college-writing assignments ask you to take the stance of an expert writing to other experts, which is the stance Matt had to take in his essay. In most college writing, you will thoroughly research your topic and join the academic conversation as an *insider* rather than an *outsider*.

Matt's Persona
Matt has taken on a more formal persona in his essay than he would take on if he were arguing with friends or writing an email to a family member. Matt uses a language that matches the academic purpose of making a scholarly argument. For example, Matt decided to use formal transition words such as *seemingly*, *conversely*, and *whereas* instead of more informal transitions such as *also* and *but*. Part of Matt's

persona as an academic writer is the way he makes us trust him and see him as reliable. He makes carefully thought-out arguments and supports his position with the words and ideas of other trusted writers who've thought and written about the same subject. Matt has also carefully edited and proofread his essay, so there are no grammatical or typographical errors, nor any awkward sentences that would interfere with communication to a reader.

Matt's Text

The kind of text Matt was asked to write is a common one in college discourse. It's a typical academic argument essay, in which the writer makes a claim and supports it with evidence from other scholars. In this type of text, writers need to take a stance and make an organized, well-reasoned, and well-developed argument. As the professor points out in the assignment, academic argument doesn't allow for claims based solely on value judgments. In the assignment, the professor also points out that students could use the course readings as models of academic argument essays.

The argument essay Matt was asked to write also has some specific *conventions*. Conventions are norms of style, form, and format that a community of writers and readers has agreed upon over time. Every community of readers and writers has a set of conventions which it tends to follow when writing for that particular community. For example, if you visit online chat rooms, it's normal to use abbreviations for words (like *lol* for "laughing out loud"). The community of writers (people who visit chat rooms) has agreed that using abbreviations is useful in chat room conversations. Using abbreviations becomes a convention: a format for writing that most people in the community agree on and use. Since Matt had to integrate and cite outside sources, he needed to follow a convention for citing them that would be understandable to the community of scholars he was writing for. He couldn't make up his own system for citing sources, since that would confuse his readers, and they would be less likely to be persuaded by his argument if they thought he didn't know the accepted conventions. Since Matt was writing this essay in an English course, in the assignment his professor listed a citation or referencing style abbreviated as *MLA* (short for *Modern Language Association*), but his professor mentioned that *APA* (*American Psychological Association*) and *Chicago* style were also acceptable. We'll talk more about the different types of citation and referencing conventions in Part III.

Matt's Context

You might think Matt's context is pretty straightforward: he's writing an essay for a college course. However, the context of any rhetorical situation is always complex. Consider the factors that create the context for Matt's writing: the essays from the textbook his class is reading, the discussions his class had been having about those essays, the response Matt received from his professor on previous writing assignments, the objectives of the course, Matt's prior experiences as a writer, Matt's level of interest in the topic – and this is not nearly a complete list of contextual factors. In Matt's case, the professor emphasized using the readings from the course textbook as models, so the wider course context was important to Matt's rhetorical situation. Closely reading the essays from the course textbook helped Matt come up with ideas for his own arguments and also provided models for Matt in deciding what persona to take on and how to organize his essay.

2.4: Learn by Doing – Reflecting on a College Rhetorical Situation

The purpose of this Learn by Doing activity is to apply what you've been reading about the rhetorical situation in college to your own college writing experiences. Write about a rhetorical situation you've encountered in one of your college writing assignments this semester or term (or a previous term, if you don't have a writing assignment in your other courses this term). What was the purpose of the rhetorical situation? Who was the audience? What kind of persona did you take on? What type of text (genre) did you write? What was the context for your writing?

Genres as Responses to Rhetorical Situations

Genres develop...because they respond appropriately to situations that writers encounter repeatedly.
>   —Professor Amy Devitt, Department of English, University of Kansas
>   (Devitt, 1993: 576)

Genre has become a term that refers to complex oral or written responses by speakers or writers to the demands of a social context.
>   —Professor Ann M. Johns, Department of Rhetoric and Writing, San Diego
>   State University (Johns, 2002: 3)

Genres are forms of texts or textual organization that arise out of particular social configurations or the particular relationships of the participants in an interaction.
>   From the book, *Multiliteracies* (Cope and Kalantzis, 2000: 21)

2.5: Writing to Learn – Exploring "Genre"

The purpose of this Writing to Learn activity is to help you reflect on the definition of *genre* by connecting the concept of genre (which may be a new concept for you) to something you're familiar with – a genre of music you listen to. Think of a type of music you listen to (country, hip-hop, techno, reggae, or other) and write about the rhetorical situation of the type of music you have selected. What topics are common in the type of music you chose? Who is the typical audience for the music? What are some conventions of the songs in the genre? Do any songs break these conventions? What kind of persona do most singers take on in the genre? What social contexts are there for the music (for example, cultural, economic, or political contexts)? How has the genre of the music you have chosen changed over time?

Genre is a complicated concept, so it might help to start with a simple example: a grocery list. Think of buying groceries as a rhetorical situation. Your purpose is to make sure you get all of the different types of food that you've run out of. Your audience is yourself – you simply need something you can use as a reminder for yourself, and it doesn't need to be anything formal or to be written with an engaging style. The rhetorical situation is one that occurs again and again – every time you run out of groceries. The grocery list is a genre that has grown out of this repeated rhetorical situation. Everyone writing a grocery list has the same basic purpose and audience, and most everyone uses the same type of text: a list of groceries on a sheet of paper or notecard. The context of the grocery list can affect the way it's organized. Since I shop at the same grocery store every time, I try to organize my list by the order of the aisles. When I'm short on cash, my grocery list is brief; when I'm giving a party or have money in the bank, I make a long list of grocery items. The genre of the grocery list has evolved over time as a useful response to a repeated rhetorical situation, but it's also still evolving. Instead of using a piece of paper or notecard, you might now save your grocery list in an iPod touch or Blackberry, or you might even record what groceries you need using a voice recorder in your cell phone. A genre, then, is a typical response to a recurring rhetorical situation that has evolved over time – and continues to evolve. A genre (such as the grocery list) has similar purposes, audiences, and conventions each time it occurs. As you can see with the grocery list example, a genre is more than just a format: it's a way of getting something done.

In college, you're going to encounter a wide variety of genres, some of which are connected to specific academic fields, and some of which are common in almost any field. Since we're going to focus on the ways that genres differ in specific academic fields later in this book (Part III), let's take a look at a genre that is common across the curriculum: the scholarly book review. The assignment from Professor Kia Bentley's social work course that I used as a model of college-level writing at the beginning of Chapter 1 is an example of the genre of the scholarly book review. Let's take another look at Professor Bentley's book review assignment:

> Every student in the class will be asked to write a book review of one of the supplemental texts listed in the syllabus. Your five page (maximum, double-spaced, perfectly APA formatted) review should include a rich but brief description of the book's content and style, a thorough review of its strengths and weaknesses from your perspective, an analytical discussion of its potential contributions to the field, and its specific impact on your thinking and your learning. Reviewing already published book reviews (found in most social work journals) has been helpful to other students in getting a "feel" for a book review's usual style. Be prepared to discuss your reviews with your classmates on the due date.

2.6: Writing to Learn – The Book Review as a Genre

The purpose of this Writing to Learn activity is for you to explore the concept of genre by thinking about Professor Bentley's book review. Reread Professor Bentley's assignment and define the rhetorical situation for the genre of the book review described in the assignment. Discuss the purpose, audience, persona, text, and context of Professor Bentley's book review.

Scholarly book reviews typically have the purpose of briefly summarizing the content of a book and evaluating a book's strengths and weaknesses. The audience is usually other scholars who are interested in the subject area of the book being reviewed but haven't read it yet. The audience might be using the reviewer's judgments to decide if they want to read or to buy the book or not, so part of the context for the writer is the responsibility of helping other scholars make this decision. In a book review, the writer takes on a persona of authority, since the writer has read the book closely and carefully in order to make a fair judgment. The rhetorical situation for the scholarly book review evolved over time: as more and more academic books were being published each year, scholars needed a way to find out about new books and new ideas in their field without having to read every book published. Academic journals began including book reviews as a way to meet this need. For the book review, genre was a social action, arising out of a specific rhetorical situation and meeting the social needs of communities of scholars (discourse communities). Like all genres, the book review continues to evolve. For example, as more and more books and other kinds of texts are published online, the book review genre will need to change to adapt to this new medium.

One important thing to notice in Professor Bentley's book review assignment is that she wants students to discuss the impact of the book on their personal thinking and learning. Some college professors who assign a book review might ask you to relate the ideas in the book to your thinking and learning, and some will want you to focus specifically on evaluating the book itself. Genres aren't templates for writing which let you just "plug in" what you write to a formula. Even a common genre like the book review will differ in purpose, organization, and persona in each academic field and for each writer. Each writer and each academic field will have a different approach to writing even a common genre like the book review. A genre like the book review will also take on different forms depending on whether it's a scholarly book review or a book review meant for a less specialized audience, such as a review of a Stephen King novel in a Sunday newspaper or popular magazine, or a customer review of a cookbook on Amazon.com.

Sample Student Essay

Let's take a look at an example of a scholarly review. The scholarly book review below is by Feras Sleiman, a student at the University of Michigan. It was published in the *University of Michigan Journal of Political Science*. Read the review and think about how it displays the conventions of the genre of the scholarly review that we've been discussing. As you read, also pay attention to my annotations of the review, where I point out some of the features of Sleiman's review that are typical of the scholarly book review as a genre.

Review of *Dying to Win: The Strategic Logic of Suicide Terrorism*
by Feras Sleiman
Published in University of Michigan *Journal of Political Science*

Robert Pape demonstrates a clear and precise command of the phenomenon of suicide "terrorism" with a remarkably original, methodical, and scholarly contribution to strategic thinking today. This controversial topic is one that sparks divisive debate over who the West's enemies are, why "they" hate the West, and

Sleiman gives a clear overall evaluation of the book.

what the West should do to better protect itself from "terrorist" attacks in a post-9/11 climate. Some purport the belief that Islamic fundamentalists, inspired by a perverted version of Islam, are engaged in a symbolic culture war against the West. Contrarily, Robert Pape argues that Western policies (particularly the stationing of Western troops in Islamic countries) create a legitimating ideology for "terrorist" organizations to commit acts of suicide "terrorism." In other words, Pape contends that "they" hate us for what we <u>do</u>; not for what we <u>are</u>. If so, how do we determine the <u>real</u> causes for the high frequency of suicide "terrorist" attacks in the last twenty-five years? In *Dying to Win*, Pape raises this vital question to go to the heart of a volatile debate over this growing threat – a threat that has manifested itself before and will continue to threaten the security of the West. Yet, he insists that the path to countering this threat involves a frank understanding of the problem grounded in fact, not politics, and a reevaluation of American foreign policy.

Sleiman summarizes the author's central argument in the book.

Pape makes his argument on the basis of what he believes to be a complete listing of all suicide "terrorist" attacks between 1980 and 1994 – a worldwide total of 315 attacks. With data from more than 460 attackers – including the names of 333 – we now know that these individuals were not mainly poor, desperate criminals or uneducated religious fanatics but were often well-educated, middle-class political activists. Pape suggests that the cause of these attacks is usually to rid a homeland from foreign (Western) forces. In his view, even al-Qaeda is not fighting for the sake of religion but instead is primarily driven toward the expulsion of the United States and its allies/clients from Muslim countries.

Sleiman presents some of the evidence the author of the book uses to make his argument.

Pape attempts to unravel several misconceptions regarding suicide "terrorism." For example, the LTTE (Liberation Tigers of Tamil Elam) in Sri Lanka thus far carry out the majority of all suicide bombings in the world, and they operate from a Marxist-Leninist ideology in Hindu communities, and not from Islamic fundamentalism. The LTTE is in fact the originator of the use of a human bomb. Vast, organized militant organizations carry out 95% of all suicide bombings in the world. Suicide bombings arise from political entities, such as al-Qaeda, Hamas, and the LTTE. Pape offers the following authoritative assertion underlying his work: the goal of suicide "terrorism" arises from secular, nationalistic political demands while religion comes into play as a secondary ideological platform. Even groups that one would characterize as "religious" (such as al-Qaeda, Hizballah, etc.) possess secular, political goals often buttressed by <u>secondary</u> religious/ theological rhetoric. Such groups engaging in suicide terrorism are to be taken as instrumentally rational and educated groups, who conduct their missions with the utmost calculation and clarity of purpose. As Pape sees it, "In general, the perpetrators are not crazy and not particularly deprived." Instead, they are fiercely opposed to the status-quo of Western policies of occupation of Islamic peoples and/or hegemony in the affairs of said peoples. The US and other Western powers should not expect suicide "terrorism" to decrease as long as it maintains policies that can be received as hegemonic interference by the "terrorist" groups. Suicide "terrorism" has been on the rise in the last twenty plus years because suicide terrorism <u>pays</u>; it is an effective method to attain the goals of "terrorist" groups against democratic nation-states. For Pape, it is crucial to acknowledge – perhaps with reluctance – that even world superpowers like the United States have made concessions in the face of suicide "terrorism" and "terrorists."

In short, *Dying to Win* debunks myths surrounding suicide terrorism and also serves as a source of wisdom on how to <u>understand</u> our enemies so we can better combat them and the abominable acts they commit. Under Pape's approach, to understand suicide "terrorism" is to fight a more effective "war on terror" and, in turn, better protect America from further "terrorist" attacks. As former President Carter's National Security Advisor Zbigniew Brzezinski commented recently, "It is a self-delusion for Americans to merely accept that

Sleiman evaluates the author, using words like "authoritative."

Sleiman includes a direct quote from the book that reveals the author's tone.

Sleiman concludes with an overall assessment and summary of the book.

the 'terrorists' are motivated mainly by an abstract
'hatred of freedom' and that their acts are a reflection
of a profound cultural hostility. If that were so,
Stockholm or Rio de Janeiro would be as much at risk
as New York City." (Sleiman, 2006: 127–130)

Sample Student Essay

Now that you've learned about the conventions of a scholarly review, try doing a
rhetorical analysis of a scholarly review focusing on genre conventions. David
Winchell was a sophomore at the University of Pennsylvania when he wrote the
scholarly review below of *The Revolution Will Not Be Televised*. It was published in
Res: A Journal of Undergraduate Research and Writing at the University of Pennsylvania. Read Winchell's review and complete the Writing to Learn activity that
follows.

Review: *The Revolution Will Not Be Televised*
By David Winchell

Politics is a dirty game won and lost, not by gentlemen, but by cunning and sometimes ruthless strategists who know just how to manipulate the public into voting for
their candidates. At least, that's the way it used to be. As manager for the Dean for
America campaign in 2004, Joe Trippi saw what he believes was a fundamental change
in the methods and focus of electioneering: the large-scale success of Internetcentric
organizing and fundraising. Trippi's convincing book *The Revolution Will Not Be
Televised: Democracy, the Internet, and the Overthrow of Everything* explains in detail a
paradigm shift in political campaigning and organizing resulting from the Dean campaign's tactics during the 2004 race for the presidency.

Trippi's authoritative narrative takes his readers on a journey through the experiences that have shaped his political perspectives. From his days as a wide-eyed deputy
on Ted Kennedy's 1979 bid for the presidency and Jim Moran's congressional push in
1988, he moves regressively toward the heart of the book: the Howard Dean campaign.
In Trippi's eyes, the Dean campaign was the first major example of "open source"
political organizing, leveraging an emerging digital culture to motivate potential supporters. He makes the distinction between the "top down" approach, in which politicians begin organizing at the national level and work their way down, and the
"bottom up" approach employed by the Dean campaign. With Dean's philosophy, the
heavy focus of organizing and fundraising was on ordinary citizens who came to care
deeply about a particular candidate.

Under Trippi's guidance, the Dean campaign attracted a veritable army of volunteers – 640,000 to be exact – and raised millions of dollars through many relatively small donations. These impressive results were achieved primarily through the campaign's innovative uses of technology to communicate, advertise, and collaborate. Meetings organized through the Meetup.com website brought thousands together to work on the campaign. For many people, it was their first involvement with political campaigning. Trippi enthusiastically explains how a "revolution" in blogging promoted unity among those in the campaign and educated outsiders much more effectively than could television or other media: "It was as if the world were shifting right before our eyes…the future [was] happening right now. To us." Through the book, Trippi conveys a great sense of nostalgia and pride for what he calls "the first campaign owned and operated by the American people." And perhaps most interesting is that when it all comes crashing down, Trippi is there to provide a true insider's view of the problems, accidents, and oddities that preceded the end.

The term "end," is something of a misnomer, however. Though the Dean campaign's momentum sputtered and finally died in the months leading up to the election, Trippi makes it clear that the campaign's influence lives on. "From here," he writes, "the world changes faster than you can imagine. This is where it gets good, where it gets thrilling, frightening, inevitable." Perhaps this is why the book's penultimate chapter, "The End," is followed immediately by "The Beginning."

It isn't often that the general public is afforded the level of insight into the machinations of political campaigning provided here by Trippi. With a matter-of-fact tone and a legion of details, he portrays political strategizing as an exciting and important, if unforgiving, profession. Simultaneously, he elucidates technology's ability to impact society and thereby change social norms and expectations. It is in the combination of these two fields – politics and technology – that the book succeeds most spectacularly, lending a sense of relevance and urgency to its message: established political systems must either change to accommodate modern society or be forgotten as relics of the past. While the fate of the "revolution" remains to be seen, there can be no doubt that, for the moment, Trippi's hopes for a more informed, active citizenry are alive and well. (Winchell, 2006: 80–81)

2.7: Writing to Learn – Analyzing the Genre of the Scholarly Book Review

The purpose of this Writing to Learn activity is to connect what you've been learning about genre (and the genre of the book review) to David Winchell's review of *The Revolution Will Not Be Televised*. Analyze Winchell's review as an example of a scholarly book review. Discuss the purpose, audience, persona, conventions, and organization of the book review. Give specific examples from the review to support your analysis.

Tips for Writing in Academic Genres

We'll be taking a closer look at college genres across the curriculum in Part III of this book, but I'll close this section with some general strategies for writing in academic genres – strategies you can use in any course in any academic field. To make these strategies for writing in academic genres more concrete for you, I'm going to connect them to my experiences writing in a common academic genre: the textbook. When I began writing *Exploring College Writing*, I had to think about the advice I give to my own writing students when they're working in a new genre. Some of the strategies I used as I wrote this textbook are described below.

- **Look for models of the type of genre you're writing in.**

   Before I began writing this textbook, I skimmed through about a dozen different textbooks that focused on introducing students to college writing in order to get a better sense of the genre of the first-year writing textbook. I paid close attention to the subjects the textbooks covered, the way they were organized, and the writing style. When you're asked to write in a genre you're not familiar with, a helpful first step is to examine how other writers have responded to the rhetorical situation you're facing. When I read through the textbooks, I was thinking about what I could use as a model for my own textbook, but I was also thinking about what I wanted to do differently and also what I wanted to add to the genre of the first-year writing textbook.

- **Don't worry if you're struggling at first as you learn to write in a new genre.**

   My first drafts of this book weren't anything like this final draft. I knew that writing a textbook would be a big project and it would require a lot of revising, so I didn't put any pressure on myself for everything to be perfected in the first or even the second draft. I focused on putting down my main ideas in a rough form, and then later I went back and revised my text many times to develop and organize my ideas. In college you'll encounter many genres that you're not familiar with, and you should expect to struggle at first as you learn these new genres. It will take you some time to find the right voice or persona and to figure out how to organize your ideas, what kinds of outside sources to include, and how to integrate those sources. Don't be afraid of undeveloped or disorganized first drafts, and give yourself plenty of time to revise and get feedback.

- **Get feedback from someone knowledgeable about the genre you're writing in.**

   When I began drafting the chapters of this book, I got feedback from other writing professors on every chapter. These professors helped me to see how my textbook might be used in different classrooms, which parts were most useful, and which activities would work best in their courses. If you're struggling to write in a genre that's new to you, it's a good idea to get feedback from your professor by having a conference during office hours or by scheduling an appointment for a different time. If your school has a writing center, you can visit a tutor or consultant for feedback. Don't be reluctant to seek help – even experienced writers want feedback.

- **Be aware of the rhetorical situation of the genre.**

As I began drafting this textbook, it helped me to constantly keep the rhetorical situation in mind. I had to keep reminding myself that my audience was new college students, so I didn't want to use too much jargon from my academic field, and when I did, I needed to define the jargon (like the term, *rhetoric*). I also had to remember that a variety of professors with different teaching styles would be using the book, so I tried to design a variety of types of activities. When you're writing college genres, keep the rhetorical situation in mind: the purpose that the professor has outlined in the assignment, the academic field and the goals of the course, the intended audience, and any evaluation criteria your professor has mentioned.

2.8: Learn by Doing – Analyzing Genre

The purpose of this Learn by Doing activity is to apply what you've learned about the concept of genre to your own college writing. Choose a writing assignment from one of your courses and describe the rhetorical situation of the genre. Think about the purpose for the genre, the intended audience, the persona you're being asked to take on in the genre, the way the genre is organized, the conventions of the genre, and any wider contexts you need to be aware of. Do you think the teacher and the assignment will allow you to expand on the conventions of the genre, or do you think you'll need to follow the conventions closely?

Common College Rhetorical Strategies

2.9: Writing to Learn – Defining Rhetorical Strategies

The purpose of this Writing to Learn activity is for you to think about your own definition of some key rhetorical strategies common to college writing in any academic field before reading about them below. Write your own definitions of the terms *summarizing*, *synthesizing*, *evaluating*, *analyzing*, and *arguing*. Be prepared to discuss your definitions in small groups and/or with the class as a whole.

In the examples of college writing assignments at the beginning of Chapter 1, or in the writing assignments your college professors have given you this term, you might have noticed some key verbs such as *explain*, *summarize*, *describe*, *compare*, *analyze*, and others. These key verbs help define the purpose for the writer, and chances are good that you'll encounter these key verbs defining rhetorical strategies such as summarizing, evaluating, or arguing in many college courses. In any of your college courses, no matter what the academic field, professors might ask students to summarize the main ideas of a text, synthesize the research results of different studies, or evaluate a book or performance. Each college-writing rhetorical situation and genre will draw on some of these kinds of rhetorical strategies, each of which combines writing and thinking about information and ideas in a certain way. For example, in the genre of the book review that we looked at earlier, you'll need to summarize, analyze, and evaluate. In the genre of the short-answer exam, you might be asked to define and explain, or to compare and contrast. In the genre of the reading log, you might need to analyze and respond to readings. It would be overwhelming if we tried to take a close look at every type of rhetorical strategy you might use in college, so let's focus on some of the most common strategies you'll encounter in your courses: summarizing, synthesizing, analyzing, evaluating, and arguing. To help you have a better sense of each of these rhetorical, or writing and thinking, strategies, we'll look at sample college-writing assignments and excerpts from a variety of academic genres.

Summarizing

Summarizing is an important strategy for college writing because it asks you to show your readers that you've understood the main ideas and arguments of the text you're summarizing and can explain those main ideas and arguments in your own words. You might be asked to write a reading journal in which you summarize and respond to course texts, an annotated bibliography in which you summarize research sources, or an abstract for a scientific research report in which you summarize the research and findings of the report.

Here are some excerpts from college writing assignments from different academic fields that ask for summary:

> You write an abstract to summarize for yourself and to convey to others the method-ology, the key arguments or points, and the supporting evidence for those arguments or points from an essay or book. In order to do this well, you need to read carefully and take note of the overall thesis, the arguments that contribute to the thesis, and the evidence used to support these points. (Professor Valerie D. Lehr, St. Lawrence University)

> Briefly summarize the content of the article in one paragraph, so that if you were writing an essay with 10 or 20 references you could quickly refer back to these sources as you write (that is the purpose of an annotated bibliography). (Mary Temblador, University of Florida)

> In your own words, briefly summarize the experiment, stating the hypothesis and the methods. (Professor Roger Sullivan, California State University Sacramento)

Some key ideas from the assignments above to keep in mind when you summarize are finding key points, putting ideas in your own words, and being concise.

To give you a sense of what summarizing looks like in academic writing, consider an excerpt from an academic article, "Tattooing and Body Piercing: Body Art Practices among College Students" by Judith Greif, Walter Hewitt, and Myrna Armstrong. In this social sciences study published in a nursing journal, the authors surveyed college students about their tattooing and body piercing practices. When social scientists conduct surveys and report the results, it's a convention to include a summary of the characteristics of the sample of people who were surveyed. Here's the summary of the sample from Grief, Hewitt, and Armstrong's research report:

> Ethnic representation included White (71%), Black (7%), Asian (5%), Hispanic (4%), and "others" (13%). Class distribution included freshmen (17%), sophomores (16%), juniors (23%), seniors (26%), graduate students (11%), and others (6%). Many of the respondents were first or only born (46%), had grown up with both natural parents (66%), and were raised in households with an income of $35,000 or more (73%). The respondents attended religious services between one to five times per year (33%) and another 33% never attended church. Almost one third (30%) declared their academic

majors as liberal arts, social science studies (27%), and basic sciences (22%). Nearly 60%
self-reported grade point averages of 3.0 or better.

The average cost of a respondent's tattoo was $67 and of a piercing, $50, with the
total cost for the entire 766 respondents' body art as $148.000. The highest amount
reportedly paid for a tattoo was $750 and another respondent paid $215 for a single
piercing, including the jewelry. Most students (76%) did not notify their parents of the
intent to obtain a tattoo or body piercing, even when some were minors, but eventually
the parents were informed (75%). Both those with tattoos and piercings cited the same
major reasons for their body art as self-expression (50%) and "just wanted one" (48%),
(Table 1). (Greif, Hewitt, and Armstrong, 1999: 375-376)

In a summary, you are trying to focus on the most important points of what you are
summarizing. In the case of this summary from the article by Grief, Hewitt, and
Armstrong, the authors are trying to get across to the reader the most important characteristic of the sample they surveyed: ethnicity, academic class and major, involvement in religion, and other characteristics.

A common genre you'll find in every academic field is the *abstract*. An abstract is
often found at the beginning of an academic research article, and it's typically a one-
paragraph summary of the entire article. Here's the abstract for the "Tattooing and
Body Piercing" article:

Tattooing and body piercing are increasing, especially among college students. A
study of 766 tattooed and/or body-pierced college students in 18 universities across
the Untied States and one in Australia was conducted to discover the demographic
characteristics, motivational factors and health concerns. The traditional college time of
18 to 22 years of age (69%) was when they obtained their tattoo (73%) and/or body
piercing (63%). More frequent health problems and impulsive decision-making were
noted for those with body piercing when compared to those tattooed. Three cases of
hepatitis were reported. Health professionals should openly discuss body art with
students, convey a nonjudgmental attitude, and assist with informed decision-making
information to either reduce risks or dissuade. Open communication and applicable
health education will be very important. (Grief *et al.*, 1999: 368)

An abstract in the social sciences summarizes the purpose and scope of the study, the
research methods used, and the results and implications of the study. Abstracts in the
humanities typically summarize central ideas or arguments, rather than the methods
and results of experiments or surveys.

Summaries like the abstract above can help readers gain a quick sense of the main
points of an article or book and decide if they want to read on. Writing summaries
will give you practice in thinking about the main ideas and arguments of the authors
you read and also the most important aspects of your own writing and research.

Whether you are taking notes on a professor's lecture, writing an abstract, or creating an annotated bibliography, recognizing the most important points of a text or presentation is a critical skill in many college writing situations and in every academic field.

Synthesizing

Synthesizing asks the writer to look at multiple texts and ideas and connect those texts, finding patterns and analyzing the ways the texts are similar and different. In college, you'll often synthesize ideas or texts in order to create a new idea or argument. For example, in a college research paper you might need to review prior research on your topic, finding multiple sources and making connections among what authors have written and what you're doing in your research.

Here are some excerpts from college writing assignments from different academic fields that ask for synthesis:

> Write a 12–15 page synthesis paper, following APA conventions throughout, that includes (a) a properly synthesized review of the literature on the targeted topic of your paper and (b) an exploration of pedagogical implications that emerge from the literature. (Professor Fredericka Stoller, Northern Arizona University)

> Following each major section of the course, you will write a brief summary paper that synthesizes the content covered in that section. This brief paper is not meant to be a research report, instead it is an opportunity for you to reflect on the content just covered, synthesize the readings and discussions, and provide evidence of your understanding of the content. (Professor Scott D. Johnson, University of Illinois)

> The synthesis paper is a 4–8 page (double spaced and typed) overview of what you gained professionally from this course – how the theories and models learned have influenced your approach to being an environmental/outdoor educator. (Professor Sydney Reed, University of Alabama)

You can tell from these sample assignments that synthesizing involves summarizing and analyzing. But synthesizing requires more than stringing together summaries of content from books or articles. College professors ask you to synthesize ideas to show them that you can see patterns and connections, and that you can analyze those patterns and connections. The excerpt below, from William Douglas's scholarly book, *Television Families: Is Something Wrong in Suburbia?*, illustrates the fact that synthesis means connecting and not only summarizing. In a section of the book on the roles of husbands and wives in television families, Douglas presents a review of the literature on this topic that synthesizes different studies, as follows:

Early studies consistently revealed that television confined wives to an essentially domestic role and husbands to the role of provider. J. McNeil (1975), for example, reported that female characters were more likely to be associated with family themes, in both their daily work and their interactions, and four times less likely to be presented as the primary provider than male characters. Less than a quarter of the married women in McNeil's sample were employed outside the home and those who were held less powerful positions than their male counterparts. Likewise, Seggar (1975) observed that women were less likely than men to pursue professional careers, and Feshbach, Dillman, and Jordan (1979), Signorielli (1982), and Press and Strathman (1994) noted that wives and mothers were rarely presented in work situations but, rather, were recurrently rooted in the home and family. Consistent with these findings, research has also shown that spousal relations were often portrayed stereotypically so that males acted in instrumental ways and wives in expressive ways (Fitzpatrick, 1987; Reep and Dambrot, 1989; Shaner 1982). Several authors have taken the position that the roles of nurturer/ caregiver and provider are not only value-laden but implicit in the distribution and use of domestic space. Newcomb (1974), for example, proposed a convention in which the kitchen, a place of work, is defined as a female space so that interaction occurring there must be understood as "softer, more 'feminine'." (Douglas, 2003: 45)

Notice that Douglas establishes patterns among a variety of studies and makes specific connections among the studies that reveal these patterns. Key words and phrases such as *likewise* and *consistent with these findings* reveal that the goal of the writer is to make connections among a variety of research studies. Reviewing what other scholars have said about a topic in a literature review often involves showing patterns and making connections by synthesizing.

For another example of synthesis, let's look at an excerpt from "An Assessment of HIV Research in the Last Three Years," a literature review by Jennifer Baure, a student at the University of California Davis (UC Davis). Jennifer's literature review was published in *Prized Writing*, a collection of the best writing across disciplines at UC Davis. The literature review assignment Jennifer was given asked students to "find, read, and understand a group of articles clustered around a research area of their choice, then to synthesize the information so that a reader could quickly grasp the present state of research in that area." Here's an excerpt from Jennifer's literature review:

Researchers are studying how treatments work against HIV and determining how to slow down HIV pathogenesis. Several types of effective treatments are available for HIV patients. Anti-retroviral therapies, or ART, prevent HIV replication. Protease inhibitors and inhibitors of HIV reverse transcriptase (RT) are two types of antiretroviral therapies. Amirayan-Chevillard et al. (2000) observed that both RT inhibitors and protease inhibitors prevented HIV replication by decreasing the production of certain cytokines.

ART has been shown to treat HIV-infected patients effectively. T-cells of HIV-infected patients on long-term ART reproduced less and lived longer than the T-cells of untreated HIV-infected patients (Hellerstein et al., 2003). In addition, patients treated with ART produced more memory T-cells than untreated HIV-infected patients, maintaining the balance between the numbers of long-lived and short-lived T-cells (Hellerstein et al., 2003).

Highly active antiretroviral therapy (HAART) is a combination of one HIV protease inhibitor and two HIV RT inhibitors. Amirayan-Chevillard et al. (2003) studied how HAART affects HIV replication. They found that HAART decreased production of cytokines TNF, IL-1B, IL-6, and IL-10. HAART not only effectively decreased cytokine production and HIV replication but also decreased the number of monocytes expressing the CD16 surface protein, better regulating monocyte/macrophage response. (Baure, 2003–2004: 33)

In this literature review, rather than focusing on connecting research studies, Jennifer showed how different researchers approached the same topic – the treatment of HIV. The synthesis involved looking at a broad topic and finding studies that addressed the topic. Notice that Jennifer does more than string together the results of research studies. She balances the information from outside sources with her own descriptions of what she's found in her review.

Synthesizing is a complex rhetorical strategy that challenges you to think and write in nuanced ways about what you are studying. In order to synthesize, you need to have a grasp of the main ideas or research results of the texts you are working with and a sense of the way those texts both connect to and contrast with one another. In an anthropology course, this might mean seeing how research methods are similar and different across studies; in an art history course, this might mean understanding how two movements in painting influence each other and also diverge from one another; and in a philosophy course, this might mean making connections between two theories of ethics.

Analyzing

Analysis requires methodically breaking down and examining a text to think critically about the relations between parts of the text and the author's main ideas and arguments. This might mean looking closely at the author's language, examining the logic of the author's arguments, and looking critically at the reliability of the author's sources. Your college professors might ask you to analyze a variety of kinds of texts: films, ads, books, articles, performances, Web sites, and others.

Here are some excerpts from college writing assignments from different academic fields that ask for analysis:

> Your assessment of which argument is more convincing is based on critical analysis (HOW do the authors make their arguments – this examines structure more than content. Do they use statistics, examples, and/or analogies that seem convincing?) (Lynn Klause, Ohio State University)

> Students will be working to analyze actual companies by closely examining their annual reports and other relevant sources (such as news articles, analyst reports, and press releases). (Professor Eun Mi Choi, Tallahassee Community College)

> Analyze in depth one or more of the works that we have discussed in class. The subject is up to you, but make sure to narrow your thesis enough to go into depth with your interpretation. For example, you might focus on a specific theme in a work and discuss how that theme is developed, or you might choose how the characteristics of a particular literary movement (such as romanticism) are expressed in a few different works. Your analysis should go beyond what was discussed in class. (Professor Brad Buckley, Portland State University)

All of these assignments define *analysis* as looking closely and carefully at a text or texts and pointing out patterns in the text that aren't obvious with a superficial reading. Even though analysis is defined in similar ways in all of these assignments, notice that in some of the assignments analysis means examining graphs and statistics, and in other assignments analysis means discussing themes in poems and novels. The way you analyze will be different for a biology course, a history course, a literature course, or a business course: each academic field defines analysis differently.

In her essay, "The Ubercool Morphology of Internet Gamers: A Linguistic Analysis," which is included in Chapter 6, Dana Driscoll analyzes the language use of Internet Gamers based on the research methods of the field of linguistics. Driscoll codes and analyzes the language of the Internet Gamers in her study, looking for interesting patterns. Here's an excerpt from Driscoll's analysis:

> The Gamer dialect is based on English. It has no speech equivalent and appears only in written form in IRC ("Internet Relay Chat") rooms, Gamer web sites, Gamer message boards, and within the games themselves. Although it is written, the syntax is more similar to speech than to writing. Because of the nature of the Gamer dialect, a form of typed speech, the main concern is speed. The gamers find many ways of shortening what they have to type, so they can convey meaning faster, just as shortening occurs in spoken language. Articles, apostrophes, and punctuation found in normal

writing are often omitted, and any and all shortcuts with the language are taken. This clipping is shown from the vocabulary. Phrases and single words are the most frequent modes of communication. To illustrate this point, listed below is an example, taken straight from the chat scripts studied. The name of the speaker is in <>, and the message is after the name of speaker.

<cashcowc> did Gnomes win?
<Stalin> its not over yet
<Pr0vokeR> U
<Pr0vokeR> pos
<Drewskee> spam is irksome.
<CriM> first map we won (:
<CriM> on to sludge
<Pr0vokeR> score?
<Mr_Hobbers{d1nn36}> sludge youll get raped
<CriM> 10 5 i think
<CriM> Laf
<Pr0vokeR> haha
<Pr0vokeR> that close?
<Mr_Hobbers{d1nn36}> Welp. not bad
<Drewskee> haha
<Drewskee> gj C
<Drewskee> snicker
<|-det0x-|> yes crayz?
<Mr_Hobbers{d1nn36}> Crayz, Im surprised u didnt pull ur modem. U doin pretty b4d that map
<Pr0vokeR> OVERFLOW CRAYZ
<Pr0vokeR> !!
<|-Crayz-|> bleh
<Stalin> hobbs doesnt like us
<Drewskee> hobbers is a fruit 2night
<|-Crayz-|> yea i know its pretty sad
<Stalin> since he doesnt get ops here
<|-Crayz-|> an OGL person being biast
<|-Crayz-|> ya kno?
<Stalin> aye, and he does in l337 chan

As shown through the example, the language of the Gamers, although written, is very similar to speech. To keep up with the speed of the conversation, the Gamers have developed words that allow them to convey meaning faster, such as their clips and acronyms. Almost all of the words in this study that are not unique are shortened versions of English words. The average new word created is between 4 and 5 letters. In this research, no dialect word longer than eight letters was discovered, although the Gamers will use longer English words when necessary, such as the word "surprised" from the example above. Also, alphanumeric characters, acronyms, and emoticons can help Gamers covey meaning faster than with words. (Driscoll, 2002)

In the social science field of linguistics, *analysis* means looking closely and systematically at the way a group uses language and providing evidence directly from examples of the language. This requires providing specific examples of language being analyzed to make the analysis more concrete and persuasive.

In academic writing, analysis often involves applying a theory to a text in order to think critically about it. In an essay analyzing the ways women are portrayed on prime-time television, Andrea Press and Terry Strathman apply the theory of postfeminism to critically assess the subtle messages that television programs give. Here's an excerpt from their analysis of the television comedy, *Roseanne*:

> Roseanne offers an interesting split in the representations of family and work, corresponding to earlier themes in television's portrayals of the working-class. The show's idealized portrayal of family life contrasts with a more critical depiction of the workplace. This pattern is consistent with postfeminist ideology. Postfeminist thought retains from the feminist movement its ability to confront some of the important issues for women in the workplace; but postfeminism differs from feminism in that it retreats from criticism of the family. In the postfeminist world, traditional family life appears to coexist easily with stereotypically feminist women.
>
> These characteristics are illustrated in an episode where Roseanne and her co-workers are told that there will be mandatory overtime again that evening. Repeated overtime has tired the women who all feel pressured by the demands the overtime has made on their families. The women struggle with their supervisor, but lose and are forced to work late. Roseanne comes home exhausted, unable to deal with her noisy household, and asks her husband for permission to get out for a few hours, which he cheerfully gives. She ends up in a late night coffee shop, comparing notes on her life with the waitress, a widowed, older woman, who discusses how much she misses her husband and hates her job. Refreshed by this moment of camaraderie, and thankful for what she's got, Roseanne returns home to fall asleep, exhausted, next to her husband. (Press and Strathman, 1993: 7)

In this analysis, Press and Strathman have found a theory that they can use to analyze the "text" of a television comedy show in order to look at the text more thoughtfully. Analysis of the show text required more than a quick, surface viewing. Press and Strathman needed to look closely and systematically at the text, and their analysis of the episode they use as an example to prove their assertions illustrates how carefully they looked at *Roseanne* in order to analyze it.

Even though analysis is not the same in each academic field, after looking at these assignments and essay excerpts, we can make some generalizations about what academic analysis usually entails. Most often analysis requires a close and careful reading of some kind of text, whether that text is print, visual, or oral. Often analysis requires going beyond the obvious and looking for meaningful patterns that may not be revealed in a surface reading of the text. The assertions you make about a text when you analyze it need to be supported with specific examples to persuade readers of the accuracy of your analysis. Analysis often means applying a specific theory or research method. Those are some general features of academic analysis, but we'll take a closer look at how analysis varies across academic fields in Part III.

Evaluating

Evaluating means making judgments about a text. This might mean judging the effectiveness of an author's argument or approach; evaluating an author's research methods; judging the quality of a film, work of art, or performance; or considering whether an author's evidence is reliable and persuasive. In college, you might be asked to write a book review, evaluate a proposed solution to a problem, or self-evaluate in a process memo or progress report.

Here are some excerpts from college writing assignments in different academic fields that ask for evaluation:

> What were one or two problems with this research? How could the author have done a better job of investigating the questions he or she posed? Did the author interpret his or her findings correctly, or did he or she over- or understate their importance? What would you have done differently? (Professor Lakshmi Singh, George Mason University)

> Write a 3–4 page film review/critique of *Syriana* (Gaghan, 2005) in which you comment on and evaluate the film and discuss its relevance to our historical moment. Discuss if you found the film powerful and worth seeing and give reasons for your judgment. (Professor Jyotsna Kapur, Southern Illinois University)

> Select a site and, in approximately 900 words, write an essay which evaluates it according to the criteria in *Evaluating Web Resources* and *Information Literacy: The Web is not an Encyclopedia*. Compare the quality of the information found in this website to the information which the more traditional resources on the Library's website pointed you toward. You may also bring in other criteria which you find relevant for evaluating Web sites; just make sure you adequately explain these alternative criteria prior to applying them to your selected site. (Jay Monroe, Arizona State University)

As you can see in these assignments, in college *evaluating* means much more than making a quick judgment and writing a critique without explaining the basis for the evaluation. In academic writing, evaluating means carefully considering the quality or effectiveness of what you're evaluating and providing sufficient justification for the conclusions that you reach.

Earlier in this chapter we saw an example of a genre that asks for evaluation – the book review. There are a variety of kinds of reviews you might encounter in your college courses (book reviews, film reviews, theatre reviews, and others), but all of these reviews will ask you to make evaluations. In Chapter 9 we're going to look at a film review of Quentin Tarantino's *Pulp Fiction* by Pat Dowell and John Fried. Here's an excerpt from the review:

> In general the tone of Tarantino's work is a rejection of anything resembling the "real" world. Sure, there are scenes in coffee shops "like Denny's," as the script denotes, and in old cars and suburban tract homes, but the movie exists only in the terms of other movies, and is not, as collagists like Godard might construct, an undermining of those terms. In fact, the perfection of its escapism places it squarely in the most traditional and the most contemporary wave of Hollywood moviemaking. In that respect, the two most talked-about movies of 1994, *Forrest Gump* and *Pulp Fiction*, are not so different as advertised. Their narrative structures certainly diverge, but their sensibilities are the two sides of a single coin.
>
> Just as much as *Forrest Gump*, *Pulp Fiction* rejects the notion of engagement with the reality available to most Americans. Forrest succeeds because he's too dumb to take it seriously, while *Pulp Fiction's* various protagonists succeed and fail on a relatively random basis that has little to do with their actions. Most of what they do doesn't make a difference in their destinies (since life is like a box of chocolates). A pothole or a trip to the bathroom at the wrong moment means life or death (more than once for Vincent Vega), or a kid's bad aim with a handgun becomes a miracle for Jules. So many movies now are daydreams about people surviving or succeeding because they don't connect with the world around them – the sitcom refugees of *The Brady Bunch*, the low-watt Forrest Gump, the insulated Nell. *Pulp Fiction* is a more sophisticated rendering of the spirit of helplessness and resignation that animates those films to imagine a solution. The answer Tarantino offers is to stop worrying and learn to love it. Let the new Stanley Kramers (as Tarantino has called Oliver Stone) worry about the meaning and effect of it all. (Dowell and Fried, 1995: 4)

In this excerpt, the reviewers critique *Pulp Fiction*'s lack of connection to the real world, and they support their evaluation with examples from the movie and the script, and by parallels with another film, *Forrest Gump*. You can read the full review in Chapter 9 to see how the reviewers support each judgment they make of the film.

In many academic genres, there is a close relationship between summarizing and evaluating. For example, earlier in this chapter, we discussed the genre of the scholarly book review. In this genre, writers need to both summarize the major themes of a book and make judgments about the value of the book. Here's an example of the relationship between summary and evaluation in an excerpt from a book review we looked at earlier in this chapter, David Winchell's review of Joe Trippi's book about the Howard Dean presidential campaign, *The Revolution Will Not Be Televised*:

> Under Trippi's guidance, the Dean campaign attracted a veritable army of volunteers – 640,000 to be exact – and raised millions of dollars through many relatively small donations. These impressive results were achieved primarily through the campaign's innovative uses of technology to communicate, advertise, and collaborate. Meetings organized through the Meetup.com website brought thousands together to work on the campaign. For many people, it was their first involvement with political campaigning. Trippi enthusiastically explains how a "revolution" in blogging promoted unity among those in the campaign and educated outsiders much more effectively than could television or other media: "It was as if the world were shifting right before our eyes...the future [was] happening right now. To us." Through the book, Trippi conveys a great sense of nostalgia and pride for what he calls "the first campaign owned and operated by the American people." And perhaps most interesting is that when it all comes crashing down, Trippi is there to provide a true insider's view of the problems, accidents, and oddities that preceded the end. (Winchell, 2006: 80)

In this review, Winchell both summarized important aspects of Trippi's contributions to the Dean campaign and evaluated Tripp as a writer, complimenting Trippi for his great sense of nostalgia and pride and his true insider's view. In a book review, summary and evaluation are rhetorical strategies that are operating together, and in most academic genres you will draw on a variety of rhetorical strategies.

Arguing

2.10: Writing to Learn – Defining "Argument"

The purpose of this Writing to Learn activity is for you to think about your own definition of *argument* and to compare your definition to that of your classmates. Write for five minutes about how you define *argument*. Then get into small groups and discuss everyone's definition. What were some features of making an argument that most of the group members had as part of their definition? Were there any disagreements among the group about what an argument is?

The verb *argue* might conjure up images of two people on different sides of an issue shouting at each other on a political talk show or around the dinner table. But academic argument is really more like a *discussion* than an *argument* in the common everyday sense of the word. In most academic arguments, you're not being asked to take a side on an issue and make a one-sided argument in order to beat the competition. Academic argument requires thoughtful consideration of multiple perspectives and a discussion of where you stand that also acknowledges members of your audience who might disagree with what you're saying. Academic argument requires careful reasoning and reliable evidence to support assertions.

Here are some excerpts from college-writing assignments from courses in philosophy, business, and environmental science that ask students to construct an argument:

> Your paper should be organized around a problem, philosophical or interpretative, and some claim you are making and arguing for which is connected to the solution of that problem. What you say should be relevant to and support your claim. When you present your view, consider what might plausibly be said against it and respond to this. When you criticize someone else's view, consider how that person might reply to your objections. (Professor Bill Uzgalis, Oregon State University)

> In proper memo format, write a memorandum to Lauren Thompson, the CEO of Thompson Electronics, in support of a voluntary affirmative action plan. In your memorandum, clearly discuss what affirmative action is, how it might be implemented, and the benefits that Thompson Electronics could expect from such a plan. (Professor Janet Lorretano, Kennesaw State University)

> Construct an argument showing how some aspects of the current public debate on a particular environmental issue has been influenced by, and is indebted to, the ideas of some of the authors we'll be studying. (Professor Chris Trueblood, Lawson State Community College)

You probably noticed that in these assignments, arguing did not mean "fighting" and trying to force your point of view on your reader. These assignments asked students to consider the positions of other scholars, how those scholars might reply, and the rhetorical situation of the argument, like writing a memo to make a recommendation to the CEO of a company.

In her academic research paper, "Now With 50% Less Sugar: The Transformation of Television Families From Idyllic to Realistic," which was published in *The Printer's Devil*, a collection of outstanding student writing from composition courses at Arizona State University, Lisa Potter makes claims about television families, but she does so in a balanced way that considers different perspectives. After arguing that "television fathers and real fathers alike have decreased in credibility" (Potter, 2007: 8), Lisa acknowledges that not all television fathers are inadequate:

> It would be ignorant to argue that all fathers today are complete idiots with dysfunctional families. Regardless of the general image that is usually portrayed on television, shows like 7th Heaven feature stable, secure families with reliable fathers. Reverend Eric Camden is an icon in his small church where his family is, at first glance, the perfect "church" family. The family dog is even named "Happy."
>
> After peeling away countless layers of sugary sap, the solid foundation of this family is finally revealed. The show discusses controversial issues, such as in the episode "The Long Bad Summer." Middle child Simon is involved in a car accident in which he kills a friend, and to cope with his emotional stress, starts getting involved in sex and alcohol. In the fifties, a person would be hard-pressed to find a television show about a church family that dealt with substance abuse and sex outside of marriage. Although people may say that this decade has been the beginning of shows starting to curb the inappropriate nature of television families, it is important to realize that although these shows are more like the traditional, moral fifties sitcoms than years before, they don't avoid serious topics. Producers make up for the traditional structure of moral families on television by openly addressing controversial issues. (Potter, 2007: 9)

Lisa refuses to see the portrayal of fathers on television in black-and-white extremes, and she supports her assertion that some programs do portray stable families with good fathers by giving a specific example: Reverend Eric Camden from 7th *Heaven*. Then Lisa argues that the issue is more complicated, and that shows like 7th *Heaven* may appear to be like traditional 1950s sitcoms, but they actually cover more serious topics.

Another example of academic argument comes from the first-year writing student case study in Chapter 1. In her response to the theory of education assignment she was given by her first-year composition professor, Melissa Bratt makes an argument about the value of a research paper. As you read her argument, think about the ways she avoids being one-sided about the issue.

> As much as every student dreads writing a research paper because of its structure and formality, I think students should learn to write them in order to develop their personal voice. Before a student can be allowed to run free and write their expressive opinions, explain their thoughts, and get creative with their writing they must first have a strong knowledge of their subject and know how to clearly convey their ideas. Someone who knows nothing about politics or religion, for example, would not speak up about their opinion on the subject matter because they would not have enough

information to form a decent argument. Furthermore, knowledge does you no good unless you can clearly formulate your ideas in order to express them in a way that makes sense to others. Research papers help provide you with the knowledge of your subject and teach you the best way to express your ideas so that they flow together. In order to relay the facts on a topic and creatively express your thoughts and opinions by writing with your personal voice, you must first have or be given the facts.

There are many people who oppose my theory of education. Paulo Freire, author of *Pedagogy of the Oppressed*, feels that my ideas to educate people are no more than a "banking system." Freire explains the "banking" system as a system where teachers deposit information into students or, as Freire puts it, containers. Once deposited the students, without any thinking whatsoever, "patiently receive, memorize, and repeat" (Freire 58). While Freire makes valid points, I disagree with his interpretation of a student as a container and his idea that the student doesn't think about the information they are receiving. If a student doesn't think about the information they are given then no one would ever form an opinion on the topic. Freire goes on to say, "Those truly committed to liberation must reject the banking concept in its entirety" (66). But I don't believe the banking concept should be rejected "in its entirety." The banking system does have problems, such as the teacher having too much control over the students, but those who want liberation can't completely disregard the main concept. Control can be bad, it's true, but no control whatsoever would be nothing but chaos, and not even the best person can learn in the midst of chaos. Students and teachers may try to change the way they teach and learn, but neither can admit that eliminating the banking concept altogether is the best way to educate an individual. Obviously, if the banking system has endured as long as it has, than there must be something good about it.

Melissa makes a claim – that students should learn to write research papers – and backs up her claim with specific reasons. Then she considers an opposing argument from a key scholar, Paulo Freire. Bratt explains Freire's position and acknowledges that Freire makes some good points. She admits there are limits to her argument – she says that the academic "banking system" does have some problems, like too much teacher control. Then she argues that too much control may be bad, but no control means chaos. Lisa considers multiple perspectives and acknowledges that her view is not the only view.

Most of the writing assignments you'll encounter in college will ask you to call on multiple rhetorical strategies. You might be asked to write a reading journal in which you summarize and respond to articles; a research report in which you review the literature on your topic and then make your own arguments; or an essay exam with a series of questions that ask you to define key terms from the textbook, explain different theories, and compare and contrast different concepts. As you read the sample writing in the rest of this book, and as you prepare for your writing assignments in your college courses, think about the genre you're reading or writing in and the rhetorical strategies required for the genre. Understanding what your professors mean when they ask you to summarize or synthesize or evaluate, whether it's for a ten-page research paper or a short-answer exam, will help you be a more successful college writer.

Contrastive Rhetoric: Language Diversity and College Writing

Instead of presenting academic discourse as coherent and well defined, we might be better off viewing it as...a sort of space in which competing beliefs and practices intersect with and confront one another.

—Professor Joseph Harris, Department of English, Duke University
(Harris, 1989: 20)

The way a point is appropriately made in writing in one language differs from the way it is done in another; the rules for presenting ideas and strategies for explaining or defending them that may seem self-evident are not completely interchangeable across cultures.

—Professor Ilona Leki, Department of English, University of Tennessee
(Leki, 1992: 88)

The diversity of our cultural heritage...has created a corresponding language diversity and, in the [21st] century, most linguists agree that there is no single, homogeneous American "standard."

—Conference on College Composition and Communication (1974: 7)

2.11: Writing to Learn – Your Response to "Standard English"

The purpose of this Writing to Learn activity is for you to reflect on what you already think about the concept of "standard English" before you read about language diversity and college writing. Explore your responses to the idea of a single, standard English. Do you think Americans communicate in one standard English? Who do you think gets to decide what's standard? Do you think we should all use the same standard when we write?

Throughout this chapter we've been talking about some common features of college writing – of *academic discourse*, especially that of the English-speaking world. For you to succeed in college writing, it's important for you to know what some general expectations for academic writing are, and what common thinking and writing strategies you'll need in all of your college courses. You'll also need to know the conventions of grammar and mechanics of *Academic English*. It's important to understand that what counts as good writing in college in the United States or another English-speaking country is not a world-wide standard, and academic discourse isn't a *better* way of communicating than other kinds of discourse – just a *different* way. It's also important to understand that college writing is not a set of rules that never changes, or a format that can be applied to any course in any academic field.

In this chapter, we've been focusing on *similarities* and *patterns* in college writing; but in this section of Chapter 2, I want to focus on *differences* and *diversity*. I want to discuss six points that linguists and writing teachers have made about language diversity and college writing:

1. Writers use language differently in different situations.
2. Different cultures have different writing conventions.
3. Different students have different dialects.
4. Academic writing varies significantly from one academic field to another.
5. Academic writing changes over time.
6. Writers transform academic writing when they add their voice to the conversation.

Let's take a closer look at each of these six points.

2.12: Writing to Learn – Writing for Different Rhetorical Situations

Imagine that you're writing an email message to describe your first few weeks of college, but write the message to three different audiences: an older family member (your mother, father, grandfather, or grandmother), a friend from high school, and a foundation that has given you a scholarship to attend college. Once you've written the three different emails to three different audiences, reflect on how you used language differently in each situation. How were your voice, style, attitude, word choice, and tone different in each of the email messages?

- **Writers use language differently in different situations.**

If you completed Writing to Learn Activity 2.12, you probably noticed that you took on a very different voice and style in your email message for each audience. If you think about it, you couldn't accurately claim that one email and one voice which you took on was "superior" to the others. If you wrote to your high school friend in the same voice you used to write to a foundation that has given you a scholarship, or if you wrote to your mother or father in the same style you used to write to your friend, you wouldn't be using language effectively for the situation. Each writing situation demands a different style, voice, and type of organization, whether you're text-messaging a friend, writing in your diary, requesting a refund from a company, or writing a book review for a psychology course. Consider how different your language and style would be for each of these possible college writing situations:

1. A ten-page researched essay for a history course evaluating the effectiveness of John F. Kennedy as a President;
2. An exploratory, ungraded journal entry reflecting on what you learned about your own personality at the end of a psychology course;
3. A newsletter article about maintaining a healthy diet for your children written for a non-profit family health foundation as part of a service learning project for a food and nutrition course;
4. A poem for a creative writing course;
5. A lab report on magma crystallization for a geology course.

- **Different cultures have different writing conventions.**

If you're coming from a different country to college in the United States or another English-speaking country, or if you're multilingual and you speak and write in more than one language, there are probably features of writing and language use that are much different in English than in the other language (or languages) that you speak and write. Some of these differences have to do with sentence-level features such as grammar and mechanics. For example, many languages don't use a definite article like *the*, or they have different ways of showing time. Other differences have to do with the way texts are organized. American academic writing tends to value a linear organization that gets to the point of the essay quickly by stating it in the opening paragraph or paragraphs. Many cultures prefer that writers take time to establish a relationship with the reader; but in most types of academic writing, in the United States as well as in other cultures influenced by British or American conventions, a writer is expected to give readers a clear sense of the purpose of the essay in the opening paragraphs. The concept of "voice" is also relative. Academic writing in the

English-speaking tradition tends to value originality and an individual voice, while in some cultures a communal voice may be more valued than an individual voice. This contrast between individualism and community can also apply in the way cultures define plagiarism. Academic writing in the English-speaking tradition places a high value on citing sources, but in many countries that emphasize sharing over individual ownership, citing sources is not as critical.

These cross-cultural writing patterns that I'm pointing out are generalizations, and not every student from the same region or country will write the same way. If English is your second (or third or fourth) language, or if you were born in the United States or another English-speaking country and you're multilingual, keep in mind that features of academic writing, such as conventions of grammar and punctuation, the way paragraphs are developed, the voice of the writer, and the forms of arguments that are valued in one culture, will differ from these features in other cultural traditions and languages. American academic writing preferences aren't "natural," even if teachers sometimes act as if they are. No one type of academic writing is any better (or worse) than any other type of academic writing; they are just different.

- **Different students have different ways of speaking and writing.**

2.13: Writing to Learn – Comparing School and Home Discourse

Write about how the way that you speak and write at home and among your friends is similar to and different from the way that you speak and write in college classes. Do you feel any conflict between the way you speak and write outside of school and the way you speak and write in school?

A *dialect* is a version of a language used by a specific group. Because *dialect* has a negative connotation for many people, linguists prefer to use the term *variety*. You can think of a variety as an "accent." America is multiregional, multiethnic, and multicultural: different regions of the country and different social and ethnic groups have their own varieties of English. The students in my writing courses at California State University Sacramento are representative of the diversity of varieties of English in America. I have students who speak both Spanish and English and whose parents grew up in Mexico; I have Hmong and Russian students who recently emigrated to the United States; I have students from Korea who learned English in Korea from Korean teachers; I have students from big cities such as Los Angeles and San Francisco; I have students from rural, farming areas in the middle of California; and I have out-of-state students from all across America. Each of my students speaks with a different accent, and so do I. I was born and raised in Ohio, and I have a Midwestern accent.

We all have our own varieties of English, and you can think of Academic English as another kind of variety or dialect. The specific variety of English used in college (and other educational institutions) is sometimes termed *English for Academic Purposes* (EAP) or just *Academic English*. The question of whether EAP should be thought of as the standard for college writing, and whether college students need to give up their own varieties when they write for college, is controversial. The largest organization of college writing teachers in America, The Conference on College Composition and Communication (CCCC), put out a position statement in 1974 about students having the right to their own dialect or variety – their own language. Read the position statement and think about your perspective on this debate.

CCCC Statement on Students' Right to their Own Language

We affirm the students' right to their own patterns and varieties of language – the dialects of their nurture or whatever dialects in which they find their own identity and style. Language scholars long ago denied that the myth of a standard American dialect has any validity. The claim that any one dialect is unacceptable amounts to an attempt of one social group to exert its dominance over another. Such a claim leads to false advice for speakers and writers, and immoral advice for humans. A nation proud of its diverse heritage and its cultural and racial variety will preserve its heritage of dialects. We affirm strongly that teachers must have the experiences and training that will enable them to respect diversity and uphold the right of students to their own language.

(Conference on College Composition and Communication, 1974: 7)

2.14: Writing to Learn – Your Response to Students' Right to their Own Language

Write a response to the "CCCC Statement on Students' Right to their Own Language." What is your perspective on the stance that the CCCC takes on language diversity? Feel free to use your own experiences as a writer to develop your ideas and arguments.

- **Academic writing varies significantly from one academic field to another.**

In this chapter, we've focused on expectations for writing that many college teachers share and on general features of college writing across academic fields. As you're going to investigate in Part III, academic writing in English – or English for Academic Purposes – can vary significantly from one academic field to another, and even from one teacher to another in the same field. The language of science can be very different from the language of the arts and humanities, and the voice and tone that is expected in writing assignments for one teacher might be very different from the voice and tone expected in another teacher's writing assignments, even if both teachers are in the same department.

The ways that writing expectations can differ dramatically in different academic fields can be seen in a project that was conducted by Professor Mark Waldo, the Writing Center director at the University of Nevada Reno. To help him better prepare tutors in the Writing Center, Professor Waldo asked different departments about their values for writing. As it turned out, each department gave a very different statement of what they value in student writing. Below are the statements from the English Department and the Biology Department.

University of Nevada Reno, English Department's Values for Writing

- Voice – the expression of the writer's self in the piece of writing
- Independence – thinking demonstrated in the writing that distinguishes it from the writing of others
- Meta-consciousness of language
- Vividness of detail; originality
- Awareness of rhetorical purpose and audience
- Evidence of thinking critically (effective summary, interpretation, analysis, argumentation)
- Few or no sentence-level problems

University of Nevada Reno, Biology Department's Values for Writing

- Clarity in statement of purpose (the paper's abstract includes a clearly stated hypothesis)
- Adherence to appropriate form (report writing contains the following sections: abstract, introduction, methods and materials, discussion, and conclusion) and placement of material in pertinent sections

- Coherent integration of secondary sources
- Accurate citation of secondary sources
- Accurate description of graphs and tables
- Evidence of thinking critically (problem solving, data analysis and interpretation, argumentation)
- Evident commitment to experimentation and to written description
- Few or no sentence-level errors

(Waldo, 2003: 15-16)

It's clear that the English Department and the Biology Department at University of Nevada Reno have very different definitions of good academic writing. You might even say that each department has its own "dialect" or variety of academic writing. The English Department is focused on voice, originality, and independent thinking; the Biology Department is more concerned with clarity and adherence to scientific reporting conventions. "Critical thinking" in English is focused on interpretation and analysis of texts, but "critical thinking" in biology is focused on interpreting and analyzing data and presenting data in charts and graphs.

To get a better sense of the ways writing in academic fields can differ, take a look at the excerpts below from academic books in three different fields.

Excerpt from a Sociology Book, *A World Full of Women* by Martha Ward

Human beings transcend sex or biology with gender. We assign social roles and determine how people defined as females will act, dress, speak, get married, or be friends with others; the same is true for males. These are basic gender roles. Then human beings assign symbols and spell out the social meanings to being male or female. These are called gender ideologies; they include the prescriptions and sanctions for what is considered appropriate female or male behaviors, and cultural rationalizations or religious explanations for the social and political relationships that are believed to exist between the genders.

The basic point is that gender is a construct. Through time and in adaption to their environment, groups of people construct, build, forge, or fabricate what they think women are really like and what they believe men are really like. Looking across human cultures, it is clear that what is "naturally" feminine, either in roles or personalities, is a matter of local conventions. It is very difficult to put the blame or the credit on biology or on culture exclusively. Our behavior and belief systems are the complex interaction of many factors – social, organic, random, historical, chance, or mischance. (Ward, 1996: 3)

**Excerpt from an Astronomy Book, *Disturbing the Solar System*
by Alan Rubin**

Stars spend most of their lives in a state of balance between their tremendous gravity, which pushes matter inward, and the gas pressure caused by the energy released during nuclear fusion – the transformation of hydrogen into helium – which pushes matter outward (figure 1.1). But toward the end of their lives, stars run low on hydrogen and begin to release energy by creating heavier elements in their nuclear-fusion furnaces. Very massive stars can fuse helium into carbon and oxygen, and carbon into oxygen, neon, sodium and magnesium. Eventually silicon, phosphorus, and sulfur are produced and fused into iron. The fusion of heavy elements is a massive star's attempt to stave off the crushing effects of gravity, but it is a competition the star is doomed to lose. When enough iron is built up in the core, the energy spigot is turned off because it takes extra energy to split iron into lighter elements or fuse it into heavier ones. (Rubin, 2006: 1)

**Excerpt from a literary criticism book, *The Signifying Monkey*
by Henry Luis Gates**

In *Their Eyes Were Watching God*, Janie uses the metaphor of the tree to define her own desires but also to mark the distance of those with whom she lives from these desires. There are well over two dozen repetitions of the figure of the tree in this text. The representation of Janie's narrative to Phoeby commences with the figure of the tree:

> Janie saw her life like a great tree in leaf with the things suffered, things enjoyed, things done and undone. Dawn and doom was in the branches. (p. 20)

"Dawn and doom," we are to learn so poignantly, are the true stuff of Janie's tale. "Dawn and doom <u>was</u> in the branches," an example of free indirect discourse, reveals precisely the point at which Janie's voice assumed control over the text's narration, significantly in a metaphor of trees. (Gates, 1988: 186)

2.15: Writing to Learn – Language Diversity and English for Academic Purposes

The purpose of this Writing to Learn activity is for you to reflect on the diversity of English for Academic Purposes by comparing the three excerpts above. Reread the excerpts above and compare the voice the writers take on in each excerpt. Consider each writer's style, tone, word choice, use of specialized terms, and level of formality. Write about the differences among the excerpts, and be prepared to discuss these differences in groups or with the class as a whole.

- **Academic writing changes over time.**

Sometimes textbooks present "rules" for academic writing as if these rules have been handed down "from above" and will last forever. However, the qualities of college writing aren't some mysterious list of rules that never change. The features of college writing evolve – whether it's the grammar and mechanics of Academic English, the format for organizing a lab report, or a teacher's "rule" about whether or not writers can use the personal pronoun (*I*) in academic writing. After all, these features are simply ways of writing that academic language communities have agreed upon, and communities change. New members join the community, new situations call for new kinds of writing, and new technologies transform the way we write.

To get a sense of how academic writing changes over time, take a look at this excerpt from a writing textbook published in 1899, John F. Genung's *Outlines of Rhetoric*:

> To write an essay or any kind of formal composition seems to most people, and doubtless is, a much more difficult thing than to converse. But why should it be so? At bottom it is virtually the same thing, except that it is done with a pen instead of with the voice. The purpose is the same, namely, to make others see a subject as the author sees it; and it ought to be just as natural, just as spontaneous, just as characteristic of the man, to write his thoughts as to speak them. If we could always bear this obvious truth in mind, and feel perfectly at ease with our pen in our hand, composition would cease to be the bugbear that it now too often is.
>
> (Genung, 1899: 1)

Genung was writing in the college textbook discourse style of the turn of the century, but his style would be seen as old-fashioned if his textbook was being published today. Today Genung's style would be considered too formal and wordy for a textbook and a student audience. Some of the words and expressions Genung uses are no longer in style in textbook writing, such as *to converse*, *formal composition*, or *bugbear*. Genung's writing would also be considered sexist by today's standards for academic writing, since he says *characteristic of the man* and *his thoughts* instead of using gender-neutral language.

Many of the "rules" of academic writing that Genung includes in his book are no longer "rules" today. For example, Genung devotes two pages of his book to discussing the rules concerning when to use *shall* and when to use *will*, but it would sound old-fashioned and formal to use *shall* in a college essay today – it's an aspect of grammar that's no longer in use in American English (though it is still common in British English). The point to keep in mind is that academic writing isn't either uniform or static. The "rules" for grammar, mechanics, and style will be very different twenty, fifty, or a hundred years from now, as new writers enter the conversation of college writing and bring new perspectives and new ways of using the English language – or rather, the different English languages.

2.16: Learn by Doing – Changes in Academic Writing

The purpose of this Learn by Doing activity is to help you gain a sense of the ways the English language changes over time. Visit your school's library and find a book written before 1900 (most libraries have search engines that allow you to set date parameters when you search). This could be a textbook, a scholarly book, a novel, or any other kind of book. Photocopy a page from the book and take some notes about how the grammar and style of the book differs from current English. Be prepared to discuss these differences in small groups and/or with the class.

- **Writers transform academic writing when they add their voice to the conversation.**

All college writers transform academic writing when they add their voices to the conversation of other academic writers. Even though part of your role as a college student is to be an apprentice who is learning the conventions of academic writing, simply by writing from your perspective and adding your voice to the academic community, you're playing a role in changing those conventions by changing what academic writing is and what subjects academic writers talk about. This doesn't mean that every paper you write in college will completely transform academic writing as we know it. But it does mean that the farther you go in your college career, the more you will add to the conversation – and even change the conversation.

To emphasize how writers can transform academic writing by adding their perspective and their voice to the conversation, let's look at two writers who've helped change the way writing teachers think about language diversity: Geneva Smitherman and Gloria Anzaldúa. Both of these scholars write about what it means to be multilingual, and they both have added a new perspective that has contributed to changing the way many writing teachers – myself included – think about English and about academic writing. Smitherman and Anzaldúa both write academic books in a multilingual style that expands the conventions of academic writing. Below are excerpts from two of the books they've written.

Excerpt from *Talkin and Testifyin: The Language of Black America*
By Geneva Smitherman

We're talking, then, about a tradition in the black experience in which verbal perform-ance becomes both a way of establishing "yo rep" as well as a teaching and socializing force. This performance is exhibited in the narration of myths, folk stories, and the semiserious tradition of "lying" in general; in black sermons, in the telling of jokes; in proverbs and folk sayings; in street corner, barbershop, beauty shop, and other casual rap scenes; in "signifying," "capping," testifing," "toasting," and other verbal arts. Through these raps of various kinds, black folks are acculturated – initiated – into the black value system. Not talking about speech for the sake of speech, for black talk is never simple cocktail chit-chat, but a functional dynamic that is simultaneously a mechanism for group approval and recognition. Even in what appears to be only casual conversation, whoever speaks is highly conscious of the fact that his personality is on exhibit and his status at stake. Black raps ain bout talkin loud and sayin nothin, for the speaker must be up on the subject of his rap... (Smitherman, 1986: 79–80)

Excerpt from "How to Tame a Wild Tongue"
By Gloria Anzaldúa

I remember being caught speaking Spanish at recess – that was good for three licks on the knuckles with a sharp ruler. I remember being sent to the corner of the classroom for "talking back" to the Anglo teacher when all I was going to do was tell her how to pronounce my name. "If you want to be American, speak 'American.' If you don't like it, go back to Mexico where you belong."

"I want you to speak English. 'Pa hallar buen trabajo tienes que saber hablar el inglés bien. Qué vale toda tu educación si todavía hablas inglés con un 'accent,'" my mother would say, mortified that I spoke English like a Mexican. At pan American University, I, and all Chicano students were required to take two speech classes. Their purpose: to get rid of our accents.

Attacks on one's form of expression with the intent to censor are a violation of the First Amendment. El Anglo can cara de inocente nos arrancó la lengua. Wild tongues can't be tamed, they can only be cut out. (Anzaldúa, 1987: 53–54)

2.17: Writing to Learn – Unconventional Academic Writing

Write about the ways that Smitherman and Anzaldúa go against traditional conventions of American academic writing. In what ways do Smitherman and Anzaldúa still exhibit the features of academic writing which we've been discussing in this chapter?

One of the challenges of college writing is understanding your teachers' different attitudes about academic writing. Some teachers will expect you to write in a formal style and follow every "rule" of Academic English without exception, while some teachers will prefer that you write in a voice and style that you're most comfortable with. Some teachers will want you to closely follow the conventions of writing in their field, while some teachers will encourage you to expand on those conventions. The kind of writing assignment you are given also matters. Personal literacy narratives or informal reader response journals will demand a different type of language and a different level of formality than a biology lab report or a psychology case study. Each different writing assignment, each course, and each teacher will present you with different expectations for academic writing, and that's one of the biggest challenges of college writing and also one of the reasons you'll grow so much as a writer from your first year to your last year of college. Even though we've been focusing on some general features of college writing in this chapter, keep in mind that when you're exploring the question, *What is college writing?*, there's never just one simple answer.

Review of Key Ideas in Chapter 2

- Each writing assignment you're given in college will present you with a new rhetorical situation. Some of the most important factors of a rhetorical situation include purpose, audience, persona, text, and context.
- Genres are rhetorical situations that have similar purposes and conventions each time they occur. Every academic field has its own set of genres that are connected to the ways of thinking and making knowledge in that particular field.
- Genres are more than simply templates for writing. Genres are responses to rhetorical situations, and they are the ways that writers make meaning in the social context of different academic fields. Because genres are dynamic and not static, they change over time and new genres are always being created.
- Each college rhetorical situation and genre will require communication by means of strategies such as summarizing, synthesizing, analyzing, evaluating, and arguing. Most college writing assignments ask or expect you to use multiple rhetorical strategies. The way different academic fields define different rhetorical strategies such as analyzing or arguing will vary. For example, *analyzing* in a literature course might mean reading a poem closely and discussing use of metaphor or simile, but *analyzing* in an economics course might

mean crunching numbers and putting data into graphs or charts.

- A defining feature of academic arguments is that they are not shouting matches, win/lose contests, or simple pro/con debates. College writing assignments that ask you to construct arguments typically require you to consider different perspectives on an issue and make claims that are well supported by reasons and evidence.

- Academic writing is a way of thinking and communicating that you'll encounter in college, but it's not the one right or only way to write effectively. Academic writing doesn't follow a single set of rules, and each academic field will have different expectations for academic writing. What counts as good academic writing in one country and culture can be different from what counts as good academic writing in a different country or culture – including the "culture" of a particular academic department or field.

- Academic writing isn't static. The definition of good college writing changes over time, as language changes and as new members of academic communities add their voices and their experiences to the conversation.

2.18: Writing to Learn – Reflecting on Genres

Make a list of the genres you've encountered in college so far. Are there any genres that are more common than others? Which genre was the most difficult to write in, and why? What strategies did you learn in this chapter that can help you to better understand the genres you're assigned in future college classes?

Writing Projects for Part I

Each chapter of Part I includes frequent Writing to Learn and Learn by Doing activities. The Writing to Learn activities are informal and they focus on brainstorming and using writing to "think out loud" on paper. The Learn by Doing assignments are a little less informal, but they are fairly short and focused. This section of *Exploring College Writing* invites you to do some more formal and extended thinking and writing. Your professor might ask you to work on one or two of these writing projects, or all three. Your professor might change these writing projects to match the goals of the class, or give you different projects.

Writing Project I.1: Literacy History Narrative

Prompt

Write a 4–6 page literacy history narrative describing the most significant moments in your writing history. You can talk about struggles with writing, successes, or both. You can focus on a specific time frame (for example, middle school, high school, or your first year of college), specific teachers, family members who had an influence on your writing, specific books that affected you, or some other focus of interest to you.

Purpose

The purpose of this literacy history narrative is to get you to reflect on your writing experiences, to think about how those experiences shaped you as a writer, and to consider how you've evolved over time as a writer. By writing a narrative of your literacy experiences, you'll be able to get a better understanding of where you've been and where you're going as a writer. This is also a chance to tell your professor and peers a little bit about your previous experiences with writing so they can respond to your writing more effectively.

Audience

A literacy history narrative usually has two audiences: the writer and the readers who would be especially interested in the writer's history. For example, two well-known literacy narratives are Malcolm X's "A Homemade Education" and Richard Wright's "The Library Card." Both of these literacy narratives are by African American writers who are trying to confront and comprehend the racism they faced in their past. As one purpose or theme of their work, Malcolm X and Richard Wright are writing to reflect on their own experiences. Malcolm X and Richard Wright are also writing to African American readers who may have had similar experiences. Both writers also have a broader audience of general, educated readers of all races who need to be made more aware of the inequalities Malcolm X and Richard Wright faced. In your literacy narrative, you're writing to yourself – to explore your own experiences – and also to your classmates and professor, so they can understand what good and bad experiences have shaped you as a writer.

Genre

The literacy history narrative is a storytelling genre. Usually when we tell stories, we're trying to make sense of our experiences to ourselves and also trying to relate those experiences to others. In the literacy history narrative, you're telling stories of your experiences writing. You can use descriptive language and details to get your experiences across to your readers, and you may even want to write scenes with dialogue. Your literacy history narrative can have a theme that helps organize it – for example, your favorite books or struggles with writing. You don't need to sound "academic" in a literacy narrative. This is your story, and it should be in a voice that feels right for what you want to say. For an example of the genre of the literacy narrative, reread Melissa Bratt's literacy narrative, "Bound for the NSA," in Chapter 1.

Conventions

A storytelling genre like a literacy narrative doesn't need to follow any specific essay structure (you don't need an introductory and concluding paragraph or a thesis). However, most stories have certain conventions that you may find useful to borrow from: an opening that draws the reader in and hints at the theme or focus of the story, vivid description and details, scenes that reveal a lot about the character (and in this case, you're the main "character"), a closing that gives a feeling of closure without simply summarizing everything that's been said. Even though most stories are told in the voice of the storyteller, you should make sure to edit your final draft so that your readers will be able to enjoy and understand your narrative without being slowed down by errors.

Evaluation Criteria

Focus on choosing significant experiences and making these experiences vivid for your readers. Your readers should be able to move smoothly from one experience to the next as they read your narrative, and they should also gain an understanding of how your literacy experiences shaped you as a writer. Your voice and style as a writer should help capture your readers' interest and also help them understand your point of view.

Writing Project I.2: Writing Inventory

Prompt

Fill out the high school writing inventory below and then write a 3–4 page reflection essay in which you explore the results of the survey and discuss your strengths and weaknesses as a high school writer and the ways you think college writing will build on the writing you did in high school.

Purpose

The purpose of this project is to get you to reflect on your high school writing experiences and think about the transition you're going to need to make from high school writing to college-level writing. By filling out the high school writing inventory and reflecting on your high school writing experiences, you'll get a sense of how prepared you are for college writing and what the similarities and differences will be between high school writing and college writing.

Audience

Since the purpose of this writing project is self-reflection, *you* are the primary audience. Write your reflection as though you're "talking to yourself" in order to use writing to explore your own experiences. Of course, since eventually your peers and your professor will read what you've written and give you feedback, your reflections should be understandable to them. By reading about your experiences as a high school writer, your peers and professor will get to know you better as a writer and they'll be able to give you more useful feedback on the writing you do for class.

Genre

A reflection essay is a type of writing you'll probably encounter in your college career. Your professors might ask you to reflect on your writing process in a portfolio reflection letter; they might assign a reflection essay in the beginning of the semester to get you to reflect on your current knowledge of a subject; or they might assign a final reflection essay to get you to think about what you've learned over the course of a semester. In the reflection essay, you'll want to make sure you think about how well your high school writing has prepared you for college writing, and what areas you might need to improve on to succeed as a college writer. You should also think about the similarities and differences between high school and college writing. Since you're the primary audience, your writing tone and style can be personal and conversational, but make sure that your final draft is edited so that your peers and professor will be able to understand what you're trying to say.

Conventions

This is an exploratory essay, and there's no specific organizational structure you need to follow, or a specific type of persona you need to take on. Don't worry about organization in your reflection letter and focus more on exploring your experiences and making comparisons. When you fill out the inventory, write one or two well-developed paragraphs (more than a few sentences) in response to each question.

Evaluation Criteria

The most important aspects of this project are the quality and depth of your thinking. Do a thorough job of reflecting on your high school experiences and think hard about what you'll need to do to make the transition from high school to college writing. You don't need to sound "academic" in this reflection, and it's perfectly acceptable to write this in a conversational tone. You want your peers and professor to be able to understand your reflections, so it's important to edit your final draft, but focus more on content than grammar and mechanics.

Writing Inventory

1. Describe and reflect on your best high school writing experience.
2. Describe and reflect on your worst high school writing experience.
3. How much writing did you do in your junior and senior years in high school?
4. How challenging was the writing you did in high school?

5. Describe the longest and most complex piece of writing you were assigned in high school and how you handled that assignment.
6. What were the most common genres you were assigned in high school?
7. What were the most common thinking strategies you used in high school writing (summarizing, synthesizing, analyzing, evaluating, arguing)?
8. What audiences were you asked to write for in high school?
9. Describe the roles your teachers played as audiences for your writing in high school.
10. What was your strongest quality as a writer in high school?
11. What aspect of your writing do you most need to work on as you make the transition from high school writing to college writing?

Writing Project I.3: Academic Writing Rhetorical Analysis

Prompt

Write a 3–4 page rhetorical analysis of one of the readings you've been assigned in your classes this semester. This could be an essay, an article, a book, a textbook, a Web site. Analyze the purpose, audience, persona, context, and genre of the reading and talk about how the reading exemplifies (or works against) the definitions of academic writing we discussed in Chapter 1.

Purpose

The purpose of this writing project is to connect the discussions of the definition of academic writing in Chapter 1 with your own experiences as a college writer. Another goal of this writing project is for you to practice rhetorical analysis skills that you can apply to any of the readings you're assigned in college. Understanding how to rhetorically analyze something you've been assigned to read will make you a better college reader and writer.

Audience

Think of your audience for this writing project as the classroom community from which you're choosing the reading – your peers in the class and the professor of the class. As you analyze the reading, think about the context of the class. What other readings in the class can help you think about the reading you're analyzing? Have there been class discussions or lectures by the professor that can help you analyze the reading?

Genre

You'll probably be asked to write a number of papers in college in which you analyze essays, books, documents, films, musical works, paintings, or other artifacts. Professors will ask you to write these kinds of analysis papers to get you to read or observe closely and carefully and to think deeply about what you're reading. A rhetorical analysis, a type of genre analysis, asks you to focus on rhetorical features such as purpose, audience, persona, genre, and context. In this writing project, the focus is analyzing a piece of academic writing and talking about the ways it reflects (or doesn't reflect) the definitions of academic writing discussed in Chapter 1.

Conventions

College analysis essays usually include sample lines or passages from the reading being analyzed as a way to show readers you're looking closely at the text. Usually the analysis is organized and systematic – so this writing project is not "narrative" or "exploratory" like the previous projects, but "analytical." Review the discussion of common college thinking and writing strategies in Chapter 2 to remind yourself of what "analysis" means for college writing.

Evaluation Criteria

The most important aspects of this writing project are the depth and quality of your analysis and the way you compare the example of academic writing you've chosen to rhetorical features of academic writing discussed in Chapter 1. Apply the different aspects of the rhetorical situation and of genre that we discussed in Chapter 2, and as you analyze the reading, give specific examples to support your analysis. Your analysis should be well organized and written in a clear and concise style.

Part II

Exploring Academic Reading, Writing, and Researching Processes

3   Academic Writing Processes

Over the last few years, I have learned that college-level writing is as much about process as it is about product.
—Kimberly Nelson, a student at the University of Iowa (Nelson, 2006: 293)

Composing does not occur in a straightforward, linear fashion. The process is one of accumulating discrete bits down on the paper and then working from those bits to reflect upon, structure, and then further develop what one means to say.
—Professor Sondra Perl, a writing professor specialist and researcher at
Lehman College (Perl 1979: 34)

I take a lot of time on revision, which is where my papers come together.
—Kristen, a student at George Mason University, in the book, *Engaged Writers and Dynamic Disciplines* (quoted in Thaiss and Zawacki, 2006: 128)

Exploring Academic Writing Processes

Part I of *Exploring College Writing* talked about some of the ways college reading, writing, and researching processes are similar to and different from high school reading, writing, and researching processes. Part II explores college reading, writing, and researching processes more closely and discusses strategies for improving those processes. Notice that we're using the word *processes*, not *process*. As you read this chapter and as you complete writing assignments for your college courses, you'll find that there's not one uniform writing process which all writers go through for every paper. Each writer has different strategies for selecting a topic, drafting and revising, and editing and proofreading. Each writing assignment and each genre of college writing will also require different writing processes. Every factor in the rhetorical situation will influence your process as a college writer – your purpose in writing and the intended audience; the genre, social context, course context, and academic field of the course; your prior experiences as a college writer; and maybe other factors as well (e.g. the availability of computers or quiet places to write). When you consider all of these factors, it's clear that college writing processes are complex. This chapter will help you gain a better understanding of your own writing processes and give you some useful strategies for college writing processes that will make you a more confident and successful college writer.

3.2: Writing to Learn – Writing Processes Quiz

Before we discuss some myths about college writing processes, let's see what you already believe about writing processes. Take the True/False quiz below and discuss the answers in your class.

1. Experienced writers get everything right on the first draft.
   __ True __ False
2. Experienced writers seek out feedback during the writing process.
   __ True __ False
3. Revising means using a spell checker and changing a few sentences.
   __ True __ False
4. There's no such thing as a "born writer."
   __ True __ False
5. Writing is mostly inspiration.
   __ True __ False

Five Myths about College Writing Processes

Myth #1: Good college writers create a perfect draft on the first try.

No college writer ever writes an "A" essay in one draft – or even two drafts. Most college writing assignments are complex and require sophisticated thinking and organization, and this means college writers need to go through many drafts in order to discover what they think about a topic, to develop their ideas enough to persuade a college-level audience, and to organize their thoughts in a way that's not formulaic. Successful college writers give themselves plenty of time to take their writing through a long process that might include making lists of ideas, free-writing, rereading the assignment, reading samples of the genre they're writing in, writing multiple rough drafts, getting feedback from readers, and editing and proofreading a final draft.

Myth #2: Successful college writers don't need any help during the writing process.

The most successful college students take advantage of one their best resources: the professor. Don't be shy about taking a draft of your paper to your professor during office hours to ask for some feedback. Also, be sure to pay careful attention to the written comments your professor makes on your paper. Usually these comments will let you know what your strengths are and also what you need to work on to improve as a college writer. Your institution's writing center is another good resource; and don't go there only at the last minute or when you're struggling. Even your professors have editors who help them make their writing better. All writers can benefit from feedback, no matter where they are in the writing process and how well they're doing. Some novice writers have a romantic myth of the individual writer working alone to find inspiration, but even famous novelists like F. Scott Fitzgerald or Jane Austen had friends and editors who gave them feedback during the writing process. You can also ask for help from other writers who've faced the same kinds of rhetorical situations that you're facing. Experienced writers know that all writing is *intertextual*. This means that they draw on other texts they've read when they write their own texts. Experienced writers will read samples of whatever kind of genre they're writing in to use as models for their own text.

Myth #3: Some people will never be good college writers.

Writing is like every other kind of skill: you improve with practice and feedback. The ability to write isn't a lucky gift or mysterious talent that some people are born with. Learning to write at the college level takes a lot of practice and a lot of help, but you'll be amazed at the progress you'll make from your first semester to your senior year. If you read a lot, take courses that require plenty of writing, and seek out feedback from peers, professors, and your college writing center, you can be a successful college writer, even if you struggled with writing in high school. Of course, it's important to keep in mind that college writing assignments are more difficult than high school writing assignments, and the expectations are higher in college than they are in high school. You'll face a learning curve when you first enter college, and an even bigger learning curve when you enter your major. Everyone experiences this learning curve, so don't be discouraged if you struggle with writing in college at first, and then struggle with writing again when you begin taking courses in your major. Just make sure you keep reading, keep writing, and keep getting help. With practice and feedback, anyone can be a successful college writer.

Myth #4: You can use the same writing process for every college writing assignment.

Let's say you're someone who likes to write at the last minute, and your writing process involves an afternoon of intense revising. This might work when your college professors ask you to write a two-page response to an article or a brief personal reaction to a performance, but if you have to write a ten-page research report for a psychology course or a company profile for a business course, you'll need to give yourself more than a few days to conduct research and to draft and organize your writing. It's always safer to give yourself plenty of time to write than to try to rush the process and find yourself turning in a "C" essay that could have been an "A" if you had had a few more weeks or days to revise it. Start planning and researching as soon as you are given a writing assignment.

Myth #5: Revising means simply changing a few words or sentences.

Nancy Sommers, an Education professor at Harvard University, studied the differences between the writing processes of experienced adult writers and novice student writers. Sommers found that most of the novice student writers didn't do a lot of rewriting. They only wrote one draft and then "fixed" a few words or sentences. Here are the ways the novice student writers described revision:

> I read what I have written and I cross out a word and put another word in; a more decent word or a better word.

Reviewing means just using better words and eliminating words that are not needed. I go over and change words around.

Redoing means cleaning up the paper and crossing out. It is looking at something and saying, no that has to go, or no, that is not right.

(Sommers, 1980: 381–384)

Contrast what these novice student writers had to say about the revision process with what the experienced writers said:

In one draft, I might cross out three pages, write two, cross out a fourth, rewrite it, and call it a draft. I am constantly writing and rewriting.

Most of the time I feel as if I can go on rewriting forever. There is always one part of a piece that I could keep working on. It is always difficult to know at what point to abandon a piece of writing. I like this idea that a piece of writing is never finished, just abandoned.

My first draft is usually very scattered. In rewriting, I find the line of argument.

(Sommers, 1980: 385)

As these quotes reveal, experienced writers separate revising and editing. Experienced writers aren't "married" to their first draft. They see the first few drafts as exploration and discovery, and they save editing sentences for the end of the process.

Even though experienced writers edit after they've revised, it's important to keep in mind that writing is not an exact, step-by-step process. Most writing professors agree that writing processes are *recursive*. When writing professors say that writing processes are recursive, they mean that writing is not a simple "paint by numbers," linear process. It's more like circles within circles, with brainstorming, drafting, revising, and editing recurring at each point in the process. For example, you might start writing a research paper by freewriting and then writing a rough draft; but then when you begin to revise the second draft, you realize that the topic you really want to focus on is different from the topic you focused on in your first draft. You might start the process again by freewriting on the new topic and coming up with another rough draft. Because you've changed your topic, you might need to do more research and integrate new information from new sources. This new information might lead you to new ideas and new arguments, and if so, additional writing and revision will be needed.

Just as there's no single, linear writing process, there's no set of rules for a writing process that will work for everyone. Some people can only write when it's completely quiet, and other people prefer to have music playing when they write. Some writers work best in the morning, and other writers are "night owls." Some writers like to create outlines, and others like to freewrite. The important thing is that you figure out what kinds of writing processes work best for you, and then follow these.

3.3: Writing to Learn – Reflecting on a Recent Writing Process

Think back to the last paper you wrote in school (high school or college). Describe your writing process. Was your process linear or recursive? How did the purpose, audience, and genre of what you were writing affect your writing process?

Understanding your Professors' Writing Assignments

The first step of a college writing process is understanding the writing assignment your professor gives you. Typically, your college professors will give you a writing assignment as a handout or as part of their syllabi. The key to starting on the right track with a college writing process is knowing what to focus on when your professor gives you an assignment. Read the following writing assignment from Professor Debra Salata, a history professor at Lincoln Memorial University, and think about what you would need to focus on if you were given this assignment.

Guidelines for a History Book Review

A book review essay is different from other history papers in that it does not ask you personally to discuss what happened in the past; instead, it asks you to discuss what one specific author/historian has said about what happened in the past. A review tells the reader what the author's goal was in writing the book under consideration, and whether the author fulfilled that goal or not. A review also should effectively describe the material presented by the author in order to sustain his/her thesis. This entails some summary of the book's contents, but it also asks you to consider the following questions:

Why has the author written the material (e.g. propaganda, historical records, nostalgia, personal advancement)? Determining the author's purpose will often tell you something of the author's choice of approach and evidence.

If possible, put the book into context with other books you have read on the subject. Does this author's presentation of the material agree or disagree with other information you have about the topic in question.

Consider what new ideas the book or article gave you about the topic in question. Do these "new ideas" make you change your way of thinking about the topic?

Ask yourself why the reading was assigned to you. This is another way of asking what is significant or important about it.

Ask yourself what information is missing from the book which you need to know in order to understand and criticize the author's argument. Is this "neglect" a fault of the author or the reader? Does the author assume too much?

Audience: Do not write the review directly to or for the instructor in the course, but direct your review to an unnamed, intelligent individual who could benefit from your careful assessment of the book. A review should be aimed at individuals who have <u>not</u> read the book already. That means you cannot assume they know anything about the topic even though they might be very intelligent and well educated. Tell your readers where the topic of the book fits in time and place.

Format: The review must be typed on unlined, white, 8½-by-11-inch paper, using a ribbon dark enough to produce legible type. It should be double-spaced, typed in a ten- or twelve-point font, and have a one-inch margin on all sides. Number each page. Staple the pages together in the upper left-hand corner. Do not use a cover sheet. Do not use a folder of any kind.

Book reviews (like other brief papers) should not have subheadings or separate sections; they chop up the flow of your thoughts without contributing anything useful. Instead, use sentences that make the transition from one thought to another.

Length: Check the syllabus for the required length of the review. The grade for the review will be penalized if the review is more than one page too short or too long.

3.4: Writing to Learn – Book Review Assignment Analysis

Individually or in small groups, use the questions below to analyze Professor Salata's book review assignment:

1. What are the key verbs in the assignment?
2. What are the most important features of the genre of the history book review?
3. How will the intended audience affect the style, tone, organization, and content of the review?
4. What do you think Professor Salata will focus on when she evaluates the review?

Strategies for Understanding Writing Assignments

- **Look for key verbs such as *define, argue, compare, summarize,* and others.**

As we discussed in Chapter 2, most college writing assignments have key verbs that reveal the kinds of rhetorical (thinking and writing) strategies that are required for the genre of the assignment. For example, in the Writing to Learn 3.4 book review assignment, the key verbs are *summarize, describe,* and *criticize,* which are all typical thinking and writing strategies for the genre of the book review. The goal of the assignment is to accurately and thoroughly describe the central arguments of a history book and then critique those arguments. Sometimes professors explain what they mean by these key verbs in the assignment, and sometimes they don't. If they don't explain the key verbs, don't be afraid to ask your professor, "What do you mean by *synthesize?*" or "What do you mean by *describe?*"

Chapter 2 made the point that rhetorical strategies like *describe* will require different approaches for each course you take. For example, *describe* in an art history course might mean using descriptive imagery to paint a verbal picture of a work of art, but *describe* in a business course might mean using charts and graphs to describe the way the economy of a country works. Try to think of the key verbs in a writing assignment in relation to what you've been doing in the course and in relation to the academic field of the course. We'll take a closer look at these kinds of differences among different academic fields in Part III.

- **Think about the genre of the writing assignment and try to find examples of this kind of genre to use as models.**

In Chapter 2, *genre* was defined as a common writing situation that has similar purposes, audiences, and conventions each time it occurs. Many of your college writing assignments will be recognizable genres that are common to the academic field of study of the course. For example, in natural science courses you might be asked to write genres such as lab reports or experimental reports, and in social science courses you might be asked to write genres such as case studies or breaching papers (where you breach a social norm and then write about what happened when you did it). If your professor doesn't provide samples you can use as models, it wouldn't take much research to find your own samples. For example, in the book review assignment of Writing to Learn 3.4, you could go to the library and find a history journal that includes a book review section. Reading a few of these samples will give you a sense of the style, tone, organization, and content of history book reviews. Looking at samples of the genre you're writing in can also help you generate ideas and find a topic.

- **Think about the intended audience.**

Sometimes professors will create a real or hypothetical audience for a writing assignment. In the book review assignment, the intended audience is not the professor but an intelligent individual who would be interested in reading the book but isn't familiar with it. If an audience isn't specified in the writing assignment, you might ask the professor questions about the intended audience. Looking at models of the genre you're writing in can again be helpful, since a specific genre will usually have a specific type of intended audience.

- **Ask your peers and your professor questions about the writing assignment.**

Writers rarely work alone: writing always has a social context, and most writers seek help at some point in the writing process. One way to get help if you're having trouble understanding one of your professors' writing assignments is to talk with other students in the course. It's also important not to be reluctant to ask your professor questions. Some students won't ask their professor questions if they're having trouble understanding an assignment because they don't want to look stupid or uninformed, but most professors are glad when students ask them questions in class or office hours. Professors naturally pay more attention to students who speak up and feel more connected to students they interact with in class or office hours. Professors are glad to know that students are thinking carefully about their writing assignments, and they also want to know if their writing assignments are confusing so they can revise them and make them clearer.

- **Take your writing assignment to your institution's writing center.**

Most colleges have a place where students can have free tutoring or help with assignments – a writing or tutoring center. Rather than struggling to understand a writing assignment and getting off track right from the start, make an appointment to see a tutor or consultant and get help. Writing center or learning assistance center tutors or consultants have experience working with writing assignments from professors in different departments, so it can be valuable to visit your institution's writing or learning assistance center for extra help.

3.5: Learn by Doing – Writing Assignment Analysis

The purpose of this Learn by Doing activity is for you to apply what we've been discussing so far in this chapter to one of your own college writing assignments. Using this section of Chapter 3 as a guide, write a one- or two-page analysis of a writing assignment you haven't started yet from a course you're taking this semester. In your analysis, discuss things such as key verbs, purpose, audience, genre, and conventions.

Finding Topics

3.6: Writing to Learn – Strategies for Finding Topics

Before you read about some strategies for finding topics, consider how you usually go about finding topics for writing assignments. Think about times that professors have let you choose a topic for a writing assignment. Individually or in small groups, come up with a list of strategies you've used for finding topics. Be prepared to discuss this list with others in the class.

The initial steps in a writing process, when you're trying to discover a topic, are what writing professors call *invention*. Invention can occur in your head as you're thinking about an assignment or as you read and find ideas for topics or on paper when you brainstorm. Invention isn't always the first step in writing processes – you might find yourself using some of the invention techniques we're going to discuss after you've already written a rough draft, if you decide to change topics or completely revise a section of your paper. Sometimes college professors will give you a topic, which means you might not have an extensive invention process. But most often in college writing you'll have some choice of topic, and it will be important that you find a topic which is interesting to you and to your readers. When you do have some freedom of choice, consider using some of the strategies described below for finding a topic:

Strategies for Finding Topics

- **Create an authority and interest list.**

You'll be more engaged with a writing assignment if you can find a topic that you're an authority on or that you want to know more about. Without putting any pressure on yourself, come up with a list of twenty to thirty things that you're an authority on or have personal experience with. These could be hobbies, areas of expertise, academic areas, or places you've lived or spent significant time in. Then come up with a list of twenty to thirty things you aren't familiar with but would like to know more about. After you've made these lists, brainstorm topics related to your lists. For example, if "WNBA (Women's National Basketball Association) basketball" was on your authority list, one topic for a sociology course research paper could be "gender roles and the WNBA."

- **Use freewriting to generate topics.**

Freewriting is a good technique for letting ideas flow and not feeling blocked before you even begin. Think about the writing assignment, and then start writing whatever comes to mind. Don't worry about grammar or organization or whether the ideas will make good topics or not – just write, write, and write some more. Keep your pen moving, and don't make any value judgments about what you're writing. Turn off your inner critic and let your mind wander. Oftentimes, by taking the pressure off yourself and using writing to explore your thoughts, you can eventually start a good train-of-thought going and come up with a good topic.

- **Try blind writing with the computer screen turned off.**

If you have trouble freewriting or writing (very) rough drafts because you're tempted to stop writing and to go back and edit sentences or fix errors, try "writing blind." Turn off the screen of your computer and freewrite. You'd be surprised at how much writing can flow out when you can't read what you've written and so are not tempted to go back and edit it.

- **Try talking about your subject and recording while you talk.**

Many college students have a hard time writing down their thoughts, but when they talk about their topic, the words flow out of them. These students can try recording their thoughts on their subject, using a tape recorder, their computer's voice recorder, or even the voice recorder on their cell phone. If you record yourself talking about your topic and happen to come up with a phrase or even entire sentences you like, you can always transcribe what you've said.

- **Surf the Internet to brainstorm topics.**

Let's say you know that you want to write an essay about global warming for an environmental science course, but you're not sure how to narrow your topic down to one aspect of global warming. You could search for "global warming" using an Internet search engine and browse whatever Web sites come up. Most Web sites also have links to other related Web sites. Five or ten minutes of browsing can lead you to plenty of related topics and different aspects of your subject – and you just might hit on an aspect of your subject that you never even considered.

- **Read and research to generate ideas for a topic.**

Earlier in this chapter we discussed the ways that writing is *intertextual*, which means new texts are always in conversation with texts that have already been written about a topic. Experienced college writers draw on their reading experiences to generate ideas for topics. For example, let's say you're writing a research paper on cloning in a biology course, and you need to find an aspect of cloning to write about. In addition to the course readings, you could find magazine, newspaper, or academic journal articles about cloning, or skim through some books about cloning. Finding out what other writers have said about a topic can help you generate ideas and even help you figure out what topics *not* to write about. Some topics (e.g. arguments for or against the death penalty) have been written about so often that they might be less appealing to your audience and more difficult for you to find something interesting to add to the conversation.

- **Meet with your professor during office hours to discuss topic ideas.**

Most college professors like it when students visit them during their office hours and ask for feedback on ideas for paper topics. Your professors can help you get headed in the right direction early in the process, which saves them time later when they respond to your final draft. Professors are impressed when students care enough about their writing to seek help early in the process.

- **Visit your institution's writing center.**

A writing center is not only a place to go for help when you already have a complete draft of a paper. Writing consultants or tutors can help you brainstorm topics for assignments, and they can give you feedback on topic ideas you're considering. It's helpful to bring your writing assignment with you when you visit the writing center, so that the tutor or consultant will have a clear sense of the assignment.

- **Narrow broad topics.**

It's fine to begin with a broad topic, but narrowing a topic down to a manageable size will help you focus your research and your writing. For example, the topic, "Negative Campaigning," would be far too broad for a five-page research report in a political science course. You could write an entire book on negative campaigning, and you could spend years in the library collecting articles and books on such a broad topic. Some ways to narrow this topic could be by focusing on a location ("Negative Campaigning in Ohio"), a group ("Negative Campaigning by Republicans or Democrats"), a time period ("Negative Campaigning in the 2010 Midterm Elections"), or a type of campaigning ("Negative Campaigning Using Television Ads"). Even these topics would probably be too broad for a five-page paper, so you could continue narrowing the subtopics you've come up with (e.g. "Negative Campaigning by Republicans in Ohio during the 2010 Mid-term Elections").

- **Use clustering to generate or narrow a topic.**

Clustering involves writing down your main topic and branching off from that topic to create related topics or subtopics in a kind of tree structure with many branches. For example, on your computer screen or a blank sheet of paper, you might write down "Civil Rights Movement" as a possible topic in an ethnic studies, history, or sociology course. Then you would brainstorm subtopics such as "Malcolm X," "Martin Luther King," and "Rosa Parks." Next you would choose some of the subtopics and create more topics. If you choose "Malcolm X," you might write down subtopics such as "Nation of Islam," "The Ballot or the Bullet speech," and "Relationship between Malcolm X and Martin Luther King."

Drafting and Revising

The "believing game" and the "doubting game" are terms invented by the writing professor Peter Elbow that can help you write and rewrite your first drafts (Elbow, 1976). Elbow tells writers not to be too critical of their writing in early drafts, and not to worry about editing for grammar and mechanics until the very last draft. His idea is for writers to play the "believing game" when they write rough drafts. Playing the believing game means writing whatever comes to mind and not being critical of your writing in early drafts – just believing in your words and letting them flow. Some college writers feel they need to make sure every sentence is perfect before they move on to the next sentence, but usually this makes it difficult for them to get their ideas out on paper. Only after you've done some drafting (and hopefully gotten some feedback) is it time to revise with a more critical eye. Elbow (1976) calls this critical approach that you need for revising your writing the "doubting game." Playing the doubting game means looking for places in your writing where you need to develop your ideas, consider different perspectives on your topic, and make your thoughts clearer to your readers. Remember that rough drafts are exploratory. All writers write messy, disorganized, or otherwise imperfect first drafts, because first drafts are brainstorms or practice runs when writers allow themselves to take risks, explore ideas, and play with language and structure. Focus on generating ideas in rough drafts. Play the believing game and save the doubting game for later drafts when you start sharpening your focus and language.

Strategies for Drafting

- **Write down what you already know about a topic and what questions you have about a topic before you begin drafting.**

Before you begin to research a topic and write a draft, write down everything you already know about the topic. Create a list of things you know or believe about your topic, and a list of questions you have about the topic. This list can help guide your research and your drafting.

- **Write a discovery draft.**

A *discovery draft* (or "zero-write," i.e. starting from nothing) is a kind of focused freewrite when you discover what you have to say by trying to write a rough draft of an entire essay or a big chunk of an essay in one sitting without worrying about organization, spelling, or grammar. The key is not to put any pressure on yourself – play the believing game and let any ideas that you have come out. You can use parts of this discovery draft when you start your formal drafting process, or you can choose the strongest section of the discovery draft and write another discovery draft using that section as a starting point.

- **Try the talk-and-transcribe technique.**

Sometimes it's easier to talk about your topic as a way to discover what you have to say about it than it is to write a discovery draft. In the *talk-and-transcribe technique*, you record your voice on a tape recorder or other device (e.g. a computer or a cell phone) and draft by talking. For example, you might talk about why you feel the way you do about a topic, or pretend you're explaining a concept to your audience. You can then play back what you said and transcribe anything that might be useful for your paper.

- **Don't edit in early drafts.**

Sometimes when we write a first draft we forget that no one is going to see that first draft but the writer. Think of your first draft as like the first exploration of a place you've never been: it's *exploratory*. Trying to make every sentence perfect or every idea complete and organized in the first draft interrupts your train of thought and makes the writing process much more difficult. Let your ideas and sentences flow in early drafts, and save revising and editing for later in the writing process. After all, why bother editing sentences and paragraphs that you might delete later on? You might even change your entire topic or argument once you've begun drafting.

- **Start with what you're most interested in or confident about writing.**

There's no rule that says when you write your first draft you need to start with the introductory paragraph and then write in logical order from there to a concluding paragraph. Let's say you're writing a critical analysis of the poetry of Adrienne Rich for a literature course, and you're most confident about writing about her poem, "Diving into the Wreck" (Rich, 1973). You might write this section first, and then go back and write other sections of the paper afterwards.

3.7: Writing to Learn – Your Revising Strategies

Before you read about some strategies for revising college writing, consider what strategies you already use when you revise your writing. Individually or in small groups, create a list of revising strategies. Share these with the class as a whole and generate a list of the most helpful strategies.

Strategies for Revising

- **Remember the differences between revising, on the one hand, and editing and proofreading, on the other.**

Because writing in college is complex and no one ever writes a perfect first draft, it's a mistake to think that revising means simply editing sentences or looking for errors to correct (proofreading). Revising requires rethinking larger issues than individual sentences and words. When you revise, don't be afraid to change the focus of your topic, to question your theoretical perspective, to move and reorder paragraphs, and to delete and add examples.

- **Give yourself time to look at what you've written with a fresh eye.**

When a professor gives you a writing assignment, it's a good idea to get an early start and give yourself enough time to put down your rough draft for a day or two and then come back with a fresh eye. Every writer has a hard time creating some distance from what he or she has written, and if you give yourself some time between drafts, you'll have a more objective perspective as a reader of your own writing. When you go back to your essay after you've put it down for a while, try to play the role of your audience and think about what they would want to know more about or what they might be confused by.

- **Get feedback from the professor.**

College professors often have a hard time getting students to visit them during their office hours. Students can be shy, easily intimidated, or worried that the professor will think they aren't smart enough to complete the assignment. Actually, most professors appreciate students who visit them during their office hours to request feedback on a draft of a writing assignment. Seeking out feedback shows professors that you're putting a lot of effort into their assignments and trying to do a good job. It also helps to build your professor's interest in and attention to you as a student and a writer.

- **Get feedback from peers.**

Some professors ask students to form pairs or small groups and give each other feedback on their essays. Peer response is common in first-year writing courses. However, many college professors outside of English departments are not familiar with peer response, and they'll leave it up to you to form groups outside of class time if you want responses from your peers. If you can find two or three peers who are willing to share drafts in each of your courses that require writing assignments, you can gain some valuable feedback. You might think your peers won't provide as valuable feedback as your professors will, but feedback from an outside reader is always helpful, even if you simply have peers point out places where they were confused or wanted to know more.

- **Get feedback from your institution's writing center.**

Most colleges have a writing center where students can have free assistance from experienced tutors or consultants. Bringing a draft of your essay to the writing center, along with any written instructions that the professor has given you can be one of the best ways to improve as a writer. Don't only visit the writing center when you're struggling with a writing assignment or near the deadline for turning it in. Even when you are in the early stages of researching or planning a paper, and even when things are going well, writers need feedback.

Some Questions for Revision

What you focus on when you revise will depend on the writing assignment, the course, and the professor. There are, however, some general questions you can ask yourself as you revise college writing that will apply to many of your writing assignments:

- Is the purpose of the writing clear to your readers?
- Are your assertions supported by enough evidence to persuade readers?
- Have you considered different points of view on the topic?
- Is the writing organized so that readers will be able to follow your ideas without becoming lost or confused?
- Is the style and tone appropriate for the rhetorical situation (the purpose, audience, and genre)?
- Does the opening capture readers' interest and offer enough information about the topic to lead smoothly into your discussion?
- Does the closing synthesize the points of the essay without being redundant or mechanical?

3.8: Writing to Learn – Improving your Writing Processes

Now that you've read about some strategies for revising, reflect on your own writing processes and write about what you can do to improve your revision processes. What revision strategies do you already use that you should continue to use in your college career? What new strategies could you use to improve your revision processes for college writing?

Editing and Proofreading

3.9: Writing to Learn – Editing Strategies

Before you read about some strategies for editing college writing, consider what strategies you already use when you edit your writing (when you focus on improving your sentences). Individually or in small groups, create a list of editing strategies. Share these with the class and generate a list of the most helpful strategies.

Revising means making big changes to the content of your essay, such as changing the topic, changing the organization, adding and deleting paragraphs, or adding more information and ideas from researching. Editing means focusing on sentence-level issues: making your sentences clearer, working on grammar and mechanics, considering word choice, and other sentence-level issues. Once your essay is edited, it's time to proofread. Proofreading means checking for mis-spellings, grammatical errors, missing words, and other mistakes. Editing and proofreading are the final stages of a writing process for a number of reasons. If you try to edit and proofread as you draft, you'll have a more difficult time putting your ideas on the page. You might get so caught up in trying to make the sentences perfect that you'll lose your train of thought or become bogged down in details. Another reason to save editing and proofreading for the final stage of the writing process is that it's a waste of time to edit and proofread sentences or paragraphs that might not even be there in the final draft.

Even though experienced college writers save editing and proofreading for last, it's still an important part of the process. Your college professors will have high expectations for the content of your essays *and* for the way you communicate that content. Part of this communication is making sure that your readers can understand your sentences. It's also important to edit and proofread carefully in order to gain the trust of your readers. After all, would you trust the information in a newspaper article or the arguments of the author of a book if what you were reading was riddled with grammatical errors and missing words? Of course, if you're multilingual, some of your sentence-level "errors" may actually be part of your writing "accent," just as we have an accent when we talk. Some college professors will focus on the content of your writing and won't be put off by your writing "accent," but most professors will want you to write in the "accent" of American academic English. The purpose, audience, genre, and context of the writing assignment will also play a role in how much focus the professor will put on grammar and other sentence-level features of writing. Regardless of the writing situation, it's important to give yourself time to carefully edit and proofread your paper, and to make use of strategies that experienced college writers use to edit and proofread their papers.

Strategies for Editing and Proofreading

- **Read what you've written out loud or have someone else read it to you out loud.**

It's usually easier to *hear* run-on sentences, unclear passages, and missing or overused words when you're reading aloud than it is to *see* them when you're reading silently. This is because people tend to read for overall meaning and not to notice errors when reading silently. Reading out loud can help you hear your mistakes and also your voice as a writer and whether it sounds the way you want it to. If you're shifting between conversational and academic language, if you're using too much jargon, repeating a certain word too often, or have too many long (or short) sentences in a row, you'll be able to hear this when you read out loud.

- **Give your essay to an outside reader to edit.**

When your professors submit an article to an academic journal to be published, they have editors who look over their article to find grammatical and typographical errors ("typos"). Even your college professors need some help spotting errors in their final drafts, and this means finding an outside reader. It's not up to your professor to edit every student's essay, and your institution's writing center is not an editing service, but you can ask a friend or a peer in the course to edit your essay before you turn it in, and then return the favor.

- **Keep an editing journal.**

Most of us have our own writing trouble spots. These trouble spots are aspects of style, grammar, and word usage that we tend to have trouble with in most writing situations. Editing isn't easy, and all college writers have language problems that they work on throughout their college writing career. Keeping an editing journal is a good way to work on your writing trouble spots and improve your editing process. In an editing journal, you keep track of the top three or four language problems that you struggle with repeatedly. For example, if your college professors tell you that you need to work on comma splices, sentence fragments, and run-on sentences, you can write down the rules for these grammatical problems and keep track of examples of these problems in your own writing. If they tell you that you overuse *so* or that your sentence structures lack variety, you can note alternative sentence structures and wordings. Keep in mind that when you're writing in a new genre or tackling an especially challenging and complex writing assignment, you're bound to have more of a struggle with word usage, grammar, and mechanics – in that case, having more problems is actually a sign of trying something new. If you're a bilingual or multilingual writer, keep in mind that these trouble spots might actually be sentence structures, grammatical features, or word usages from your first (or second or third) language that have found their way into your English writing.

- **Work on patterns of error with your professor or a tutor.**

Writing scholars have done a lot of research on the best ways for students to improve their grammar and mechanics. The research shows that the best way to improve any problem with sentence-level errors is to focus on one or two patterns of error at a time. Trying to learn all of the grammatical rules for every little error you have in a paper can be overwhelming, and it's better to focus on a few of the most frequent errors. For example, if you notice that in your college writing your professors comment on noun and pronoun agreement and singular versus plural word forms, then it's a good idea to keep an eye out for those two kinds of errors when you edit your final drafts. You might be able to get some help for working on these patterns at your institution's writing center, but keep in mind that it's not the writing center's job to proofread your paper or go on an "error hunt."

- **Read, read, read.**

Studies that have investigated how college students learn to improve their grammar, mechanics, and word usage have shown time and again that the best way to improve grammar is not to memorize rules or take grammar quizzes, but to read, read, read. The more you read, and the greater the variety of kinds of reading you do, the greater the sense you'll have of how words are used and how sentences are constructed in different genres and academic fields. When you read the texts you're assigned in college, pay close attention to the style of the writing, to how and which words are used, and to the way sentences are structured. You can learn a lot about grammar and you can expand the range of words and expressions you are able to use in your writing by being a careful reader. Learn to read like a writer.

- **Don't be frustrated if you struggle with errors in your college writing career.**

College professors have high expectations for your writing, and they expect essays that are carefully edited and proofread. This is understandable – after all, if you want to get your message across to your readers, they need to be able to understand the words and sentences which you've used to express your ideas. Try not to become too frustrated if you find yourself making more sentence-level errors in college than you did in high school. Often errors are a sign of growth. In college you're going to experience new genres, the new language and discourse of different academic fields, and challenging and complex writing assignments. This means you're going to struggle and to make mistakes as you learn these new genres and expand your writing style. You don't have to be frustrated by these errors – keep practicing, keep reading, and keep working on improving your editing skills.

Timed Writing

3.10: Writing to Learn – The Challenges of Timed Writing

Think back to times in high school or college when you had to take a timed writing test. Write about the challenges you faced in writing under pressure. Is writing under time pressure more difficult for you than other kinds of writing situations? Why or why not?

The writing processes we've been discussing are for ideal college writing situations when you have plenty of time to analyze the assignment, think about a topic, draft and revise, get feedback during the process, and carefully edit a final draft. But often in college the writing situation won't be this ideal. If you're taking an in-class essay examination, you won't have time to engage in the kind of writing processes we've been discussing. Since timed writing limits the amount of revising a writer can engage in and doesn't give writers the chance to get feedback from readers, why do college professors assign timed writing? Some professors ask you to write in-class essays so they can have a better sense of your writing style as well as your strengths as a writer and what you need to improve. It's also common for college professors to give timed essay exams if they teach in large courses, since the writing will be less extensive and it won't be overwhelming for them to respond to and grade their students' essays. Unfortunately, timed writing tests (e.g. the essay portion of the SAT) give the public the impression that a brief, timed writing task can measure how well a student can think and write. If you don't do well on timed tests, or if you were a successful writer in your high school courses but didn't do well on the SAT, this is not as negative as you may think. Researchers who study writing processes have shown that timed essay tests don't really measure how well a student can write or think critically about a topic, since there's not enough time to think deeply about the topic, plan and draft, and extensively revise and edit: and as we've discussed in this chapter, writing *is* revising. Writing is a social and intertextual process, and timed examinations deny writers the chance to gain feedback and seek out models of the genre they're writing in. Writing for examinations is therefore quite different from writing with less time pressure.

Even if you feel nervous when you have to take a timed essay examination or you know that you write much better when you have time to revise and get feedback, the reality is that throughout your college career you'll likely have to do some timed writing. The good news is that when you do have a timed essay test, there are some strategies you can use so you'll be well-prepared and confident.

Strategies for Timed Writing

- **Prepare ahead of time by studying possible writing topics and writing practice essays.**

You'll be much more confident and much less nervous going into a timed writing situation if you're well prepared. Give yourself time to study your notes and course readings well before the day of a timed essay exam. Write some practice essays ahead of time to get a feel for how long you'll have to write and what you might say. Sometimes your professor will give you questions ahead of time, and sometimes you'll just have to practice by making an educated guess about what you think the essay exam might cover.

- **Carefully read and reread the question and underline key words.**

When you read the timed exam question or questions, don't panic. Take a deep breath and give yourself time to read and reread the question to make sure you have an understanding of what the professor is asking you. Look for key verbs that point to the kind of thinking and writing strategies the question is asking for, such as *summarize*, *define*, *evaluate*, and *argue*.

- **Tap into course lectures and discussions.**

In timed essay exams, professors will often ask you to respond to questions that were raised in lectures or course discussions. Try to recall what the professor discussed in his or her lectures or what your peers talked about in class discussions.

- **Do some brainstorming and planning.**

It's worthwhile to devote some time to brainstorming ideas, planning, and rough drafting before you start writing a more organized response. You could use some of the strategies discussed in this chapter, such as making lists, clustering, or creating a rough outline. You won't have time to engage in an extensive drafting and revising process, but you might have time to write a quick rough draft, or on a separate sheet of paper write a "no pressure" discovery draft of the essay or a section of it that you're stuck on.

- **Don't approach the drafting of a piece of timed writing with the same approach you use for other kinds of writing assignments.**

If you're writing a research paper that you have two months to write, there's plenty of time to develop complex arguments, support your ideas to the fullest, and write in a sophisticated style. In a timed essay examination, you'll need to simplify things. Depending on how much time you have, you may need to find a simple way to organize your ideas or strategies for supporting your arguments more concisely than you would in a ten-page research paper. You might also simplify your writing style somewhat. Usually professors are focused on the content of students' essays in a timed examination, and they're not looking for a sophisticated writing style.

- **Don't worry about surface errors while you're writing, but save some time for a final edit.**

In timed writing situations, you can't let yourself become bogged down in making each word choice perfect and each sentence grammatically correct. Don't edit as you go, but save five minutes or so at the end to look over what you've written and do a final edit. Most professors don't have the same expectations for grammatical correctness in timed essays that they would in an essay you had weeks to write, revise, and edit. However, as in all writing, in a timed essay your sentences need to be understandable.

Getting Feedback

Throughout this chapter the argument has been made that writing is *socially constructed*. This means that experienced college writers don't just sit alone at a desk waiting for inspiration, and they don't turn in a final draft without getting feedback first. Successful college writers gain as much help with their writing as they can. They talk with their professors about ideas for topics, ask friends or classmates to look at rough drafts, or take a draft to the writing center. In this section of Chapter 3, we'll focus on three strategies for gaining feedback during the writing process: peer response, writing groups, and writing centers.

3.11: Writing to Learn – Guidelines for Peer Response

If you've participated in a peer response workshop before, write a list of the most helpful kinds of feedback you received and another list of the least helpful kinds of feedback you received. Share this list with others in your class to generate some guidelines for peer response.

Peer Response

Several times during the semester, your instructor will ask you to read and respond to first drafts written by your classmates. These responses are often called *peer critiques* or *peer reviews*. Writing peer responses demands that you develop your powers of critical reading. Moreover, as you carefully observe your classmates' strategies while tackling the same assignment, you often learn valuable writing strategies that you may employ later in writing and revising your own essays.

— from the *Student Guide to First-Year Writing*, University of Texas Division of Rhetoric and Writing (University of Texas Division of Writing, 2010)

The group workshops always helped when you were writing an essay. The other students would read your work and give their opinion on it. Whether it was positive or negative, there was always something you could improve in your essay.

— a first-year writing student at Florida State University (quoted in Cook, 2006)

Writers rarely write in a vacuum. Writers need response, need a community of other people with whom they can discuss their work.

— Professors Robert Brooke, University of Nebraska, Ruth Mirtz, Ferris State University, and Richard Evans, University of Nebraska (Brooke, Mirtz, and Evans, 1994: 13)

In peer response, students are formed or form themselves into pairs or small groups and give each other feedback on a draft of an essay. This is a common activity in first-year writing courses, and it's likely that some of your professors in other academic fields will also ask you to respond to drafts of your peers' writing. Professors who use peer response know that what you can learn from your peers can be just as helpful as what you can learn from your professor.

Professors feel that peer response has other benefits as well:

- Peer response gives you feedback early in the writing process.
- Peer response provides you with a real live audience for your writing.
- Peer response gives you the chance to ask direct questions to readers.
- Peer response lets you see how other students are responding to the writing assignment.
- Peer response helps you become a better evaluator of your writing by learning how to evaluate your peers' writing.
- Peer response discourages you from waiting until the last minute to write.
- Peer response helps create a classroom community of writers.

Advice for Responding to your Peers' Writing

- **Try to balance praise and constructive criticism.**

Sometimes in peer response students are trying not to hurt someone's feelings, so they only make positive comments about an essay. It's good for the writer to hear what's working in an essay, but in order to give the writer ideas for what and how to revise, you also need to offer constructive criticism and let the writer know where you were confused or lost interest. At the same time, you don't want to just tear apart the writer's work. Give *constructive* criticism.

- **Don't comment on grammar and mechanics in rough drafts.**

Experienced writers save editing and proofreading for the final stage of writing processes, and unless your professor has a special peer editing workshop for final drafts, it's best not to comment on grammar and mechanics in peer response. There's no sense in editing a sentence or paragraph that may not even end up in the final draft. Don't play the role of error corrector or the "grammar police" in peer response.

- **Ask the writer what he or she needs help with before you read and respond.**

Sometimes writers will have specific questions they'd like their peer readers to address, such as: "Does the introduction draw you in?" or "Do I have enough evidence in paragraph #3?" Before you begin discussing another student's essay or writing your response, ask the writer if he or she has specific questions for you to address.

Writing Groups

It's common for first-year writing professors to ask students to form peer response groups, but unfortunately it's not as common for professors in other academic fields to organize peer response groups in their courses. It's always a good idea to form a peer response group on your own if your professor doesn't organize one for you. You can ask a few classmates if they'd like to meet outside of class to exchange papers, or you can exchange papers through email. If you're lucky, you'll find a few peers who can form a writing group for your entire college career, and you can all learn from each other. A group like this takes some effort to set up and to keep going, but it's worth the effort as a source of feedback on your college writing before you turn it in for a grade.

Some Questions for Responding to Someone's Writing

If you're in a writing group, here are some general questions you can ask yourself when you respond to someone's writing:

- What did you like best about the paper and why?
- What did you want to know more about?
- Where in the paper were you confused as a reader?
- Was the writer's persona and voice appropriate for the rhetorical situation of the writing assignment?
- Did the writer provide enough support for his or her argument?
- What other perspectives could the writer consider?
- If research was required, how well did the writer integrate outside sources, and how reliable and appropriate were the sources?
- Was the paper well organized?
- Was the organization appropriate for the genre?
- Was the opening and closing effective? Why or why not?
- What are the two or three most important things the writer should focus on improving in the next draft?

Writing Centers

The Writing Center at the University of Miami strives to help all members of the university community learn more about writing and become better writers. Writers at all levels can benefit from sharing their writing with someone who is both knowledgeable and trustworthy, someone who is not grading them or evaluating their work.

—from the University of Miami Writing Center's mission statement
(University of Miami Writing Center, 2010)

Since we are a teaching center, writers should be able to use our services at any phase of their writing process, whether they have just received an assignment and are brainstorming for ideas or are in the final phases of their writing project.

—from the Colorado School of Mines Writing Center's mission statement
(Colorado School of Mines Writing Center, 2010)

We provide a comfortable environment where you can work to become more confident in your own writing. To help you succeed, we will ask you many questions and provide useful feedback. Of course, we are not an editing service—our goal is to offer supportive guidance to help you become a better writer!

—from the Web site of the Northern Virginia Community College Writing Center (Northern Virginia Community College Writing Center, 2008)

Most colleges have writing centers where students can go for free help with their writing. Typically, these writing centers are staffed with tutors or consultants who are experienced writing professors, peer counselors, or undergraduate and/or graduate students who have been given special training in how best to help students with their writing. Most writing center tutors or consultants can help you with a writing assignment in any course, but some colleges have a separate writing center only for English or composition courses. Some colleges even have writing centers for specific academic fields, such as engineering, business, or the natural sciences. Writers can benefit greatly from one-on-one feedback, and visiting the writing center frequently can be your key to college writing success.

Advice for Visiting Your Writing Center
Below I offer some advice for visiting your institution's writing center.

- **Bring the course writing assignment along with your draft.**

The more information the tutor has about the writing assignment, the more the help you receive will be tailored to your assignment. If your professor doesn't give you a written assignment, make sure you write down how your professor described the assignment so you can describe it well to the tutor.

- **Don't wait until the last minute to go for help.**

You need to give yourself time to revise after you receive feedback from a tutor. If you visit the writing center the day before the paper is due, you won't be able to engage in a writing process. Remember that writing center tutors can help you at any stage in the process: understanding the assignment, finding a topic, revising, and working on improving your editing skills.

- **Visit the writing center even if you're having success in your college writing.**

A writing center is not only for students who are struggling with their writing. Even successful writers seek out feedback for improvement.

- **Don't try to get help with revising and editing in one session.**

Writing center tutors know that writing is a process and that experienced writers save editing for the final stage of the process. Visit the writing center early in the process for help with drafting and revising (focusing your topic, improving your organization, supporting your ideas). Then, when you're just about finished writing the essay and you've given it a good edit yourself, you can take it to the writing center for further help with editing techniques and for finding the mechanical or grammatical errors you still have in the essay. But remember that even though most writing centers can help you become a better editor of your own writing, they won't just edit and proofread for you.

- **Don't expect the writing center to revise or edit your essay for you.**

The goal of a writing center is to help students improve as writers, not just to help them obtain a good grade on a single paper. If the tutor or consultant tells you how to organize your essay or corrects patterns of grammar errors for you, you'll never learn to revise or edit your own writing. Writing centers can help you develop editing strategies and learn how to recognize patterns of error you have in your writing, but tutors are not proofreaders.

- **Visit the writing center (or other learning resource center) for help with your reading assignments as well as your writing assignments.**

Reading and writing are closely connected: most good writers are also good readers. In most of your college writing assignments, you'll be asked to respond to a text or support your arguments with outside sources. College reading is usually difficult. The ideas are complex, and each academic field has a different terminology and different genres. At some writing centers, or in separate learning resources centers at most colleges, you can ask for help not only with your writing process, but also with your reading process. You can bring in the text or texts you are struggling with and work one-on-one with a tutor. Writing or learning resources tutors can also help you develop some general strategies for reading college material as well as your own writing.

- **Visit the writing center regularly to improve as a writer, not only to work on one piece of writing.**

Don't think of the writing center as an "emergency room" that you only visit when you're in big trouble and need help fast. Most writing centers would like you to visit regularly throughout your college career so you can improve as a writer. They prefer to focus on the student as a writer rather than focusing on only one writing assignment for one course.

3.12: Learn by Doing – Writing Center Interview

Interview a tutor or consultant at your institution's writing center to find out what kind of help is available to students. If your college doesn't have a writing center, it may be that the place which offers free tutoring is called the *Learning Center* or *Academic Success Center*. Arrange to meet with a tutor and ask him or her about what is done in a tutoring session, what common writing issues students are working on, and what other help in addition to tutoring is available.

Creating a Writing Portfolio

What is a Writing Portfolio?

A writing portfolio is a collection of your work, including rough and final drafts. Many first-year writing professors ask students to prepare a portfolio of their work rather than only collect and grade individual essays. Each professor will have different guidelines for what goes into a writing portfolio, but most professors will ask for final drafts of the essays you've written for the course, a rough draft or multiple rough drafts of the essays, and a cover letter in which you discuss your writing processes and evaluate the strengths and weaknesses of the portfolio. Some professors ask students to choose two or three of their best essays in the portfolio, rather than including all of their essays, and reflect in their process memo about why they chose those particular essays. Portfolios can be assembled in a folder, binder, or online as electronic portfolios (a screen shot of a student's electronic portfolio is shown as an example in the section on document design in this chapter).

Why Do Professors Use Portfolio Evaluation?

Portfolio evaluation has a number of advantages for professors and students. Portfolios give students time to fully engage in writing processes and revise their writing throughout the entire semester. Students can take more chances and experiment more in their writing, knowing that they have time to revise before they're given a final grade. Portfolios reward students for the effort they put into revision, since the professor can observe students' writing processes by looking at the drafts included in the portfolio. Portfolios reward a student for growing as a writer, since the professor evaluates each student's entire body of work. Portfolios also encourage students to reflect on their own writing processes and evaluate their strengths and weaknesses as writers. Professors like portfolios for all of these reasons, and also because students pay more attention to professors' comments if they know they can revise the essay based on the comments before they are given a final grade.

What is a Portfolio Cover Letter?

Most portfolios include some kind of an introduction to the portfolio and how it was created, often called a *cover letter*, *process memo*, or *reflection*. This introduction usually has two audiences: the writer and the reader. The writer is doing some self-reflection and self-evaluation, and the writer is also giving clues to the reader about what to look for in the portfolio and how best to evaluate it. Because the ability to critically self-reflect on your writing processes is such an important part of improving as a writer, many first-year writing professors ask students to include an entire self-reflection essay, and not just a cover letter.

Questions for a Portfolio Cover Letter or Reflection
Here are some questions you can ask yourself about your portfolio when you're preparing the cover letter or reflection:

- What does my portfolio reveal about my strengths and weaknesses as a writer?
- How has my writing history influenced the writing in my portfolio?
- In what ways does my college writing persona connect to or conflict with the persona I take on in the writing I do for myself or for communities that I belong to outside of college?
- What aspects of writing do I still need to practice and improve upon for my future college writing?
- What new things did I learn about writing this semester?
- What kinds of writing processes did I engage in for each essay?
- In what ways did my essays change from the first draft to the final draft?
- How did the rhetorical situation and genre affect my writing processes in each essay?
- What does the reader need to know about my writing processes and my writing history to evaluate the portfolio?
- What does my reader need to know about the final products to evaluate the portfolio?
- At what places in my portfolio do I have evidence that I've met the learning outcomes of the course?

Collaborating: Group Writing Projects

It is fairly common in some of the social sciences for researchers to work in teams – to collaborate... It is even more common for professionals outside the academy to collaborate on writing tasks, so it is worth understanding how to do it well, as there is a high possibility you will work and write with others at some point in your life.

—Professor Kristine Hansen, Brigham Young University (Hansen, 2003: 34)

Remember that in group work we expect all group members to take responsibility for keeping all of their group mates up to speed and to take personal responsibility for contributing everything they are capable of. "The whole is greater than the sum of its parts"; this is especially true when working in groups.

—Purdue University Department of Physics Web site (Purdue University Department of Physics, 2008)

3.13: Writing to Learn – Your Experiences Working in Groups

Before you read about collaborating and group writing, reflect on your own experiences collaborating. Have you participated in a group writing project in high school or college? What were the advantages of working in a group? What were the disadvantages?

As the quotes above reveal, group writing is becoming more and more common in college and in the workplace. College professors are beginning to realize the benefits of having students work with their peers on writing projects. One benefit of group writing, then, is that team projects are very common in the workplace. Even if you're not a big fan of working in groups, you'll need to learn how to work with others successfully no matter what job you have after you graduate. Another benefit of group writing is the amount of information and feedback you are able to obtain when you work in groups. A text written by a group benefits from the different perspectives and ideas of each group member. If the group works as a real team, writing in a group can be a great experience. It's easy, however, for groups to run into problems if there aren't some ground rules. Some advice for writing in a group is given below.

Strategies for Group Writing

- **Set clear and fair writing objectives and roles for each group member.**

Each group member should choose a role that will play to his or her strengths. Although everyone should be involved in writing the final product, you might have each person take a primary role such as organizer, editor, researcher, or graphic designer.

- **Take advantage of each person's writing strengths.**

Each writer has a different strength: researching, planning, organizing, creating charts and tables, editing and proofreading. Divide up the writing duties based on each writer's strength.

- **Divide the project into different parts.**

Just as you can divide up the writing duties, you can divide the project into stages or parts. For example, you might start with researching, then drafting and revising, and then editing and design. Or you might break the project into sections and have each person or pairs work on a section.

- **Set a drafting and revising schedule.**

Group projects require more organization and planning than individually written projects. Setting a schedule and assigning a group leader to keep everyone on schedule will lead to a more successful writing process.

- **Allow time for the writing process.**

Collaborative writing projects always involve a more extensive revision process than usual since so many writers are involved. Don't wait until the last minute to begin drafting.

- **Exchange rough drafts and give each other feedback.**

Sharing drafts gives each writer feedback during the process and helps to create a more unified final product. Give both positive feedback and constructive criticism, and focus on content in the initial drafts (organization, tone, development) and on clarity and sentence-level issues in the final draft (word usage, grammar, mechanics, format).

- **Allow extra time to integrate each section of the project into a single voice.**

One of the biggest challenges of collaborative writing is to give the project a feeling of unity. Allow extra time to read the project in its entirety and edit for a unified tone and style.

Document Design

In Chapter 2, we talked about the definition of *rhetoric*, and the focus was on rhetoric as the art of communicating effectively to your audience. In college writing, communicating effectively often means writing texts, but it also means using visuals such as graphs, charts, photos, and graphic design elements. Communicating effectively using visuals means being skilled at *visual rhetoric*. There's even an entire field of study for *digital rhetoric*, and in a digital environment the use of visuals such as digital images or video files is common. This section will provide you with some strategies for effective visual rhetoric.

3.14: Writing to Learn – Thinking about Visual Rhetoric

The purpose of this Writing to Learn activity is to help you to think about visual rhetoric and what contributes to a well-designed document before you read some design principles in this section. Take a close look at the two samples of visual design below: Layla Quinones's electronic portfolio index page, which can be found at http://www.eportfolio .lagcc.cuny.edu/scholars/doc_fa09/eP_fa09/Layla.Quinones/index.html, and Professor Tess Wynn's scientific poster presentation, which can be found at http://www.writing. eng.vt.edu/courses/presentations/poster3.pdf.

Individually or in small groups, write about or discuss whether or not these two documents are effective visually, and why they are or aren't effective. Be prepared to discuss your opinions with your peers.

Layla Quinones's electronic portfolio and Professor Wynn's poster presentation were responses to two very different rhetorical situations. Layla's goal in creating an electronic portfolio was to present her best qualities as a student and professional-in-training to her professors and to future employers. Since she was working in a digital environment, she had to think about graphic design for the Internet and effective use of hyperlinks. Professor Wynn's purpose in creating a scientific poster was to display the results of a research study in a concise and visually attractive way to attendees of a scientific conference. Every college rhetorical situation that calls for the use of visuals will be different: a PowerPoint presentation in a business course, a Web site for a communication studies course, a brochure for a service learning project, a poster for a science course. But there are some basic visual design principles to consider no matter what kind of visuals you're working with.

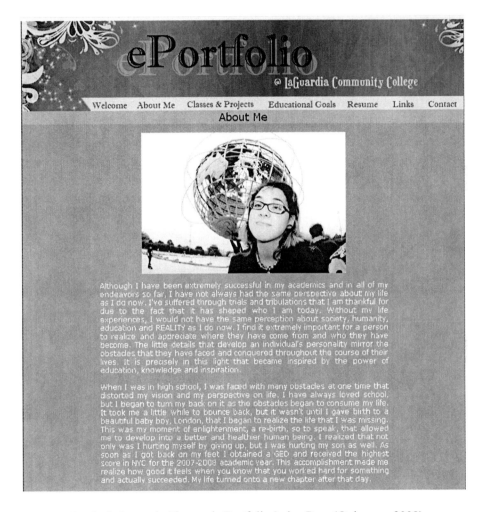

Layla Quinones's Electronic Portfolio Index Page (Quinones, 2009)

Proposal to Study the Effects of Woody and Herbaceous Vegetation on Streambank Erosion

Tess Wynn, *Virginia Tech*

Justification for Study

Streambank erosion can be a large source of sediment, as much as 80% of the total watershed sediment yield [1, 2].

Sediment is the primary pollutant of rivers [3, 4].

Streambank erosion also causes
- Increased flooding
- Increased need for dredging
- Undermining of in-stream structures
- Degradation of reservoirs

Collapse of near vertical bank after high flows have scoured the toe of the bank.

Objectives of Proposed Research

Compare the effects of woody and herbaceous vegetation on
- Stream hydraulics at bankfull discharge
- Soil moisture and temperature regimes
- Soil strength

Methods

(1) Perform monitoring at two field locations on a stream near Blacksburg, Virginia. Locations will have sections with herbaceous and wooded riparian buffers.

(2) Continuously monitor the following:
- Air temperature and precipitation
- Stream stage
- Soil moisture and temperature

(3) Sample the following:
- Suspended sediment (weekly)
- Bank material (texture, friction angle, root area ratios)

(4) During two storms with 1-2 year return periods, measure the following:
- Stream velocity and discharge
- Sediment concentration
- Bedload

Background: Grass Versus Trees

Research has shown that streams are significantly narrower with grass buffers than with forested buffers [5, 6]. The photos below support this finding.

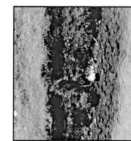

Two adjacent stable reaches of Spruce Run, an alluvial stream near Newport, Virginia. (top) riparian buffer of meadow grass; (bottom) buffer dominated by trees and shrubs.

References

[1] Trimble, S. W., "Contribution of Stream Channel Erosion to Sediment Yield from an Urbanizing Watershed," *Science*, vol. 278 (1997), pp.1442-1444.

[2] Simon, A., A. Curini, S. Darby, and E. J. Langendoen, "Streambank Mechanics and the Role of Bank and Near-Bank Processes in Incised Channels," in *Incised River Channels: Processes, Forms, Engineering and Management*, ed. by Darby, S. E., and A. Simon (Chichester: John Wiley and Sons, 1999) pp. 123-152.

[3] US EPA, *National Water Quality Inventory: Report to Congress* (USEPA: Washington, DC: US EPA, 1990).

[4] US EPA, *Managing Nonpoint Source Pollution. Final Report to Congress on Section 319 of the Clean Water Act* (Washington, D.C.: US EPA, 1990).

[5] Trimble, S. W., "Stream Channel Erosion and Change Resulting from Riparian Forests," *Geology*, vol. 25, no. 5 (1997), pp. 467-469.

[6] Clifton, C., "Effects of Vegetation and Land Use on Channel Morphology," in *Practical Approaches to Riparian Resource Management. An Educational Workshop*, ed. by Gresswell, R. E., B. A. Barton, and J. L. Kershner (Billings, Montana: USDI/BLM, May 8-11, 1989), pp. 121-129.

Acknowledgments:

U.S. Environmental Protection Agency Office of Research and Development Science to Achieve Results Program Grant No. 91534101

Professor Tess Wynn's Scientific Poster Presentation (Wynn, 2001)

Some General Visual Design Principles

- **Consider your rhetorical situation.**

It helps to think about rhetorical factors such as purpose, audience, genre, and persona whenever you're designing a visual. For example, in her electronic portfolio, Layla Quinones's persona is both friendly and professional, and this persona is effective for her purpose (keeping a visual record of her work as a student) and audience (professors and future employers). Layla uses conventions associated with effective Web writing, such as a uniform header at the top of each page.

- **Be consistent in your design.**

Whether you're composing a Web site, a brochure, a poster, or a PowerPoint presentation, consistency helps your audience. If you're consistent in your layout, colors, and fonts, it will be easier for readers to make transitions from one Web page or PowerPoint slide to the next, and readers will know where to find information. Layla used the same template for all of her Web pages, with a header that repeats on every page in a uniform format, with uniform colors and uniform fonts. As readers navigate her Web site, they never feel lost because they can always find her index page and the primary links she's included.

- **Understand how to use color, contrast, and emphasis.**

Whether you're creating a pie chart or a full color newsletter, think carefully about how you're using color, contrast, and emphasis. When you're considering colors to use in your visuals, think about issues such as being consistent with your use of colors, using color combinations that will make your text clear to your readers (including visually impaired readers), and using colors that work well together. Colors can be used effectively for emphasis, but it's also easy to overwhelm your audience if there are too many different colors in your Web site or brochure or graph. In her electronic portfolio, Layla uses color for emphasis and for contrast. For example, each of her hyperlink headings is a dark blue color that provides emphasis and also contrasts well with the light gray background. Layla also uses the contrast of a white font on a green background for her main text. Color is one way to add emphasis to a visual, but you can also use text boxes, bullets, increased or varied fonts, and other graphic tools.

- **Create visually appealing organization and formatting.**

The way you organize your visuals is key to effective visual rhetoric. Think about features such as the balance of words and images, the use of margins and white space, the placement of images, and the use of columns or text boxes. Professor Wynn's poster presentation, for example, is well-balanced in terms of how the different parts are organized and presented on the page. There are four columns of equal width, and each column has a heading in a bold and larger sized font. The pictures are also nicely balanced in terms of their location on the page, with a larger picture in the far left column and two smaller pictures to the right. Professor Wynn uses a sans-serif typeface for her poster presentation. Sans-serif typefaces like Arial and Verdana tend to be better for visuals such as posters and Web sites, and serif fonts like Times New Roman and Courier work better for documents that have a lot of text. Serif typefaces have small lines at the ends of letters; sans-serif typefaces don't have these lines, so they're easier to read on the screen. It's also a good idea to match your font to your theme. Professor Wynn wouldn't want to use a Comic Sans font, which is a "playful" font, or Brush Script font, which is a highly decorative font, since she's trying to present the results of her research in a formal and scientific persona.

3.15: Writing to Learn – Comparing Composing in Print with Composing Online

The purpose of this Writing to Learn activity is to have you think about some of the differences between composing in print and composing online. Individually or in small groups, create a list of the differences between composing a print essay and composing a Web site. Think about differences between rhetorical features like organization, style, and audience, and also think about how composing processes differ between online and print composing. Be prepared to discuss your list with other students in your class.

Before we talk about strategies for creating effective Web writing, let's look at an example of Web writing, the index page of the Purdue University Online Writing Lab (OWL), which you can visit at http://owl .english.purdue.edu/owl.

The principles of effective visual design we discussed in the previous section can be seen in the Purdue Online Writing Lab Web site. The Purdue OWL is well-organized, consistent, and easy for readers to navigate. It uses color and contrast to highlight links and increased fonts for emphasis. It has features that are common conventions of Web writing, such as lists of hyperlinks and text chunking rather than conventional paragraph format.

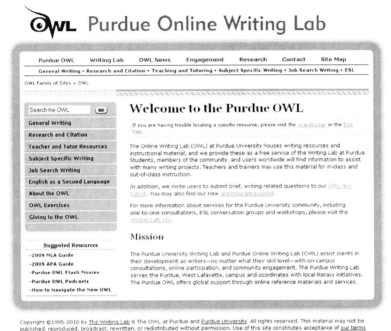

OWL Purdue Online Writing Lab

| Purdue OWL | Writing Lab | OWL News | Engagement | Research | Contact | Site Map |

General Writing • Research and Citation • Teaching and Tutoring • Subject Specific Writing • Job Search Writing • ESL

OWL Family of Sites > OWL

Search the OWL   [GO]

General Writing
Research and Citation
Teacher and Tutor Resources
Subject Specific Writing
Job Search Writing
English as a Second Language
About the OWL
OWL Exercises
Giving to the OWL

Suggested Resources
-2009 MLA Guide
-2009 APA Guide
-Purdue OWL Flash Movies
-Purdue OWL Podcasts
-How to Navigate the New OWL

Welcome to the Purdue OWL

If you are having trouble locating a specific resource, please visit the search page or the Site Map.

The Online Writing Lab (OWL) at Purdue University houses writing resources and instructional material, and we provide these as a free service of the Writing Lab at Purdue. Students, members of the community, and users worldwide will find information to assist with many writing projects. Teachers and trainers may use this material for in-class and out-of-class instruction.

In addition, we invite users to submit brief, writing-related questions to our OWL Mail Tutors. You may also find our new grammar blog useful.

For more information about services for the Purdue University community, including one-to-one consultations, ESL conversation groups and workshops, please visit the Writing Lab site.

Mission

The Purdue University Writing Lab and Purdue Online Writing Lab (OWL) assist clients in their development as writers—no matter what their skill level—with on-campus consultations, online participation, and community engagement. The Purdue Writing Lab serves the Purdue, West Lafayette, campus and coordinates with local literacy initiatives. The Purdue OWL offers global support through online reference materials and services.

The Index Page of the *Purdue Online Writing Lab* (*OWL*; Writing Lab at Purdue, 2010)

It's becoming more and more common for college students to compose online in digital environments such as Web sites and Weblogs (*blogs*). You might be asked to create a digital portfolio of your essays for a composition course, to design your professional online résumé for a business course, or to create a politically themed blog for a political science course. Web sites and blogs have their own conventions that are very different from the conventions of print genres such as a lab report or a research paper or an essay examination. Some of the strategies below for creating Web sites are similar to strategies for composing in print, but some are also specific to the conventions of composing online.

Strategies for Creating Effective Web Sites

- **Find models of the kind of site you're creating.**

Just as you might look for examples of the type of print text genre you're writing in, if your professors ask you to create a Web site, it would be helpful to find models. For example, if your political science professor asks you to go to

Blogger.com and create a political blog, you could find models of political blogs simply by typing the phrase *political blogs* in an Internet search engine. By searching for models you can also gain an idea of what kinds of Web writing *aren't* effective for the genre of Web writing you've been assigned.

- **Think about the rhetorical situation for your Web site.**

Like print-based assignments, writing for the Web is always done in the context of a rhetorical situation. Creating a professional online résumé for a business course will present a much different rhetorical situation than creating a personal Web site for a first-year experience course. It's also important to keep in mind that writing published on the Web could have wider and sometimes unintended audiences. Remember that eventually almost everything published on the Internet finds its way into a search engine.

- **Create a map of your site before you begin to construct it.**

For experienced Web writers, an initial stage in the writing process often involves creating a map of their Web site before they begin to build it. One of the most important aspects of creating Web sites is deciding how many pages to include, how the pages will be linked, and what information will be included on each page. Let's say that you've been asked to create an electronic portfolio of your college writing. You might begin sketching out a plan for the structure of your Web site by drawing a map of your site (see opposite page).

Creating a map of your Web site can help you gain a sense of how easy it will be for readers to navigate, how many links you might include in a header or sidebar on your index page, and whether or not you may be trying to put too much information and too many links on each page. Just as when you sketch an outline for a print essay, you don't need to be wedded to your map as you begin to create your Web site. As you create your Web site, you'll probably think of new pages to add and you'll probably discover different ways to organize your site.

- **Create a unified and consistent look.**

In the examples of Web writing we've looked at in this chapter – Layla Quinones's electronic portfolio and the Purdue Online Writing Lab – each page of the site has a consistent look. The same organization, frames, and colors are used on each page. This kind of consistency can help the reader stay focused and organized, and it makes the site easier to navigate. It's also helpful to have a navigation bar on the top or side of each page. If you include the most important links on each page in a navigation bar, readers won't become lost as they move

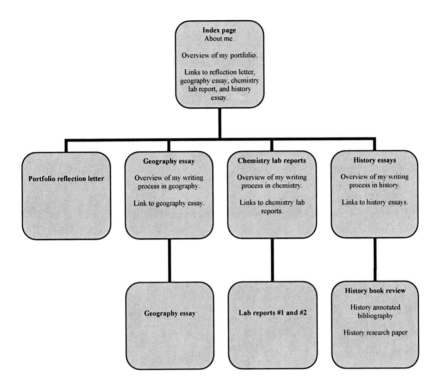

farther and farther away from the index page. A recurring navigation bar also helps separate content from navigation, which makes your site easier for readers to browse.

- **Use Web writing styles such as headings and text chunking.**

The writing style of your Web site will depend on your purpose and audience, but there are stylistic conventions that are associated with writing for the screen. Most of these conventions have to do with the rhetorical situation for reading and writing online. Most Web surfers are reading for information rather than reading for pleasure, so Web writers try to make their sites easy to navigate and skim. For example, most Web writers use headings for major sections of their site, and they usually emphasize these by increasing font size, changing font style, and/or changing the color of the font. Instead of writing in print essay style, using long series of paragraphs with an indent at the beginning signaling a new paragraph, Web writers often chunk paragraphs in blocks with a space between blocks. The use of frames and boxes to organize and emphasize information and links is another convention of Web writing. Since on the screen it's easier to read single-spaced text than double-spaced text, most Web writing is single-spaced. Another convention of Web writing is the use of short pages that fit on one screen with links to further information, rather than long pages that readers need to scroll through from one screen to the next.

- **Make sure your site is easy to download.**

When you're writing for the Web, it's tempting to fill up your site with pictures and clip-art. But keep in mind that the more pictures and clip-art you include on your site, the more slowly the site will download for visitors. Also, a Web site that's cluttered with photos or clip-art can overwhelm readers.

- **Make your site accessible to readers with disabilities.**

Keep in mind that some Web surfers who visit your site may be hearing impaired or visually impaired. If you've included images on your site, include a description of the images for those who can't (easily) see the colors. If you're using more than one color, make sure the colors provide a strong contrast for readers who are color-blind. If your site has sound, be sure to include captions. Conversely, it is good Web design for maximum accessibility to include both audio and print versions of information. Letting readers know that the information on your site is available in alternate formats is also helpful. For more on how to make your Web site accessible, visit the accessibility guidelines at the Web Accessibility Initiative site: http://www.w3.org/TR/WAI-WEBCONTENT/.

3.16: Learn by Doing – College Web Site Evaluation

The purpose of this Learn by Doing activity is to encourage you to think about the qualities of an effective Web site by looking at your own institution's home page. Go to the home page of your college, look it over carefully, and think about whether or not it's an example of effective Web writing. Discuss why the site is or isn't effective Web writing, keeping in mind the visual design principles and strategies for effective Web writing that we've been discussing as well as the rhetorical situation of your institution's home page.

Integrating Visuals

At different points in your college career, it's likely that you'll be asked to write in genres that include visuals such as charts, tables, and photos. These visuals are often fundamental to the way certain genres and academic fields make meaning: for example, in the sciences, reporting data is critical for sharing knowledge, and charts and graphs are common visual tools for making the quantitative results of data clear to readers. When you integrate visuals, there is some advice to keep in mind, as discussed below.

- **Refer to visuals in print before they appear.**

To prepare your readers for the visual, make sure you mention the visual in the body of your paper before it appears. For example, you wouldn't want your readers to wrestle with a complicated graph without first preparing them by introducing the information in the graph and discussing the graph's purpose. This will give your readers the context needed for understanding the graph.

- **Connect visuals to the text.**

In addition to introducing visuals, explain their significance for the rest of the text. Make a connection between your ideas and arguments and the visuals you use. For example, if you've included a pie chart to provide support for an argument that Americans spend too much of their budget on entertainment, refer to the chart as evidence when you make your argument; don't simply drop it in and force your readers to make the connection themselves.

- **Use visuals to enhance content and not simply take up space.**

If you're a little short on page length, you might be tempted to include visuals to take up a little extra space. But beware: readers know when a writer is using visuals as an effective part of their argument and when writers are adding extra visuals simply to take up space (or with no thought as to their purpose). Just as you don't want to add meaningless words to meet a page requirement, you don't want to add images simply to take up more space.

- **Match the purpose and tone of your visuals to the purpose and tone of your paper.**

In the formal genre of the lab report, it wouldn't be appropriate to include cartoon clip art. A complex graph might be excellent evidence for an economics course report on the history of interest rates, but a complex graph in a PowerPoint presentation aimed at classmates might confuse or frustrate your audience. Think about aspects of the rhetorical situation (e.g. purpose, audience, and persona) when you integrate visuals.

Common Types of Visuals

Following is a brief overview of common types of visuals you might integrate into your college writing.

Bar Graphs

Use bar graphs to make quick, easy comparisons. Bar graphs can help highlight differences between groups or sets of data. Take, for example, the bar graph below from a sample lab report on the foraging habits of beavers that we will look at in Chapter 7. With a relatively quick scan of the bar graph, readers can make comparisons between the circumference of trees selected by beavers.

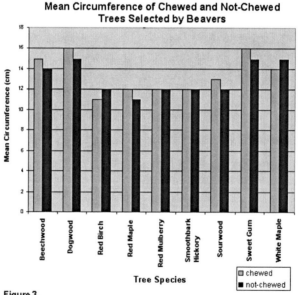

Figure 3.

North Carolina State University (2004)

Tables

Use tables when you want to emphasize numerical information. Tables can relate complex data more easily and clearly than bar graphs. Consider the amount of information and the number of categories that are contained in the table below from the United States Department of Health and Human Services (2001).

TABLE (Continued). Percentage of high school students who reported sexual risk behaviors. by sex, grade, race/ethnicity, and survey year — United States, Youth Risk Behavior Survey, 1991, 1993, 1995, 1997, 1999, and 2001

Characteristic	Ever had sexual intercourse		≥4 sex partners during lifetime		Currently sexually active†		Condom use during last sexual intercourse§		Alcohol or drug use before last sexual intercourse§	
	%	(95% CI*)	%	(95% CI)	%	(95% CI)	%	(95% CI)	%	(95% CI)
Race/Ethnicity††										
Black										
1991	81.4	(±3.2)	43.1	(±3.5)	59.3	(±3.8)	48.0	(±3.8)	13.7	(±2.9)
1993	79.7	(±3.2)	42.7	(±3.8)	59.1	(±4.4)	56.5	(±3.8)	12.2	(±3.5)
1995	73.4	(±4.5)	35.6	(±4.4)	54.2	(±4.7)	66.1	(±4.8)	19.2	(±4.6)
1997	72.6	(±2.9)	38.5	(±3.6)	53.6	(±3.2)	64.0	(±2.8)	18.1	(±3.1)
1999	71.2	(±8.2)	34.4	(±10.3)	53.0	(±8.9)	70.0	(±5.4)	18.1	(±7.9)
2001	60.8	(±6.6)¶	26.6	(±3.7)¶	45.6	(±5.4)¶	67.1	(±3.5)¶ **	17.8	(±2.6)¶
Hispanic										
1991	53.1	(±3.5)	16.8	(±2.6)	37.0	(±3.6)	37.4	(±6.2)	17.8	(±4.2)
1993	56.0	(±4.1)	18.6	(±3.1)	39.4	(±3.7)	46.1	(±4.4)	18.2	(±4.8)
1995	57.6	(±8.6)	17.6	(±3.7)	39.3	(±7.1)	44.4	(±11.1)	24.9	(±5.2)
1997	52.2	(±3.6)	15.5	(±2.4)	35.4	(±3.9)	48.3	(±5.6)	25.3	(±5.3)
1999	54.1	(±4.8)	16.6	(±3.6)	36.3	(±4.0)	55.2	(±4.2)	22.5	(±4.0)
2001	48.4	(±4.5)	14.9	(±1.7)	36.9	(±3.2)	53.5	(±5.1)¶	24.1	(±2.8)¶
White										
1991	50.0	(±3.2)	14.7	(±1.8)	33.9	(±2.8)	46.5	(±4.6)	25.3	(±3.7)
1993	48.4	(±2.8)	14.3	(±2.1)	34.0	(±2.1)	52.3	(±3.9)	24.4	(±2.7)
1995	48.9	(±5.0)	14.2	(±2.4)	34.8	(±3.9)	52.5	(±4.0)	26.6	(±3.1)
1997	43.6	(±4.2)	11.6	(±1.5)	32.0	(±3.1)	55.8	(±2.0)	26.0	(±2.5)
1999	45.1	(±3.9)	12.4	(±2.1)	33.0	(±3.3)	55.0	(±5.1)	27.4	(±4.8)
2001	43.2	(±2.5)¶	12.0	(±1.4)¶	31.3	(±2.2)	56.8	(±3.0)¶	27.8	(±2.2)
Total										
1991	54.1	(±3.5)	18.7	(±2.1)	37.4	(±3.1)	46.2	(±3.3)	21.6	(±2.9)
1993	53.0	(±2.7)	18.7	(±2.0)	37.5	(±2.1)	52.8	(±2.7)	21.3	(±2.0)
1995	53.1	(±4.5)	17.8	(±2.6)	37.9	(±3.4)	54.4	(±3.5)	24.8	(±2.8)
1997	48.4	(±3.1)	16.0	(±1.4)	34.8	(±2.2)	56.8	(±1.6)	24.7	(±1.8)
1999	49.9	(±3.7)	16.2	(±2.6)	36.3	(±3.5)	58.0	(±4.2)	24.8	(±3.0)
2001	45.6	(±2.3)¶	14.2	(±1.2)¶	33.4	(±2.0)	57.9	(±2.2)¶ **	25.6	(±1.7)¶

* Confidence interval.
† Sexual intercourse during the 3 months preceding the survey.
§ Among students who are currently sexually active.
¶ Significant linear effect (p<0.05).
** Significant quadratic effect (p<0.05).
†† Numbers of students in racial/ethnic groups other than white, black, or Hispanic were too small for meaningful analysis.

United States Department of Health and Human Services (2001)

Pie Charts

Pie charts can be used to show parts in relation to a whole. A pie chart can become overwhelming if it has too many parts, so consider how accessible your chart is to your readers. Pie charts focus on static data, and they don't show changes over time. An example is the pie chart below, which shows age group by population in the United States in the year 2000.

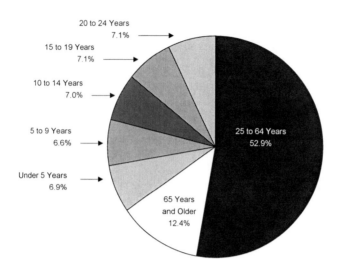

United States Census Bureau (2000)

Line Graphs

Line graphs show changes over time. Line graphs allow you to include different variables and make comparisons between variables. The line graph below traces four variables over twenty-seven years.

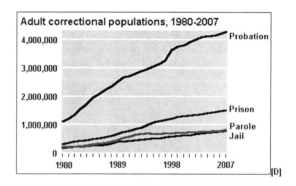

United States Bureau of Justice Statistics (2007)

Diagrams

Diagrams are used to make relationships and hierarchies clear. A flow chart is a common type of diagram that you may be familiar with. The flow chart below was designed to give students and professors at Weber State University a clear sense of the hierarchy of courses in the Information Systems and Technology Department, and also how the courses are related.

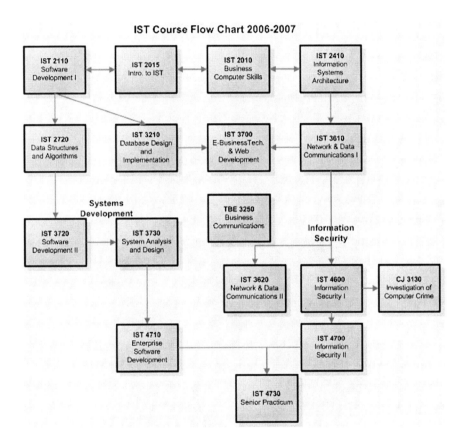

Information Systems and Technology Department, Weber State University (2010)

Photos

Often photos are used to give readers a strong visual sense of what writers are describing in the text. Sometimes photos are used to personalize a text (e.g. when someone adds pictures of themselves or their college to their blog), and sometimes photos are used for dramatic effect (for example, when a newspaper shows photos of charred land and homes after a big fire). If you were writing a report on Victorian architecture for a humanities course, you might include images like the one below to give readers a sense of the style of the kind of architecture you were discussing in the report.

Review of Key Ideas in Chapter 3

- The first step in college writing processes is to closely examine your professors' writing assignments. Look for key verbs in the assignments (e.g. *argue*, *evaluate*, *explain*) and think about the rhetorical situation of each assignment in terms of purpose, audience, genre, and context. Ask your professors questions about their assignments if you're unclear about them.

- College writing is a recursive and collaborative process that requires multiple drafts and feedback from readers. Successful college writers allow plenty of time for invention, drafting, revising, editing, and proofreading, and they seek out feedback on their drafts from peers, the professor, and the college writing center.

- Experienced college writers know that no one writes a perfect first draft, and they make significant changes to the content of their writing when they revise. Experienced writers save editing and proofreading for the final draft.

- Peer response is a valuable way of gaining feedback from readers. When you're responding to your peers' drafts, focus on content and not grammar or mechanics, and give the writer both praise and constructive criticism. In college courses where the professor doesn't organize peer response groups, it's helpful to find two or three classmates who are interested in forming a writing group outside of class.

- Your college writing center is an excellent place to get feedback on your writing. Try to visit the writing center frequently, rather than dropping in a day before a paper is due. When you visit the writing center, bring your writing assignment and any questions you have about the assignment or your draft. Remember that the writing center is not an editing and proof-reading service – their goal is to help you become a better college writer, not to rewrite your paper for you or to fix all your errors.

- Writing portfolios are collections of student writing that typically include rough drafts, final drafts, and a process memo or reflection letter describing the writing purpose, process, and product. Professors who use portfolio evaluation want to encourage you to engage in an extensive writing process throughout the entire semester and to use feedback from peers and the professor to revise and improve the content of your writing. Portfolios encourage reflection and self-evaluation, both of which help you to become a better writer.

- Group writing is common in college and in the workplace. Professors assign group writing because they want students to learn to work together on writing processes and products. Professors who assign group writing believe that knowledge is *socially constructed*: in other words, academic writing and thinking is a conversation, and people collaborate to make meaning. It's important to allow plenty of time for the group writing process and assign everyone a specific role that matches their strengths.

- Visual rhetoric is an important aspect of college writing. Your professors might ask you to compose Web sites, blogs, newsletters, brochures, PowerPoint presentations – and other types of visual texts. You can also expect to be asked to write papers that include charts, tables, photographs, and other kinds of visual inserts. Visual design principles of consistency, balance, effective use of color and contrast, clear organization, and appropriate formatting are important considerations when your professors ask you to compose a document that includes visuals.

3.17: Writing to Learn – Reflecting on Your Writing Processes

Now that we've looked at some advice for the college writing process, make a list of the new strategies for coming up with topics, drafting, revising, and editing that you learned in this chapter.

---

4   Academic Reading Processes

Reading in college has been more of an independent learning experience where you're trying to expand your mind as much as learn for a test. The texts themselves have been more challenging, and I have to read through them a couple of times.

> —Laura Ceideburg, a first-year student at California State University,
> Sacramento

Critical reading is difficult. It involves more than turning pages or even remembering the words on those pages – a process of passive consumption. Rather, it involves understanding the material and asking questions about it – a process of active and creative participation.

—Professor Diana Laulainen-Schein, History Department, University of Minnesota

No longer is reading thought to be simply a passive taking in of information; rather, it is now regarded by most researchers – and from a variety of disciplines and perspectives – as a complex, active process.

—Professor Kathleen McCormick, English Department, Purchase College
(McCormick, 1994: 3)

Writing and reading are related. People who read a lot have a much easier time getting better at writing. In order to write a particular kind of text, it helps if the writer has read that kind of text. In order to take on a particular style of language, the writer needs to have read that language, to have heard it in her mind, so that she can hear it again in order to compose it.

—National Council of Teachers of English (NCTE, 2004)

4.1: Writing to Learn – Similes for Reading

The purpose of this Writing to Learn activity is for you to think creatively about your attitude towards reading by using similes. Come up with five similes for the way you feel about reading: for example, "Reading is like traveling" or "Reading is like going to the dentist." Be prepared to share these similes in small groups or with the class.

Expectations for College-Level Reading

4.2: Writing to Learn – High School Reading Survey

In this Writing to Learn activity, you're going to reflect on your reading experiences in high school by filling out the high school reading survey below. After you've filled it out, compare your answers with those of your peers.

High School Reading Survey

1. In high school, I read (a) less than 5 pages a day (b) between 5 and 20 pages a day (c) more than 20 pages a day.
2. I would describe most high school readings as (a) easy (b) somewhat difficult (c) very difficult.
3. If I was confused by something I read in high school, I would (a) ask a peer for help (b) ask the teacher for help (c) not ask for help.
4. In high school, I took notes as I read. (a) True (b) False
5. In high school, I would often need to reread passages or entire texts to understand them. (a) True (b) False
6. In high school, I would often "cram" and do the required readings the night before a test. (a) True (b) False

---

Contrasting High School and College-Level Reading

To gain a sense of expectations for college-level reading, let's compare an excerpt from a high school history textbook and an excerpt from a college history book. The first excerpt is from a textbook aimed at high school seniors, *The American Journey*. The second excerpt is from a history book aimed at college-level readers, Howard Zinn's *A People's History of the United States*.

Excerpt from the High School Textbook, *The American Journey*

Cultural Perceptions and Misperceptions

When members of these societies met for the first time, confusion inevitably resulted. Even simple transactions produced unexpected results. When Columbus showed swords to Caribbean islanders, for example, "they took them by the edge and through ignorance cut themselves" because they had never touched metal weapons. French explorers were similarly taken by surprise when they choked while smoking Iroquois tobacco, which they thought tasted like "powdered pepper." These were relatively minor mishaps and were soon overshadowed by more substantial interactions which seemed to exaggerate the differences between Indians and Europeans.

Religion was extremely important to both Native Americans and Europeans, but differences in forms and practices encouraged misunderstandings. Most Indians believed that the universe contained friendly and hostile spiritual forces in human and other-than-human forms (such as plants, animals, and stars). People interacted with the spirit world through ceremonies that often involved exchanging gifts and performing certain rituals. To Europeans accustomed to worshiping one God in an organized church, Indian traditions were incomprehensible. Indians, in turn, often found Christianity confusing and at first rejected European pressure to convert.

Different understandings of the roles of men and women provided another source of confusion. Europeans assumed that men were naturally superior to women and should dominate them and rule society. They disapproved of the less rigid gender divisions among some Native American peoples. Europeans, accustomed to societies in which men did most agricultural work, also objected to Indian women's dominant role in farming and assumed that men's hunting was more for recreation than subsistence. They often concluded that Indian women lived "a most slavish life." Indians, in turn, sometimes thought that European men failed to make good use of their wives. In Massachusetts, some native men ridiculed colonists "for spoiling good working creatures" by not making their women work in the fields.

These were some of the many cultural differences that separated Indian and European societies. In order for natives and newcomers to get along peaceably with each other, each side would have to adapt to the new circumstances under which both groups now lived. At first, such harmony seemed possible. But it soon became clear that Europeans intended to dominate the lands they discovered. Only three days after he arrived in America, Columbus announced his intention "not to pass by any island of which I did not take possession" and soon speculated on the possibility of enslaving Indians. Such claims to dominance sparked vigorous resistance from native peoples everywhere who strove to maintain their autonomy in a changed world. (Goldfield, Abbott, DeJohn Anderson, Argersinger, J. E., Argersinger, P. H., Barney, and Weir, 2007: 24)

Excerpt from a College-level Book, Howard Zinn's _A People's History of the United States_

To emphasize the heroism of Columbus and his successors as navigators and discoverers, and to deemphasize their genocide, is not a technical necessity but an ideological choice. It serves – unwittingly – to justify what was done.

My point is not that we must, in telling history, accuse, judge, condemn Columbus _in absentia_. It is too late for that; it would be a useless scholarly exercise in morality. But the easy acceptance of atrocities as a deplorable but necessary price to pay for progress (Hiroshima and Vietnam, to save Western civilization; Kronstadt and Hungary, to save socialism; nuclear proliferation, to save us all) – that is still with us. One reason these atrocities are still with us is that we have learned to bury them in a mass of other facts, as radioactive wastes are buried in containers in the earth. We have learned to give them exactly the same proportion of attention that teachers and writers often give them in the most respectable of classrooms and textbooks. This learned sense of moral proportion, coming from the apparent objectivity of the scholar, is accepted more easily than when it comes from politicians at press conferences. It is therefore more deadly.

The treatment of heroes (Columbus) and their victims (the Arawaks) – the quiet acceptance of conquest and murder in the name of progress – is only one aspect of a certain approach to history, in which the past is told from the point of view of governments, conquerors, diplomats, leaders. It is as if they, like Columbus, deserve universal acceptance, as if they – the Founding Fathers, Jackson, Lincoln, Wilson, Roosevelt, Kennedy, the leading members of Congress, the famous Justices of the Supreme Court – represent the nation as a whole. The pretense is that there really is such a thing as "the United States," subject to occasional conflicts and quarrels, but fundamentally a community of people with common interests. It is as if there really is a "national interest" represented in the Constitution, in territorial expansion, in the laws passed by Congress, the decisions of the courts, the development of capitalism, the culture of education and the mass media. (Zinn, 1999: 8–9)

4.3: Writing to Learn – Comparing a High School and College Textbook

Individually or in small groups, create a list of the differences between the excerpt from the high school textbook and the excerpt from the college book. When you think about the differences, consider things like purpose, audience, style, and vocabulary.

If you completed Writing to Learn activity 4.3, you probably found a number of big differences between the high school textbook and the college-level book, such as those discussed below.

Purpose

Although the authors of the high school textbook present different points of view about Columbus and about the cultural differences and conflicts between Europeans and Native Americans, the tone is fairly objective. The author of the college-level text, Howard Zinn, has a series of forceful arguments about the way we should think of history and the United States. Zinn's purpose is not to objectively provide information about history, but to make an argument about the way historians should talk about history. Most scholarly writing takes a position within an academic conversation, and often this position goes against the grain and forces readers to question common assumptions. For example, Zinn argues that written history is usually untrustworthy because it's told by those in power. He further argues that the idea that there is a single "national interest" of the United States, or even a single "United States," is a false assumption. Whether you agree or disagree with Zinn's claims, the important thing to think about is that the purpose of most academic writing is not only to convey information in an objective way, but also to create new knowledge in an academic field by presenting claims and evidence to support those claims and by questioning common assumptions. Zinn does not merely deliver a series of facts about Columbus: he creates a theory of history. Your goal as a college reader is not to passively take in facts and information, but to think about whether or not you agree or disagree with the arguments and theories you're reading, and to consider how what you're reading challenges your own assumptions.

Audience

The audience for the high school textbook is not *insiders* but *novices*. The authors of *The American Journey* don't expect their audience to be familiar with the subject they're discussing, and they're careful to explain each cultural misperception between Europeans and Native Americans in a straightforward way. The audience for *The People's History of the United States* is history *insiders*. Because he's not writing for a novice audience, Zinn often includes references to insider information that he assumes his audience is familiar with. For example, he uses "Kronstadt and Hungary" as an example of a time we accepted atrocities as necessary for progress, a reference that novice history readers (and most college students) probably wouldn't be familiar with. One of the biggest challenges of college reading and writing will be that the farther along you go in college, the more your professors will expect you to take on the role of an insider and join in the conversations and arguments going on in their academic fields. This will require some researching on your part, which means looking up information about references and topics that you aren't familiar with or that you can't obtain from the context of the reading.

Style

The writing style of the excerpt from the high school textbook, *The American Journey,* can be described as simple and straightforward. There are few complex and lengthy sentences, and each paragraph has a topic sentence that signals to the reader what the paragraph is going to focus on. The author's voice has a neutral, objective tone. The writing style of the college-level book, *A People's History of the United States*, is more sophisticated and challenging. Sentences are lengthy and complex (notice, for example, how many commas and hyphens Zinn uses), and paragraphs don't necessarily focus on one simple idea. This is not to say that the writing style of *The American Journey* is poor quality or that college-level texts have a superior style. The purpose of *The American Journey*, like most high school texts, is to give students an introduction to the subject, and it's aimed at a novice, high school audience. The writing style of *The American Journey* is effective, considering its purpose and audience. College-level texts, such as *A People's History of the United States*, usually are working with more complex theories and arguments than high school texts, and college-level texts usually have an audience of insiders who are already familiar with a field of study. Naturally, then, the writing style of college texts is going to be more complex.

Vocabulary

When you read the excerpt from *The American Journey*, you probably didn't come across many words you didn't understand or had never seen before. Since high school textbooks are aimed at an audience of non-experts, the vocabulary which authors use is meant to be clear to novices of an academic field. In college-level writing, you can expect to frequently encounter vocabulary that's unfamiliar to you. In the excerpt from *A People's History of the United States*, Zinn uses words and phrases you might not have come across before, such as *ideological, in absentia,* and *learned sense*. Since Zinn is writing to other scholars and to students studying history, he assumes his readers will either know these words and phrases or will look them up in a dictionary or work to understand them based on their context.

4.4: Learn by Doing – Analyzing College Reading

The purpose of this Learn by Doing activity is to expand on the previous discussion of college-level reading by having you do a rhetorical analysis of a page from one of the readings you've been assigned this semester. Choose one page from a book, textbook, or article you've been assigned to read in one of your courses and write a 1–2 page rhetorical analysis in which you analyze its purpose, audience, style, and vocabulary. Once you've analyzed the reading, reflect on the ways it's similar to and different than the kinds of readings you were assigned in high school.

Features of College Reading

The sample textbook excerpts and Learn by Doing activity 4.4 have helped you think about some differences between reading in high school and reading in college. As with writing, some of the kinds of reading you do in college will be similar to the reading you did in high school. But there are some general differences to think about.

- **Most college reading assignments are challenging and complex.**

College professors don't assign challenging and complex readings just to make life difficult for you. One reason college professors assign challenging texts is that they want you to grow as a reader, just like they want you to grow as a writer. Another reason college readings are more difficult than high school readings is that the subject matter is more complex. College professors want to introduce you to the most important ideas in their academic fields, and these ideas aren't simple. Being introduced to an academic field means learning new and complicated concepts and key terms. It also means reading texts that are aimed at an audience of insiders – people who are interested in the specialized conversations going on in whatever subject you're reading about. In high school, your professors gave you a basic introduction to different academic fields, but in college you're going to go much deeper and explore each field or academic area (the natural sciences, the social sciences, the arts and humanities) in much more detail. All college students struggle as they're introduced to the ideas and key terms in different academic fields, so you are in good company if you do not fully understand the first time you read the texts you're assigned in college. You're not a poor reader if you struggle with college-level reading – all readers struggle when they're reading difficult texts on topics they're not familiar with.

- **College reading is a process.**

In high school, just as sometimes you could write a paper the night before it was due and still obtain a passing grade, you could probably get away with reading a textbook chapter the night before a test and still pass the test. Because college texts are more challenging and complex than high school texts, you probably won't be able to understand what you've read if you try to read something once at the last minute. College reading requires rereading. It also requires annotating, which means reading with a pen or pencil in hand and underlining, highlighting, and writing down questions or comments. We'll discuss some annotating strategies later in this chapter.

- **You'll do a lot more reading in college than you did in high school.**

Most college professors use books and articles as the basis of class discussion and the subject of writing assignments. First-semester college students are surprised by how much reading they're assigned, and many of them fall behind when they are in college because they're used to doing much less reading in high school. You can expect each of your college professors to assign books and articles as well as other kinds of texts such as Web sites and films. Since most of these texts are focused on complex topics, they're not short: besides doing more reading in college than you did in high school, you'll be reading longer texts. Your college professors want to immerse you in the conversations that are taking place in their field, and in order to do this, they need to assign plenty of reading. They also want you to conduct research, which means you'll do a lot of independent reading as well. The best part of doing all this reading is that you'll not only learn a lot in only four years of college, but your writing will improve dramatically, since reading generally improves writing.

- **College reading assignments often ask you to respond to texts and not just read for information.**

It's not uncommon in high school for reading to be associated with tests and quizzes. In many high school courses, students read textbooks only for information that they need to memorize for a test. Even in college, you'll be asked to memorize information and take exams, but often college professors will want you to respond to the readings and join the academic conversation on whatever topic you're reading about. Instead of looking for facts to memorize as you read, most college reading assignments ask you to both gain an understanding of an author's main points and to think about your perspective on an author's central arguments.

This is called *critical reading*. In the next section, we'll take a closer look at what it means to be a critical reader.

College Reading is Critical Reading

In Chapter 3, we looked at a sample writing assignment for a history book review from Professor Debra Salata. As part of the book review assignment, Professor Salata gives her students the following guidelines for critical reading:

> Critical reading is difficult. It involves more than turning pages or even remembering the words on those pages – a process of passive consumption. Rather, it involves understanding the material and asking questions about it – a process of active and creative participation. One does not simply absorb information but rather makes something of it.

> First, read the table of contents, the preface, and the conclusion – or in the case of any article, read the first and last pages and the section headings. In this way, you can form a mental map of where the author will lead you.

> Then read the book or article, keeping up your side of the conversation by underlining, comments, questions, or angry exclamations in the margins (if you own the book). Do not let yourself get stuck on trivial points. THEN GO BACK AND TAKE NOTES.

> Think about what you have read and written. Better yet, talk about it with someone. You understand material best when you have to explain it clearly to someone else. (Debra Salata, Lincoln Memorial University)

Rodney Larsen, a professor of classics at Duke University, has a similar description of critical reading in the analysis guide he wrote for his students:

> Analyzing an article involves evaluating and reflecting upon what the writer has said, how the writer had said this, and what the writer means by it. Your goal as a critical reader is to determine whether this perspective is reasonable and relevant.

> As you re-read the article, note any sections that you agree or disagree with, that are not clear to you, and that you find contradictory or irrelevant. You may also consider some of the following questions as guides to your analysis.

> - The issue: Is it examined thoroughly? Has anything been left out? If so, why might this be the case?
> - Thesis: Is it clearly stated? Logical? Convincing? Do you agree or disagree with it? Why?

- Supporting details: Do they support the thesis in a logical and convincing way? Are there enough details (relevant evidence, experience, and/or information) to support the thesis completely? If there are not, what is lacking?

These two descriptions of critical reading provide a general overview of what critical reading means for college reading, writing, and researching. Like Professor Salata and Professor Larsen, most of your college professors will ask you to be critical readers and not passive readers. Below I give a summary of what it means to be a critical college reader:

- **Critical reading means being an active reader and not a passive reader.**

Critical readers are not sponges, absorbing and memorizing information from the text. Critical readers are active readers: they look for the main points an author is making, question the author's assumptions, and annotate the text as they read.

- **Critical reading means interacting with the text.**

Critical readers read with a pen or pencil in hand. They underline key points, write responses or questions in the margins, and take notes about the text in their own words. Later in this chapter we'll look at some strategies for interacting with texts.

- **Critical reading means questioning assumptions and claims.**

One myth that some readers believe is that if something is written in a book or an article, it must be true. In college you're going to discover that even scientists disagree about what is true and what isn't. Every college text you read will be from the point of view of an author or authors, and all authors have political and cultural perspectives and assumptions, even when they're trying to be objective. Most of your college professors will expect you to challenge assumptions that you disagree with. Being a critical reader doesn't mean that you have to criticize every author you read and challenge every point an author makes. It's good to read with an open mind and try to understand an author's perspective and what evidence they're using to prove their point. But in college you also need to have the confidence to think for yourself and draw your own conclusions about what you're reading.

- **Critical reading means evaluating evidence.**

In your college reading, pay careful attention to the evidence authors use to support their claims. Most of your college professors will ask you to respond to, analyze, and evaluate the assigned texts, and this means deciding whether the evidence authors use is persuasive. Is the evidence from reliable sources? Does the evidence appear to be too biased to be persuasive? Is there enough evidence to be convincing? These are the kinds of questions you want to ask yourself as you read in your college courses.

- **Critical reading means thinking about where and to what extent you agree and disagree with the author.**

Every text is a kind of argument. Even a textbook that appears to simply summarize important events in American history is making the argument that some events are more important than others. In college, most professors will expect you to not only understand an author's argument, but also to think about to what extent you agree and disagree with the author. Keep in mind that most academic arguments aren't *all or nothing*. In other words, most of your college professors will expect you to consider a variety of points of view on an issue, and not think in a simple, "either/or" or "black and white" way. Your college professors will most often want you to carefully consider what other scholars have said on a topic and not only argue from your own experiences.

- **Critical reading means considering the rhetorical situation and genre of the text.**

In Chapter 2, we talked about how every college writing assignment presents a new rhetorical situation and a new genre. Keep this idea of the rhetorical situation and genre in mind as you read college texts. Ask yourself questions such as: What is the author's purpose? What is the author's personal background? What is the author's political and cultural perspective? What type of genre is this text? How are the ideas organized? What is the author's style and tone? Who is the author's intended audience? How does the text relate to previous reading assignments or classroom discussions?

- **Critical reading means talking with other readers about the text.**

Most of your college professors will devote class time to discussing the assigned readings. College professors know that critical readers don't read in a vacuum. Critical readers want to know what other readers think about a text. Critical reading is like a conversation between the author, the reader, and the community of scholars who have decided to join in the conversation. In college, this community of scholars will include your professor, your classmates, the authors of the course readings, and the authors you discover in your own research. Think of going to college as joining a conversation that was started before you arrived and will continue after you've graduated. The texts you're assigned are always in conversation with other texts from other scholars who've written about the topic. You're attending college not merely to sit back and listen to the conversation like a passive observer, but to join in and add your voice to the discussion.

4.5: Writing to Learn – Critical Reading

Think back to a time in high school or college when you read like a *critical reader*. Describe your purpose for reading. What strategies did you use as you read the text in order to be a critical reader? Was the reading assignment connected to a writing assignment, and if so, what was the writing assignment?

Reading and Writing Connections

4.6: Writing to Learn – Reading and Writing Connections

In this Writing to Learn activity, you'll think about the ways reading and writing are connected. Think back to a time in your life that reading helped improve your writing, or that writing helped you understand what you were reading. Describe the ways that reading and writing were connected.

Even though *Exploring College Writing* devotes a separate chapter to reading, it's important to keep in mind that all of the chapters in Part II of this textbook are connected. Reading, writing, and researching are all part of the same act: when you read, you're writing your own version of the text in your mind, and when you write, you're writing in relation to other texts you've read. In what follows, I describe some ways that reading and writing are connected.

- **Your college readings can serve as models for your college writing.**

Good college writers are usually good college readers, and part of the reason for this is that good writers use their readings as models for what they're writing. As you read in college, I suggest doing two things at once: read to understand and respond to the text, but also read like a writer. Reading like a writer means paying attention to how texts are constructed and applying what you've noticed as a reader in your own writing. As you read in college, ask yourself these questions:

What kind of genre is this text, and what can I learn about writing in this genre from reading the text?

What is the style of the writing, and how does the style connect to the rhetorical situation?

How does the author support his or her arguments? What kind of evidence is presented?

What techniques does the author use in the opening and the closing?

How does the author organize his or her ideas and make transitions from one idea to the next?

How would you describe the author's tone and voice?

What kind of formatting does the author use?

How does the author incorporate visuals such as charts, graphs, and photos?

- **When you read a text, you're also writing the text.**

This might sound odd at first, but just think about it. When you read, you're not simply inputting information into your mind like you input data into a computer. You're an active participant in creating the meaning of a text. You bring your own personal and cultural background to every text you read: your own opinions, experiences, and interpretations. Whether you're analyzing a poem or reading an argument in a psychology book, there's no single *correct* interpretation of the reading. Reading is a transaction between a writer and a reader, and every reader and every writer has his or her own point of view. Even an objective science or history text that is full of facts has its own point of view and its own interpretation. Think about the difference between an American history book written by a Native American and one written by a European American, or a science book from two hundred years ago full of "facts" about how the shapes of people's heads determine their intelligence. All of this means that you shouldn't be passive as you read college texts. You're not an empty container being filled with facts and information. In college, you need to be an active and critical reader.

- **Writing about a text is the best way to understand the text.**

When you skim an article to find key facts in order to cram for a quiz, you memorize information, but do not *learn* it. If you write a summary and response journal or an essay about the article, you're much more likely to understand the ideas in the article and to engage in depth with the ideas. Writing is a tool for thinking, so it makes sense that writing about a text will help you think about its content and meaning. When you write about a text, it's important to both summarize and respond. Try to understand the main ideas, but also think about your own response to those ideas. More techniques for writing about what you've read will be discussed in the next sections of this chapter.

Exploring Academic Reading Processes

4.7: Writing to Learn – Reflecting on Your Reading Process

The purpose of this Writing to Learn activity is for you to reflect on your own reading processes before you explore academic reading processes in this section of the chapter. Think back to the last challenging reading assignment you were given in school (high school or college). This could be a book, a textbook chapter, a poem, or an article – whatever kind of reading you found difficult. Now describe your reading process. Did you have to read parts of the text or the entire text more than once? Did you underline or highlight while you read? Did the professor ask you to respond to the reading or to keep a reading journal? If there were places in the reading that you did not understand, did you ask other students or the professor for help?

Once you come to see that reading and writing are similar kinds of acts, it's easy to understand that, like college writing, college reading is a process. When you read an email from a friend or an article about a movie star in *Entertainment Weekly* or on the Internet, you probably don't need to reread any passages (unless you become distracted), and you probably don't take notes or underline key ideas. If you try to use this same *read it once* strategy when you tackle your college reading assignments, you're not going to be a successful reader. Like college writing, college reading requires an extensive process. You're going to need to read and reread, underline and highlight, and respond to reading in class discussions and in writing assignments. The next section of this chapter gives you some strategies for successful college reading processes. As background for talking about reading strategies, let's look at some common myths students have about college reading processes.

Five Myths about College Reading Processes

Myth #1: Good college readers understand what they've read the first time they read it.

The first time you read a book about existential philosophy or a textbook chapter on statistical analysis and population sampling, you're going to face some difficulty. The authors are going to use key words, concepts, and vocabulary that you're not yet familiar with. Successful college readers don't expect to read something only once and understand it. They know that college reading requires rereading and asking questions. Good college readers don't throw their hands in the air and give up when they're confronted with a text they can't understand on the first reading. Instead, they know they need to read difficult material more than once.

Myth #2: Good college readers don't need any help understanding texts.

Just as writing is collaborative, reading is collaborative. Like successful college writers, successful college readers have learned how important it is to gain feedback and ask questions. Asking questions about reading assignments during class discussions is one of the best ways to get help. Some students won't ask questions during a discussion of an assigned reading because they don't want the professor to think they're not smart readers. But the reality is that smart readers ask questions and seek help. You can also seek help from other students in class, make an appointment to talk about the readings with the professor one-on-one, or visit your school's writing center and bring the text you're having trouble understanding to your tutoring session.

Myth #3: Some people will never be good readers.

If you've struggled with reading assignments in the past, don't let that cause you to think you'll never be a good reader. The more you read, the better reader you'll be. The more reading strategies you have at your disposal, the better reader you'll be. The more you write about what you've read, the better reader you'll be. Just as writing isn't a natural ability that some people are born with, no one is born to be a reader. If you use the reading strategies discussed in this chapter throughout your college career, you're going to be surprised how much you improve as a critical reader from your first year in college to your final semester.

Myth #4: You can use the same reading process for every college reading assignment.

If you use the same writing process and style for writing a lab report as you do for writing a poem, you're going to struggle with college writing. If you use the same reading process and strategies for reading a lab report that you use for reading a poem, you're going to struggle with college reading. Good readers adapt to the reading situation, and every college course is going to present you with a different type of text to read and a different purpose for reading that text. What you need is different sets of strategies for different reading situations and purposes. You need to think about the academic field of the course, the genre of the text you've been assigned to read, and the ways your professor is asking you to respond to what you've read. This section of Chapter 4 will provide you with some general strategies for college reading, and Part III will help you develop specific strategies for reading in different academic fields.

Myth #5: Reading means memorizing information.

High school students who are used to reading for quizzes, when they have to memorize information from a text and then regurgitate it, have a mistaken idea that reading is primarily *fact finding*. Most college professors don't want you to be a passive sponge, soaking up information. They want you to be a critical reader. This means questioning assumptions, looking with a skeptical eye at the arguments authors make and thinking about your own stance on the issue. Even if your professor asks you to summarize a text, he or she is challenging you to think critically about what the author's main points are. Some college professors will give you the same kind of reading quizzes you might have gotten in high school, but most college professors will ask you to think carefully and critically about what you're reading. They will ask you to engage with the readings in class discussion and in writing assignments.

Prereading Strategies

If you're visiting a city you've never been to before, it's a good idea to look at a map before you travel there. Think of prereading as looking at a map before you visit a place you've never been to. Prereading includes all of the things you might think about and do before you begin to read a book, an article, or a textbook chapter assigned by one of your college professors. Some prereading strategies are described below.

- **Think about what you already know and believe about a subject before you read about it.**

At the beginning of each chapter of this book, there's a prereading Writing to Learn activity that asks you to think about the subject of the chapter before you read about it. For example, at the beginning of this chapter, I asked you to come up with five similes for reading. If you completed the prereading Writing to Learn activity at the beginning of the chapter, it helped start you thinking about your attitudes toward reading before you read this chapter. Tapping into what you already know and think about a subject before you start reading about that subject helps you connect your prior knowledge to the new ideas you're going to read. Pondering what you believe about a subject before you read new ideas on that subject can also help make you a more critical reader, since it encourages you to consider to what extent you agree and disagree with the author. Even though you may have strong beliefs about a subject before you read, if you keep an open mind as you read, you will find that your beliefs change and grow as you read in college.

- **Think about your purpose for reading before you begin to read.**

Before you start reading a college text, take a moment to think about your purpose (or purposes) for this particular reading assignment. If your purpose is to take in information for a final exam, you'll need to focus on understanding and remembering key terms and concepts as you read. If you're writing a response journal on an assigned reading, you'll need to focus on the author's claims and think about whether or not you agree with them. If you're reading a sample student essay that your professor has provided as a model for an assignment, you'll want to pay close attention to the features of organization, development of ideas, and style. We'll look more closely at different college reading purposes later in this chapter.

- **Think about the genre of the text.**

In Chapter 2, *genre* was defined as a common writing situation that has similar purposes, audiences, and conventions each time it occurs. If the text you've been asked to read has a recognizable genre, you can think about some specific ways to approach your first reading. For example, let's say your biology professor has asked you to read a scientific research report. These types of reports almost always start with an abstract (a brief summary of the experiment and the findings). Reading this abstract before you read the report will help you focus and get a sense of what you're about to read. An abstract will also reveal the major research methods and the most important findings of the study. When you read the whole report, you'll be looking in more detail and with a critical eye at the research methods and findings. In most scientific research reports, a final reflection on the important findings of the experiment is in a section titled *Summary* or *Conclusions*. When you come to this section, you'll need to pay careful attention to the major findings of the study. Knowing the genre of what you're reading helps you understand where to focus and what to expect as you read.

- **Skim the text before you read as a way to preview its content.**

Let's go back to the metaphor of visiting a city for the first time. In order to keep from getting lost, before you visit a new city you'll probably look at some maps and guidebooks to figure out the layout of the city: where the major roads are, where the downtown area is, where the parks are. Skimming a college text before you read is like looking at a guidebook of the city before you visit. If you have the basic organization of the city in your head, you're less likely to get lost when you visit. If you skim a college text before you read, you're less likely to get lost in its content or structure as you read. For example, when you found out that your writing professor was using this textbook for the class, it would have been a good idea to skim through the table of contents and maybe the book as a whole. You would have gotten a sense of how the book is organized and what topics are discussed, and this would've helped prepare you to read the book. When your professor asked you to read this chapter, did you skim it first? If you did, you probably have a good idea of what topics are coming up after this section, and you'll be better prepared and more focused. When you skim a text, pay close attention to:

The table of contents
Chapter summaries or abstracts

Chapter titles, section headings, and subheadings
Introductions
Conclusions
Words in bold, italic, or underline styles
Lists and bullet points
Tables and figures
Information highlighted in text boxes or bubbles

Reading Difficult Texts

When experts read difficult texts, they read slowly and reread often... They interact with the text by asking questions, expressing disagreements, linking the text with other readings or with personal experience.

—Professor John Bean, English Department, Seattle University
(Bean, 2001: 134)

Take notes, jot down pithy quotes, and if the book or article belongs to you, underline, circle, and record your reactions in the margins. You will learn much more by writing while you read than if you just read something straight through.

—Professor Dana Dunn, Department of Psychology, Moravian College
(Dunn, 2004: 42)

There will be a fair bit of reading in this course – and it is mostly pretty difficult. It would be a shame to spend hours and hours reading and come away able only to say that you passed your eyes over all the words. Though we will only be *tasting* parts of some works, those parts are worth chewing on, thinking about carefully, and talking about. My role is not to give you any particular interpretation of these works – you have to interpret and evaluate them yourselves.

—Professor Sophia Isako Wong, Department of Philosophy, Long Island
University, Brooklyn Campus, in a course syllabus for
Introduction to Philosophy

4.8: Learn by Doing – Think-Aloud Reading Protocol

Before we discuss reading difficult texts, this Learn by Doing activity will help you reflect on your reading process when you're confronted with a difficult text by doing a think-aloud reading protocol. First, form small groups of 3 or 4. Then read the excerpt below from a book by the philosopher, Francis Bacon. As you read the excerpt, try to do two things at once: read the excerpt, but also talk out loud to the other group members and tell them what you're thinking as you read. For example, let them know if you become lost or confused, if you're rereading words or sentences, if you're annotating, and what you're doing when you annotate. The group members will write down the strategies you used to read this difficult excerpt, and you can write down your group members' reading strategies when they do their think-aloud protocol. Once all members of the group have done a think-aloud reading protocol, come up with a list of strategies for reading difficult texts that seemed effective, and another list of strategies that didn't seem to be effective. Here's the excerpt:

There are four classes of idols which beset men's minds. To these for distinction's sake I have assigned names, calling the first class *Idols of the Tribe;* the second, *Idols of the Cave;* the third, *Idols of the Market-place;* the fourth, *Idols of the Theater.*

The formation of ideas and axioms by true induction is no doubt the proper remedy to be applied for the keeping off and clearing away of idols. To point them out, however, is of great use, for the doctrine of idols is to the interpretation of nature what the doctrine of the refutation of sophisms is to common logic.

The Idols of the Tribe have their foundation in human nature itself, and in the tribe or race of men. For it is a false assertion that the sense of man is the measure of things. On the contrary, all perceptions, as well of the sense as of the mind, are according to the measure of the individual and not according to the measure of the universe. And the human understanding is like a false mirror, which, receiving rays irregularly, distorts and discolors the nature of things by mingling its own nature with it.

The Idols of the Cave are the idols of the individual man. For everyone (besides the errors common to human nature in general) has a cave or den of his own, which refracts and discolors the light of nature; owing either to his own proper and peculiar nature or to his education and conversation with others; or to the reading of books, and the authority of those whom he esteems and admires; or to the differences of impressions, accordingly as they take place in a mind preoccupied and predisposed or in a mind indifferent and settled; or the like. So that the spirit of man (according as it is meted out to different individuals) is in fact a thing variable and full of perturbation, and governed as it were by chance. Whence it was well observed by Heraclitus that men look for sciences in their own lesser worlds, and not in the greater or common world.

(cont.)

4.8 (cont.)

There are also idols formed by the intercourse and association of men with each other, which I call Idols of the Market-place, on account of the commerce and consort of men there. For it is by discourse that men associate; and words are imposed according to the apprehension of the vulgar. And therefore the ill and unfit choice of words wonderfully obstructs the understanding. Nor do the definitions or explanations wherewith in some things learned men are wont to guard and defend themselves, by any means set the matter right. But words plainly force and overrule the understanding, and throw all into confusion, and lead men away into numberless empty controversies and idle fancies.

Lastly, there are idols which have immigrated into men's minds from the various dogmas of philosophies, and also from wrong laws of demonstration. These I call Idols of the Theater; because in my judgment all the received systems are but so many stage-plays, representing worlds of their own creation after an unreal and scenic fashion. Nor is it only of the systems now in vogue, or only of the ancient sects and philosophies, that I speak: for many more plays of the same kind may yet be composed and in like artificial manner set forth; seeing that errors the most widely different have nevertheless causes for the most part alike. Neither again do I mean this only of entire systems, but also of many principles and axioms in science, which by tradition, credulity, and negligence have come to be received.

(Bacon, 1620)

College reading is critical reading, and critical reading is *active* reading. Successful college readers annotate the text as they read, underlining key terms and concepts, and write questions and responses in the margins. Successful college readers aren't afraid to reread when they're struggling to understand a difficult text (like the text by Francis Bacon in Learn by Doing Activity 4.8): they know that just as revising is necessary for college-level writing, rereading is necessary for college-level reading. Active reading is a skill that requires practice, and you'll need a set of strategies for active reading that you can use throughout your college career. What follows are some active reading strategies that should help you read challenging college texts.

Active Reading Strategies

- **Read with a pen or pencil in hand and annotate the text as you read and reread.**

In high school, you might have been in a situation where you weren't allowed to write in your textbooks because you had to turn them in at the end of the semester so they could be reused. In college, this rule doesn't apply. You need to be comfortable writing in the books you purchase for your courses. For starters, it's a good idea to underline key words and concepts so you can review them later. Sometimes it's difficult to tell what to underline, and some students underline almost the entire text because they aren't sure what the most important ideas are. When you're annotating the main ideas and key concepts, keep these points in mind:

If you're reading a difficult text, read through the text once without annotating, and then read it a second time and annotate it. If you save annotating for rereading, you'll have a better sense of what to underline.

Pay close attention to the introductory paragraph or paragraphs. In most American academic writing, the main idea or ideas of the text (the central points the author is trying to make) are usually laid out in the opening paragraphs.

Keep in mind that in most academic texts, each paragraph has a central focus. Typically, authors make a point and then develop that point with supporting evidence. If you underline every bit of supporting evidence, you won't be able to tell what the main focus of the paragraph is.

Keep an eye out for annotating that the text already does for you. For example, in textbooks it's common for key terms to be highlighted, such as in text boxes or in bold font.

Here's an example of an annotated academic text:

What does she mean by *high* and *low* culture?

Although zoos were popular and proliferating institutions in the United States at the turn of the twentieth century, historians have paid little attention to them. <u>Perhaps zoos have been ignored because they were, and remain still, hybrid institutions</u>, and as such they fall between the categories of analysis that historians often use. In addition, <u>their stated goals of recreation, education, the advancement of science, and conservation have often conflicted</u>. Zoos occupy a middle ground between science and showmanship, high culture and low, remote forests and the cement cityscape, and wild animals and urban people. Furthermore, <u>although zoos have always attracted diverse audiences, they are middle-class institutions</u>. This may explain why historians of recreation and of popular culture, who have focused on parks, for example, as arenas of working class rebellion, have overlooked zoos. Zoos also may have been passed over by historians because of the

four reasons why zoos have been ignored by scholars

lowly status of their animal inmates.

Historians of science may have dismissed zoos as too entertaining, connected to neither museum-based zoology nor laboratory science, or simply unscientific "places of spectacle and dilettante scientific interest." To be sure, unlike European zoos, the first American zoos had few ties to university zoology departments. The director of the National Zoo, when he visited the Amsterdam Zoo in 1929, commented – without irony – that "It was interesting to find zoology being studied in a zoo." The study of dead specimens in museums contributed far more to the advancement of scientific knowledge around the turn of the century than did observations of zoo animals. But amateur interest in science bears examination both in itself and in its relationship to professional science. This study has benefited from recent work that focuses on how popular culture is made and used, that looks at issues of scientific practice and the history of natural history, and that seeks to understand cultural representations of nature.

The few scholars who have looked at zoos in their historical context have tended to focus on individual institutions and to emphasize the power relations implicit in the human gaze at caged animals, interpreting it as symbolic of imperial power over colonial subjects. Other writers have looked at zoo animals as stand-ins for humans, comparing zoos to prisons, for example, or analyzing the ways zoo visitors anthropomorphize animals. While zoos do express human power over the natural world, and until relatively recently they depended on colonial commerce to supply exotic animals, the process of collecting and exhibiting wildlife has been more complex than a display of dominance. Collecting, for example, has a history as a scientific endeavor, which zoos used in their attempts to raise their cultural status. It seems likely too that zoo audiences, particularly in countries without colonial empires, have seen zoo animals as more than surrogate colonials, and that the meaning of animals – elephants and eagles, for example – changes in different national contexts, and over time. (Hanson, 2004: 32).

Margin notes (left): I think I agree with this view…most zoos still have the animals behind bars like a prison!

Margin notes (right): This sentence was confusing

Margin notes (right): What does she mean by *surrogate colonials?*

- **Create your own *text map* as you read.**

A *text map* or *concept map* is a kind of note-taking that helps you see the skeleton of an author's argument. College texts can be dense and complex, and it's easy to get lost in details as you read. A text map will help make sure you don't lose sight of the main ideas and organization of the author's argument. In a text map, you chart the author's main points as you read. Here's a sample text map of Matt Miles's essay "Personal Appearance and its Implications of Sexuality" from Chapter 2:

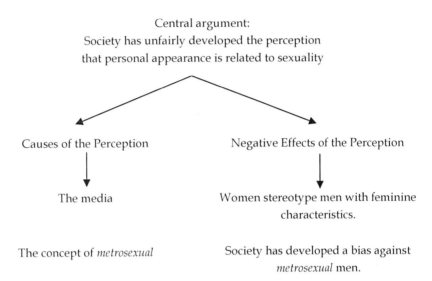

Central argument:
Society has unfairly developed the perception
that personal appearance is related to sexuality

Causes of the Perception   Negative Effects of the Perception

The media   Women stereotype men with feminine characteristics.

The concept of *metrosexual*   Society has developed a bias against *metrosexual* men.

- **Use a double-entry journal when you read.**

A double-entry journal is a kind of reading log. When you know that you're going to need to understand the main ideas of a text and respond to the ideas, a double-entry journal is a useful tool to record your thoughts as you read and keep your mind active and engaged. On a notebook or on the computer, make a journal with a line down the center. On one side of the line, record the author's main ideas, important supporting details, and key terms. On the other side of the line, write your questions and responses to those ideas. This technique encourages you to interact with the text you are reading and note the questions you have, and it helps you stay clear on which ideas are the author's and which are yours – which turns out to be very important in writing.

Here's an example of the beginning of a double-entry journal for an article about molecular technology in a chemistry journal:

Author discusses two paradigm changes in biology: systems biology and preventative medicine.	What does the phrase *paradigm change* mean?
Key term: *time-variant*	Time-variant = four-dimensional
Author argues that biologists and technologists should work together to make advances.	In what ways do biologists and technologists approach molecular biology differently?

- **Make predictions as you read.**

When you're driving your car, you're constantly thinking about what's ahead of you. You're watching for red lights and other cars turning into your lane, and you're thinking about where you need to turn and which lane you need to be in. Active readers are like good drivers, in the sense that they're always thinking about what's coming up next in the text and making predictions about what lies ahead. Making predictions keeps your mind alert and focused and helps you anticipate what you're going to be reading. Let's look at an example of predicting. Let's say you're taking an education course, and you're reading a book about school desegregation. Here's the opening line of the introduction:

> The changes wrought by school desegregation since the 1954 *Brown v. Board of Education* decision have been at times dramatic, uneven, and subject to reversal.
>
> (Clotfelter, 2006: 1)

Active readers would begin to make some predictions about the road ahead as soon as they read this opening sentence. You can predict that the next section of the reading is going to talk about the changes brought on by school desegregation. Since this is an academic book for a college-level audience, most likely the author will give many specific examples of these changes. The author will probably focus on how these examples of changes were "dramatic, uneven, and subject to reversal," since that's the emphasis in the opening sentence. Let's take a look at the next sentence of the introduction:

As illustration, consider two school districts in the formerly segregated South.

(Clotfelter, 2006: 1)

The transition, *as illustration*, should catch your attention as you are making predictions as a reader. Phrases such as *for example* or *as illustrated by* signal to readers that some specific support for an author's claims are coming up next. Our original predictions were correct, and now we can predict that the author is going to devote some well-developed paragraphs to the two examples of school districts in the South. As you're making predictions, look for other key transitional expressions such as *on the other hand*, *contrary to*, and *in addition to*.

- **Think about the pattern of organization of the text you're reading.**

In the discussion of prereading strategies earlier in this chapter, we talked about the importance of knowing the genre of the text you're reading. In addition to having some common genres, academic writing has some common patterns of organization. These patterns of organization are strategies that authors use to make arguments, to report, and to otherwise organize their ideas. Here are some basic organizational patterns that are common in academic writing:

> *Thesis and support*: A claim followed by evidence.
> *Point and counterpoint*: Arguments and counter-arguments with rebuttals.
> *Synthesis*: An exploration of what different arguments or approaches have in common.
> *Compare and contrast*: An exploration of the similarities and differences among two or more arguments or approaches.
> *Cause and effect*: An examination of the causes of a problem or situation and the effects that are the result of the problem or situation.
> *Problem and solution*: The presentation of a problem and an argument for a solution or solutions to the problem, which often involves evaluating the advantages and disadvantages of other proposed solutions.

As you read college texts and make predictions, keep these basic patterns of organization in mind. Academic writing is complex, and often authors will use a variety of these patterns, or they might create a different type of organization to fit the needs of the rhetorical situation. Knowing some basic patterns of organization for academic writing can help you understand what an author's purpose is and make predictions about what to expect as you read.

- **When you're having difficulty understanding a text, reread.**

In Chapter 3, we discussed how college writing processes are *recursive*, meaning that writing is not strictly an ordered sequence but involves both forward progression and backwards movement in a continual process of writing, revising, and rewriting. The same is true of college reading processes. Needing to reread a college text is not a sign that you're a poor reader; in fact, just the opposite is true. Successful college readers are rereaders. When you struggle with a challenging college text, you can expect to reread it and rethink it, often multiple times, before you understand it well. This might mean rereading and rethinking a sentence, a paragraph, or an entire chapter in order to have a better idea of what it means. You'll also do a lot of rereading in college in order to prepare for a test or write an essay. This is when good annotating skills can really help. When it comes time to review a textbook chapter for a test or to reread parts of a book to find passages you want to include in an essay, your life will be much easier if you kept a double-entry journal or carefully annotated the text.

Even though rereading is an important part of college reading processes, it's also a good idea not to spend too much time on any one sentence or phrase as you read. A common feature of academic writing is repetition. In order to communicate their points clearly to their audience, academic authors often will explain a key term or a complicated theory in more than one way. For example, an author might explain a theory and then give three examples of how that theory applies to specific situations. If you don't understand the author's definition of the theory the first time you read it, and then you reread again and still don't understand, instead of spending an hour struggling with one passage of the text, keep reading. Maybe after you've read about how the theory is applied in specific situations, you'll begin to understand it. Then you can go back and read the definition again, but with a better understanding.

When you do a first reading of a college text, it's important not to worry about every word you don't know or understand. Often you can gain a sense of what a word or phrase means by looking at the context: in other words, by looking at the word in the context of the sentence, the paragraph, and the author's argument. For example, take the phrase, *in absentia*, in the excerpt from *A People's History of the United States* at the beginning of this chapter. Here's the excerpt again:

> My point is not that we must, in telling history, accuse, judge, condemn Columbus *in absentia*. It is too late for that; it would be a useless scholarly exercise in morality. But the easy acceptance of atrocities as a deplorable but necessary price to pay for progress (Hiroshima and Vietnam, to save Western civilization; Kronstadt and

Hungary, to save socialism; nuclear proliferation, to save us all) – that is still with us. One reason these atrocities are still with us is that we have learned to bury them in a mass of other facts, as radioactive wastes are buried in containers in the earth. We have learned to give them exactly the same proportion of attention that teachers and writers often give them in the most respectable of classrooms and textbooks. This learned sense of moral proportion, coming from the apparent objectivity of the scholar, is accepted more easily than when it comes from politicians at press conferences. It is therefore more deadly.

(Zinn, 1999: 8–9)

Since the phrase, *in absentia*, is in the first sentence of the paragraph, and the sentence starts out "My point is not," it's probably important to understand the gist of what Zinn is arguing in that first sentence. But if you don't understand the phrase, *in absentia*, when you first read it, rather than stopping your reading entirely, try going on to the next sentence. Notice that the next sentence says "[i]t is too late" to accuse and judge Columbus. Why is it too late to accuse Columbus? In the next sentence, Zinn argues that even though atrocities like Hiroshima and Vietnam are over, what's still with us today is the acceptance of atrocities as the price to pay for progress. You might be able to figure out that it's too late to accuse and judge Columbus because he's dead: accusing him *in absentia* means accusing him in his absence (notice how the modern word *absent* is in the Latin word, *absentia*, which is another clue). Even if you're not sure about the definition of *in absentia* after reading the rest of the paragraph, as long as you understand the author's main point – that historians shouldn't focus on accusing and judging people who committed atrocities in the past but instead should focus on the ways we bury atrocities in a mass of facts – you can understand the paragraph without knowing exactly what *in absentia* means.

When you come across concepts or terms that you can't understand, even after you've used the strategies mentioned here or others your professor might have suggested, be sure to make a note in the text. Then you can look up these terms or ask for help from other readers (e.g. other students or your professor).

- **Talk about the text with other readers.**

Most college professors feel that knowledge in their field is *socially constructed*. This means that people don't read and write and think in a vacuum, but in conversation with others. Knowledge is constructed through conversations about texts. Your professor and each of your peers will have a different interpretation of and response to the assigned texts. Talking about texts with your classmates and professor in class or online discussions as well as outside of the course will help you think more deeply and critically about what you've read. Interaction with others about a text can also help you think through parts of the text that are unclear to you. If you're struggling with a challenging text, it's a good idea to seek out help from your peers, your professor, or a tutor at your institution's writing or learning center.

- **Match your reading speed with your reading purpose.**

There's no connection between successful college readers and fast college readers. As a matter of fact, the most successful college readers are actually *slow* readers. Most college texts are too difficult to breeze through like a speed reader. Using active reading techniques such as annotating and predicting means reading more slowly and carefully. Have you ever had the experience of reading an entire page but, since your mind was wandering while you were reading, you actually didn't take in a word? If you're using active reading techniques, you can avoid this problem of your mind wandering, but you're going to have to read at a slower pace. This means that you need to give yourself plenty of time to complete your college reading assignments. Don't wait until the night before class to read that assigned article or chapter.

When you read a popular magazine such as *Sports Illustrated* or *People*, you can probably read the articles pretty quickly. Usually the ideas discussed in these magazines aren't complicated, and there's little need for the authors to provide examples to support their claims or to discuss what other writers have said about their topic. It's not that these magazines are inferior to what you're going to read in college, but rather that they have a different purpose than college texts. Don't use the same reading speed for college texts that you use for these kinds of popular magazines. Think about how your purpose for reading will affect your reading speed. If you need to read a brief article to prepare for a classroom discussion, you won't have to take as much time in your reading as you would if you needed to read a chapter of a difficult academic book and write a three-page summary and response paper about the chapter. We'll look more closely at purposes for college reading in the next section.

Common College Reading Purposes

4.9: Writing to Learn – Reading Purposes

The purpose of this Writing to Learn activity is for you to think about the ways that reading processes are connected to reading purposes. Make a list of everything you've read in the past week, from email, to shopping lists, to the campus newspaper, to books and articles for your classes. Next to each item on your list, write down the primary purpose for reading (e.g. to get information, for entertainment, or to pass a test). Choose one of the items on the list and explore in writing how the purpose of the reading affected your reading process.

Just as every college writing assignment will present you with a purpose or purposes as a writer, every college reading assignment will present you with a purpose or purposes as a reader. There are countless purposes for college writing and countless purposes for college reading. Even though you're going to be challenged to read for a variety of purposes in college, there are a few basic reading purposes that you'll encounter again and again in your college reading assignments. These purposes include summarizing, comparing, evaluating, analyzing, and responding. Most of your college reading and writing assignments will require some combination of these reading purposes. We'll look at some examples of assignments that ask for these reading purposes, but first let's define each purpose.

Summarizing

Summarizing means describing the most important points of a text. This might mean describing the author's purpose and thesis, central arguments, key terms, important concepts, and key examples and evidence.

Comparing

Comparing means pointing out the similarities and differences between two or more texts written by the same or a different author. This might mean showing how the arguments of the two texts are similar and different, how authors support their arguments using similar or different types of evidence in the different texts, how the concepts and theories of the two texts are similar and different, or how the research methods of the two are similar or different.

Evaluating

Evaluating is the process of making judgments about a text. This might mean judging the effectiveness of an author's argument or approach, evaluating an author's research methods, or considering whether an author's evidence is reliable and persuasive.

Analyzing

Analyzing means closely examining parts of a text to think critically about the author's argument. This might mean looking closely at the author's language, examining the logic of the author's argument, and looking critically at the reliability of the author's sources.

Responding

Responding is giving your own opinion about the ideas presented in a text. This might mean agreeing or disagreeing with the author's thesis or central arguments, connecting the author's points to class discussions or other texts, or connecting the author's ideas to your own experiences.

Let's take a look at some college reading and writing assignments to gain a sense of what some of these reading purposes will look like in actual college assignments. First, we'll look at an assignment from Professor Edward Capps, a classics professor at the University of Mississippi:

> Write a comparison of the *Homeric* version of Demeter & Persephone with Ovid's version. Note and briefly summarize the episodes that the two versions have in common, the episodes from the "Homeric" version that Ovid has omitted, and the episodes that he has added to that version. Note the differences in detail within the episodes that the two versions share (in reference to the characters, locations, descriptions, motives, etc.)

This assignment focuses on two reading and writing purposes: summarizing and comparing. If you were given this assignment in a college course, you would need to think about these purposes before you read the Ovid and Homeric versions of the myth of Demeter and Persephone. One strategy might be to create a text map of both versions and then compare the text maps. This would help you summarize each scene and figure out which scenes both versions have in common and which scenes are omitted from one version or the other. Since the assignment requires you to "note the differences in detail within the episodes that the two versions share (in reference to the characters, locations, descriptions, motives, etc.)," as you write your text map, you'll want to be sure to include these kinds of details.

Now let's look at a reading and writing assignment from Professor Mona Ibrahim, a psychology professor at Concordia College:

> For each assigned chapter, you are asked to turn in a reading log on the day we are scheduled to begin discussing it in class. Late reading logs will not receive any credit. Logs are designed to keep you up to date with the readings, to stimulate class discussion, and to encourage you to think about the class materials as both psychological scholarship and as personally relevant. Occasionally, you will be asked to share your log with the class.
>
> Your log should be about 1–2 pages. You should print two copies of the log. I will collect one copy and you will use the second copy to help with class discussion. At the top of the reading log put your **Name**, **Chapter Number**, and the **Chapter Heading**. When referring to a specific passage in the readings, please cite page number(s).
>
> Use the following format and headings in **boldface** for each log:
>
> 1. **Key statements**: Discuss passages that you really liked from the readings. It could be something you strongly agree with or something that contributed to a positive emotional reaction. Speaking from your own experience, intellectually and personally, why did you like this passage?
>
> 2. **Questions**: What questions, if any, would you like to ask? Indicate anything from the reading assignment that was confusing or unclear or that raised a question for you that was not answered in the reading.
>
> 3. **Reactions**: Discuss a passage that you strongly reacted to or one that stimulated you to think of some ways of changing how things are done in our society to make it more inclusive? What ideas did the passage give you?

The focus of these reading logs is responding. Professor Ibrahim is looking for students' personal responses to the chapters: their emotional reactions, their experiences, their ideas, and their questions. Because the focus is on responding and not just summarizing, if you were given this reading log assignment in one of your college courses, your reading strategy should focus on aspects of the chapter that you felt strongly about, or places where you had questions. You would want to annotate the chapters as you read, but rather than underlining every main idea, you'd focus on ideas that you strongly agreed or disagreed with. You might read the chapter with a pen or pencil in hand and jot down your responses in the margins or note places where you were confused or had questions.

Let's look at one more reading and writing assignment. This assignment is from Professor Stanley Schultz, a history professor at the University of Wisconsin:

> To improve your critical thinking and writing skills, we require a brief critical paper, either a book review of an academic history book or a historical analysis of a work of fiction. This assignment offers you a chance to investigate a theme, person, event, or process in American history in greater detail, while also allowing you to display your understanding of the major themes of the course in a setting less rigid than the examination format.
>
> This project should be a critical analysis of the text, which means much more than a simple summary of the book's contents. What we are looking for is an analysis of the work's major points: What is the message of this text? Is the argument plausible, and is it backed up with credible evidence? Is the argument ultimately convincing? Does this work neglect other points of view, and, if so, how does this affect the value of the argument? These are just a few of the questions you should be pondering when analyzing any piece of historical scholarship or fiction. To see examples of first-rate analyses, read some published book reviews. For example, select a historical journal such as *Reviews in American History* and observe how various reviewers have tackled their assignments.

This writing and reading project asks for evaluation and analysis. The emphasis is on critical thinking, which means you will need to be a critical and active reader. Notice that Professor Schultz is looking for "much more than a simple summary of the book's contents." Many college professors say that since high school students are so used to summarizing ideas for tests, sometimes students have a difficult time understanding the difference between summary and analysis. In this case, analysis means finding the major arguments of the book and evaluating whether or not those arguments are effective by looking at the evidence presented and considering other points of view. To read an entire book and analyze its arguments is a challenging task, and it requires a set of active reading strategies. One strategy might be to use a double-entry journal. You could jot down all of the main arguments of the book in the left-hand column, and write your analysis and evaluation of these arguments in the right-hand column. As

Professor Schultz points out, a book review and analysis is a common academic genre, and you can easily find examples of this genre in academic journals like *Reviews in American History*. So another reading strategy would be to go to the library, look up *Reviews in American History* or another history journal, and find a few sample book reviews to use as models. You would want to *read like a writer* when you look at these models. You would pay close attention to how the author of the review analyzes the book under review and how the review is organized.

4.10: Writing to Learn – Reading Strategies

In this Writing to Learn activity, you will apply what you learned about active reading strategies and college reading purposes to three sample college reading and writing assignments. Imagine that you were given the three assignments below in your college courses. Individually or in small groups, come up with a list of reading strategies for each assignment and share these strategies with the whole class.

Assignment #1

Read the articles, "The Impact of Global Warming" by Maria Sandoval and "The Global Warming Hoax" by Richard Cheney. Compare Sandoval's and Cheney's arguments concerning the threat of global warming. In what ways do the two authors disagree about the impact of global warming? What kinds of evidence does each author provide to support his or her arguments? Which argument do you feel is more persuasive, and why?

Assignment #2

Visit the Web site of a Fortune 500 company and write a 2–3 page rhetorical analysis of the site. In your analysis, answer the following questions:

- Who is the audience for the Web site? Does the site do an effective job of connecting to the intended audience?
- How is the site organized? Is the organization effective?
- What information about the company is included on the site? Is the presentation of the information effective?
- Describe the graphic design of the site. Is the site effective at visual persuasion?
- If you were the Web master for this company, would you make any changes to the site?

(cont.)

4.10 (cont.)

Assignment #3

In this assignment, you will practice writing an abstract for a chemistry journal. An abstract is a one- or two-paragraph summary of an article that appears just before the article in a journal. The abstract gives the readers of the journal an overview of the purpose of the experiment, the research methods, and the results of the experiment. I will give you three chemistry journal articles to choose from. Even though an abstract is only a paragraph or two long, don't think that this assignment will be easy! The articles you are choosing from are written for an audience of chemists, so it will be a challenge for you to understand the experiment and figure out what the most important results of the experiment are.

Reading Visual Images

4.11: Writing to Learn – Reading Images

The purpose of this Writing to Learn activity is to start you thinking about strategies for *reading* images. Bring an example of an interesting piece of visual rhetoric to class – an image of a painting, a CD cover, a Web site, a photograph, or other visual image. In small groups, share the images and tell your group what you found interesting and meaningful about the image you chose to bring to class. Then write down a list of strategies the group used for reading and understanding their images.

Examples of Visual Images

You may not associate reading with understanding and interpreting visual images, but experts in visual rhetoric argue that we *read* visual images using many of the same strategies we use when we read printed text. Just as your college professors are going to ask you to read and analyze printed texts, you'll occasionally be asked to understand and interpret visual images such as paintings, photographs, or Web sites. For example, a sociology or communication studies professor might ask you to analyze an advertisement like this one from Adbusters, a social activist media group and magazine devoted to critiquing the mainstream media:

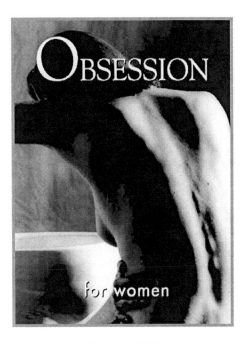

Adbusters, 2009b

To analyze this image, you might consider the rhetorical situation, just as you would with a print text. You could ask yourself questions such as: What is the purpose of the ad? Who is the intended audience? How does the ad comply with or break from the conventions of advertisements? What is the broader social context that this ad is reflecting and responding to?

4.12: Writing to Learn – Practicing Visual Analysis

The purpose of this Writing to Learn activity is to practice the kind of visual analysis discussed above. Write a rhetorical analysis of the second of the Adbusters ads. Consider the ad's purpose, audience, genre, and wider social context. Your professor might ask you to discuss your analysis in small groups and/or with the class as a whole.

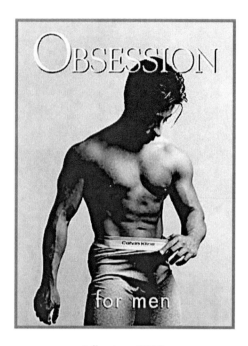

Adbusters, 2009a

Strategies for Reading Visual Images

- **Consider the rhetorical situation of the image.**

Remember that just like printed texts, images are responses to rhetorical situations. All images have purposes, whether it's to help readers of a newspaper see and feel the consequences of a natural disaster or to persuade college students to buy a credit card or to interpret a scene from nature in an oil painting. Just like texts, images are created with an audience in mind, and are often working within the conventions of a genre such as abstract art, scientific poster presentations, or PowerPoint slides. And just like printed texts, images are never created in a vacuum. New images are influenced by prior images and by social contexts – think, for instance, of how important prior images and social contexts are to interpreting the Adbusters ads shown here.

- **Consider the genre of the image.**

Just as print texts such as a lab report or a book review develop as genres because they help writers respond effectively to recurring rhetorical situations, images can become genres. Movie posters are an example of a visual genre that evolved over time as a response to a recurring rhetorical situation: the need for film companies to advertise new movies in a visually appealing way to draw audiences in. If a professor in a film studies class asked you to analyze a movie poster, you could think of the context of other movie posters and the ways in which the poster follows the conventions of the genre. Just as with print texts, sometimes visual texts are significant because they break with the conventions of the genre. For example, Adbusters ads attract attention because they parody the conventions of mainstream ads. To understand and analyze the Adbusters ads shown here, you'd need to be aware of the convention of perfume ads in fashion magazines.

- **Consider the composition of the image.**

In Chapter 3, we talked about some general considerations for creating visuals: color, contrast, emphasis, and organization. Keep these aspects of visual design in mind when you're reading and analyzing images. For example, in the first Adbuster ad, the shadows on the woman's body created by the contrast of black and white and the way the shadows emphasize her spine and bony shoulders affect the meaning of the image.

4.13: Learn by Doing – Reading an Image

The purpose of this Learn by Doing activity is to apply what you've learned about reading images to an image from readings for your own college courses. Choose an image that you'll need to analyze in one of your courses this semester. This could be an image from a textbook or other course text, an image from a Web site or PowerPoint lecture slide, or an image for a project you've been assigned (for example, to analyze a building or visit a museum and analyze a painting). Write a 1–2 page rhetorical analysis of the image, using the strategies we discussed in this section. Be prepared to share your image and discuss your analysis with the class as a whole.

Review of Key Ideas in Chapter 4

- Most college texts will be longer, more challenging, and more complex than high school texts. This is because college professors want you to grow as a reader and thinker, which means reading more difficult texts than you read in high school. They also want to introduce you to the key concepts, theories, and arguments in their academic fields, and this requires reading texts that are written for an *insider* audience.

- College reading is critical reading. Critical reading means trying to understand authors' arguments as well as questioning their assumptions, evaluating the evidence presented by authors, and thinking about your own perspective on the arguments which authors are making.
- College reading and college writing are closely connected. Writing about a text helps you think more deeply about what you're reading, and your college readings can serve as models for your college writing. When you read college texts, read like a writer: think about what you can learn about writing from the author's style, voice, organization, type of evidence used, and other aspects of the text (e.g. headings, formats, and fonts).
- College reading is a process. College texts are complex, and in every course the readings will present you with new terms and theories. This means you can't *speed read* college texts or wait until the night before a test to read the assigned text.
- Since college reading is critical reading, you need to be an active reader and not a passive reader when you are given a college reading assignment. Active reading means prereading, annotating, predicting, rereading, and discussing what you've read with peers and the professor.
- College reading assignments will present you with a variety of purposes, including summarizing, comparing, synthesizing, evaluating, analyzing, and responding. Think about your purpose for reading before you read, and use the active reading strategies that match your purpose.
- In college you'll sometimes be asked to *read* images just as you would read a text. When you're analyzing a visual image, consider the rhetorical situation of the image: the purpose, audience, genre, and social context.

4.14: Writing to Learn – Applying Reading Strategies

The purpose of this final Writing to Learn activity is to reflect on what we discussed in the chapter and apply it to your own reading process. What recommendations from this chapter for successful reading do you already use in your own reading process? What reading strategies from this chapter will you try to use in the future to improve your reading processes?

5 Academic Researching Processes

True research papers are more than a loose collection of anecdotal memories or a patchwork of data pulled from several books. But while new to most first-year students, a research paper can be incredibly exciting, rewarding, and even comforting to write because it finally allows you to really get into a subject you care about...

—Sarah Hamid, a tutor at the Purdue University Writing Center (Hamid, 2010)

I was really scared about doing a research paper. In high school we would just find a bunch of quotes and string them all together... But in ENC1102 we needed to express our opinion about our topic. This helped make it more interesting because it's my argument, not somebody else's.

—A first-year writing student at Florida State University (quoted in Melzer, 2002)

I go to the library to get the feel of the topic. I research little by little. I have a little notebook, gather all the data, look it over carefully. Sometimes it's difficult when you have a lot of data and you don't know where to begin. I gather all my research, prepare an outline, look over the research again. I start to write a rough draft in my notebook, check it over, talk with the professor if I'm stuck or confused.

—Linda, a student from the City College of New York, in the book, *Time to Know Them* (quoted in Sternglass, 1997: 213)

The writing process is a fluid one. As you do your research, you will come across material that you did not expect to find, but may work well with your paper, and possibly change the topic or tone of it. That is O.K.! That is what research is supposed to do! As you read the material that you have gathered, you may uncover information that you did not expect to find. It fits your topic, but may take your paper into a different direction. That is O.K. too!

—Jason Schilling, Writing across the Curriculum, American River College (Schilling, 2006)

5.1: Writing to Learn – Reflecting on your High School Researching Processes

Before you read about expectations for college-level research, reflect on your high school researching experiences. Think back to a research paper you wrote for a high school class. What kind of research did you do? Did you search for information online? At the library? On academic databases? Did you conduct your own research through observations or interviews or surveys? How many outside sources did you find? How much time and effort did you put into finding your sources?

Expectations for College-Level Research

In high school, most students are given a general introduction to conducting a research project. You probably did some basic library and online research in high school and wrote research papers that were a little longer and more in-depth each year, from your first year of high school to your senior year. Your college professors will build on this foundation, but they'll help you take your research and writing skills to another level. College research will be more extensive, and college research projects will be lengthier and more complex. You might have had some good practice for college writing if you did a big research project in high school – for example, a senior project. In a senior project, students take an entire semester to engage in an involved research process. They find an interesting and original topic to explore, conduct thorough research on their topic until they become experts, and draft and revise a lengthy research paper that contains a balance of their own thoughts on the topic and information from a variety of outside sources. Most of the research papers you're assigned in college will be similar to a senior project. You'll need to do more than merely search for a few sources online or find a few books at the library and then report on your topic by stringing together some quotes.

Sample Student Essay

To gain a sense of the differences between high school and college research writing, let's take a look at a college research paper. Lydia Tolman wrote "The Rise of Starbucks" when she was a first-year student at Arizona State University (ASU). It was published in *The Printer's Devil*, a collection of award-winning student essays written in ASU composition courses. As you read the essay, think about some of the similarities and differences between Lydia's research paper and research papers you wrote in high school.

The Rise of Starbucks
By Lydia Tolman

Published in *The Printer's Devil*, a collection of award-winning student writing from the Arizona State University Writing Program (Tolman, 2004–2005)

    While silently pondering the merits of a venti wet latte made with nonfat milk, an extra shot of espresso, a few pumps of caramel flavor, and a dollop of whipped cream in the Starbucks line of Arizona State's Memorial Union, I had a mathematical epiphany one morning, which is an amazing fact, considering I had not had my daily dose of caffeine. Count with me. There is a Starbucks in the ASU Memorial Union, a Starbucks in the W.P. Carey Business School of ASU, a Starbucks in the Palo Verde East dorm, a Starbucks right off campus on Mill Avenue, and a Starbucks in the local Safeway. There are five Starbucks in and around the ASU community — at least, to my immediate knowledge. Further investigation, however, led me to the conclusion that there are actually twenty-five Starbucks within a five-mile radius of ASU ("Store"). Numbers alone should be enough to prove that coffee or, to be more exact, Starbucks coffee, is a huge trend, but if you will not take my word for it, take the words of the entrepreneur and CEO of Starbucks himself, Howard Schultz: "[T]here are people living their lives around Starbucks. You'd never guess coffee was so important in people's daily lives, but it is" (quoted in "Interview"). Why has Starbucks grown more than fifteen hundred percent in the last ten years (Markman)? And, more importantly, how is this new obsession quietly changing the lives of millions of Americans? The once simple, ten calorie cup of joe has become a pricey, fattening, calorie-laced status symbol phenomenon, of which we cannot seem to get enough (Linn).

According to the National Coffee Association of USA Inc., over 109 million Americans, or half of the adult U.S. population, drink coffee every day, and another twenty-five percent drink it occasionally (ElBoghdady). Even fifty years ago, these numbers may have not been that shocking, since people have been consuming coffee to perk up in the morning for years. However, what is surprising is the additional report that the biggest gains in coffee drinking are "among the daily and occasional drinkers of 'gourmet' coffee of the kind popularized by Starbucks" (ElBoghdady). The numbers in that category rose from about 87 million drinkers in 1997 to 150 million drinkers in 2001. The key to Starbucks' success may not just lie in the type of coffee beans used to brew my daily caffeine dose. Starbucks, like cell phone and computer companies, has created a new need that was "non existent in this country only two decades ago" (ElBoghdady). Behind Starbucks' success are brilliant business maneuvers that make us want to part with those three or four dollars for a cup of coffee. The statement that Starbucks is literally everywhere is not hyperbole. It is a fact that can be proven by a few keystrokes into Starbucks .com's store locator, which informed me there are approximately five Starbucks for every square mile around Arizona State University ("Store"). Although conventional business wisdom has dictated that a retailer should space its stores, Starbucks has "embraced self-cannibalization as the fastest way to expand its business" (ElBoghdady). Surprisingly enough, the tactic has worked by providing convenient, quick, and trendy locales for rushed coffee buyers. The strategy also has the added benefit of free advertising by simply being everywhere.

To attract even more customers, Starbucks has also created what founder Schultz calls the "third place" of American life (Markman). Rose, a teenager who is a supporter of the Starbucks trend, explains that she can get "more than a drink for $3 or $4. She buys a chair and a table of her own where she can chat with friends or populate her sketchbook with cartoon characters for as long as she wants — and that's a pretty good deal" to her (Sommerfeld). However, as I walked out of my local Starbucks to rush to my next class, I realized that I hardly ever use the provided over-stuffed couches and pseudo-intellectual board games, so there must be something more to this Starbucks trend than just Schultz's "third place" and the fact that Starbucks seems to be plastered in every state, city, and town across the United States.

Surprisingly enough, as coffee drinking has been on the rise, smoking has been dropping dramatically among teens across the United States (Sommerfeld). Coffee appears to be the new "social lubricant and image enhancer," the new trend, and the new addiction among teenagers (Sommerfeld). This fact alone may be enough reason for Starbucks' explosive growth. I say, who can blame the kids? The Frappucinos are the equivalent of a milkshake with a shot of caffeine. Jessica Frederick, a senior in high school and a Starbucks coffee connoisseur, explains carefully, "Sometimes carrying around a cup of coffee helps complete a look. A pair of capris, flip flops, and a coffee — and it has to have the cardboard sleeve — is very trendy" (quoted in Sommerfeld). In fact, one does not even need the actual substance in the cup to be cool — just the Starbucks branded piece of rolled up cardboard, the new status symbol, will do (Sommerfeld).

If teenagers, however, were the only patrons of Starbucks, I would write the Starbucks' coffee cup status symbol off as a long-lived fad similar to the popular brightly colored Livestrong bracelet and its many copycats. However, apparently the adult population's addiction is just as big, if not bigger, than the teen's obsession with the little white and green cups. Jon Markman calls this trend "a lust for status emblems…that we carry around in our collective cerebral cortex" (Markman). The compulsion to carry this coffee cup rather than, say, a fifty cent gas station cup of practically the same coffee is similar to the "compunction among women to paint their fingernails" and the reasons that businesspeople shake hands (Markman). When a woman paints her fingernails, for example, that woman is sending a subtle message to others that she does not do physical labor, and when businesspeople shake hands they are showing each other "that neither bears the calluses of hard labor" (Markman). In other words, by carrying an over-priced cup of coffee, I can effectively and skillfully prove that I am wealthy enough to not care about how much my coffee costs.

Many of the Starbucks drinkers out there are very aware of the tactics the Starbucks Corporation uses to lure them in and are also conscious of the fact that they are just mere members of the cardboard cup carrying community. They are complacent and happy to be a part of this trend. However, these coffee drinkers may not be aware of how much extra money they are pouring into Starbucks' wallet and how many extra calories they are pouring into their bodies. At some point in a long gone past, "a dime could buy you a cup of coffee... The company's (Starbucks') 12-ounce tall (small) latte ranges from \$2.25 in Minnesota to \$3 in New York City" (Wong). Jon Markman also notes that for forty cents, he can make a cup of Starbucks brand coffee at his own home every day, yet he still drops by his closest Starbucks every morning to pick up a cup for \$3.22 (Markman). After some careful calculation, Markman determined that he is paying around \$1.37 for the barista, or, the drink preparer, to steam some milk, a process which takes around twenty seconds. If the barista prepares steamed milk constantly, she is making Starbucks about \$246 an hour. If one even narrows the steamed milk production down to one cup a minute, the company is still getting \$175 an hour for steaming milk, "and that goes a long way to explain why the company's profit margins come in around 11.5 percent pretax" (Markman). This willingness to pay for expensive coffee does not make sense to any wary consumer, and it especially does not make sense to anyone living in the current economic decline.

While consumers' wallets are losing weight for the benefit of Starbucks, their waistlines seem to be gaining. In the time of health conscious best-sellers like Fast Food Nation and hits like the documentary Super Size Me by Morgan Spurlock, the fast food industry and the greater restaurant industry is trying to trim down the epic portions and calories that dominated during the late twentieth century. Yet, Starbucks seems to have eluded this trend. This could be because coffee is not inherently fattening. In fact, "a cup of black coffee has just 10 calories" (Linn). However, if you decide to satisfy your Starbucks addiction "with a 24-ounce Strawberries and Crème frappuccino, for example...you're sipping 780 calories, 19 grams of fat, and 133 grams of carbohydrates" (Precker). That frappucino has more calories than a Quarter Pounder with cheese and a small fry from McDonald's — combined (McDonald's). Diane Javelli, a dietician from the University of Washington in Seattle, says that "many people do not count the calories they slurp, whether it's coffee, juice, or soda," which means way too many people are probably devouring almost eight hundred extra calories a day in the form of a Starbucks drink.

With 8,337 Starbucks locations available worldwide and countless cafés proclaiming "We are proud to serve Starbucks coffee," the question of whether or not Starbucks is a national phenomenon becomes moot. Whether you are lured in out of curiosity about this coffee place that seems to be everywhere or whether you are seduced inside out of a desire to retreat to the comfortable couches with a cup of warm coffee, once you buy that cardboard cup marked by the mysterious green mermaid, you have set in action a course that cannot be reversed. You have become a part of the growing movement to pay too much for a cup of coffee. But before you sip that overpriced eight hundred calorie milkshake that passes off as coffee, remember McDonald's. The fast food restaurants are striving to improve their menus and to make the food they serve healthier and safer because of works like Fast Food Nation, Super Size Me, and the words of the public. America has finally realized that just because you are born hungry does not mean you are born wanting a Big Mac. The question that remains is this: When will America understand that just because you are born thirsty does not mean you are born wanting a grande Chai latte made with soy milk and a pump of gingerbread syrup.

Works Cited

ElBoghdady, Dina. "Pouring it on: The Starbucks Strategy? Locations, Locations, Locations." Washington Post 25 August 2002, late ed.: H1.

"Interview: Howard Schultz has made a fortune trying to convince the world that it cannot get through the day without a tall skinny latte. But, for the Chief Executive of Starbucks, world domination may not be enough." The Independent 24 May 2000, late ed.: Business 1+.

Linn, Allison. "Your Health." St. Louis Post 9 August 2004, late ed.: Health & Fitness 4.

Markman, Jon D. "Starbucks' Genius Blends Community, Caffeine." 16 February 2005. 2 March 2005 <http://moneycentral.msn.com/content /P107679.asp?Printer>.

"McDonald's USA Nutrition Facts for Popular Menu Items." 10 March 2005 <http://www.mcdonalds.com/app_controller.nutrition.index1.html>.

Precker, Michael. "Starbucks is the latest heavy-hitter to see the lite Fast-food Companies list nutritional info on the Web." The Dallas Morning News 20 July 2004, late ed.: D1.

Sommerfeld, Julia. "Coffee Cool: The 'Other" Teen Drinking Scene." The Seattle Times 26 October 2003, late ed.: 22.

"Store Locator." 10 March 2005 <http://www.starbucks.com/retail/locator/>.

Wong, Brad. "Cup of Starbucks Going Up Average of 11 Cents Oct. 6: First Coffee-Price Increases Since August 2000." Seattle Post 28 September 2004, late ed.: E1.

5.2: Writing to Learn – Comparing College and High School Research Writing

Individually or in small groups, write a list of the ways that Lydia Tolman's essay, "The Rise of Starbucks," is similar to and different from the research papers you wrote in high school. Be prepared to discuss this list with the class as a whole.

It's important to keep in mind that the kind of research writing you do for each college course will be different, depending on the professor and the academic field (e.g. sociology, history, biology, psychology). Every time you write a research paper in college, you'll have a different purpose for writing and a different audience to write to. There's no such thing as a universal college research paper, and there's no magic formula for writing a college research paper. In Part III, we'll talk a lot more about how research processes and research papers are different in each academic field. Lydia Tolman's essay, "The Rise of Starbucks," provides an example of some general ways that research writing in college differs from most high school research writing. For starters, Lydia was doing a lot more than simply reporting information or repeating what other people have said about her topic. She came up with an interesting question to explore, and she related her topic to her own experiences at her university. She gave her opinions about why Starbucks is an obsession, and didn't just copy and paste what others have said and written. Even though it was her questions and her opinions that shaped the essay, she also included information, quotes, and opinions from others. You probably got the sense that Lydia was in a "conversation" with her sources, using them to help her explore her own thoughts on why Starbucks is an obsession.

Differences between High School and College Research

Reading Lydia's paper can give you some clues about differences between high school and college research writing. What follows is an overview of some of the most important differences in research writing that you'll experience as you make the transition from high school to college researching.

- **College research is a process of discovery and revision.**

Did your high school teachers ever make you write a formal outline of your research paper before you began to write? In college research, it's a mistake to think that you can already know exactly what you're going to write and how it will be organized before you even begin the researching and writing process. In most college research projects, you begin with an interesting question that you want to explore, like "Why has Starbucks become an obsession?" As you research and find out what others have said about your research question, you begin to form an opinion, but you might revise your opinion or even change the entire focus of your paper as you research and write. Like college writing and college reading, college research is a complex process. It's *recursive*, to use a key term from Chapter 3.

- **College research involves having a conversation with sources.**

In high school, students sometimes use the cut-and-paste approach to integrating sources. *Cut-and-paste* means finding a few sources and cutting and pasting quotes into your research paper. Think of college research as having a conversation with your sources, and not merely regurgitating what other researchers have already said about your topic. It's almost as if you're sitting down at a table and having a conversation with other researchers. You'll need to understand the key words and key concepts that everyone at the table is talking about, and you'll need to think about who you agree with and who you disagree with and why. Since you're being invited to sit at the table and join the discussion, you'll also need to add something to the conversation by saying something new. A college-level audience expects you to know the topic you are writing about. You need to become familiar with what other experts have said about the topic, and you need to think deeply about the topic and explore an interesting and significant question.

- **College research involves more than merely searching the Internet or finding a few books on your topic.**

Most of your high school teachers were trying to introduce you to some basic research strategies and basic techniques for writing a research paper. In most of your high school research papers, you probably weren't asked to search academic databases or conduct your own research through interviews, surveys, or experiments that you design. College professors want you to expand your research skills and become an expert on a topic in the academic field of whatever course you're taking. Becoming an expert means thinking about what other experts have said about your topic and figuring out where you stand in the conversation. This requires searching academic databases for books from scholarly presses and articles from scholarly journals (we'll talk more about what a *scholarly* source is later in this chapter). Becoming an expert also means conducting some of your own research by designing experiments, conducting interviews, creating surveys, and carrying out other kinds of research.

- **College research focuses on exploring original research questions and not just reporting on what's already been said about a topic.**

In most of your high school research papers, you probably weren't expected to add a new argument or new angle to whatever topic you were exploring. One aspect of the transition from high school to college research is the higher expectations of your readers. College-level readers expect you to add something to the conversation, not simply repeat what other researchers have said about a topic. Sometimes in college your professors will ask you write research papers which are intended only to report information that's already known, but more often your college professors will want you to add something new to the conversation. This might mean reading what others have said and then adding a new idea or argument to the conversation, finding an original solution to a problem, or conducting some of your own research through experiments, interviews, or surveys. Your college professors don't want you to merely repeat information like a parrot: they want you to become a critical and independent thinker and researcher. This means that you need to think about college research as a process of *inquiry*. In the next section, we'll look more closely at what inquiry means when it comes to college research.

5.3: Learn by Doing – High School Researching Peer Interviews

The purpose of this Learn by Doing activity is for you to reflect on your high school researching experiences and to compare them to a peer's experiences. As a class, come up with some questions which you could ask your peers about their high school researching experiences. For example, "What was your best and worst experience writing a research paper?" Or, "How did you conduct research in high school?" Once the class has generated a list of questions, get into pairs and interview a classmate about their high school researching experiences by choosing three of the questions to ask them. Be prepared to report back to the class as a whole on what you discovered in the interview.

Academic Research as Inquiry

A good education should provide multiple opportunities for students to engage in "inquiry-based learning," both independently and in collaborative teams. Through inquiry projects, students should learn how to find and evaluate evidence, how to consider and assess competing interpretations, how to form and test their own analyses and interpretations, how to solve problems, and how to communicate persuasively.

—American Association of Colleges and Universities (AACU, 2007: 30)

Above all, we want our students to view mystery as a source of inquiry, research, and writing. Mystery is an academic value; what good would an institute of inquiry be if everything was already known?

—Professor Robert Davis and Professor Mark Shadle, Writing Program,
Eastern Oregon University (Davis and Shadle, 2000: 441)

5.4: Writing to Learn – Defining *Inquiry*

Think about the definition of *inquiry*. What do you associate with the word *inquiry*? How would you define it? Can you think of specific examples of inquiry? Why do you think Robert Davis and Mark Shadle in the quote above connect inquiry with mystery? Write for five minutes and then share your thoughts in a small group or with the class as a whole.

The Nature of College Research

College research usually begins with a question. Should the United States devote money to exploring Mars? What role does gender play in communication among college students? What larger cultural trends influenced the abstract art movement in the 1960s? Usually these questions are *open-ended*. This means that there isn't a single, correct answer. Inquiry involves exploring an open-ended question and making the best argument you can after considering what others have said about the question or after conducting your own research on the topic. For example, in "The Rise of Starbucks," Lydia Tolman came up with two related questions for inquiry: why is Starbucks so popular, and what effect has Starbucks' popularity had on American society? These are debatable questions. No one can give you the *right* answer to why Starbucks is popular or what effect its popularity has had on American society. That's what makes them interesting questions for inquiry. Lydia did some research on the topic, considered what other authors have said about the questions she wanted to explore, and reflected on her own answers to these questions. It was important that Lydia chose a topic and research questions that she was curious about and that she felt connected to personally. When your college professors give you some freedom in choosing research questions, try to find questions for inquiry that you genuinely want to explore. The best kind of inquiry happens when the researcher is curious: when exploring topics that connect to the researcher's personal experiences or goals, or when asking questions the researcher really wants to know the answer to.

Examples of College Research Assignments

Let's take a look at some examples of college research assignments so you can gain a sense of what is meant by *inquiry*. Below are three excerpts from research assignments in college courses. As you read the three assignments, think about the ways each research assignment requires students to practice academic inquiry.

History Research Paper Assignment from Professor Donald Shaffer, Upper Iowa University

The ultimate assignment for the course, toward which students will be working the entire semester, is a major research paper, 15–25 pages. This assignment requires that each student present an original historical interpretation based on his or her own primary research. The essence of history is creating new interpretations of the past through primary research and analytical writing. Before graduating, students need to cap their work as a history major by experiencing this process. This course will provide that experience.

The subject of each student's paper will be one of their own choosing. However, a strongly suggested way of framing a paper will be to examine the experience of slaves in one particular state in the U.S. South. This approach will allow a student to make use of the WPA slave narratives as their main primary source, simplifying the task of locating primary sources. Please note: this approach is not required. The instructor welcomes other topic choices by students.

Students will be using secondary sources in their papers (books, articles, etc.), but primary sources will be the cornerstone.

To assist students along in the process of completing their research paper, they will complete a number of preparatory assignments along the way. These will include a library research exercise, a formal proposal, an annotated bibliography, a rough draft, and group critiques (i.e., students will be critiquing each others' papers).

Political Science Research Paper Assignment from Professor Thomas Sowers, Lamar University

The research paper is divided into three assignments. The first is to develop a research question and conduct a literature review on the question. This should be between 4 and 5 pages and is worth 30 points. The second assignment is to develop a hypothesis or hypotheses to be tested. This should also include a description on the data and the variables you plan to use. This should be between 1 and 3 pages and is worth 20 points. The final assignment is the finished paper. Students are expected to have done actual analysis applying one of the tools that we learned in class.

Psychology Research Paper Assignment from Professor Tom Shuell, State University of New York at Buffalo

This paper is perhaps the major assignment for the course. Its purpose is to provide you with an opportunity to think about, develop, and define a problem associated with the psychology of human cognition and instruction that you find interesting and to design a study that will help answer one of the questions arising from the problem.

The main impetus for the paper should come from you, but I will help you in any way I can. Perhaps you would find it useful to talk with me several times during the semester as the problem/question and the paper begins to evolve. This will give me an opportunity to react to the paper in its formative stages when my reactions may be most helpful to you. It is suggested that a draft of the paper be turned in approximately three weeks before the end of the semester; the draft will be critiqued in a manner that hopefully will help you write the final version of the paper. In this way I can provide you with feedback during the early stages of the learning associated with the paper instead of only after the paper has been completed. The final version of the paper should be written according to APA format (see the *APA Publication Manual*, Fourth Edition).

There are three major aspects to this paper:

1. State what you consider to be an important, unanswered question in the area of human cognition and instruction and some of the reasons why you consider it to be an important question. Although I will provide you with feed-

back on my perceptions of how important other psychologists and educators would view the problem/question, the major thrust of my reactions will be in terms of how well you justify the importance of the question selected.

2. What aspects of present-day knowledge are relevant to the question? In what ways do present-day research and theory relate to the question you have selected and in what ways do they fall short of providing an answer to your question? This will include reviewing <u>some</u> of the research (both theoretical and empirical) relevant to your question, but this review should consist of something more than just an annotated list of studies and theoretical positions.

3. Design a study which is capable of providing an answer to the question you selected. The design of the study should be methodologically sound and valid, although I do not necessarily assume that you already have taken relevant courses in statistics, etc. It is not necessary for you to conduct the study as part of this course, but you may want to consider conducting the study you design at some later time.

5.5: Learn by Doing – Analyzing College Research Writing Assignments

Individually or in small groups, create a list of the ways that research and inquiry is defined in each of the three excerpts from college research writing assignments. Consider the following questions as you think about the assignments:

1. Is the assignment asking you to report information, say something original, or both?
2. What kind of research and writing process is asked for?
3. What kinds of sources would you need to find to help support your ideas?

If you've been assigned any research writing in your courses this semester, choose one of your research paper assignments and discuss it along with the three research assignments presented here as examples.

Exploring Academic Researching Processes

5.6: Writing to Learn – College Research Quiz

Before we talk about college research process myths, take this college research quiz and discuss it with the rest of the class:

1. You should already have a position or definite opinions before you begin to research your topic.__ True __ False

2. The first step in writing a research paper is to create a formal outline.__ True __ False

3. You can't use *I* in a research paper. __ True __ False

4. It's fine if your entire topic changes after you start researching and writing your paper.__ True __ False

5. Research papers mostly summarize what other people have written about a topic.__ True __ False

6. You should use your own opinion in a research paper.__ True __ False

7. It's fine to use personal experiences as evidence in a research paper.__ True __ False

---

Five Myths about College Research Processes

Myth #1: Writing a research paper is a linear, step-by-step process.

In high school, you might have had professors who required you to follow a step-by-step process to complete a research paper: start with a thesis and an outline; next, find some sources on your topic, and write information from the sources on notecards; and then follow your outline and draft your paper, inserting quotes from the notecards. This linear, step-by-step process might have helped give you a basic starting point for learning how to write a research paper, but it probably won't be effective if you try to apply it to college-level research. College research is complex, and it requires you to go beyond the step-by-step formula. In Chapter 3, we talked about the ways that college writing is *recursive*, and the same is true of college research. In most college research writing, you'll start with some open-ended questions (rather than a simple and straightforward thesis) and then revise your questions and your own thinking on the topic as you explore what others have said about the topic. As you read and write, your argument and the way you organize your paper will be constantly changing, and after you consider what others have said about your topic, it's likely that you'll end up having a more complex argument than a simple one-sided, pro/con thesis. You'll probably need to conduct more research after you begin writing, because you'll discover new questions and new aspects to your topic – you might even change your topic entirely if you discover a more interesting topic or realize that you don't have anything new to add to the conversation on your original topic.

Myth #2: You can use the same research process for any research paper assignment.

In Chapter 3, we talked about the ways that your writing process will differ for each college writing assignment. The same is true for research processes. Just as there's no single, universal writing process, there's no single research process. A fifteen-page chemistry research paper asking you to conduct an experiment and report on the results will require a much different research process than a five-page theatre research paper that asks you to discuss a modern interpretation of one of Shakespeare's plays, citing Shakespeare scholars and theatre critics. Sometimes you'll be able to choose your own research question, and other times the professor will give you a specific topic. Sometimes you'll find a research question and stick with it throughout the entire process; other times you'll change topics after doing some researching and drafting. Sometimes you'll find information by searching online databases for articles from academic journals; other times you'll collect your data from observations and interviews. It's important to be flexible as a college researcher and adapt your research strategies to the rhetorical situation of the research project.

Myth #3: Researching means finding a few books and articles at the library.

In high school, you might have had a library day when your class visited the library and found some books and articles for a research paper. In college, a first visit to the library is a good start, but most of your college research will require more extensive investigating than simply finding a few books and articles. For most of your college research projects, in addition to finding relevant books on your topic, you'll search a variety of academic databases to find articles. The articles and books you find will lead you to more references and a search for more information. It's likely that you'll return again to your search after you've done some writing and discovered new aspects of your topic – or even an entirely new topic. In addition to this library research, many college research projects require you to do some of your own original research by conducting experiments, interviewing people, creating and distributing surveys, or carrying out other kinds of original research.

Myth #4: Writing a research paper means finding relevant quotes and information on your topic, then stringing it all together to make a paper of the required length.

In Chapter 1, we talked about the ways that college professors value critical thinking and original arguments. Since college professors want you to learn to think for yourself and not simply regurgitate information, it makes sense that most college research paper assignments ask you to do more than repeat what others have said about your topic. If your essay is one quote or paraphrase after another, with none of your own ideas and responses to the information you report, then why bother writing in the first place? Yes, it's important to consider what others have said about your topic and to show that you understand what others have said in order to enter the conversation as a credible writer and researcher. At the same time, you don't want to give up ownership of your paper and let it become a mere *collage of sources*, with one quote and paraphrase after another and none of your own words, ideas, and arguments.

Myth #5: Writing a research paper means finding the truth or the right answer.

At some point in your research process, you're going to come to a crossroads. You're going to find two experts who have two completely different points of view on your topic. For example, one expert says that violent television programs don't cause children to act more violently, and another expert says that there's a direct link between watching violent television programs and violent behavior in children. What do you do when the experts disagree? It's important to remember that one of the goals of college is to encourage you to think for yourself. Critical thinkers consider all of the evidence and then reach their own conclusions. In the end, everything is an argument. College researchers aren't looking for *The Truth* with a capital *T*. Researchers are always adding to what we know about a topic, and there's always a debate about what we know. Even the experts often disagree. In college, you'll very rarely have professors who are asking for a right or wrong answer when they ask you to conduct research and explore a question or argue for a solution to a problem.

Strategies for Finding a Research Question

5.7: Learn by Doing – Finding Research Questions

Imagine that your psychology professor has given you the research assignment below. What strategies would you use for finding a research question? Come up with some possible research questions for the assignment and share them with the class.

Here's the assignment:

For this assignment, you will explore a debatable gender issue in psychology. Choose a psychology issue connected to gender in college students, and come up with a research question that you'd like to explore. The paper will be 5–7 pages long, and you'll need to look at articles from psychology journals to help you explore your topic. Choose an issue that's not too broad and that will be interesting to psychologists, and make sure your research question is debatable.

For some of your college research assignments, the professor will choose a topic or give you a list of topics to choose from. However, most of your professors want you to learn how to formulate your own research questions and find topics that are interesting to you and that you're passionate about and so will enjoy researching and writing on. When you're given a research assignment and you have the freedom to choose your own research question to explore, a number of strategies can be helpful, as discussed below.

- **Use freewriting to generate research questions.**

Sometimes when students are given a research paper assignment, they panic. They feel so overwhelmed by the idea of writing a lengthy paper, and so nervous about trying to find a good topic, that they freeze up and have trouble even getting started. Instead of putting pressure on yourself to find a perfect topic off the top of your head, do some freewriting. Try creating an authority/interest list as described in Chapter 3. Or start brainstorming and writing questions without worrying about whether they would make good topics or not. You can also try writing down some opinions you have on the topic and then try turning them into research questions. For example, for the psychology paper writing assignment in Learn by Doing Activity 5.7, you might jot down the opinion, "Because women mature faster then men, they have a better chance of success in their first semester of college." You can turn this opinion into a series of research questions you could explore: Does gender and maturity level play a role in college success during the first semester?

Do men and women mature at different rates? Are there differences in maturity levels between the men and the women I know in college, and if there are, how did these differences affect their success the first semester?

- **Draw on course readings, lectures, and discussions to come up with research questions.**

Throughout *Exploring College Writing*, we've been talking about the ways that knowledge is *socially constructed*. Even if your professors ask you to come up with an original topic for a research project, that doesn't mean they expect you to discover a research question all on your own. When college professors ask you to come up with an interesting and original research question, it usually means they want you to add something of your own to what's already been said about a topic. Think about the ways that a research paper assignment might connect to the readings assigned in the course or the material presented in lectures. Have there been any interesting questions raised in class discussion? Has the professor asked any open-ended questions for class discussion or debate?

- **Talk with the professor and your peers about research questions.**

In Chapter 3, the point was made that professors appreciate it when you visit them during their office hours with questions. Keep this in mind if you become stuck when you're trying to find a good research question. Sometimes talking to the professor or talking to a classmate about some possible research questions or general topics can help you think about which topics and questions your audience might find interesting. Talking to the professor can be especially helpful if you want to have an idea of which research questions are original and which have already been asked over and over again by experts. Another resource for working on research questions is your institution's writing center.

- **Talk with a reference librarian.**

The reference librarians at your school are experts in helping students find and narrow topics. Librarians will be familiar with the resources available on your topic, so they can be especially helpful when it comes to avoiding topics for which no resources are available or narrowing topics down to a manageable scope for research. You can also go to reference librarians for help later in the researching process, when you begin searching for outside sources. Reference librarians are usually experts in researching sources not only in libraries but also online. They can also help you find and obtain sources that your library does not have but other libraries might.

- **Start doing some research to help you find research questions.**

This advice may sound backwards to you at first. Some students might say that you should have a research question in mind before you start doing any research. Remember, however, that research isn't a simple three-step process: choose a thesis, conduct research, and then write a paper. Sometimes you might start with a general area you want to focus on but not a specific question and then do some research to see what others have said about your topic, in order to consider what you can add to the conversation. Let's go back to the psychology research writing assignment in Learn by Doing Activity 5.7. Let's say you knew you wanted to write about gender and dating in college, but you weren't sure about a research question. You might find a few books and articles about dating in college and skim them to see what interests you. Let's say that one of the articles you find claims that college women are more likely than college men to be looking for a life-long partner when they date. Perhaps this article makes you think about your own friends in college, and you can think of a few of your male friends who are looking for life-long partners. This makes you wonder if the article is valid or not. You might then decide to conduct interviews with your friends and a survey of your classmates to explore the question, "Are there gender differences in dating and commitment among college students?" If you're having trouble coming up with an interesting research question, don't panic – just read.

- **Avoid research questions that merely repeat what's already been said on your topic.**

If one of the major goals of college research is to create new knowledge about a topic, it makes sense that you'd want to avoid research questions that have already been explored so thoroughly by other researchers that it's hard to say anything new. It's difficult to come up with new and interesting research questions on topics such as "The Death Penalty" or "Euthanasia." Sometimes you can take a topic that seems overdone but find a new angle by relating the topic to a personal experience or by doing some of your own research through interviews or surveys to add something new to the conversation. In general, though, you should avoid picking a topic that doesn't really interest you just because it seems like it would be easy to find information. In addition to finding a question that you really want to explore, keep your readers in mind when you choose a topic. It's going to be more difficult to gain your readers' attention if your research question focuses on a topic that's been overdone.

- **Avoid research questions that aren't debatable.**

Research questions such as "Does eating fast food have a negative effect on your health?" or "Is there a relationship between poverty and crime?" are not debatable enough for most kinds of college research. It's been well accepted by researchers that eating fast food has a negative effect on health, and criminologists agree there's a connection between poverty and crime. But sometimes you can write an effective research paper by taking a closer look at a topic that's not really debatable and making a point that researchers have missed. Let's take the example of fast food having a negative effect on health. It's been accepted by researchers that eating fast food has a negative effect on health, but very few researchers have argued that eating fast food regularly for only a short period of time can put a person at a serious health risk. Morgan Spurlock, a filmmaker, came up with an interesting and original research question: "What would happen to a person if he ate only McDonald's food for a month?" Spurlock conducted an experiment by eating at McDonald's every day for a month, and the results were surprising. Spurlock gained twenty-four pounds, had near failure of the liver, and also suffered from mood swings and depression. He filmed this experiment in the documentary, *Super Size Me*, and one of the reasons the movie was so popular was because the results of his experiment were surprising. Everyone knew that a fast-food diet was unhealthy, but researchers and the general public were shocked by how bad the health effects were in only a month of eating nothing but typical fast food.

- **Avoid research questions that are too broad for the assignment.**

It's fine to start out with a broad research question. Starting with a broad question can keep your options open as you begin to research and write. But beware of trying to write a research paper on a question which is so broad that an entire book can be written about the subject. Let's go back to the sample psychology assignment in Learn by Doing Activity 5.7. If you tried to explore the research question, "How are college men and women different psychologically?" you wouldn't even know where to begin because the question is so broad – not to mention that you could spend years of your life researching and writing about all of the different aspects of this topic. You might narrow this broad question to: "How do gender differences in college affect educational success?" This would help you narrow your search for information, but it's still such a broad topic that you could easily write a 500 page book on it, and the professor is only asking for 5–7 pages. You could narrow the topic down further – for example, by focusing on the question, "How do gender differences affect class participation in college?"

You can narrow broad topics by thinking of an aspect of the topic that connects to your experience or interests. You can also narrow a broad topic by focusing on a specific time period, a certain group of people, a geographic location, or a specific theory or approach.

5.8: Learn by Doing – Evaluating Research Questions

Individually or in small groups, consider whether the five research questions below would be good topics for a research project in a history course. Imagine that the questions are for a ten-page research paper that focuses on a debatable issue connected to the Vietnam War. Talk or write about why each research question would or wouldn't be effective.

1. What role did the counterculture movement play in ending the Vietnam War?
2. Was the Vietnam War justified?
3. What were effects of post-traumatic stress syndrome on Vietnam War veterans?
4. What were the causes and effects of the Vietnam War?
5. What effect did the My Lai Massacre have on the American public's support of the Vietnam War?

Locating Sources

5.9: Writing to Learn – Research Sources

Create a list of every kind of source you've used in research papers in the past (books, Web sites, journal articles, interviews, and so on). Then create another list of every resource you've used to locate an outside source (Internet search engines, library databases, television, and so on). Share the two lists with the whole class.

Most college-level research requires much more than merely surfing the Internet or taking a single visit to the library to find a few books. If you want to join in the conversation on an academic subject, you need to understand the key terms and arguments and what other experts have said about the topic. You need to show an in-depth knowledge of your subject and consider it from different points of view. To reach this level of expertise on your subject, you're going to need to find more than just a few sources online or a few books on the shelves of your library. Let's take a look at a research paper scenario to have a better idea of what finding sources really means for college-level writing. Let's say that you're given the research project assignment below in an ethnic studies or education course. Read the assignment and then consider the questions that follow.

> In this research project, you will take a position on the topic of bilingual education. You need to consider what educators and politicians have argued about whether or not students who aren't fluent in English should be given bilingual instruction and take a position on the topic after considering what others have said. Your hypothetical audience for this essay is our local Board of Education.

If you were given the research project above, where would you look for sources? What kind of sources would be most effective? How many sources do you think you would need?

There's no single, correct answer to the questions above, but since the assignment is a typical college research assignment, it's helpful to think about where you might go to find sources. For starters, you might find a few books on bilingual education. It would also be helpful to find articles from educators who are experts on the topic. This would require looking at some electronic databases, and especially databases that focus on education issues. Considering that the audience is the Board of Education, it might also be helpful to find newspaper articles on the subject to find out what school officials and politicians have said recently on the topic. You might even consider interviewing some professors, school officials, or politicians. Although books and articles would give you the best chance of finding out what educators have said about the topic of bilingual education, you might also find some resources by surfing the Internet. Government and education Web sites would be especially helpful. If all of this sounds challenging, it is! College-level research is complex, and locating sources takes time and effort. In college research, you'll also need to learn how to recognize *scholarly sources* and to understand how scholarly sources are different from non-scholarly sources.

Scholarly Sources vs. Non-Scholarly Sources: What are the Differences?

Most of your college research assignments will require you to find scholarly sources. These are sources written by an expert in the field, and they're typically published by academic presses – publishers connected to a university or a professional organization. Non-scholarly sources are usually published by presses that aren't connected to a university, and they're aimed at a wider audience than experts or students studying the subject to become experts. Here's a table that shows some differences between scholarly and non-scholarly sources:

Scholarly Source	Non-Scholarly Source
Written by an expert/scholar in the field.	Written by a non-expert or by an expert writing to a non-expert audience.
Always reviewed by peers (other experts in the field) before being published.	Sometimes but not always reviewed by peers.
Published by an academic press or the press of a professional organization.	Published by a press that is not associated with a university.
Audience for the text is experts or students studying the subject in-depth.	Audience for the text is non-experts.
All sources are cited in a reference page.	Sources are not always referenced.

5.10: Learn by Doing – Scholarly vs. Non-scholarly Sources

Individually or in small groups, decide whether you think the following sources are scholarly or non-scholarly, and discuss why you came to the decision you did:

1. An article in *Time* magazine.
2. An article in *The New England Journal of Medicine*.
3. A book on the experiences of women in the military written by a former Army Colonel and published by Random House.
4. A book about the ways race is portrayed in television sitcoms written by a sociology professor and published by the University of Chicago Press.
5. A book on women in the corporate workforce published by the National Organization of Women.
6. An entry about Freudian psychology in the online reference site Wikipedia.
7. A Web site about the future of robotic engineering published by the University of Southern California Center for Robotics

Types of Textual Research Sources

5.11: Learn by Doing – Library Tour

The purpose of this Learn by Doing activity is to help you become familiar with the college research sources we'll discuss in the next section. Sign up for a tour of your institution's library, or if your college library doesn't offer tours, find a map of the library and take a self-guided tour. Once you've taken the tour, write about which library resources you might need to use for your courses this semester.

Throughout your college career, you'll rely on sources such as books, periodicals, and Web sites for your research projects. The following section provides an overview of each of these kinds of sources.

Books

Most of the books that are useful for college research are scholarly books published by academic presses (such as a university press, e.g. Princeton University Press or Cambridge University Press, or a commercial publisher specializing in academic books, e.g. Academic Press or Elsevier) or books published by professional organizations (such as the National Council for the Social Sciences or the National Education Association). These books are typically written for academic audiences. They explore a topic in depth and from different points of view, and they use multiple sources written by experts on the topic to support their arguments. Sometimes scholarly books are collections of essays by a variety of authors that have an editor who combines the essays into one book and often adds his or her own perspective in an introductory essay. These are referred to as *edited collections*. Edited books that collect literary or artistic works are called *anthologies*. Whether you rely on scholarly books, non-scholarly books, or a mix of the two types will depend on the rhetorical situation of the research assignment: the purpose, audience, and genre. Whatever type(s) of books you use, a good starting point for searching for a book is a *subject* or *keyword* search in your school library's online catalogue. Keep in mind that most books have a bibliography listing the sources the author used, and this list can help lead you to other books and articles that might be useful. If there's a book that you need for your research but that your library doesn't own, you can use interlibrary loan to obtain the book. Interlibrary loan is a way to order books from other libraries through your library, and most college libraries have a way to order books using the interlibrary loan service on the library Web site.

Reference Books

Reference books are different from scholarly books that make arguments about an issue or report on the results of research. Reference books are not meant to be read from cover to cover but to be used as a resource for finding information about a specific subject. You've probably used reference books like encyclopedias to get an overview of a subject, dictionaries to find a definition of a word, or handbooks to figure out how to cite sources in a specific citation style. When you're doing college-level research, you usually will be expected to use the most reliable kinds of each of these reference books. For example, you'd want to consult *The Encyclopaedia Britannica* before you'd look at an online encyclopedia found by searching *Yahoo!*, and you'd want to find a definition of a word in *The Oxford English Dictionary* or *Merriam-Webster* rather than from *dictionary.com*. You might not realize that every academic field (art, anthropology, chemistry, and so on) has its own specialized encyclopedias and dictionaries. We'll talk more about these kinds of reference books in Part III. One other type of reference that will be helpful to you in college is the book-length bibliography. These are lists of books and articles on a specific subject. For example, writing professors often use the *Bedford Bibliography for Teachers of Writing* as a resource for finding books and articles on subjects related to the teaching of writing. Usually book-length bibliographies are annotated, which means that they provide a summary of each source. *The Bedford Bibliography for Teachers of Writing*, for example, has a list of important articles and books on the teaching of writing and a summary of the main points of each source listed. You can view the *Bedford Bibliography* online (www.bedford stmartins.com/bb/) if you want to see an example of a book-length annotated bibliography.

Periodicals

A periodical is anything published over time and at regular intervals (each week, each month, each season). This includes scholarly journals such as *The American Journal of Psychiatry* or *Modern Fiction Studies*, popular magazines such as *Newsweek* and *Wired*, and newspapers such as *The New York Times* or *USA Today*. Some academic fields have professional journals that are aimed at professionals in a field rather than scholars. Fields like engineering and business have many journals that are published by professional organizations and aimed at working professionals. The kinds of periodicals you use as references (scholarly journals, popular magazines, newspapers, or a mix of these) will depend on the purpose, audience, and genre of the research writing assignment. Most college library Web sites will allow you to search for titles of periodicals by changing the searching parameters to "Periodical" and "Title." To find articles by keyword or subject, you'll need to search the periodical databases available on your school's library Web site. Articles in scholarly journals always include a reference page that lists the sources the author cited, and these can be a great resource for finding more information about your topic. Keep in mind that if you need an article from a journal your library doesn't own, most college libraries allow you to order articles from periodicals as well as books using interlibrary loan.

Electronic Sources

Did you know that you can sometimes have access to the full text of articles and newspaper reports in your library's electronic databases? Did you know that entire books are now becoming available online? Did you know that Google has a special search engine focused on academic resources called *Google Scholar*? Computer searching through the Internet and electronic databases gives you easy access to a lot of information. Sometimes there's so much access to so much information that it can be overwhelming. We'll break these electronic sources into different categories to make it easier to talk about what's available: Web sites, electronic databases, and electronic books.

Web Sites

One of the best things about the World Wide Web is that almost anyone can create a site and publish it online. But this is also the aspect of the Web that makes it tricky to search when you're writing college-level papers. Some Web sites are more reliable than others. For example, if you were writing a research paper arguing against electronic voting machines, you wouldn't want to use "Bob's Anti-Voting Machine" Web site for information, since there is no way to tell if "Bob" is a reliable source of information. You also wouldn't want to use the Web site for Diebold, a company that makes electronic voting machines (unless you're trying to show their point of view). Diebold's Web site address is www.diebold.com, so they have a *.com* domain. Web sites with *.com* domains are commercial, and because they're trying to sell something, they're less reliable sources of information than Web sites that are not for profit. These not-for-profit domains are *.edu* for education Web sites, *.gov* for government Web sites, and *.org* or *.net* for non-profit organization Web sites. These four types of Web sites are from non-commercial organizations, so the information they post is usually more reliable, but you still need to be a careful and critical thinker when you visit these not-for-profit domains. For example, a *.org* Web site may only present information from studies that benefit the mission of the organization, and a *.gov* Web site might present information in a way that favors the policies of the current government. We'll talk more about evaluating Internet sources in the next section of this chapter.

Another kind of Web site that is becoming more and more popular is a *blog* (short for *Web log*). Blogs are similar to personal journals, except the writer posts the entries online. Sometimes blogs allow readers to post their responses in conversation threads as well. Blogs often include pictures or video files. There's a lot of variety in the kinds of blogs you'll find on the Internet. Some are personal diaries about the blogger's day-to-day life, some are written by experts on specific topics, and some are connected to political groups. It's unusual to cite a blog in college research, only because they are less reliable than other kinds of sources such as scholarly books or academic journals (which are peer reviewed), but it's possible that you'd want to cite a blog in your research – for example, if you were doing a paper on how political groups get their message out or a study of a specific subculture that uses blogs to communicate.

The Web sites below are good starting points for doing college-level research on the Internet. These sites all focus on academic research.

> *The Internet Public Library* (http://www.ipl.org)
> *The Virtual Library* (http://vlib.org)
> *Academic Net* (http://academicinfo.net)
> *Google Scholar* (http://scholar.google.com)
> *Infomine*: Scholarly Internet Resources Collection (http://infomine.ucr.edu/)

Electronic Databases

Electronic databases are indexes for collections of journals and newspapers. You can search these databases by author, subject, or keyword. Usually these journals are print-based, but sometimes you can access the full text of the article, a summary or shorter version of the original article, online. When a database has a full text of an article available, it's usually in one of two kinds of formats: *html* or *pdf*. The *html* format provides the text of the article with only a click of the mouse. The *pdf* format is a scanned image of the article that you can download. Some of these electronic databases are very broad, and cover academic journals in many different academic fields. Some databases are only for specific academic fields of study, such as electrical engineering or chemistry. We'll talk about these specialized databases in Part III, but for now we'll look at general electronic databases. Below are some of the major general academic databases. Most of these databases should be available from your library:

FirstSearch. *FirstSearch* provides access to more than 10 million articles in journals, magazines, and newspapers. Some of the articles are available in full-text form.

EBSCOhost Academic Search. *EBSCOhost* is a database of books, periodicals, and newspapers. Some of the articles are available in full-text form.

InfoTrac: Expanded Academic. *InfoTrac* includes over 20 million articles from nearly 6,000 sources. You can limit your search to only peer-reviewed, academic articles. You can also limit your search to only full-text documents.

LexisNexis: Academic. *LexisNexis* is focused on news, business, and legal articles. Most of the information is in full-text documents. This is an especially useful database for searching newspapers.

WorldCat. *WorldCat* is the world's largest network of library collections. *WorldCat* searches thousands of libraries for books and periodicals.

Electronic Books

Some books are available online as *e-books*. These might be books that are also available in print, but some e-books are only published online. Your school's library might have access to some of these e-books, and some of them are available to anyone. Often you might be allowed only limited access to an e-book. For example, you might not be able to print something from the e-book, or you might only be allowed to view it for a limited time. Here are three of the best Web sites to visit for free e-books:

Google Books (http://books.google.com)
Project Guttenberg (http://www.gutenberg.org/wiki/Main_Page)
The Internet Public Library (http://www.ipl.org/div/subject/browse /hum60.60.00)

Primary Research Sources: Interviews and Surveys

5.12: Writing to Learn – Effective Interviews

The purpose of this Writing to Learn activity is to start you thinking about what makes an effective interview. Read the interview with a sociology professor at the beginning of Chapter 8, and individually or in small groups, write or talk about the ways that the interview was or wasn't effective. Considering the purpose of the interview, were the questions appropriate? Did they elicit helpful answers from the person being interviewed? Were there any follow-up questions which you might have asked if you were the one conducting the interview?

At some point in college it's likely that you'll be asked to conduct primary research. Primary research involves collecting data that does not already exist, often by going out *into the field* and observing human behavior or the physical world, interviewing people, or designing and conducting surveys. Earlier in this chapter we talked about the ways that college researching usually goes beyond simply summarizing what other people have said about a subject. Doing their own research by gathering data is one way that college researchers add their perspectives to the conversation on a subject. Since two common types of primary research in college research are interviews and surveys, let's take a look at some strategies for conducting interviews and creating surveys.

Strategies for Conducting Interviews

- **Arrange the interview as early as possible.**

If you wait until the last minute to schedule an interview with someone, you run the risk of not being able to find a time that fits their schedule. It's courteous to give an interviewee at least a few weeks to find an open spot in their schedule.

- **Find experts by checking your sources.**

As you conduct research, you might find some experts on your topic that you'd like to interview. Most of the time you can track down the contact information of these experts by searching their names on the Internet. Once you locate them, you can tell them that you're a college student doing some research and that you'd like to interview them by phone or email. You might be reticent about doing this, but you'd be surprised how open most experts are to being interviewed about the topic they've researched and written about.

- **Find experts by searching the Internet, the phone book, and your institution's faculty directory.**

The Internet is a great resource for finding experts to interview on your topic. Just checking search engines using keywords from your research topic can connect you to experts on your topic at universities and professional organizations. The local telephone book can also connect you to experts on your research topic. For example, if you were researching the effects of physical abuse on the mental health of children for a psychology course, you could find a child psychologist in the phone book and arrange for an interview. Another great resource is your own school's faculty directory, since your professors are experts on the topics in their field of study.

- **Prepare a list of questions ahead of time.**

It's a good idea to brainstorm a list of questions and then narrow the list down to what you think are the most important questions. If you're not sure what to ask, here are some general ideas you can start from. You could ask the person you're interviewing:

To explain something about your topic you don't understand.
To discuss the history of your topic.
To talk about what they think is the most important or surprising aspect of their research.
To clear up common misconceptions about the topic.
To point you to further research and resources on your topic.

- **Ask follow-up questions.**

Even though you want to have questions prepared before you begin the interview, when you conduct the actual interview, you might have new questions. These may be questions you hadn't thought of that come to you while you're interviewing, or follow-up questions that encourage the person you're interviewing to expand on what they're saying. During the interview, be a good listener and show the person you're interviewing that you're interested in what they have to say.

- **Take notes during the interview.**

The best way to note what was said in an interview is to use a tape recorder or digital recorder. When I conduct an interview, I like to use a digital recorder and also bring a notepad. On the notepad I make a note of something important that was said or a quote I might want to use in my paper. When you're taking notes during an interview, try using abbreviations so you can write faster (e.g. *w/* for *with*, *w/o* for *without*, or + for *and*).

Strategies for Conducting Surveys

- **Use a survey to complement your research or to help develop aspects of your topic for which you need more information.**

Since you'll only be able to survey a limited number of people (a small sample size), in most college research you won't be using a survey as the basis for your entire study. But a survey can help you complement your research or fill in gaps where you need more information. Even a small survey can help show some patterns. For example, if you're writing a research paper about how much television college students watch, if you conducted a survey of thirty college students and found that most of them watched more than twenty hours of television a week, you can use that pattern as evidence in your research paper to complement other research information you've gathered.

- **Choose the type of questions that would be most effective for the information you need.**

In a survey, you can ask multiple-choice questions, open-ended questions, or questions that use a scale. Here are examples of each of these types of question:

Multiple-choice question

How much television do you watch in a week?

    a. 0–5 hours
    b. 6–10 hours
    c. more than 10 hours

Open-ended question

Do you think that college students watch too much television? Why or why not?

Scale question

On a scale of 1–5, with 5 being "very frequently" and 1 being "never," how often do you watch television?

If you use open-ended questions, make sure the questions are specific enough to give you useful information for your research. For example, you wouldn't want to ask, "Do you watch a lot of television?" because the answer might not be specific enough. Try to avoid biased questions when you design your survey. For example, the question, "Do you think stem cell research is wrong because it kills human life?" is biased because it assumes that stem cells are equivalent to human life, which is open for debate. Also, be careful to avoid questions that can be considered sexist, racist, or otherwise offensive. It's a good idea to have a draft of your survey questions checked by your teacher (or a writing center or learning resources center tutor) and to make any necessary changes in wording before gathering your data.

- **Test your survey and get feedback before you distribute it.**

It's difficult to see a flaw in a survey question until someone actually tries to respond to your survey, and you don't want to send out your survey and then find out too late that one of your questions is too broad or is biased. It's a good idea to test your survey before you send it out by giving it to a few friends and showing it to your professor to get feedback.

5.13: Learn by Doing – Practicing Interviews and Surveys

In this Learn by Doing activity, you'll have a chance to practice creating a survey in a group. Each group will create a survey for the class about their research writing experiences and attitudes. Decide whether you want to ask multiple-choice questions, open-ended questions, questions on a scale, or a mix of these types. When your group has a draft of your questions ready, test your survey by giving it to a classmate from another group. Then revise the survey and give it to all your classmates. Be prepared to discuss each group's survey results with the class as a whole.

Evaluating Sources

5.14: Writing to Learn – Your Experience Evaluating Sources

Before you read about what makes a reliable source for college research, let's tap into what you already know about how to evaluate sources. Write about how you've evaluated sources in the research you've done for school. How can you tell if a source is reliable? What kinds of sources are most reliable? What kinds of sources are least reliable?

If you want to persuade your audience that your research is reliable, you'll need to use sources that are appropriate for college-level research papers. The kind of sources you use will depend on your purpose, audience, and genre, but there are some general questions you can ask about your sources to help you evaluate them, as discussed below

Who is the author?

In college research, pay close attention to the background of the authors that you cite. What makes them experts? Do they have an advanced degree such as a Ph.D., J.D., or M.D.? Are they affiliated with a credible university or professional organization? Do they have other publications? Are they cited by other experts on the topic? It's a safe bet that the authors who are cited the most by the books and articles you're reading on your topic will be the most reliable, since they'll be considered the top experts in the field.

Who is the publisher?

If it's a book, is it published by a university or other academic press or a professional organization? If it's a periodical, is it an academic, peer-reviewed journal? If it's a Web site, is it an *.edu*, *.net*, or *.org* domain? If it's a newspaper, is it a reputable newspaper with a national or international reputation, such as *The New York Times*, *The London Times*, or the *Washington Post*? If the publisher isn't an academic press, be sure that the publishing company doesn't only publish books with a particular political slant. Some publishing companies publish books, magazines, or newspapers with only a very conservative or only a very liberal point of view, so your audience may perceive these sources as biased. If you use a source which is biased, this can affect your credibility as an author – unless you make clear that you are aware of the bias and have a reason for using that source. In the case of a Web site, pay attention to whether it's published in a commercial domain (*.com*) or if it's published in an *.edu*, *.org*, *.net*, or *.gov* domain.

What is the date of publication?

Some kinds of college research will require that you use recent sources. If you're writing a research paper about Americans' obesity problems or recent developments in gene therapy, you'll want to cite recent research. If you're comparing advertising in the 1950s with today's advertising or investigating the social consequences of broken treaties for Native Americans in the 1800s, you'll probably need to rely on at least some sources from the time period you're exploring.

What are the conventions of the source?

Scholarly journals have specific conventions, such as the necessity of citation of sources, the use of specialized language, a consideration of different points of view on an issue, and an absence of advertisements. Articles in commercial publications such as magazines or newspapers will be written for a more general audience, and authors may or may not cite their sources. Commercial publications will have advertisements, and one of their primary goals is to make a profit. Some sources might appear to be scholarly, but present a biased point of view without carefully considering what other researchers have said about the subject.

5.15: Learn by Doing – Practicing Evaluating Sources

Imagine that your political science professor has given you the following assignment:

> Write a 10–12 page research paper exploring recent conflicts between Democrats and Republicans about immigration policies with Mexico. Consider different points of view on the issue and then make an argument about what you think the U.S. immigration policy with Mexico should be. Imagine that you are going to deliver this report to the Congress and Senate: your audience is Senators and Congressmen from both parties.

Individually or in small groups, think about whether the sources below would be reliable enough to include in the research paper. Discuss your evaluation of the sources with classmates.

Here are the sources to evaluate:

1. Statistics about the effect of Mexican immigrants on the U.S. economy from a Web site published by The American Immigration Council (www.americanimmigrationcouncil.org/).
2. Information from a book on the history of immigration from Mexico to the United States published by Princeton University Press in 1991.
3. An interview with a first-generation American citizen whose family immigrated to the United States from Mexico.
4. Quotes from an editorial on immigration policy written by a Democratic Senator and published in *The New York Times*.
5. Projected immigration trends published by the U.S. Immigration and Naturalization Service on a *.gov* domain.
6. Your personal experiences working with immigrant workers from Mexico.
7. An article by a political science professor in the *American Journal of Political Science* arguing in favor of more open borders.
8. Quotes from a political commentator who appeared on a Fox news special about immigration.
9. Information from an article about the government's immigration policies published in *Rolling Stone* magazine.
10. Quotes from a book arguing for stricter immigration policies written by a former border patrol agent and published in 2007 by Patriot Press.

Integrating and Responding to Sources

Throughout this chapter, we've been comparing research writing in college to joining a conversation. When you write a research paper, you're not just summarizing what everyone else has said about a topic, and you're also not just stating your opinions without carefully considering what other experts have said about the topic. You're having a conversation on the topic with the experts (your sources), and through this conversation you're figuring out what you think and feel.

Here's one of the paragraphs from Lydia Tolman's essay, "The Rise of Starbucks," from earlier in this chapter. As you read the paragraph, think about the ways that Lydia is *joining the conversation* and integrating sources:

> If teenagers, however, were the only patrons of Starbucks, I would write the Starbucks' coffee cup status symbol off as a long-lived fad similar to the popular brightly colored Livestrong bracelet and its many copycats. However, apparently the adult population's addiction is just as big, if not bigger, than the teen's obsession with the little white and green cups. Jon Markman calls this trend "a lust for status emblems...that we carry around in our collective cerebral cortex" (Markman). The compulsion to carry this coffee cup rather than, say, a fifty cent gas station cup of practically the same coffee is similar to the "compunction among women to paint their fingernails" and the reasons that businesspeople shake hands (Markman). When a woman paints her fingernails, for example, that woman is sending a subtle message to others that she does not do physical labor, and when businesspeople shake hands they are showing each other "that neither bears the calluses of hard labor" (Markman). In other words, by carrying an over-priced cup of coffee, I can effectively and skillfully prove that I am wealthy enough to not care about how much my coffee costs.

Notice how Lydia starts the paragraph by giving her own thoughts on one aspect of the rise of Starbucks: if teenagers were the only ones obsessed with Starbucks, she'd write it off as a fad, but it's more than a fad because adults are also obsessed. To help support this assertion and explain why Starbucks is also an obsession for adults, Lydia integrates some opinions from Jon Markman, a contributing editor to *MSN Money*. Lydia quotes a distinctive phrase that really captures Markman's voice – "a lust for status emblems...that we carry around in our collective cerebral cortex." Then Lydia integrates a few more of Markman's phrases, but she does this without losing her own voice. Notice that Lydia has smoothly integrated her thoughts and Markman's thoughts in the next few sentences. In the final sentence, Lydia summarizes Markman's ideas in her own words. She says, "In other words," and then goes on to summarize the *conver-*

sation she's had with Markman. Lydia balances her own thoughts and language with Markman's ideas and language.

Citing Sources: Hypothetical Examples

Let's say you were given the following research paper assignment in a political science course:

> Write a 10-page research paper arguing for or against one of the provisions of the USA Patriot Act. Your audience for this essay is educated readers, a group that could include conservatives, moderates, and liberals. Since your goal is to persuade your audience, you'll need to back up your assertions with information from credible sources that don't have an overt political agenda.

Now let's say that you've done some research and collected information and opinions from a variety of sources, including a book about the Patriot Act by a professor at the University of Chicago and an article about the Patriot Act in a political science journal. Consider that the information below is taken directly from these hypothetical sources that you'd like to use in your research paper:

Excerpt from *The Patriot Act Controversy*, a Scholarly Book Written by Juwanda Thomas, a Political Science Professor at the University of Chicago

Perhaps the most controversial provision of the Patriot Act is section 215, which deals with the implied right of the FBI to access library records of U.S. citizens. This provision allows the FBI to obtain a secret warrant from the Foreign Intelligence Surveillance Court (FISA) to access library records of anyone suspected of spying or international terrorism. Librarians and the ACLU have fought this provision, arguing that it violates a patron's rights.

Excerpt from the Article, "Human Rights and the Patriot Act," Written by Felix Gomez and Published in a Political Science Journal

The provision of the Patriot Act that is most often seen as anti-constitutional is the authority of government agents to search library records of those they suspect of terrorism or spying. Although the Justice Department claims that this provision cannot be used to investigate American citizens who are not suspected of spying or of having a connection with international terrorism, the ACLU has filed a lawsuit on behalf of a number of American Muslim groups that have had their library records searched without probable cause. The ACLU claims that section 215 violates the First Amendment of the Constitution. Given the history of unconstitutional FBI investigations into groups that were not a threat to the United States but simply disagreed with the political establishment (e.g. Civil Rights and anti-war groups in the 1960s), one has to remain sceptical of the Justice Department's claim that their investigation of library records will be limited to those suspected of spying or international terrorism. Suspending our constitutional rights is a dangerous path, and it's one we should go down carefully – if at all.

Let's take a look at some sample paragraphs from a hypothetical student research paper that cites these sources. Read the first sample paragraph and think about whether or not the writer has done a good job of integrating the sources:

> Perhaps the most controversial provision of the Patriot Act is section 215, which deals with the implied right of the FBI to access library records of U.S. citizens" (Thomas 24). Section 215 allows the FBI to "obtain a secret warrant from the Foreign Intelligence Surveillance Court (FISA)" and "access library records of anyone suspected of spying or international terrorism" (Thomas 24). I agree with the ACLU that section 215 violates the constitution. As Felix Gomez argues, "Given the history of unconstitutional FBI investigations into groups that were not a threat to the United States but simply disagreed with the political establishment (e.g. Civil Rights and anti-war groups in the 1960s), one has to remain sceptical of the Justice Department's claim that their investigation of library records will be limited to those suspected of spying or international terrorism" (Gomez 12).

The sample paragraph above is a case where the writer is simply "cutting and pasting" information and ideas from sources. The writer isn't really in a conversation with the sources, and there are no opinions, ideas, or reflections from the writer's point of view. Even if the writer paraphrased the information and ideas she quoted, it would just be one piece of information after another from sources, with no reflection from the student writer.

Let's look at another sample paragraph from the same hypothetical student essay:

> There's a delicate balance between respecting constitutional rights and protecting American citizens from terrorism, but one provision of the Patriot Act that fails to reach a balance is section 215. Section 215 gives the FBI the right to get a secret warrant and gain access to library records of American citizens suspected of spying or international terrorism (Thomas 24). This may not sound unconstitutional at first, but the problem is whether or not we trust the FBI to limit their searches to those citizens who are truly involved in spying or terrorism. As political scientists Felix Gomez point outs, the FBI has a history of conducting unconstitutional investigations of groups that weren't involved in spying or terrorism (12). Gomez mentions 1960s anti-war groups as an example, and who's to say that the FBI won't

search the records of groups that are against the Iraq war, even if there's no evidence that these modern anti-war groups are involved in spying or terrorism? As Gomez argues, "Suspending our constitutional rights is a dangerous path, and it's one we should go down carefully—if at all" (12). I think the U.S. has made a mistake and the Patriot Act is taking us down a very dangerous path.

In this paragraph, the student writer is not merely stringing together information and ideas from the two outside sources. The writer begins the paragraph by talking about her own thoughts on the "delicate balance" between respecting the constitution and protecting Americans, and argues that section 215 goes too far. The writer supports this argument with some ideas from Gomez, but notice how she adds to the conversation by expanding on Gomez's point about the FBI investigating anti-war groups. When the writer does quote an entire passage from an outside source, it's done to capture Gomez's voice and language.

When you're integrating sources in college writing, it's important to keep in mind the genre and academic field you're working in. For example, in scientific reports frequent or extended quotations are rare because the results of scientific research are more important than the words of individual researchers. In the arts and humanities, most genres of research writing contain frequent quotes from individual authors, and longer block quotes are common. In the arts and humanities, writers often cite outside sources to show how their own arguments add something new to the conversation, but in the sciences the purpose of citing sources is often to show how the writer's research connects to previous studies and is therefore a valid approach. We'll talk more about these differences between different academic fields in Part III, but keep in mind that looking at examples of the genre of the research writing you've been assigned can help give you a sense of the ways that outside sources are integrated.

Earlier in this chapter, I said that in college research, you're not looking for "The Truth" about a topic or the "correct" argument or answer to a controversial issue. If you were to research a topic like the Patriot Act, you'd find out that the experts disagree about whether it's constitutional. Some scholars argue strongly that it isn't constitutional, and some say that it is constitutional. Some members of Congress want to overturn the Patriot Act, and some are in favor of renewing it. Such controversy is the challenge of college-level research, and this is also what makes college research more interesting than simply reporting *objective facts* about a topic. You're going to have to think critically about what you're reading and decide for yourself where you stand.

5.16: Learn by Doing – Practicing Integrating Sources

For this activity, imagine that an environmental science professor has given you a research project that involves evaluating the effectiveness of a solution to an environmental problem. You choose to evaluate the use of electric cars as a solution to the world's reliance on oil. Use any information you want from the following hypothetical excerpts to create a paragraph evaluating electric cars as an alternative to cars that use oil:

Excerpt from page 49 of a book on alternative fuels by Peter Grandby, an environmentalist from the Sierra Club

Not only do electric cars use no oil, they create far less pollution than cars that use gasoline. An electric car emits 90% less CO_2 than a car that uses gasoline. By switching to electric cars, we can dramatically reduce global warming and prevent oil companies from drilling off coastal shores and in natural preserves in places like Alaska. If we want to save our environment, we need to think electric.

Excerpt from page 231 of an article by environmental science professor Min Lui in the *Journal of Technology and the Environment*

Some critics of electric cars argue that they are too limited in terms of their size and power to catch on in America, but these critics have misrepresented the electric car. You might not realize that electric cars look exactly like gasoline-powered cars, and they have the same interior and body. They are just as safe as gasoline-powered cars, and just as reliable. They are also just as powerful. The Tesla Roadster, a new electric sports car, can go 0 to 60 in four seconds, and can reach speeds of up to 130 miles an hour.

Excerpt from a statement by a mechanical engineer in an article on the Web site *Environmental Engineering Clearinghouse*

Environmentalists who are jumping on the electric car bandwagon have failed to consider the limitations of electric cars. Americans love their road trips, but your average electric car has a range of only 50–80 miles before it needs to be recharged. If you want perks like a radio or air conditioning in your electric car, then it's going to be a big drain on the battery. Cost is also an issue. For example, the new Tesla Roadster is $90,000, which is far more than most sports cars on the market. Environmentalists should look to other forms of alternative vehicles, such as hybrids, if they want to truly make a positive environmental impact in the near future.

Advice for Integrating Sources

- **Annotate your sources as you research.**

In Chapter 4, we discussed some strategies for annotating texts. Keep these strategies in mind as you conduct research and begin to think about what information and ideas you might integrate into the paper. The better the job you do of underlining key words and ideas and writing down your responses and questions as you research, the easier the time you'll have when you're ready to start integrating your sources. On notecards or in a research notebook or computer file, keep track of the bibliographic information (author, title, publisher, date of publication), the main ideas of the author, your initial responses, and key quotes you might integrate.

- **Keep a double-entry journal as you research**

One technique for active reading that we discussed in Chapter 4 is the double-entry journal. The double-entry journal is a great research paper tool because it helps you keep track of the main ideas of everything you're reading and also encourages you to begin responding to what you're reading. Your double-entry journal responses could be the starting point for your research paper.

- **Write summaries of your sources in your own words**

When you integrate sources, most of the time you'll find yourself putting an author's ideas or information in your own words, rather than constantly quoting passages from your sources. You don't want to simply string together quotes, and the voice of your research paper will sound more consistent if you take ideas and put them in your own words. To help you put things in your words, try writing a one-paragraph summary of every source you read. This will force you to put the ideas in your own words (but don't forget to cite your sources in your paper, even if you're putting ideas in your own words).

- **Balance information and ideas from outside sources with your own ideas and reflections.**

As you draft your research paper and begin to integrate sources, try to find a balance between what experts have said about a topic, what you think of what these experts have said, and your own arguments or solutions. Remember that you're now participating in the conversation on this topic, so don't let the other experts drown out your voice and opinions. On the flip side, don't completely take over the conversation. Remember to consider what other experts have said, and respond to what they've said.

- **Avoid direct quotes unless you're capturing an author's tone or a distinctive phrase.**

If you have direct quote after direct quote from sources in a paragraph or an entire paper, at a certain point you give up ownership of your own writing. The paper becomes primarily the voice of the sources you found, with little of your own voice. In general, it's a good idea to use direct quotes only when you're trying to capture an author's tone or a provocative thing they've said.

- **Use reporting verbs to indicate when you are quoting or paraphrasing a source.**

It's helpful to your readers when you introduce quotes or paraphrases by using *reporting verbs*, as in: "Levitz *argues*..." or "anthropology professor Sharif Ahad *believes*..." Using titles such as *anthropology professor* or *President of the National Organization of Women* along with the name and a reporting verb is a good idea, since it helps to persuade your audience of the credibility of the sources you're using. Here are some common reporting verbs:

believes	says	feels	claims	maintains
observes	notes	suggests	thinks	indicates
asserts	reports	shows	insists	points out

Although it's good to vary the reporting verbs so your writing doesn't sound repetitive, keep in mind that each of these reporting verbs has a different connotation. For example, *argues* implies a stronger assertion than *claims*, and *says* has a less assertive connotation than *contends* or *insists*. *Reports* has connotations that the author is relaying information that he or she is confident is true, but *suggests* implies that the author is not stating something that he or she believes to be a definitely proven fact.

- **If you're feeling overwhelmed by your research, write a draft without any outside sources.**

After doing a lot of research, it's easy to become overwhelmed by everything you've read about your topic. Sometimes too much information can be a bad thing. You might feel overwhelmed or lost in all of your books and articles. Try writing a draft of parts of your research paper (or even a draft of the entire paper) from only your point of view and in your own words, without using any information directly from your sources. Of course, if you've done a lot of research, your point of view will be influenced by what you've read, but you can go back and begin citing sources later, in the next drafts. You can also use this technique if you have some paragraphs that are merely a collage of sources. Try writing the paragraph without any outside sources, completely from your own point of view. Then go back in the next drafts and start integrating outside sources.

• **Read models of the genre of research writing you've been assigned to gain a sense of the conventions for integrating outside sources.**

Remember that different research genres and different academic fields have different conventions for integrating sources – there are no universal rules for integrating sources that can apply to every college writing situation. The way a social scientist will integrate outside sources in a case study will be much different from the way an art historian will integrate sources in an article for an art journal. Finding models of the kind of research genre you've been assigned can give you a sense of the citation conventions used in that genre.

Understanding and Avoiding Plagiarism

5.17: Writing to Learn – The Importance of Citing Sources

You've probably written research papers and cited your sources, but have you ever thought about why it's so important to cite your sources? In a five-minute freewrite, explore the question of why it's so important to acknowledge where you are getting ideas and information from. Be prepared to share your answers with the class as a whole.

The Need to Cite Sources

An important part of integrating sources into a college research paper in American academic culture is acknowledging the sources of any information or ideas that are not your own or that aren't common knowledge. This usually involves in-text citations and a bibliography or reference list at the end of the paper. In-text citations are the places in your essay for acknowledging where you've obtained information or ideas from outside sources, and you cite those sources in parentheses or in footnotes. A bibliography (*References* or *Works Cited* page) appears at the end of your research paper as a list of all of the sources you cited and their publication information. The different ways of citing sources might be confusing at first. You might be asking yourself, how do I decide if I should be using a Works Cited or

References page? When do I use footnotes? Why are there so many different ways of citing sources? Wouldn't it be easier if there was one way of doing it? In this section, we'll look at the most common questions students have about citing sources.

Common Questions about Citing Sources

- **Why is it important to cite your sources?**

One reason citing your sources is so important in college writing is an ethical issue. If you use someone else's information or ideas without giving them credit, it's considered a type of cheating because you're taking credit for someone else's ideas. It's also important to cite your sources so your readers can have access to them if they want to. Think of your readers, and let them know where the information and ideas you are using came from so they can find your sources to evaluate them or to connect them to research that they're doing. If academic writing is a conversation, it's important to let your readers know who you're having a conversation with. Keep in mind that this emphasis on citing your sources is part of a specific type of academic culture. In some cultures it's common for students to begin an essay with information, ideas, and quotes from well-known authors without necessarily citing the authors, and this is an accepted convention. Even though I've been emphasizing that writing college research papers is more than repeating what others have said about your topic, in some cultures, students are expected to rely on outside sources and even to repeat them verbatim in their writing as a show of respect to the cultural tradition. If you're coming to college from a country with a different academic tradition, you might need to adjust your writing to adapt to the new academic culture. Keep in mind these different cultural traditions: the more knowledge you have of different ways of writing, the better writer you'll be. Just be aware that in the culture of academic writing which you will encounter in the United States and many other countries you're expected to cite your sources any time you use someone else's words, ideas, or information.

- **Do I need to cite something that I already knew before I began my research or something that is common knowledge?**

Let's say you're doing research on identity theft, and you had a friend who was a victim of identity theft. Because of this friend, you know a lot about what steps to take to protect yourself from identity theft and what to do if you become a victim of identity theft. What if you did some research and found a book about identity theft that made some suggestions you already knew about? Do you need to cite the book? Technically, since you already knew the information, it wouldn't be necessary to cite it. But in college writing, it's not a bad idea to find sources that support what you already know about a topic, as a way to persuade your audience that the experts agree with the points you're making. In this situation you might let your readers know that you have knowledge of the topic because of what happened to your friend, but you might also cite the book for extra support. On almost any topic you write about, there will be *common knowledge* that you don't need to cite. Common knowledge is information that is shared by all of the members of a specific community. It's common knowledge that John F. Kennedy died in 1963 and that poverty is a major social problem in America. Keep in mind that *common knowledge* always depends on the rhetorical situation. If your economics professor asks you to write a research paper exploring the impact of NAFTA as if you're preparing a report for Mexican, Canadian, and U.S. economists, the common knowledge will be much different than if the research paper is aimed at general readers. For example, it will be common knowledge among your audience of economists that NAFTA is an acronym for North American Free Trade Agreement and that NAFTA is a trade agreement made among the United States, Mexico, and Canada.

- **How many different kinds of citation styles will I need to use in college, and how will I know which ones to use?**

A citation style is a convention for citing sources that's agreed upon by members of a specific academic community. For example, in the arts, foreign languages, and literature, the citation style that is most common is MLA, which is an abbreviation for Modern Language Association. In social sciences such as anthropology, sociology, and psychology, APA style is most common. APA is an abbreviation for American Psychological Association. In natural sciences such as biology, chemistry, physics, and astronomy, authors typically use CSE style, short for Council of Science Editors. You might encounter Chicago style in a history course, and there are other citation styles you might encounter as you move into your major (e.g. electrical engineering has its own citation style). Usually, your professor will let you know which citation style to use for a particular field of study, and if you're not sure, ask your professor. In Part III, we'll talk more about MLA, APA, and CSE citation styles.

- **Why are there so many different citation styles? Why can't there be one style to make referencing easier?**

In the arts, foreign languages, and literature, the reputation of the authors you're citing tends to be more important than the date a book or article was published. In MLA style, you cite the author and page number in an in-text citation, but not the date of publication. In the sciences, the year when a study was conducted is usually important, since what counts as knowledge in science changes more rapidly than it does in the humanities, and usually you need to cite the most recent studies in science research papers. Therefore, citation styles like APA and CSE emphasize the year of publication, and you include the year a book or the results of a study were published in the in-text citation. Keep in mind that some college professors emphasize correct citation style, and they will want you to follow the MLA or APA guidelines very carefully, making sure that all of the commas and periods are in the right places. Other professors will be more focused on making sure that you've acknowledged your sources and that readers won't have a problem finding your sources, and these professors won't mark you down for a missing comma or putting a period in the wrong place.

- **What is plagiarism, and how can I avoid it?**

Plagiarism is such a serious issue in college writing that it's worth devoting time and attention to it. The final section of this chapter is all about understanding plagiarism.

What you Need to Know about Plagiarism

5.18: Writing to Learn – Your Definition of *Plagiarism*

Before you read a definition of plagiarism from the Council of Writing Program Administrators, let's see what you already think about what exactly plagiarism is. Write about how you would define plagiarism. Be prepared to share your definition in small groups or with the class as a whole.

In your definition of plagiarism in Writing to Learn Activity 5.18, did you think about the differences between intentional plagiarism and unintentional plagiarism? The definition of plagiarism from the Council of Writing Program Administrators focuses on *deliberate* use of someone else's ideas without acknowledging them. Here is the WPA's definition of plagiarism:

> Plagiarism occurs when a writer deliberately uses someone else's language, ideas, or other original (not common-knowledge) material without acknowledging its source. (Council of Writing Program Administrators, 2003)

If you try to cite your sources, but you use the wrong format or incorrectly use quotation marks, you're not going to fail a course or be suspended from school for plagiarism. Plagiarizing means *deliberately* presenting someone else's ideas as if they were your own. The Internet makes access to term paper mills easy, and some students give in to the temptation to buy an essay online and turn it in as if they'd written it. Turning in an essay you've bought or copied and acting as if it is your own work is a serious kind of plagiarism with serious consequences. If you do this, you could not only fail the course, but you could be suspended or even forced to leave school. If you integrate one or more outside sources in your essay but then never cite the source(s) in your text or in a bibliography, that's also a form of plagiarism. Using an essay you've written in one course for a different course is another form of plagiarism (*self-plagiarism*). Most colleges have an honor code that discusses the consequences for plagiarism, and it would be a good idea to check out your school's honor code.

5.19: Learn by Doing – Understanding Plagiarism

Practice recognizing what is and what isn't plagiarism by looking at some sample paragraphs. The excerpt below is from an article about college education by Ernest Boyer:

> The focus on individuality, on the personal benefits and the utility of education, has a right tradition in American higher education. Throughout the years, students have come to college to pursue their own goals, to follow their own aptitudes, to become productive, self-reliant human beings, and, with a new knowledge, to continue learning after college days are over. (Boyer, 2003: 31)

What follows are some hypothetical sample paragraphs from a student essay that integrate Boyer's ideas. Read over each of these passages, and in small groups or with your class as a whole discuss whether or not there is any plagiarism and why or why not. If there is plagiarism, does it appear to be intentional or unintentional?

Student Essay Paragraph #1
A focus on individuality, on the personal benefits of education, has a strong tradition in American colleges. I think that throughout time, students have attended college to pursue their own goals, to become productive human beings, and to continue to learn after college.

Student Essay Paragraph #2

I think that a focus on the individual is a significant tradition in colleges in America. Students have always attended colleges to "pursue their own goals, to follow their own aptitudes, to become productive, self-reliant human beings, and, with a new knowledge, to continue learning after college days are over."

Student Essay Paragraph #3

I agree with Boyer's argument that the focus on individuality is an important tradition in U.S. colleges. Boyer feels that students come to college to "pursue their own goals, to follow their own aptitudes, to become productive, self-reliant human beings, and, with a new knowledge, to continue learning after college days are over" (31). I am a perfect example of what Boyer is arguing, because I came to college to find a career that matches my abilities and to gain new knowledge I couldn't get anywhere else.

Review of Key Ideas in Chapter 5

- College professors will ask you to go beyond the basic research skills you learned in high school. College research projects are lengthier, require more extensive research, and require more than simply finding a few book or articles.

- Much of your high school research probably involved reporting information, but college research focuses on adding something new to the conversation on your topic and not just regurgitating what others have said. This might mean conducting some original research, taking a stance on an issue, or arguing for a solution to a problem.

- College research is focused on inquiry. Inquiry involves exploring an open-ended question, thinking about what others have written, and then forming your own position. Inquiry could also involve designing an experiment or conducting some of your own research through interviews or surveys.

- Like college writing and college reading, college research is a process. Each research assignment you have in college will require a different process: there's no one right way to conduct research or a formula for all of college research. Most research writing assignments, however, require you to find a research question, locate a variety of sources, and integrate and cite these sources.

- Most of your college research assignments will require you to find scholarly sources. These are peer-reviewed sources written by an expert in the field, and they are typically published by academic presses – publishers connected to a university or a professional organization.
- Most college research requires you to find a balance between integrating sources and presenting your own responses to the sources, ideas, and arguments about the topic. Integrating sources means having a conversation with other experts on your subject, and not merely stringing together quotes.
- It's important to make a distinction between intentional and unintentional plagiarism. If you try to cite your sources, but you use the wrong format or incorrectly use quotation marks, you're not going to fail a course or be suspended from school for plagiarism. However, using a paper from an online term paper mill or deliberately using information without citing sources is a serious offense.

5.20: Writing to Learn – Reflecting on Researching Processes

Now that you've explored college researching processes in depth, write down three things about researching processes that you learned from this chapter, and three questions you still have about researching in college. Share these questions in small groups and with the class as a whole.

Writing Projects for Part II

Writing Project II.1: Reading, Writing, and Researching Processes Self-Survey

Prompt

Fill out the reading, writing, and researching processes survey below and then write a 3–4 page reflection on the survey in which you reflect on the strengths and weaknesses of your literacy processes and think about how you could improve your literacy processes as a college student.

Purpose

The purpose of this self-survey is to help you to reflect on your own reading, writing, and researching processes and to begin to think about how you could improve as a reader, writer, and researcher in college. One way to "take stock" of your own literacy is to fill out a survey. By filling out this survey and reflecting on the results, you'll become more aware of your own reading, writing, and researching habits, and you'll have a better idea of what you need to improve upon in college.

Audience

Since the purpose of this survey is for you to explore your own literacy processes and reflect on them, *you* are the primary audience for this writing project. Your professor will be reading your reflection on the survey and evaluating how carefully and in-depth you've thought about your own reading, writing, and researching processes; but the primary audience for this project is you. Write your reflection as though you are "talking to yourself." Of course, since eventually your peers and your professor will read what you've written and give you feedback, your reflections should be more structured than a freewrite done only for yourself.

Genre

A reflection letter or reflection memo is a type of writing you will probably encounter in your college career. Your professors might ask you to reflect on your writing process in a portfolio reflection letter; they might assign a reflection essay in the beginning of the semester to have you reflect on your current knowledge of a subject; or they might assign a final reflection essay to have you think about what you've learned over the course of a semester. In this reflection memo, you'll want to make sure you evaluate your strengths and weaknesses as a reader, writer, and researcher, and think about how you could improve your literacy processes as a college student; but it's up to you to decide how you want to organize the reflection. Since you're the primary audience, your writing tone and style can be personal and conversational, but make sure that your final draft is edited so that your peers and professor will be able to understand what you're trying to say.

Conventions

The reflection letter is exploratory, and there's no specific organizational structure you need to follow. Since this is an exploratory and personal essay, and since *you* are the primary audience, your grammar and mechanics don't need to be perfect. But make sure that your final draft is edited well enough that any mechanical problems or other types of errors don't interfere with your professor's or your peers' ability to understand what you have written.

Evaluation Criteria

The most important aspects of this project are the quality and depth of your thinking. Think hard about your strengths and weaknesses and do a thorough job of explaining what you need to improve on in your college career and why. You don't need to sound "academic" in this reflection, and it's perfectly acceptable to write this in a conversational tone, as if you're talking to yourself. You want your peers and professor to be able to understand your reflections, so it's important to edit your final draft, but focus more on content than grammar and mechanics.

Survey Questions

Multiple choice: Circle all answers that apply.

1. *I usually write essays for school* (a) in one draft (b) in two or three drafts (c) in more than three drafts.

2. *In my typical writing process for school assignments, revising means* (a) editing for errors (b) changing a few sentences or paragraphs (c) rethinking the purpose, organization, and content of my essay.

3. *I usually edit for grammar and mechanics* (a) while I'm writing my first draft (b) after the first draft but before the final draft (c) when I have a final draft.

4. *When I'm having difficulty writing an essay, I usually* (a) struggle through it on my own (b) get help from a friend or classmate (c) get help from the teacher.

5. *When I am given a writing assignment, I usually start writing* (a) a day or two before the assignment is due (b) a few weeks before the assignment is due (c) soon after the assignment is given.

6. *In my reading for school (high school or college), in the last year I've read* (a) 1 book (b) 2–4 books (c) more than 4 books (d) I haven't read a book for school in the last year.

7. *When I'm confused by something I read for a school assignment, I* (a) ask a peer for help (b) ask the teacher for help (c) do not ask for help.

8. *When I am given a reading assignment, I usually start reading* (a) the night before the reading is going to be discussed in class (b) a day or two before the reading will be discussed in class (c) soon after the reading assignment is given.

9. *In high school, my primary purpose for reading was usually* (a) memorizing information for a test (b) understanding the author's main points (c) thinking critically about the author's ideas.

10. *When I conduct research for a research paper, I usually* (a) just surf the Internet for sources (b) try to find a few books and articles on the topic (c) search the Internet, search academic databases, and search for scholarly books or articles.

11. *To find a research question or topic, I usually* (a) try to find one on my

own (b) start doing some research to help me find a topic (c) discuss ideas for research questions with my teacher (d) discuss ideas for research questions with a reference librarian.

12. *In high school, I conducted primary research through* (a) experiments (b) interviews (c) surveys (d) I did not conduct primary research in high school.

13. *For research paper assignments, I've used* (a) MLA style (b) APA style (c) other referencing styles besides MLA and APA (d) I've never been asked to use a referencing style.

14. *The longest research project I've ever written was* (a) 5 or fewer pages (b) 6–10 pages (c) 11–20 pages (d) more than 20 pages.

15. *Usually when I conduct research I* (a) annotate the sources (b) keep some kind of a research journal (c) keep notecards on the sources (d) I do not keep notes when I research.

True or False: Circle (a) True or (b) False depending on whether the statement applies to you.

1. *I usually write essays in one draft.* (a) True (b) False

2. *In high school I wrote something for classes every day.* (a) True (b) False

3. *My final draft is better if I get feedback during the writing process.* (a) True (b) False

4. *The main goal of writing in school is to give teachers what they want.* (a) True (b) False

5. *When I don't understand something, I reread it.* (a) True (b) False

6. *I read with a pen or pencil or highlighter in hand and take notes as I read.* (a) True (b) False

7. *The main purpose of reading in school is to get information.* (a) True (b) False

8. *In most of my experiences with writing research papers, I just report what others have said about the topic.* (a) True (b) False

9. *It's better to come up with a thesis before you start researching a subject.* (a) True (b) False

10. *For most research papers, you can do all of your research on the Internet.* (a) True (b) False

Writing Project II.2: Reading, Writing, and Researching Advice for Future College Students

Prompt

As a class, write a college reading, writing, and researching guide for future college students. The guide can be in the form of a series of handouts, a pamphlet, a small book, a Web site, PowerPoint slides, or even a video saved on a CD or DVD, or posted on *YouTube* or another video sharing Internet site. Your professor might have each student write an individual part of the guide, or have you work in small groups to create parts of the guide (e.g. one group might focus only on researching).

Purpose

The purpose of this project is to take the information about college reading, writing, and researching provided in Part II and your own personal experiences with college literacy and put that information in your own words. Writing a guide to college writing will help you review what you've learned and also help future college students, since your professor can make the guide available to future classes. This project will also give you practice writing to a wider audience beyond the classroom. Since this is a collaborative class project, you'll be gaining experience with collaborative writing and learning.

Audience

Your audience for this essay is future college students. Keep in mind that you're not writing this guide to your professor. The goal is not to show the professor what you know, but to provide useful information to other college students. Think of ways to write and format the guide to appeal to your audience. This might mean using words *and* images, or if you're creating a Web site, using links and even sound. If you have video editing equipment, you could even add video to your Web site or create the guide in the form of a video burned to a CD or DVD or posted on YouTube.

Genre

You've seen a variety of different genres of informative guides in such forms as books, handouts, instruction sheets, pamphlets, PowerPoints, Web sites, and others. You can use these models to help you create your class guide. Usually an informative guide is not written in an essay format, with an introduction, a conclusion, and standard paragraph formatting. Typically, guidebooks or Web sites that focus on giving information and advice are concise and easy to read, with bulleted lists of advice and examples to illustrate ideas for the reader. Informative guides will have some interesting graphic design to appeal to the reader, and the author will make use of elements such as headings, colored fonts, images, and other attractive and attracting features to catch the reader's eye, so keep in mind what you've learned about visual rhetoric. Even though you want to appeal to the reader through graphic design, the content still needs to be good enough to keep the reader interested. You need to give your readers solid advice that they will find useful.

Conventions

There's no single format for a guide book or informative Web site. Since your audience will probably skim your guide for information, you might want to use short sentences and design features such as bulleted lists or boxed text. If you create a Web site or pamphlet that has long paragraphs in essay form, you might lose your readers, since they're reading for quickly accessible information and not for detailed description or analysis. Find some examples of whatever kind of guide you're writing (book, pamphlet, Web site, DVD) and note the conventions of these models. Even though you will probably want to write this guide in an informal or conversational style (since your audience is future students), you'll still want to edit the final draft carefully. Your audience may not trust the advice you're giving them if the writing isn't carefully edited.

Evaluation Criteria

Audience will play a big role in how this guide will be evaluated, in addition to selectivity and originality. You should focus on providing useful advice, appealing to your audience through your writing style, and using formatting and graphic design tools to capture your reader's interest. You will be evaluated both on your ability to select and to present key information, and on what you can add to the advice offered in this book: don't just repeat what's already been said in Part II, but add your own advice from your own experiences and in your own voice.

Writing Project II.3: Researched Academic Argument Portfolio

Prompt

Choose one of the student academic writing journals below and write a researched academic argument for possible submission and publication in the journal. In order to gain a sense of the conventions of the journal you might submit your essay to, before you begin writing your researched argument, do a 2–3 page rhetorical analysis of the journal (see Writing Project #3 in Part I for advice about writing a rhetorical analysis). As you draft and revise your essay, save each draft in a separate file, and when you've completed the essay, write a 1–3 page process memo discussing your writing and researching processes and what you think are the strengths and weaknesses of the essay. Include the rhetorical analysis, the rough drafts, the final draft, and the process memo in a final portfolio.

Here are some college writing journals and writing contests that accept submissions from undergraduate students in any region:

Pittsburgh Undergraduate Review (www.pur.honorscollege.pitt.edu/)
Lethbridge Undergraduate Research Journal (http://www.lurj.org/)
Neo-Vox International Student Online Magazine (http://neovox.cortland.edu/weblog/)
Public Writing (http://scholarlyexchange.org/ojs/index.php/PW/index)
Young Scholars in Writing (http://cas.umkc.edu/english/publications/young

scholarsinwriting/index3.html)
Teen Ink Magazine (http://www.teenink.com/index.php)
The Nation student writing contest (www.thenation.com/node/33447)
The Atlantic student writing contest (www.theatlantic.com/)

You can also check to see if your college has an undergraduate writing or research journal.

Purpose

The purpose of this project is for you to practice a genre of college writing that you'll encounter throughout your college career: the academic research paper. Most college professors assign research papers because researching a debatable issue to find out what others have said and then taking a position within the debate is an important way to create new knowledge in every academic field. This project will give you practice applying the reading and researching skills we discussed in Chapters 4 and 5, and you'll also practice making the kinds of academic arguments we focused on in Chapter 2. By reflecting on your writing process in the process memo, you'll have a chance to discuss some of the aspects of writing processes we looked at in Chapter 3. This project will also give you some practice conducting a rhetorical analysis and writing for an audience and context beyond the professor or other students in a particular course. As you draft and revise your researched academic argument, be sure to refer back to the section on writing academic arguments in Chapter 2 and the section on academic researching processes in Chapter 5. Chapter 5 has advice for finding a research topic, locating and evaluating sources, and integrating and responding to your sources.

Audience

Your primary audience for the researched argument essay is the editors and readers of whatever journal you're writing for. In your rhetorical analysis, think carefully about this audience and consider the kinds of research genres published in the journal, the conventions of format and style of the essays published in the journal, and the purpose and target audience of the journal. When your peers and the professor respond to your researched argument, they can play the role of the editor and readers of the journal, since your ultimate goal is to publish an article in the journal.

Genre

Researched arguments are a common genre in any academic field. Exploring open-ended questions and taking a stance on a debatable issue is one of the primary ways scholars discuss subjects, explore issues in depth, and create new knowledge. Researched argument genres are different from informative report genres. When your professors ask you to take a position or write an argumentative research paper, they want you to do more than simply summarize what other writers have said about a topic. In a researched academic argument, the writer explores an open-ended question and takes a stance within a debate about a significant issue. Taking a stance doesn't usually mean arguing for or against something in a one-sided way. As we discussed in Chapter 2, academic arguments usually involve careful consideration of many different perspectives in the debate, and the inclusion of different voices in the conversation through citation of outside sources. The academic researched argument is usually focused on inquiry, as we discussed in Chapter 5. Refer back to Chapters 2 and 5 to review the genre of the academic researched argument.

Conventions

The rhetorical analysis you conduct of the journal you're writing for will dictate the conventions of your researched argument essay. Think about conventions of style, organization, format, citation, page length, and any other relevant factors when you conduct your rhetorical analysis. Also consider whether the essays published in the journal always stay within a specific set of conventions, or whether some of the essays expand on those conventions or even break with them entirely. Reread Lydia Tolman's "The Rise of Starbucks" and Matt Miles's "Personal Appearance and its Implications of Sexuality" to help you think about the conventions of academic researched arguments.

Evaluation Criteria

Your professor will play the role of the editor and reader of the journal when evaluating the final draft of your researched argument. Your professor will consider whether or not you've written in a style and form appropriate for your target journal, whether you've taken a stance within the debate or merely reported on what others have said, whether you've convinced your readers of your stance through support for your claims, and whether you've synthesized the ideas and arguments of other voices in conversation with your own position. Your professor will also consider if you've fully engaged in a process of drafting, revising, and editing, and if you've reflected on your process and evaluated the strengths and weaknesses of your essay in a process memo. The depth of thought in the rhetorical analysis of your target journal will also be an important part of the evaluation criteria, since it's critical that you have an understanding of the rhetorical situation for your researched argument.

Part III

Exploring Reading, Writing, and Researching across the Curriculum

6   Introduction to Writing across the Curriculum

You may discover that your professors in different fields have different expectations about how you should write, and part of the task you face in becoming a better writer is to identify and understand these differences.

—from *Writing Prose*, Yale University's student writing guide
(Yale University, 2001).

Academic writing is a single thing only in convenient arguments. If you collect samples of academic writing, within or across the disciplines, it has as many types and categories...as writing grouped under any other general category: magazine writing, business writing, political writing, sports writing.

—Professor David Bartholomae, English Department, University of Pittsburgh
(Bartholomae, 1995: 62)

Writing is so complex an activity, so closely tied to a person's intellectual development, that it must be nurtured and practiced over all the years of a student's schooling and in every curricular area.

—Professor Barbara Walvoord, Department of English, University of Notre Dame (Walvoord, 1990)

6.1: Writing to Learn – Your Communities

Write a list of the different communities you're a part of. For example, your list might look something like this:

My dorm
My college classes
The debate team
My family
Facebook
The restaurant where I work
Madden gamers online

Once you've made a list, compare the conventions of two different communities that you're a part of. What kind of language do people use when they talk or write? Are there texts that are part of the community? Are there *unwritten rules* that community members follow when they communicate?

Disciplines and Discourse Communities

Academic fields, such as psychology, civil engineering, and music history, are often referred to as *disciplines*. A discipline is a community of readers, writers, and researchers who use similar ways of thinking about the world to research and write. A community of scholars in a discipline such as biology, for example, will use similar research methods, write in similar genres, and follow similar conventions. The community of biologists have agreed that they will use the scientific method of hypothesis-testing as their primary research method, and as a community they have developed genres such as the lab report to share the results of their research among community members. These kinds of communities are often called *discourse communities*. John Swales, a writing scholar who has studied academic discourse communities, says that the defining features of a discourse community are that it has a common goal, a forum available to all of the participants, shared conventions and genres, specialized terminology, and a mix of expert and novice participants in the community (Swales, 1990). Here are the ways some other writing scholars have described disciplines and discourse communities:

> Disciplines are separate language communities with their own values, purposes, and forms for writing...
>> Professor Mark Waldo, English Department, University of Nevada Reno
>> (Waldo, 2003: 30)

> A "discourse community" is a group of people who share certain language using practices.
>> Professor Patricia Bizzell, Department of English, College of the Holy Cross
>> (Bizzell, 1992: 222)

> The academic discourse community isn't a complete or unified community to be initiated into. It already contains portions of the discourses that students... bring with them.
>> Professor Tom Fox, English Department, California State University Chico
>> (Fox, 1999: 59)

Even though disciplines share common texts, genres, and research methods, just like any discourse community, they don't always agree. In the discipline of composition professors, referred to as Rhetoric and Composition, there's a conflict about what kind of writing students should be doing in first-year writing courses. Some members of the discourse community of Rhetoric and Composition think students should write about personal topics and personal experiences. Other discourse community members in Rhetoric and Composition think students should write in the conventions of academic discourse so that they're better prepared for their courses beyond first-year writing. Other discourse community members challenge those who think that we should teach students a certain type of academic discourse in order to initiate them into academic writing, and they argue that students should also be taught to think critically about academic writing and to challenge the conventions of academic discourse. Even though the members of the field of rhetoric and composition disagree about many issues, they still consider themselves a discourse community: they talk on listservs, meet at conferences, read and publish in the same journals, and share specialized terminology.

The word *discipline* is used in flexible ways. Sometimes a discipline can be defined broadly, e.g. the social sciences, and sometimes a discipline can be defined in a narrow way, e.g. anthropology. Your school might have a College of Social Sciences that's made up of social science disciplines such as anthropology, sociology, and political science. There are also subdisciplines, e.g. cultural anthropology. The important thing to remember is that a discipline is a community of scholars with shared genres, texts, and research methods.

6.2: Learn by Doing – Investigating Disciplines at your College

The goal of this Learn by Doing activity is for you to think about disciplines by exploring the way your college Web site is organized. Go to the index page of your institution and find a link to academic departments or colleges. Does your institution have different colleges, and if so, how are they grouped? Which departments are represented in each college? Choose a department from each college and go to the index page of the department (if your institution isn't divided by colleges, choose any three different departments). Are there different subdisciplines within the departments? What are the subdisciplines, and how many are there? If there are subdisciplines, are there any further breakdowns of disciplines within any of these subdisciplines (e.g. can you tell if faculty have certain specialty areas within sub-disciplines)?

Reading, Writing, and Researching in General Education Courses

---

6.3: Writing to Learn – Goals of a College Education

Write about what you think are the major goals of a college education. You might explore questions like:

1. To what extent should a college education focus on workplace skills or academic skills?
2. Should students explore different fields of study their first few years of college, or should they pick a major subject right away?
3. To what extent is going to college about improving intellectually, and to what extent is it about getting a good job?

Most colleges have a general education or core curriculum program that's required of all students before they enter their major. The general education program usually involves taking introductory courses in a variety of academic fields – from the natural sciences, to the social sciences, to the arts and humanities. General education courses introduce you to reading, writing, and researching *across the curriculum*. In this context, *curriculum* means the courses and assignments in every department, across the entire institution. General education courses will give you your first taste of the reading, writing, and researching in different fields. In these introductory general education courses you'll practice some of the genres of different fields and you'll read books and articles that will introduce you to the ways of thinking and making arguments in different fields. After reading Part III of *Exploring College Writing* and doing the writing and reading activities in each chapter, you'll have a good idea of what to expect as you take introductory (general education or core curriculum) courses in the natural sciences, social sciences, and arts and humanities. You'll be better prepared for your general education courses and more confident about the reading, writing, and researching you'll be assigned.

Examples of General Education Mission Statements

One way to talk about what general education courses are is to look at some mission statements from general education programs at different colleges. A *mission statement* is a summary of the major goals of a business, an institution, or a program. Below are given the general education mission statements from Washington State University and the University of North Carolina at Asheville.

Washington State University's General Education Mission Statement
(http://gened.wsu.edu/overview/atWSU/)

Higher education is more about acquiring skills than assimilating an inert body of knowledge. To that end, WSU's General Education prepares students for life-long learning, equips them with research skills, and builds competence in evaluating information and constructing knowledge in multiple ways. Fundamental to all these skills is the ability to think critically.

WSU's General Education Program is designed to serve the following aims:
Provide a Foundation for the Major
To function well in the workplace, it is necessary to see beyond it. The General Education curriculum encourages integration of students' anticipated careers

within larger, more encompassing and multiple contexts. Exposure to different values, perspectives, and cultural traditions is a valuable preparation for the kinds of work that college graduates do, and this knowledge can significantly enrich awareness of the context and meaning of careers.

Realize Individual Student Potentials

A traditional purpose of higher education is to foster and develop potentials in the individual. General Education offers opportunities for personal enrichment and serves a variety of intellectual, aesthetic, and creative interests. The curriculum provides opportunities for introspection and testing one's own values as well as for enlarging one's vision. The several kinds of study required in General Education are designed to contribute to the development of higher intellectual skills, such as critical thinking, and essential communication skills.

Prepare for Membership in the Community

General Education prepares students for citizenship in a free society. The curriculum represents an effort to provide elements of the ever-changing body of valuable common knowledge. Shared knowledge and values growing out of common educational experience help to bind society together and make communication possible. Writing proficiency and information literacy are high priorities at WSU, and the foundation of these skills is laid in the General Education courses. The curriculum also provides opportunities for hands-on service learning and emphasizes study of the relevant past as a way for students to understand and engage contemporary issues.

Facilitate Integration of Knowledge

The breadth of General Education requirements reflects our historical experience of how new knowledge has been acquired and how it is likely to be acquired in the future. Consequently, the curriculum facilitates the acquisition of a working knowledge of a broad range of scholarly methods, from the arts and humanities to the sciences. One of the goals of General Education is to assist students to understand the characteristic ways of acquiring knowledge in different fields of study, and methods of verification and communication.

The University of North Carolina at Asheville's General Education Mission Statement
(http://www2.unca.edu/genedrev/Mission%20Statement%20and%20Goals.htm)

A liberating education—one that emphasizes humane values in thought and action and promotes the free and rigorous pursuit of truth—creates good citizens, individuals who assume responsibility for their thoughts and actions and their impact on the world. Their personal development is inextricably linked to the contributions they make to their scholarly, social, and political communities. To be good citizens, people must be able to think critically and to communicate their ideas. In serving UNCA's liberal arts mission, the General Education Program works alongside the majors to help people develop and improve these skills by immersing them in an interdisciplinary community of mutually supportive scholars.

At UNCA, primary responsibility for developing the ideas and methodologies to communicate within a disciplinary community lies with the major department. The purpose of the General Education Program is to provide a broader context for the discipline. General education offers exposure to the ideas essential for students to understand how their work in the major is part of a larger range of human concerns. With these ideas, people can make connections across the liberal arts. General education helps specialists learn to communicate with people in different scholarly communities and enables them to understand problems outside their areas of study. By promoting the integration, synthesis, and application of knowledge, general education provides individuals with an awareness of their role in a diverse culture and highlights their responsibilities to the larger community.

6.4: Writing to Learn – Reflection on the Mission of General Education

Reread the general education mission statements above and explore the following three questions:

1. What is the relationship between general education courses and coursework in the major, according to the two mission statements?
2. What are the key words in the two mission statements that help define *general education*?
3. To what extent do you agree or disagree with the statements made about general education in these two mission statements and why?

Be prepared to discuss what you've written with the class as a whole.

6.5: Learn by Doing – Exploring General Education at your College

The goal of this Learn by Doing activity is for you to look closely at general education or core curriculum courses and requirements at your college and think about the goals of the general education portion of the college curriculum. You may already have taken some general education (or core curriculum) courses, but even if you have, it's useful to reflect on your school's general education core curriculum program. For this Learn by Doing activity, you'll write a 1–2 page essay about your school's general education program. This essay may be read and responded to by your peers or your professor, so you'll want to communicate your ideas in a clear and organized way for your readers.

The first step in this activity is to visit the part of your school's Web site and/or catalog that describes the curriculum and specifically the requirements for general education courses. When you've found the Web site or catalog description, see if there's a mission statement, and if there is, read it over carefully. Next, take a look at what kind of courses are required. Which fields of study are represented? If you're at a four-year college, are there general education courses required for upper-division (junior and senior) as well as lower-division (first-year and sophomore) years of study? Once you've looked over the Web site, compare your school's general education program to the relevant sections of the mission statements from Washington State University and the University of North Carolina at Asheville. How are they similar and how are they different? If you've already taken general education courses, have you found that they match with the goals described on the college's Web site or in the school catalog?

Differences between the First-Year Writing Course and Writing in General Education Courses

First-year writing courses were created to help students make the transition from high school to college writing, and you're going to find that the writing practice and feedback you receive in first-year writing will help you in any general education or core course you take. Engaging in academic research and reading challenging texts in first-year writing is good practice for reading and researching across the curriculum. If you're asked to develop arguments and use evidence to support your positions in first-year writing essays, you're practicing a skill that you will need for almost all of your general education courses. Improving your own writing processes by practicing revision in first-year writing will translate to better writing processes in the papers you write for general education courses. Despite all of this practice and preparation, there is no way one or two first-year writing courses can prepare you for all of the kinds of writing you'll experience across the curriculum. As you make the transition from first-year writing to writing in your general education or core courses, keep in mind a few differences between the two:

- **First-year writing courses are small and designed to give you feedback on your writing from peers and the professor. General education courses are often larger and professors may not give you as much feedback on your writing.**

In your first-year writing course (or courses), you learn just how helpful it is to have feedback from an outside reader during the writing process. As you take general education courses, seek out feedback from classmates or your school's writing center, and don't be reluctant to visit your professors during their office hours to get feedback.

- **First-year writing courses give you a broad introduction to college writing. General education courses give you a broad introduction to writing in different disciplines.**

If the main purpose of a first-year writing course is to introduce you to college writing, the main purpose of an introduction to sociology or a history survey course is to introduce you to the ways of thinking and writing in that specific discipline. Each discipline has different genres, different research methods, and different types of readings. A first-year writing course can give you a solid foundation, but there's no way it can prepare you for all of the different kinds of reading, writing, and researching you'll do in your general education courses.

- **In first-year writing courses, you'll often be able to decide what voice you will write in, how your essay will be organized, and what kinds of evidence you'll use to support your ideas. In general education courses, you'll often need to learn the genres and conventions of the different college disciplines.**

In many first-year writing courses, professors encourage students to use *I* and to write about their personal experiences as evidence. First-year writing professors often ask students to let the purpose and audience of their writing dictate the form that it takes, and some even encourage students to mix genres or create their own genres. But in many of the genres students encounter in different disciplines, they won't be able to use *I* or write about their personal experiences because that's not part of the conventions; and in many courses, there will be forms and formats that students will be expected to learn before they can break out on their own. Genres in different disciplines are constantly changing and evolving, and new students like you will bring new ideas and new voices to the conversation of college writing and researching. It's important to keep in mind that general education courses will be your first experience with thinking and writing like a historian or a physicist or a sociologist, and you may need to learn the essentials of the genres and conventions and to demonstrate that knowledge before you attempt to expand on them.

Reading, Writing, and Researching in the Major

You make a transition from high school writing to college writing in your first-year writing course, and then you make a transition from first-year writing to writing across the curriculum in general education courses. In addition, there's one more big transition you'll need to make in your undergraduate career – the transition to writing in your major subject. Taking courses in your major means learning how to read, write, and research like a specialist in your chosen academic field. As you enter your major you're an *apprentice*, and you can expect to struggle a bit as you learn the expectations for reading, writing, and researching in your major. Even if you received good grades on your lower-division writing assignments, don't be surprised if you take a step backwards in your writing as you learn the conventions of writing in your major.

Sample Writing Rubrics and Assignments in the Major

To gain a sense of the high expectations for writing in the major, let's take a look at some rubrics for writing in the major from different departments at George Mason University and then at a sample assignment. Professor Terry Myers Zawacki, the director of the Writing Across the Curriculum program at George Mason University, worked with departments to develop the writing rubrics to help professors assess their students' writing. (The writing rubrics for each of the departments Professor Myers Zawacki worked with are available at http://wac.gmu.edu/assessing/assessing_student_writing.php#part3.)

George Mason University Writing Rubrics

Scoring Sheet for Writing Assessment of Laboratory Research Papers
Department of Psychology

By Prof. James F. Sanford and Terry Myers Zawacki with assistance from members of the Psychology Department Undergraduate Committee

1. Content is clearly stated, including adequate justification of hypotheses, appropriate level of detail throughout, and reasoned/logical presentation of research. Literature review studies are applicable and used appropriately, and the review includes adequate and appropriate documentation. Method section includes sufficient detail to enable reader to replicate the study.
   More than satisfactory_____ Satisfactory_____ Unacceptable_____

2. The text "flows" well. Flow includes (a) organization (clear, well-developed hypotheses; clear topic sentences; good transition between ideas; all sections of paper tie together) and (b) tone (language is professionally appropriate; word choice is accurate; text demonstrates appropriate voice for writing task).
   More than satisfactory_____ Satisfactory_____ Unacceptable_____

3. APA style and format are used correctly, including format of reference section and agreement between references cited in text and those in reference section.
   More than satisfactory_____ Satisfactory_____ Unacceptable_____

4. Mechanics are correct. These include grammar, syntax, spelling, punctuation, and use of correct homonyms/near homonyms (e.g. affect, effect; compliment, complement) while avoiding non-word errors (e.g. alot).
   More than satisfactory_____ Satisfactory_____ Unacceptable_____

5. Paper is written for the appropriate audience, namely, individuals who read research articles.
   More than satisfactory_____ Satisfactory_____ Unacceptable_____

Biology Scoring Sheet for Writing Assessment

1. Demonstrates understanding of scientific writing

- abstract summarizes key points and sections
- each section has content appropriate to the section
- discussion section synthesizes results with literature

- understands what needs to be cited
- graphics integrated into and integral to the paper
- shows evidence of analytical thinkin

More than satisfactory	Satisfactory	Unsatisfactory	Unacceptable

2. Content, comprehension, and development of ideas

- follows assignment
- has sufficient data and/or information
- evidence of original work
- paraphrases correctly and accurately
- conclusion captures main points

- has a title that fits paper
- has appropriate and challenging content
- defines technical terms, used appropriately, not gratuitously
- stays on topic

More than satisfactory	Satisfactory	Unsatisfactory	Unacceptable

3. Structure and organization

- clearly organized
- flows (has topic sentences, repetition of key words, other transitions)
- shows an understanding of paragraphs

- introduction sets up paper and points follow in order
- topic sentences focus paragraph

More than satisfactory	Satisfactory	Unsatisfactory	Unacceptable

4. Documenting and Citing

- has adequate citing
- sources are introduced appropriately
- follows appropriate documentation style

- paraphrases without excessive quoting
- citations match references

More than satisfactory	Satisfactory	Unsatisfactory	Unacceptable

5. Mechanics (any paper that receives an "unacceptable" in this section must receive an overall score of unsatisfactory)

- correct labeling and referencing of tables and graphs
- correct tenses
- punctuation, esp. comma use
- correct sentence structure and syntax

- correct word choice
- subject/verb agreement (e.g. data are)
- correct use of italics
- concise language appropriate to science

More than satisfactory	Satisfactory	Unsatisfactory	Unacceptable

Overall Score (any paper that receives an "unacceptable" on one or more items must be assessed as unsatisfactory overall.)

More than satisfactory	Satisfactory	Unsatisfactory

School of Management

Criteria for Competent Writing

By Professors Karen Hallows, David Beach, and Alison O'Brien. Revised by Professor Beth Schneider.

1. **Content of Argument:** The content is clearly stated and includes sufficient knowledge of the material or topic. The assignment includes conceptual sophistication and analysis appropriate for the assignment and writing level.
   Strong _____ Adequate _____ Weak _____

2. **Format of the Argument:** The deliverable has a well-stated thesis/objective, relative points to support the thesis, and provides an appropriate conclusion. Paragraphs and statements are balanced, supported, and presented in a logical sequence with smooth transitions.
   Strong _____ Adequate _____ Weak _____

3. **Content purpose and audience:** The deliverable contains the proper techniques and organization to achieve the intended purpose of the assigned task (to inform, persuade, instruct or record). The use of voice, tone, and diction is appropriate for the intended audience (superior, expert, general, or subordinate).
   Strong _____ Adequate _____ Weak _____

4. **Format and Structure:** The deliverable is developed following the appropriate guidelines for the specified business format (memorandum, letter, report). Business writing criteria is demonstrated through clear, economical and active language. The document is professional in appearance.
   Strong _____ Adequate _____ Weak _____

5. **Documentation and Citation:** Research has been incorporated to sufficiently support the thesis or argument. One designated citation format has been adequately used through internal citation (paraphrasing and quoting) and in reference sections.
   Strong _____ Adequate _____ Weak _____

6. **Style and Mechanics:** The paper demonstrates proper grammar, syntax, spelling, and punctuation. The paper uses standard, English language appropriate for business.
   Strong _____ Adequate _____ Weak _____

7. **Overall,** this deliverable is:
   Strong _____ Adequate _____ Weak _____

Dance Department

Writing Assessment Scoring Criteria

Writing Competency in the Department of Dance will be met when a student:

1. Shows a serious, thoughtful attempt to understand dance. Discusses the meaning of the dance using mature, sophisticated ideas.
    More than Satisfactory _____ Satisfactory _____ Unsatisfactory _____

2. Uses imagery (vivid "pictures" in prose — simile, metaphor, concrete adjectives, or active verbs) and are able to relate this imagery to the intent of the dance. Uses terminology related to dance performance.
    More than Satisfactory _____ Satisfactory _____ Unsatisfactory _____

3. Displays opinions/ideas that are well-supported using specific examples from the dance. Gives sufficient detail and depth to support opinions/ideas.
    More than Satisfactory _____ Satisfactory _____ Unsatisfactory _____

4. Demonstrates clear organization and includes an introduction which provides a context for the whole by including relevant information such as program information, title of work, composer, etc; and a conclusion which reflects on the overall experience or provides the bigger picture to end the piece.
    More than Satisfactory _____ Satisfactory _____ Unsatisfactory _____

5. Pays attention to technical correctness (spelling, grammar, sentence structure, punctuation, and paragraphing).
    More than Satisfactory _____ Satisfactory _____ Unsatisfactory _____

6.6: Writing to Learn – Comparing Writing in General Education and Writing in the Major

The purpose of this Writing to Learn activity is to think about the ways that expectations for writing in the major are different from expectations for general education classes. Compare the writing rubrics for the Psychology, Biology, Management, and Dance Departments at George Mason University and the general university writing rubrics in Chapter 1. What are some of the differences in terms of reading, writing, and researching expectations between the George Mason departmental rubrics and the university rubrics given in Chapter 1?

In Chapter 8, you'll see an example of writing and researching in the major in the case study of Bethany Coston, a senior sociology student writing in a course in her major, sociology, at a small liberal arts college in the Midwest. To get a more concrete sense of what writing and researching in the major is like, let's take a look at a research assignment Bethany was given and some excerpts of Bethany's response to the assignment. The first part of the assignment is shown below.

Final Paper and Presentation (A&S 360 — *INTIMATE VIOLENCE*)

Pending IRB approval, your final assignment will revolve around the campus survey we will be conducting as part of the class. Upon completion of data entry, each student will receive a copy of the data set. Students should begin thinking about what specific variables they want to focus on for the final paper, consult with me to make sure their topics are unique, and then begin data analysis.

Given the pre-requisites for this course, students will be expected to conduct bivariate data analysis at a minimum, and possibly multivariate analysis for those students who have received training in SPSS. We will discuss data analysis more in class after Spring Break. There are thorough literatures for all of the issues covered in our survey, so locating resources for your literature review should not be a problem.

I will allow some students to conduct their own research on topics not addressed in our survey, so that we cover a variety of intimate violence issues during the last part of the course (student presentations). IF YOU WILL BE CONDUCTING YOUR OWN RESEARCH, please see the next two paragraphs for key information…(if you are using survey data, turn to page two)

RESEARCH METHODS: **If you do not use our survey data, you must conduct some other form of original research.** You can do *interviews* with relevant volunteers (see me if you want to do this), pass out *surveys* (see me), do *content analysis* (examine relevant current/historical documents first-hand; see me), or *do some observation* (e.g. attend a court case; see me). You must obtain approval from me PRIOR TO CONDUCTING YOUR RESEARCH. **Failure to obtain approval for your research method prior to conducting your research will result in a failing grade for the entire assignment.**

This assignment reflects some common expectations for writing in the major, as described in the next section.

Common Expectations for Writing in the Major

- **Original research and ideas**

The assignment asks students to pick a "unique topic" and to do some "original research." The further along you progress in college and in your major, the more you will be asked to add to the disciplinary conversation and contribute something original from your own work.

- **Specialized disciplinary terms**

This assignment has terms you probably won't be familiar with if you're not a sociologist or a sociology major: for example, *bivariate*, *multivariate*, and *content analysis*. Disciplines create specialized terms to describe discipline-specific ideas and research methods. In this case, *bivariate* and *multivariate*, types of statistical analysis, and *content analysis*, a type of research method that does not necessarily involve statistical analysis, are terms and procedures which sociologists need to know.

- **Complex disciplinary research methods**

The research methods discussed above are not easy for apprentice sociologists. Bivariate and multivariate analysis involve simultaneously analyzing multiple variables by statistical means to see if they're related. Since sociologists look for patterns in human behavior and connect those patterns to variables such as race, class, and gender, this analysis method reflects ways of analyzing behavior and making meaning in sociology. Students have to take an introductory sociology and a research methods course before they can take the course that Bethany is writing her research paper for, Intimate Violence. It takes time, practice, and multiple courses before students can move from apprentices to insiders in their chosen major.

- **Complex disciplinary genres**

The type of research paper Bethany was asked to write is similar to the kind of research reports found in scholarly journals in sociology. Bethany's professor said: "Final research papers mirror those of a journal article. Students must utilize multiple theories, incorporate relevant material from inside and outside of the course, conduct original research, report findings, and discuss the findings in the context of their theories and literature." Apprentice sociologists would need some practice and some feedback if they were attempting to write in a complex disciplinary genre like the one Bethany was assigned. Because the genres you're asked to write in become more and more complex as you move through your major, don't be surprised if you struggle a bit as you develop from an apprentice to an insider in your chosen major field of study.

To gain a sense of how Bethany conducted her analysis and wrote it up in her report, let's look at some excerpts from her final paper. In the opening of her paper, Bethany establishes the originality of her focus. Here's an excerpt from her introduction:

> Rape in fraternity, athletic, and group settings has been studied by researchers in the past, but this research seems limited. Mainly, the research available has looked at group setting in terms of fraternity rape, and therefore gang-rape. While gang-rape is an important aspect of violence in the culture of fraternities, and the socialization of masculinity, it is also essential to look at the connection between fraternity membership and sexual assault and rape within intimate partner relationships.

As a senior in sociology writing the kind of research report published in sociology journals, Bethany is expected to do original research, and she was able to find an aspect of her topic that hadn't been fully explored by researchers: fraternity sexual assault and rape within intimate partner relationships.

Bethany had enough experience as a sociology major to successfully engage in the kind of analysis that the assignment asks for, and she reported the results of her research in tables. The following is an excerpt from the *Findings* section of her paper. (The name of Bethany's college was changed to *X College* for publication in this book to keep the name of the school anonymous; and note that Bethany uses *Greek* to mean "fraternity" as college fraternities are typically named in Greek and abbreviated as Greek letters.)

Hypothesis 1: *Greek men on X College's campus will have more patriarchal opinions than non-Greek men.*

> There were not considerable differences between Greek men and non-Greek men on the subject of patriarchal opinions (Table 1). On average, the Greek males tended more towards agreeing than non-Greek males, but were still mostly split between Agree and Disagree for the questions about men being in charge, troubles between couples remaining private, and women paying for dinner on first dates. The Greek males also disagreed less strongly on the issue that being a man means being ready to use violence, and forcing someone to have sex if they wouldn't get caught; however, overall, all men disagreed with these questions. All men, Greek and non-Greek alike, disagreed very strongly with the issue of forcing someone to have sex, with the means being 3.89 and 3.9, respectfully.

Table 1 shows the relationship between Greek affiliation and patriarchal opinions.

	incharge	private	womenpay	menready	forcesex
Greek Males	2.69	2.24	2.24	3.38	3.89
Non-Greek Males	3	2	2.49	3.48	3.9

Hypothesis 2: *Greek men will be more likely to have committed acts of abuse than non-Greek men.*

This hypothesis had the most support (Table 2). While non-Greek men committed almost no acts of forced sexual contact or physical abuse, Greek men committed an average of 2.4 acts in these categories. Even more startling is that these acts were committed against fellow students, and at X College, more than away from X College; whereas non-Greek males committed only 2 failed forcible sexual acts away from X College, and 1 act of physical violence against a girlfriend/ boyfriend.

Verbal abuse was highest among both groups, with 9 acts being committed against girlfriends/boyfriends, and 4 acts against someone the respondent was dating, for non-Greek males. For Greek males, the numbers were startlingly higher. These men committed 17 acts of verbal abuse against girlfriends/boyfriends, and 4 acts against someone they were dating.

Table 2 shows the relationship between Greek affiliation
and self-reported acts of abuse.

	Greek Males	Non-Greek Males
utouchxcollege	4	0
utouchstudent	5	0
utouchaway	3	0
utriedxcollege	2	0
utriedstudent	2	0
utriedaway	2	2
uforcexcollege	2	0
uforcestudent	1	0
uforceaway	1	0
uverbgb	17	9
uverbdt	4	4
uphysgb	0	1
uphysdt	2	0

Bethany's research methods and the way she reports her research in tables reflect the complexity of senior-level sociology research. She wouldn't have been able to do this kind of research if she hadn't taken preparatory courses such as Introduction to Sociology and Social Sciences Research Methods.

In addition to gaining expertise in sociology research methods, Bethany has learned to use the specialized language and key terms that scholars use when discussing her subject. For example, take a look at her statement of the purpose of her research:

> The purpose of this paper is to explore a somewhat new territory of intimate violence, and examine all of the factors that may lead college-aged men to be violent towards their partners. I hope to study this issue from a gender-based critique; considering that patriarchy, male social power, is bad for both men and women, in that it not only diminishes women's existences, but also reduces men to *objects* of their gender. In doing this, and keeping in mind that social change is slow, I desire to reach a new understanding of intimate violence between dating partners and the effects of fraternity membership on relational aggression.

Bethany is using specialized terms that would be recognizable to her audience – the discourse community of sociologists. *Gender-based critique*, *patriarchy*, and *relational aggression* are important terms for sociologists who study the subject Bethany is exploring, and using them connects Bethany to the discourse community of sociologists interested in her topic and establishes her own credibility – her ethos – as a researcher.

Reading, Writing, and Researching across the Curriculum

6.7: Writing to Learn – Writing across the Curriculum

Before we look at some myths about writing across the curriculum, let's tap into your own experiences with writing in different departments. If you've already had general education classes, write about the ways the professors' expectations for writing were different for each class and also the ways they were similar for each class. If this is your first semester of college, you can base this freewrite on the syllabus your professors have given and any writing assignments you've had so far.

Five Myths about Reading, Writing, and Researching across the Curriculum

Myth #1 Good writing is pretty much the same across the curriculum.

Even though we focused on some general features of academic writing in Chapter 1, it's important to realize that what counts as *good writing* will be different for each discipline. Complex sentence structures and descriptive language may be considered features of good writing in the humanities, but the discipline of science tends to value clear and concise writing. You will likely be using data from experiments and research studies in the natural sciences and the social sciences, but in the arts and humanities your evidence will more likely come directly from your analysis of the texts you're reading or your own arguments in conversation with other scholars. Active voice is valued in most humanities courses, but in the natural sciences it's common to use passive voice when reporting the results of an experiment. One of the challenges of college writing is to begin to learn what counts as *good writing* in different disciplines.

Myth #2 Every professor in a department will have the same expectations for writing.

Even though you can make some general statements about the expectations for writing in the natural sciences, the social sciences, or the humanities, it's not as though professors share a rule book for writing in their discipline that they all follow. Disciplines are communities, communities are made up of people, and no two people think exactly alike. Writing is too complex an activity for there to be standards and rules that are written in stone for each discipline. You need to pay close attention to each professor's syllabus and the way they talk about their writing assignments. Ask yourself what your professors seem to value in writing, and how that is similar to (or different from) what we talk about in Part III. Your professors will try to represent their fields when they ask you to write and when they respond to your writing, but disciplines don't have a list of rules about writing that everyone must follow.

Myth #3 You can use a similar research strategy in every course.

Just as there are no standardized genres or list of rules for writing across the curriculum, there's also not a single research process or research method. The natural sciences and social sciences will tend to use research methods that focus on designing and conducting experiments or systematic observations to test a hypothesis. Research in the arts and humanities tends to focus on reading and interpreting texts (including artwork and performances). Even within a discipline, researchers use different methods.

Myth #4 Reading means the same thing across the curriculum.

In a course in biology or chemistry, reading might mean interpreting data from graphs. In courses in art or theatre, reading might mean looking closely at a painting or viewing a play. A course in philosophy might require reading dense and difficult texts, while a course in music might require the reading of lyrics from songs. Each of these types of reading will require different kinds of reading strategies and different reading processes.

Myth #5 General education courses focus on learning information about a discipline and then showing that you've learned the information on tests.

Paulo Freire, the educator Melissa Bratt mentioned in one of her essays in Chapter 1, contrasted what he called the *banking* model of education, in which professors deposit knowledge in students through lectures and tests, with the *critical* model, in which students learn to become critical thinkers through inquiry (Freire, 1986). Most college general education programs focus on critical thinking, and even in introductory courses most college professors want you to learn to use the tools of a discipline to think for yourself and explore open-ended questions. It's possible that some of your professors in general education courses will use the banking method and just deliver information in lectures to have you regurgitate it on exams. But most of your professors in these courses will use reading, writing, and researching as tools to encourage you to practice inquiry in their discipline, that is, to practice the ways of thinking and making knowledge in the discipline.

6.8: Learn by Doing – Assignments across the Curriculum

The goal of this Learn by Doing activity is for you to reflect on the five myths about reading, writing, and researching across the curriculum that I just reviewed by looking at some actual writing assignments from courses across the curriculum at your institution and writing a two-page analysis of the assignments. In this Learn by Doing activity, you'll do a rhetorical analysis of three writing assignments from three different courses and three different disciplines. The first step in this activity is to gather writing assignments from courses across the curriculum. You can collaborate on this as a class if everyone brings in five copies of an assignment from one of their courses. Once you've chosen three different assignments from three different disciplines to analyze, you'll read the assignments carefully and consider the rhetorical situation of each assignment. Here are some questions you can ask when you do your rhetorical analysis:

(cont.)

6.8 (cont.)

1. What are the genres of each writing assignment, and how do these genres differ across disciplines?
2. What are the expectations for writing for each assignment? How are the expectations for writing similar and different in each discipline?
3. What kind of reading is asked for in each assignment? Are there differences in the readings for each discipline?
4. If the assignments require research, what research methods are required? Do these research methods vary in each discipline?

6.9: Writing to Learn – Your Prior Knowledge of Writing across the Curriculum

The purpose of this chapter is to give you a broad introduction to writing across the curriculum, but you probably already know some things about reading, writing, and researching in the natural sciences, the social sciences, and the arts and humanities. Individually or in small groups, create a table with three vertical columns and three horizontal rows. Label the columns *Reading, Writing, Researching* and the rows *Natural Sciences, Social Sciences, Arts and Humanities*. Then fill in each box with what you already know about reading in the natural sciences, writing in the natural sciences, and so on. You can draw on previous writing experiences in these different disciplines, or just make an educated guess. Be prepared to share your answers with the class as a whole.

In the remainder of Part III, we'll be looking closely at what it means to read, write, and research in courses in the natural sciences, the social sciences, and the arts and humanities. Before we consider each discipline, it would be helpful to look at some examples of student writing from each of these disciplines and to think about how this writing reflects the research methods and writing styles and conventions of the discipline. Provided below are three student research essays: one from the natural sciences, one from the social sciences, and one from the arts and humanities. The first essay, "The Blob that Attacked Waikiki," was written by Katrina Outland and published in *The Journal of Young Investigators*, an undergraduate journal that publishes scientific articles written by college students. The second essay, "The Ubercool Morphology of Internet Gamers," was written by Dana Driscoll, a student at the California University of Pennsylvania, and published in the *Undergraduate Research Journal for the Human Sciences*. The third essay, "Blurred by Our Cultural Lens: Issues with Oral Literature and the American School System," was written by Stephanie LeBlanc for an oral literature course at James Madison University and won an award in the JMU student writing contest *Write On* and published on the contest Web site. As you read the three texts, think about how they differ in terms of style, tone, organization, research methods, citation of sources, and other rhetorical features.

Sample Student Essay in Physical Sciences

The Blob that Attacked Waikiki: The Box Jellyfish Invasion of Hawaii
By Katrina Outland
Published in *The Journal of Young Investigators* (Outland, 2008)

They come ten days after the full moon, swarming to shore, nearly invisible and wielding poison-loaded tentacles. A few days later, they disappear just as mysteriously as they had come, leaving behind their microscopic spawn. No, this isn't the plot of another science-fiction movie; it is a real, monthly occurrence on the beaches of Oahu, Hawaii. These creatures are aliens, but they aren't from space. They are an alien species of box jellyfish that has been invading Hawaii's waters for almost two decades. Lifeguards, tourists, and scientists all keep a wary vigilance for this particular box jelly, called *Carybdea alata*.

Named for their square shape, box jellyfish are the most highly evolved and the most dangerous of the jellyfish. Like corals and other members of the phylum Cnidaria, jellyfish tentacles are lined with microscopic cells called cnydocites that each house a powerful stinging thread called a nematocyst. When triggered, each nematocyst is released in a powerful spring-like action, piercing whatever might touch it. Box jellyfish not only have the most potent poison of all jellyfish in their nematocysts, but they have even developed complex eyes that can detect light. They don't just drift around — they can actively pursue prey.

Hawaii's C. alata is not the largest or the deadliest box jelly (a status reserved for the infamous sea wasp of Australia), but it is still a dangerous nuisance. Nearly every month brings a string of news reports about jellyfish stings, mostly on the southern and eastern shores of Oahu. For example, on a single day in July 2004, 318 people were stung at the tourist destination Waikiki, along with 45 stings at other beaches. No one is immune to a sting's pain; as lifeguard Landy Blair told reporters in 2001, "I have sent 30-year-old muscular surfers in tears and with breathing difficulties to the hospital."

Where are they from, where are they going?

Hawaii's box jellies are unique in their predictable arrivals: they come near shore to spawn 8 to 12 days after each full moon. John Culliney, Professor of Biology at Hawaii Pacific University, said that other members of the same phylum, including corals, also time their spawns based on the lunar cycle.

"They do this because it's easier to concentrate the eggs and sperm all together," Culliney said. What is unique about *C. alata* is that nowhere else in the world are box jellyfish quite so reliably on-time. No one is yet able to answer why.

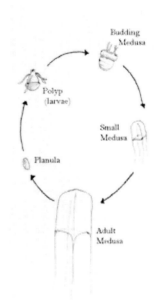

The box jellyfish lifecycle. The sexually reproductive medusae bud off of the asexual polyps. Source: *Ruppert and Barnes, Invertebrate Zoology: 6th Ed.*

To add to the mystery, very little is known about the box jelly's lifecycle. A jellyfish, also called a medusa, is actually only one stage of the lifecycle; the medusae bud off of larval-stage polyps that are attached to the sea floor. According to Culliney, a box jellyfish polyp is longer-lived than other jellyfish polyps — perhaps even indefinite. The problem is that no one knows where the polyps live.

"There might be a chance to control the population if we knew what substrate [the polyps] live on," said Culliney, "but no one's been able to find them."

After spawning, the adult jellyfish disappear again, just as suddenly as they came. Where do they come from? Where do they go? How long do they live? So far, there are no answers.

Coming to Hawaii

Carybdea alata received its name from its place of origin — the Caribbean. So how did these mysterious invaders reach Hawaii? Researchers have several theories, though none have been proven. Some believe that the medusae were carried in ballast water in ships. Others, including Culliney, think it is more likely that the polyps were transported by attaching to the bottom of ships. Whatever the method of arrival, this box jellyfish has now spread worldwide.

First appearing on Oahu in the late 1800s, this box jelly has shown up regularly near beaches since the 1980s. "Always before then they'd disappear for a few years between sightings," said Culliney. "Now it looks like they're spreading around Oahu."

Originally only found on Oahu's south and east (leeward) shores, C. alata has been showing up more recently on the north and windward shores. With no means of controlling their numbers, many worry that the jellyfish may spread to the rest of Hawaii. Predictions are not promising. According to Culliney, "It's only a matter of time before they get to neighbor islands."

Oww! I've been stung!

So far, no one in Hawaii has died from a C. alata sting, but it can cause nasty welts, and even breathing difficulties and dizziness in people more sensitive to the venom. So, what should you do if you happen to encounter a box jelly? Some say to use vinegar, others say meat tenderizer, and still others say to urinate on stings. Traditional "remedies" are so numerous that they can be more confusing than helpful. Few of these treatments have been scientifically tested until recently, and many of the results are contradictory. What really works and what doesn't?

There are a few things on which everyone can agree. For any species of jellyfish, white vinegar poured over the wound helps to deactivate the nematocysts, preventing further stings. After being doused in vinegar, any remaining tentacles should be picked off. Finally, never rub the wound with anything, as that can discharge any nematocysts that are still on the skin.

As for other remedies, studies are not conclusive. Traditional pain relief usually calls for a cold pack, but more recent research contradicts this idea. Dr. Craig

Thomas and Susan Scott, authors of *All Stings Considered*, published a study in the Hawaii Medical Journal in 2001 that found application of a heat pack to a jellyfish sting could provide moderate pain relief. Another study, published in 2002 in the *Medical Journal of Australia*, also reported that heat could reduce the lethality of venom for other box jellyfish species.

Traditional treatments, including applying meat tenderizer, freshwater, alcohol, steroid cream, and even human urine to jellyfish stings, are not supported by solid evidence; some of these remedies may even be harmful in certain instances. The general rule is: If it isn't proven, don't risk it.

The invasion continues

C. alata has become one of the more recent additions to the long list of alien species introduced into Hawaii. Whatever effects it might have on the islands' unique ecosystem is only another unknown surrounding this creature. The only things about which we can be sure are that *C. alata* is unwelcome, and that it is not leaving any time soon.

Author's Note

14 March 2006: It has been recently brought to my attention that *Carybdea alata* has not been confirmed as an invasive species to Hawaii; there are ongoing studies to determine if this box jellyfish is introduced or native. I apologize for any confusion I might have caused in using the terms "invasive" or "alien." In addition, evidence has also been presented to me to disprove the hypothesis that *C. alata* might have been introduced via ballast water, as ships during the late 1800's used dry ballast instead of water. — Katrina Outland

References

Carrette T, et al. (2002). Temperature effects on box jellyfish venom: a possible treatment for envenomed patients? Medical Journal of Australia. http://www.mja.com.au/public/issues/177_11_021202/car10576_fm.html

Fenner, PJ and JA Williamson. (1996). Worldwide deaths and severe envenomation from jellyfish stings. The Medical Journal of Australia. 165; 658.

Thomas, CS and SA Scott. (1997). All stings considered: First aid and medical treatment of Hawaii's marine injuries. University of Hawaii Press.

Thomas CS, Scott, SA, Galanis, DJ, and RS Goto. (2001). Box jellyfish (Carybdea alata) in Waikiki: their influx cycle plus the analgesic effect of hot and cold packs on their stings to swimmers at the beach: a randomized, placebo-controlled, clinical trial. <u>Hawaii Medical Journal</u>. 60(4): 100–7.

---. (2001). Box jellyfish (Carybdea alata) in Waikiki. The analgesic effect of sting-aid, Adolph's meat tenderizer and fresh water on their stings: a double-blinded, randomized, placebo-controlled clinical trial. <u>Hawaii Medical Journal</u>. 60(8): 205–7, 210.

Sample Student Essay in Social Sciences

The Ubercool Morphology of Internet Gamers: A Linguistic Analysis
By Dana Driscoll
California University of Pennsylvania
Published in the *Undergraduate Research Journal for the Human Sciences*
(Driscoll, 2002)

The Internet connects a number of diverse people and groups. Language is one of the main distinguishing characteristics from group to group, with each group having its own unique words and expressions. Such diversity is similar to different professions or ethnic groups employing a dialect. Communication features that are constant across the Internet dialect groups include the emoticons, e.g. ":)," and common abbreviations, e.g. "lol," but there is a great deal of diversity as well. This study focuses on the morphology of a dialect of a specific Internet group — Gamers. The Gamers are simply a large group of people who play online games. Most of these Gamers devote hours of their time each day to playing. They play such games as "Everquest," "Ultima Online," "Asheron's Call," "Unreal Tournament," and "Quake." Many gamers play more than just one game. A commonality between all of the aforementioned titles is that the players of such games form teams, which they call <u>guilds</u> or <u>clans</u>. This research has been focused on the Quake players, specifically the players of Action Quake II. The research has been done primarily on their clan chat rooms on IRC (Internet Relay Chat) and through in-game observation. The chat rooms and in-game discussions are the clan's primary means of communication, and therefore the best environment to study their language.

Surprisingly, few linguistic studies have considered the topic of Internet dialects. The studies that have been conducted focused on the Internet dialect as a whole and did not look at the diverse groups on the Internet that communicate differently. Studies in the communications field have focused on the main Internet dialect as well, although those studies did not look at the language from a linguistic point of view. Studies in sociology discussed Gamers overall, but did not linguistically analyze language. Furthermore, almost all of the studies found are dated, and the language has changed from the time of the research. Because of the apparent lack of linguistic studies in the field of Internet dialects, this research is one of the first of this type. No study has looked at the specific dialect groups of the Internet. If nothing else, this study will prove that there is more to Internet language than a single dialect and that language of the World Wide Web is extremely diverse and segmented.

The first studies that will be discussed dealing with the Internet are not linguistically oriented, but rather come from the communications field. The first, a book dealing with Internet language as a whole, is called Flame Wars: The Discourse of Cyberculture (1997). It consists of sixteen articles by various authors about the dark side of cyberculture and its language. The article for which the book was named, "Flame Wars," briefly discusses emoticons, or text expressions. Another article, "New Age Mutant Ninja Hackers: Reading Mondo 2000," discusses the computer Hackers. It does mention some words they use; however, the article's focus is on a computer conference, Mondo 2000. None of the articles discusses Internet language in detail. They only scratch the surface.

The second study was an undergraduate research project completed by Reid (1991). She discussed how "internet relay chat" or IRC posed problems for current theory in communications. She discussed the nature of IRC and listed many of the common words that were found on IRC. The study is very dated. Many of the expressions that she claimed are popular have become extinct, and many new expressions are not mentioned.

Breeze (1997) wrote an overview about the Quake gamers from a sociological standpoint. She gave an overview of the game, focused on the Gamer's sense of community, and briefly discussed their language. Besides these three specific examples of non-linguistic oriented studies, many "Internet dictionaries" are available. Such titles include Webster's Computer and Internet Dictionary (2000), Net Speak: The Internet Dictionary (1994), and The New Hackers Dictionary (1996). Interestingly enough, The New Hackers Dictionary does focus on one specific group's language, Internet Hackers. Unfortunately, no linguistic analysis of the hacker language is present, as the book is simply a dictionary.

Two linguistic studies also have been done on the Internet dialect. Hodges (1999) discussed a specific Internet language feature in her master's thesis, "Deciphering the Pragmatic Content of Extralinguistic Items in Email." She was specifically interested in the use of extralinguistic items such as "emoticons" and "acronym'" in email communication. She also studied how the use of extralinguistic items differed by gender. Because her project was completed in 1999, it is one of the most recent ones that I have located.

Davis and Brewer (1997) also did a linguistically oriented study of Internet language. They discuss it in their book, Electronic Discourse: Linguistic Individuals in Virtual Space. They document how the language of electronic communication has the speech characteristic of immediacy but has the writing characteristic of permanence. The study shows how communication that is solely through electronic sources is different than both writing and speech.

Because of the apparent lack of linguistic studies in the field of Internet dialects, this research is one of the first of this type. No study has examined the language of a specific Internet group. If nothing else, this study will show that there is more to Internet language than a single dialect and that language of the World Wide Web is extremely diverse and segmented. The specific research question is: How do the Online Gamers form specific words that contribute to their dialect?

Methodology

Research was conducted in chat rooms of the Quake clans. The chat rooms were located in Internet Rely Chat, or IRC. Because it was impossible to monitor all of the chat rooms for hours each night, log files were used instead. Log files are simply chat sessions that are saved and can be viewed at any time. Approximately seventy-five log files dating over a period of six months were studied. These log files were received from several gamers who had them saved. Everything was done anonymously. First, names that are used in the log files are nicknames the gamers use for themselves when playing. Second, any specific gamer names were changed before use within this paper.

The language from the log files was sorted in two ways. The researcher documented each time a word (or form of the word) was spoken and who spoke it. An analysis was completed to determine which words were in frequent use and which words were new coinages that may not be used by the majority of speakers. The speaker was important because it had to be determined whether a single person or small group, or a majority of speakers used the word. The standard words were determined by number of speakers and number of occurrences. Each word in the standard dialect was analyzed for morphology, multiple forms, and definition. Throughout the course of the research, it was discovered that many of the terms and phrases the gamers used were incomprehensible even in context, so this researcher enlisted the help of a "Gamer veteran," a person who was part of the Gamer group for over seven years, to help with the definitions. After the research was complete, the words and morphemes were analyzed to determine how they were formed. Working definitions were also formed for each word.

Results

The following is a list of the results of the research. The words have been classified according to the way they were formed. Each type of morphological formation is listed along with common words and definitions. Other information has been included that is a large part of the Gamer dialect, such as alphanumeric symbols and voiced pauses. After the list of results, some statistical data are provided on the types of formation.

Clips: Clips are some of the more frequently used words in the Gamer vocabulary.

<u>altho</u>- although
<u>prolly</u>- probably
<u>foo</u>- fool
<u>cuz</u>- because
<u>bout</u>- about
<u>thx</u>- thanks
<u>wether</u>- whether
<u>id</u>- I'd minus the ' (Note- the deletion of the apostrophe is very common)
<u>spec</u>- clip of spectator, means to watch or be a spectator
<u>msg</u>- message
<u>peeps, ppl</u>- people
<u>doods, d00ds</u>- dudes
<u>dling, dl-ing, dl</u>- downloading
<u>g'night</u> - goodnight
<u>pwd, pw</u>- password
<u>newbies</u>- inexperienced players/users
<u>k</u>- ok, okay
<u>pl</u>- packet loss, game term
<u>frag</u>- game term meaning kill, taken from war
<u>gf, g/f</u>- girlfriend

Acronyms: Some of these acronyms are used in the common internet dialect, although others are unique to the Gamers. The more common acronyms, which I found in a standard Internet dictionary, are marked with an asterisk.

n\m- never mind
nm- never mind
rofl- rolling on the floor laughing *
np- no problem
dl- downloading
bbiab- be back in a bit *
lol- laughing out loud *
brb- be right back *
gj- good job

Compounds:

awhile- a while
ahold- a hold
moreso- more so
ina- in a

Blends:

wanna- want to
lemme- let me
usin- using
welp- kind of like well... (as in "welp im going now")
thatd- that would, gamers rarely use '

Suffixes:

-age- suffix, when added to a word it indicates action, or replaces the –ed suffix (for
example- "I owned him" would become "I had ownage" or "it was ownage").
It assumes the place of the object
-or,0r, -zor- suffx, I am doing, use or after vowel sounds and the letter x
(as in sexor or b0x0r), and zor after all other consonants (as in "I need
foodzors" or "sleepzor").

Prefixes:

uber- means very, can be prefixed to any word, such as "youre ubersexy" or "that
was uber-cool." Most of the time it is joined with a dash. This can also be a
free morpheme.

Unique words: I have also included any standard English words which
have new definitions in this category.

uber- multiple meanings- a) large, b) very, c)group nature (as in uber cool)
w00p, woop- joyus exclamation, similar to 'hurray!'
w00t, woot- joyus exclamation, similar to 'hurray!'
Ho- multiple meanings- a) greeting, b) whore
own, owned- multiple meanings- a) ownership, b) to win over someone or
something, c)an excellent performance
elite, l337, l33t- used very frequently, derogatory term, means the opposite of the
normal 'elite' definition. Often associated with "fakeness." The newer

definition stemmed from the overuse of the word by "newbies."

m4d, mad- very, as in "m4d l337"

bogged- overloaded

unf- sexual sound

ort- sexual sound

spectate- to observe

nog- affirmative

phat- cool

r00t, root- administrator of computer server* interesting usage (I got r00t on your b0x0rs)

Heya (greeting)

b0x0rs, boxors(rare)- computer servers

woops- I goofed up, like whoops or oops

egads- exclamation, used extremely surprising but very non serious situations

muh- me

ya- you

Aye- very rarely will they use the word yes, but rather use aye as affirmation

gah- exasperation

ringers- game term, when a person not of the team plays for that team, incognito

hammer- to repeatedly do something, especially in reference to logging on to a server or ftp

lamer- loser

sweet- multiple meanings, a) standard meaning- sweet tasting–very rarely used b) pretty, nice, good

yer- your, you're

j00- you

Also included in the research were other language elements that were common in the Gamer dialect. These elements convey meaning and give a more complete picture of the different aspects of the dialect.

Voiced Pauses: Because the gamers are not face to face, typed voiced pauses are used in the same manner they are used in speech.

Uhm, uhhh, hrm (signifies thinking), heh, erm, uh, hmmm

Laughter: This is also impossible to signify without typing something. There are many ways the games signify laughter, the three listed are the most common.

hehe, laf, lol

Alpha-Numeric Substitutions: These are very common in the Gamer dialect. Any or all letters can be substituted. Some of the more common substitutions are listed in the unique words section and the alternative spellings section.

1- L,l
3- e (most common)
4- a
5- s
$- s
7- T,t
8- B,b
0- o (most common)
@- at
* - "star"

Alternative Spellings:

doods- people (derived from dudes)
4 (instead of for)
2 (instead of too, to) example: "it happens 2 me 2 :("
lewser- loser
b4- before
ph34r- fear
l337,l33t- see unique words section
b0x0r, 80x0r- see unique words section

Expressions: Here are some examples of the emoticons that were found in the Gamer Dialect. Many of these are also found in the main Internet dialect.

:/
=(
shrug
sigh
:P
=]
arrrggh
:) :(
:0 :o
:[:]

The following data are statistical calculations dealing with the different types of morphological formations. The first set of data represents just the different ways of forming words, without the unique coinages. The second set includes all words, but does not include the alphanumeric symbols, emoticons, voiced pauses, or laughter.

Total number of words (not including unique coinages):	43
Clips	24 — 55.81%
Acronyms	10 — 23.26%
Blends	5 — 11.63%
Compounds	4 — 9.30%

Total number of words including unique coinages	72
Unique coinages	29 — 42.27%
Clips	24 — 33.33%
Acronyms	10 — 23.25%
Blends	5 — 11.63%
Compounds	4 — 5.55%

Discussion

The Gamer dialect is based on English. It has no speech equivalent and appears only in written form in IRC ("Internet Relay Chat") rooms, Gamer web sites, Gamer message boards, and within the games themselves. Although it is written, the syntax is more similar to speech than to writing. Because of the nature of the Gamer dialect, a form of typed speech, the main concern is speed. The gamers find many ways of shortening what they have to type, so they can convey meaning faster, just as shortening occurs in spoken language. Articles, apostrophes, and punctuation found in normal writing are often omitted, and any and all shortcuts with the language are taken. This clipping is shown from the vocabulary. Phrases and single words are the most frequent modes of communication. To illustrate this point, listed below is an example, taken straight from the chat scripts studied. The name of the speaker is in <>, and the message is after the name of speaker.

<cashcowc> did Gnomes win?
<Stalin> its not over yet
<Pr0vokeR> U
<Pr0vokeR> pos
<Drewskee> spam is irksome.
<CriM> first map we won (:
<CriM> on to sludge
<Pr0vokeR> score?
<Mr_Hobbers{d1nn36}> sludge youll get raped
<CriM> 10 5 i think
<CriM> Laf
<Pr0vokeR> haha
<Pr0vokeR> that close?
<Mr_Hobbers{d1nn36}> Welp. not bad
<Drewskee> haha
<Drewskee> gj C
<Drewskee> snicker
<|-det0x-|> yes crayz?
<Mr_Hobbers{d1nn36}> Crayz, Im surprised u didnt pull ur modem.
U doin pretty b4d that map
<Pr0vokeR> OVERFLOW CRAYZ
<Pr0vokeR> !!
<|-Crayz-|> bleh
<Stalin> hobbs doesnt like us
<Drewskee> hobbers is a fruit 2night
<|-Crayz-|> yea i know its pretty sad
<Stalin> since he doesnt get ops here
<|-Crayz-|> an OGL person being biast
<|-Crayz-|> ya kno?
<Stalin> aye, and he does in l337 chan

As shown through the example, the language of the Gamers, although written, is very similar to speech. To keep up with the speed of the conversation, the Gamers have developed words that allow them to convey meaning faster, such as their clips and acronyms. Almost all of the words in this study that are not unique are shortened versions of English words. The average new word created is between 4 and 5 letters. In this research, no dialect word longer than eight letters was discovered, although the Gamers will use longer English words when necessary, such the word "surprised" from the example above. Also, alphanumeric characters, acronyms, and emoticons can help Gamers covey meaning faster than with words.

The Internet is unique without borders or boundaries. People from everywhere in the world can be a part of the Internet community. The Internet has many different groups, all speaking a specific dialect. There are people who spend time in chat rooms, and the studies have studied general chat rooms. Other groups, such as the Hackers, Gamers, Phreakers, and Techies — all have dialect differences. Those groups share some dialect similarities with the general Internet dialect, such as acronyms and emoticons, but they have a much larger vocabulary and more defined expressions. The best way to describe the sub-dialect groups may be through an analogy of the dialects of America. The standard American dialect is much like the standard Internet dialect. Americans share and understand expressions and words regardless of their sub-dialect. Specific geographical regions and/or specific groups, such as the North, South, and speakers of Black English, are very similar to the many groups on the Internet.

This study is by no means complete. The research task of determining the morphology of Gamer words was completed, but little attention was paid to the rest of the Gamers' speech. During the research, it was also surprising to discover that there are sub-sub-dialects of the Gamer dialect. These dialects are based on the type of game played. The main group studied was a group of people playing a first action shooter game. Another major group is those players of the massive multiplayer online role-playing game or MMORPG. Many similarities in dialect exist between the two, but there are some major dialect differences. Besides the Gamer dialect, other dialects, such as the Hacker and Techie dialects, are wide open to study. It would be interesting to see what the variation is between the Internet sub-dialects and the standard Internet dialect.

References

Breeze, M. A. (1997). "Quake-ing in my boots: Examining Clan: Community Construction in an online gamer population" [On-Line], Cybersociology Magazine (Vol. 2). Available: http://www.socio.demon.co.uk/magazine /2/is2breeze.html

Davis, B. H., & Brewer, J. P. (1997). Electronic Discourse: Linguistic Individuals in Virtual Space. New York: State University Press.

Dery, M. (Ed.) (1991). Flame Wars The Discourse of Cyberculture. London: Duke University Press.

Fahey, T., & Prevost R. (Eds.) (1994). Net Speak: The Internet Dictionary. Hayden Books.

Hodges, S. (1999). Deciphering the Pragmatic Content of Extralinguistic Items in Email. Unpublished master's thesis, Georgetown University, Washington, D.C.

Margolis, P. (2000). <u>Webster's Computer and Internet Dictionary</u> (3rd ed). Random House Reference.

Raymond, E. (1996). <u>The New Hackers Dictionary</u>. Boston: MIT Press.

Reid, E. (1991). <u>Electropolis: Communication and Community on Internet Relay Chat</u>. Unpublished Manuscript, University Of Melbourne, Australia.

Sample Student Essay in Arts and Humanities

Blurred by our Cultural Lens: Issues with Oral Literature and the American School System
By Stephanie LeBlanc
James Madison University
Published in *Write On* (LeBlanc, 2009)

There are significant problems with how oral literature is defined and taught in the American school system because of the country's inclusion in Western culture. And the solutions for these problems are not far from our reach. In order to understand how the American definition of oral literature is misconstrued, we must arrive at a general definition for literature itself. Literature is the organization of language used artistically. The history of literature follows two paths. One path is the African, Asian and Native American view of literature as originally oral, then splitting into oral and written literature, with no hierarchy of the two. The authors of this path always acknowledge the oral origins of their writing. The other path, decidedly Western, is one that Americans follow. This history holds that writing was the first form of literature, eventually adding oral literature as Western culture was introduced to it. The problem with this path is that until very recent times oral literature was seen as inferior to written. Since Americans are historically and culturally conditioned to view oral literature in this way, we will examine how oral literature is either taught in a biased fashion or not taught at all, how there actually is no American oral literature besides that of Native Americans, and what academic issues arise from the general misunderstanding of oral literature. Then we will see how there are perfectly achievable solutions for these problems.

The largest problem with the way that oral literature is treated in America today is that it either is not taught in schools as an alternative form of literature or that it is taught under biased conditions. Based on my own schooling, I only remember being informed briefly of ancient and primitive societies telling stories by firelight to pass the time in their uncivilized cultures because they didn't have the capacity for written language. It never occurred to me that these cultures could have the knowledge of written language and choose oral literature instead. I also never realized the derogatory impact that words like "primitive" and "uncivilized" had on my opinion of those lifestyles. To have all American children taught in that same fashion creates a hierarchical view of societies. Oral literature is very different than written literature and cannot be taught by being compared to written literature. The problem is that the cultural lens of American society tells the learner that in order to understand something new, they must compare it to what they already know. Taking off the cultural lens is necessary to understanding the oral literature in an objective context.

Small steps are being taken to correct the flawed education of oral literature. More members of the higher academic community are taking interest in this field of study. One scholar, Gerald Haslam, realizes the importance of oral literature and its needed inclusion in American education. In his essay, "American Oral Literature: Our Forgotten Heritage", he laments that oral literature has been "long ignored in classrooms" (709). Since oral literature has been brushed aside in American education, more attention must be given to the study for it to be fully understood and respected as an equal of written literature. To be a true English scholar, all forms of literature must be studied and understood. The issues in education even extend to the university level. As a "conventional English major", studies in oral literature are rare and often taught in the bias perspective that is so undermining of academic thinking (709). However, only bringing greater attention to oral literature is not enough to correct the problems of how it is taught.

Racist and derogatory diction is a serious issue in the discussion of oral literature. Most scholars do not even realize that they are using language that carries false connotations to describe oral literature and the societies that practice it. In his essay "Oral Literature", William P. Murphy creates a great environment for the further discussion of oral literature by outlining the issues with language describing it. The difficulties lie in the fact that for so many years those who've studied people of oral societies used derogatory language, creating racist ideas connected to the use of such literature. For example, dealing with the term "folklore," Murphy notes that "although professional folklorists argue that they use the term technically without these associations, it is an unavoidable fact that...ethnocentrism weighs heavily on the term in its present day usage" (114). After some debate, he decides that the term "oral literature" has the least negative connotation and is best for scholarly discourse. Nevertheless, even after all that productive awareness, Murphy uses racist language like "'tribal' or 'primitive' peoples of non Western nations" (115). The cultural lens is so encompassing that even knowing it's there is not enough to remove it. Even worse, Murphy's language and descriptions create a hierarchy among the societies he is speaking of. By calling non Western oral cultures "primitive" and Western oral cultures "folk", a clear distinction is drawn between the two. The term "primitive" has a decidedly more negative implication than "folk". Parallel with almost all text about societies that use oral literature, he describes the literate society of Europe as the "European academic life" (115). We cannot create hierarchies among societies if we hope to ever attempt to understand other cultures. American teachers must be aware of the consequences of their language and the light in which they describe non Western societies.

Because of the problems with how oral literature is portrayed, the American definition of that particular use of language was written under cultural judgment. In more cases than not, academic minds cannot even agree on a definition of oral literature. Murphy defines the word as "a form of communication which uses words in speech in a highly stylized, artistic way" (113). This definition is close to our previously stated definition of literature. Haslam, however, doesn't directly define oral literature, but relies on the assumed cultural implications of his audience. And in actuality, he writes more about "spoken rhetoric" than oral literature (710). While he cites oral expressions of African American and Native American societies within America, he also claims that modern songs, sermons, and speeches are oral literature. His understanding of what oral literature is has affected the academic integrity of his paper. Those examples are of written literature that is spoken out loud. If Haslam had considered removing his cultural lens, he would have realized that members of societies that use oral literature wouldn't see the point in writing their literature down. The meaning and effect of such literature would be compromised. Americans, as the nationality is understood today, do not have oral literature. The foundations of our nation are rooted in written language.

Stemming from the problems with defining oral literature in the American school system, understanding how to study oral literature is a difficulty that scholars and students face. The first thing that we must understand in order to reliably study oral literature is that it is a whole different type of prose than written. This means that tools and theories used to study written text cannot be used to analyze oral literature. The foundation of understanding oral literature is comprehending the cultures practicing it and knowing the differences that exist between written and spoken prose. If this foundation isn't solid, nothing can be built upon it. This is the area where scholars of oral literature run into the most difficulties.

In his essay, Murphy analyzes different theories that attempt to study oral literature. These theories, however, are Western ideas and are obviously going to run into problems fitting oral literature into their written literature mold. The first issue that is confronted is the difficulty in creating genres for oral literature and making the spoken stories fit into written genres. This is a perfect example of how tools used to organize writing cannot be used to organize spoken words. The next problem is the authors' misunderstanding of the meaning of the stories they're studying. When oral stories are placed on paper, much of the meaning and impact of the story is lost. All oral "literary forms [are] in favor of the hidden or unconscious meaning" (Murphy 121). The meaning of their stories is woven into that specific culture's way of life. Outsiders, like those trying to study oral literature, cannot understand that meaning when the stories are transcribed on paper.

A worse offense than not understanding the meaning of the stories is not understanding the cultures they come from. Some of the theories in Murphy's essay make the claim that the "'natives' do not understand the true significance of their words and symbols" (121). Only someone who doesn't understand oral literature would make that assumption. The characters and themes in oral literature represent the cultural ideals of the people that use those stories. Only children who have yet to learn the full meaning of the words spoken to them might not completely grasp what's being explained to them. Some nature mythologists, as Murphy says, "felt that the original meaning [of the stories] had been lost and their job was to uncover it" (118). These mythologists importantly recognize that oral literature is always adapting to changes in the world of the societies using it. They need to take their understanding a step further, however, and conclude that previous meanings may not be relevant anymore to those people or that the focus of the story could be on another meaning more applicable to their life.

If the meaning of spoken stories is misunderstood, then the function of oral literature will be misunderstood as well. Some of the scholars in Murphy's essay claim that its function is "on the 'distortion' or 'deformation' of meaning" or to entertain (121). Oral literature's function in those societies is to educate, to contain history, and to display the values of the people. It is a significant part of the culture. The entertainment value of the spoken stories is necessary to keep them interesting and alive throughout generations but it is not the only function by any means. Gerald Haslam makes a better point by saying that "literature is for enlightenment just as it is for inspiration" (712). Oral literature is no different. We need to keep reminding ourselves when studying this form of creative language that it is on the same level as written literature. Its function is just as important to its people as written literature is to our American culture.

Despite the criticisms of "Oral Literature", some credit must be given to Murphy and his study. Obviously, it is a step forward for the field of oral literature that any study like this is being performed. Regardless, he doesn't quite reach the level of objectivity needed for fair academic discussion. First, it is important that he realizes that "social context is crucial not simply to understand social life but to better interpret the text" (125). Again, the meaning of a story performed orally is essential to the context of its presentation. Yet, even after realizing that, Murphy claims that studying oral literature as a story written down and studying it in its "communicative event" is a "shift in focus from text to context" (125). This is untrue. The text of oral literature can only be understood in its context. Secondly, he touches on the problem of creating genres in oral literature. He notes, "the form and content of the legend genre is influenced by the audience's shared knowledge of the beliefs underlying the legends" (126). He is dually realizing that oral genres change constantly with the audience and that the audience plays a large role in the meaning of the story. He only needs to understand that there can be four or five written genres within a piece of oral literature. One performance can contain a story, song, proverb, joke, trick, or any combination of those. To complicate the understanding of genres of oral literature even further, genres cross over and change from one culture to another. The creation of a new way to categorize the stories of oral literature, without the influence of a cultural lens, needs to be created to solve this problem.

Professors and professors alike should resist the temptation to teach oral literature as an introduction to written literature. Haslam hold's this opinion in the highest esteem. He claims that oral literature "should be used as a supplement" to other types of written prose (722). He advises professors to "begin an introduction to poetry…with the sung verse" (720). While oral literature may have advanced into written text into some societies, it has grown and developed into an equally sophisticated form of literature. To view oral literature as an introduction to written is like saying that the development of literature is linear: oral to written. And taking it a step further, our cultural lens then wants us to view civilization in that linear path as well: primitive to advanced. Not only are these statements untrue, but also sustain the nonacademic hierarchy in literature. Oral literature should not be taught as an introduction to other forms of literature because, as stated previously, they are completely different fields. If teachers educate their students in this way, the false assumptions that are stunting the progression of the study of oral literature today will persist.

American history has a large impact on its educational practices because Americans are conditioned partially by the actions and beliefs of those that lived in the country before them. Understanding how and why Western civilization changed Native American society and its practice of oral literature is essential to removing the biased ideas that are taught in this country. There were ten million American Indians living in the country before European contact; less than a quarter million survived that contact. The population collapse was due to "epidemic disease, warfare, and genocide" (Snipp 354). In fact, Europeans affected Native American's even before they decided to move onto their land by bringing disease with the first explorers. All of these historical events were no doubt worked into the oral literature practiced among all of the different Native American peoples. Before European contact, Native Americans had a much more pure form of oral literature. The subjects and uses for it pertained only to their cultures and relation with the world. As the way they related to the world changed with the introduction of Western civilization, their stories changed too. Because Native Americans were forced onto reservations, their culture was contained inside those places. Europeans committed not only a destruction of lives, but also the "destruction of tribal culture" (Snipp 355). The European way of life soon dominated the country. The Europeans who conquered the country had only ever used and understood written language as literature. This is the only form of literature to be taught to every child to pass through the American school system. The fact that other forms of literature exist isn't general knowledge. Why should those of Western culture pay attention to aspects of a culture it nearly destroyed, especially if those aspects are different than their own? In another essay titled "Who Speaks for the Earth?" Gerald Haslam comments, "American Indian thought offers...an entirely different way of viewing our world" (44). The conditioned American mind set is that if we over powered the Native Americans, they must be inferior to us and their culture and practices must be inferior to ours. American education, life and culture are based on written literature. Why learn about anything else? Haslam explains better than I could why we should study oral literature: "Oral prose is of great value in altering one's perceptions of the cultures producing it, for literature, rather than popular stereotypes, candidly reflects the aspirations and assumptions of its creators" (715). We only need to make sure that we don't let our popular stereotypes affect our study of it.

Let us now try to remove our cultural lenses and look at what oral literature truly is. After knowing what it is, we can then finally continue forward and analyze it. Oral literature changes as the cultures producing it change. The meaning changes when it is taken out of the culture in which it was created. There are four main aspects necessary to the meaning of an oral piece: the performer, the audience, the setting, and the occasion. Performance is central to understanding the meaning of a piece. There is no way to duplicate a performance and the supposed text of an oral story has a different meaning because of who is performing it. In the foreword of a collection of oral literature of American Indians, Barre Toelken describes, "the stories must remain oral to be alive" (Lopez xiii). Because of our cultural lens, American society has the tendancy to view oral literature as old and solidified, like a genre of literature. Oral literature is none of those things. It continuously changes as the cultures creating it change. As we attempted to force Native Americans to assimilate into our culture, we affected their way of life, including their oral literature. Oral literature is also not history. It may contain historical facts as a way of reminding its people of past events or ideas, but it also contains so much more. This leads into the false idea that oral literature is more simple than written. Barry Lopez explains, in the introduction of his book, that "there were great complexes of stories, some that strung together, could be weeks in the telling. Other stories were told only once in a person's lifetime" (xviii). Oral literature is very complex, although not all of the stories are as long as Lopez describes. Their complexity is "of an entirely different order than most written modes" (Murphy 710). If the professors in the American school system can learn these few facts about oral literature and even about the cultures that create it, we wouldn't have many of the problems with the education of oral literature.

We have looked at many of the problems with studying oral literature in a Western school system, as well as, some solutions to those problems. We must now work towards fixing the exclusion of oral literature from the American education system, our understanding of American oral literature and attempt to solve the academic problems caused by our misunderstanding. The solution to all the problems of the education of Americans relating to oral literature lies in the realization of the cultural lens and then its removal. In this way, not just oral literature, but many aspects of foreign cultures can be studied in a fair, engaging way. As minds of higher education, we need to begin to produce this change. We need to be aware of all types of literature and treat them as equals, to attempt to fully understand the field we're studying, and to be wary of the social implications of our language.

Works Cited

Haslam, Gerald. "American Oral Literature: Our Forgotten Heritage." The English Journal 60.6 (1971): 709723. JSTOR. 2 Feb. 2009 <http://www.jstor.org/search>.

--. "Who Speaks for the Earth?" The English Journal 61.1 (1973): 4248. JSTOR. 11 Feb. 2009 <http://www.jstor.org/search>.

Lopez, Barry. Giving Birth to Thunder, Sleeping with His Daughter: Coyote Builds North America. New York: Avon, 1977.

Murphy, William P. "Oral Literature." Annual Review of Anthropology 7 (1978): 113132. JSTOR. 2 Feb. 2009 <http://www.jstor.org/stable2155690>.

Snipp, C. Matthew. "Sociological Perspectives on American Indians." Annual Review of Sociology 18 (1992): 351371. JSTOR. 2 Feb. 2009 <http://www.jstor.org/search>.

6.10: Writing to Learn – Analyzing Writing from Across the Curriculum

Reread the three essays above and, individually or in small groups, answer the following questions:

1. What kinds of research methods were used in each essay? How did these methods differ for each discipline?
2. What was used as evidence to support each author's arguments? How did the evidence differ for each discipline?
3. How would you describe the voice and style of each author? How did the voice and style differ for each discipline?
4. What kinds of organizational strategies were used by each author? How did these strategies differ for each discipline?

The three essays presented above give a sense of how the natural sciences, the social sciences, and the arts and humanities differ in terms of research methods, writing style, and conventions. Before you read about each of these disciplines in more detail in Chapters 7, 8, and 9, consider some basic ways these three disciplines differ.

Reading, Writing, and Researching in the Natural Sciences

- Scientists use reading, writing, and researching to explore questions about the physical universe.
- Scientists use observations to make hypotheses and then test these hypotheses by designing experiments, building on what other scientists have observed and reported in academic journals and books.
- Scientists report the results of their experiments in written genres such as lab reports and scientific research reports.
- Because scientists follow the research methods of observation and hypothesis-testing using experimentation, genres like the lab report and the scientific research report are organized in sections that correspond to the systematic, scientific approach to research: an introduction describing the hypothesis and background for the study, a section describing the research materials and methods, a section reporting the results of the study, and a discussion section that explores the significance of the results.
- Because scientists try to report accurately on complicated natural phenomena, they value concise and precise language and formal conventions.
- Even though scientific research methods and conventions are fairly formal, some scientists break out of these conventions (e.g. by writing personal stories about their work or writing for general audiences).

Reading, Writing, and Researching in the Social Sciences

- Social scientists use reading, writing, and researching to explore questions about human interaction.
- Social scientists, like natural scientists, inquire by forming hypotheses, but social scientists' hypotheses focus on human behavior. Social scientists test these hypotheses by designing social or psychological experiments, collecting data through interviews or surveys, or systematically observing human behavior, building on what other social scientists have observed and reported in academic journals and books.

- Social scientists conduct research using quantitative methods (methods that result in numbers and statistics) and qualitative methods (methods focused on observing, describing, and analyzing social behavior, social artifacts, and social institutions).
- Social scientists report the results of their experiments, data collection, or systematic observations in the written genres of case studies, surveys, interviews, ethnographies, and research reports.
- Social scientists build theories of human behavior based on their research, and these theories are constantly being debated by social science discourse communities of writers and researchers.
- Because social scientists study human behavior using a variety of approaches and genres, the level of formality and conventions of social science writing will depend on the writer's purpose, audience, and genre. In general, social scientists tend to value writing that is precise and logically organized and that follows the conventions of whatever social science genre they're writing in.
- Even though social science genres have purposes and conventions that have been agreed upon over time by communities of social scientists, these genres are constantly evolving, and social scientists are always creating new genres and new conventions.

Reading, Writing, and Researching in the Arts and Humanities

- Arts and humanities scholars use reading, writing, and researching to explore questions about the meaning and value of human experiences and artistic creations.
- Arts and humanities scholars make arguments and support their arguments by using the application of theories, close readings of texts and other artifacts, and discussions of personal experiences. When arts and humanities scholars make arguments or develop theories, they build on the conversation of academic discourse communities taking place in scholarly journals and books.
- Arts and humanities scholars publish their arguments in a variety of written genres such as reviews, critical analysis papers, interviews, creative writing, and scholarly books.
- Because arts and humanities scholars focus on exploring ideas and arguments rather than conducting systematic experiments, arts and humanities genres tend to be less prescriptive than scientific genres in terms of lan-

guage and form. Because the theories and arguments expressed by arts and humanities scholars are often personal and subjective, a personal voice and engaging style is often valued in arts and humanities writing.

Review of Key Ideas in Chapter 6

- Academic fields such as the natural sciences, the social sciences, and the arts and humanities are referred to as *disciplines*. A discipline is a discourse community of readers, writers, and researchers who share similar ways of thinking and making knowledge, and similar genres and research methods.

- Most colleges have a general education or core curriculum requirement that allows you to take introductory courses in the natural sciences, social sciences, and arts and humanities before you enter your major. This general education/core curriculum requirement is important because it gives you an introduction to the ways of reading, writing, and researching in different fields.

- What counts as *good writing* will be different for each discipline, and even different professors in the same department will have different ideas about what good writing means.

- The writing and researching process you practice in a first-year writing course will help prepare you for writing across the curriculum, but it's impossible for one course to prepare you for the variety of kinds of reading, writing, and researching you'll encounter across the curriculum.

- In general, natural scientists use reading, writing, and researching to explore questions about the physical universe; social scientists use reading, writing, and researching to explore questions about human behavior and social systems; and arts and humanities scholars use reading, writing, and researching to explore questions about the meaning and value of human history and artistic creations.

6.11: Writing to Learn – A Question about Writing across the Curriculum

Write down one question you have about writing in the natural sciences, one question about writing in the social sciences, and one question about writing in the arts and humanities. Keep these questions in mind when you read Chapters 7–9.

7 Reading, Writing, and Researching in the Natural Sciences

Learning how to write about science…is as important as learning how to understand theories, formulate hypotheses, perform experiments, and analyze data.
—Professor David Porush, Literature and Media Studies, Rensselaer
Polytechnic Institute (Porush, 1995: 3)

The major goal of a scientific paper…is to report descriptive or experimental observations that relate to a particular question. Because of this priority, some conventions have evolved that most scientific writers follow. When you first try these you may feel confined and awkward, in somewhat the same way as in writing a first haiku or sonnet. Challenge yourself to stay within the confines of these conventions while still writing as well as you possibly can.

—Dickinson College Biology Department writing guide
(Dickinson College Biology Department, 2010)

When you write scientific papers, your primary reasons for writing are to communicate information and to persuade others of the validity of your findings.

—Professor Karin Knisely, Biology, Bucknell University
(Knisely, 2005: 19)

7.1: Writing to Learn – Your Prior Knowledge of Writing in the Natural Sciences

The purpose of this Writing to Learn activity is to think about your experiences with writing in the natural sciences before you read this chapter. Think back to the writing you've done in science courses (in high school or college or both). Write about some of the features of the science writing you've done. What were the purposes and audiences for writing? What conventions did you follow? How would you describe the persona you took on in writing for science classes?

Writing and Critical Thinking in the Natural Sciences

The last part of Chapter 6 gave you an overview of some of the features of reading, writing, and researching in the natural sciences. Take another look at this overview to refresh your memory of the way I described writing in the natural sciences:

- Scientists use reading, writing, and researching to explore questions about the physical universe.
- Scientists use observations to make hypotheses and then test these hypotheses by designing experiments, building on what other scientists have observed and reported in academic journals and books.

- Scientists report the results of their experiments in written genres such as lab reports and scientific research reports.
- Because scientists follow the research methods of observation and hypothesis-testing using experimentation, genres such as the lab report and the scientific research report are organized in sections that correspond to the systematic, scientific approach to research: an introduction describing the hypothesis and background for the study, a section describing the research materials and methods, a section reporting the results of the study, and a discussion section that explores the significance of the results.
- Because scientists try to report accurately on complicated natural phenomena, they value concise and precise language and formal conventions.
- Even though scientific research methods and conventions are fairly formal, some scientists break out of these conventions (for example, by writing personal stories about their work or writing for general audiences).

At most institutions, the natural sciences include biology, chemistry, environmental science, physics, astronomy, and geology. Let's take a look at some assignments from science courses to get a better sense of the features of writing in the natural sciences. Read the three sample natural science writing assignments given below and think about the professor's expectations in each of the assignments and how those expectations connect to the overview of the features of writing in the natural sciences as discussed above.

Sample Natural Sciences Writing Assignments

Physics Assignment from Professor Hank Yochum, Sweet Briar College Skyline Community College

Hints on writing a lab report

Title Page
Include your name, the names of your group members, and the date the experiment was performed. Include your abstract on the title page.

Abstract
WHAT IS THE PURPOSE OF THE LABORATORY EXPERIMENT??? What are you trying to measure? Do not put procedure in the purpose. This need not be lengthy, a few sentences is often enough. As a scientist it is your job to convey *exactly* what you did and measured.

Introduction

This should contain background information about the physical concepts explored and the derivations of important equations tested or used. Under what conditions are the equations you are using valid? Is there any historical or technological importance to the quantity you are measuring or theory you are testing?

Procedure and Equipment

State what equipment you used. A sketch is usually useful here. Very briefly outline your procedure. What quantities did you measure? How many times did you measure them and why?

Data

A nice looking table or tables of the data you took. Make sure this is well organized! Columns should be labeled and units given. I want ALL the data you took, though it does not necessarily need to be in the lab report body, it can be placed in an appendix. If your data is in your notebook, simply photocopying the notebook is fine. In general we will not have large data sets so putting all data in the report will be ok. Remember, use only the data *you* collected in class! Using other groups' data is cheating.

Data Analysis and Results

Show your data and error analysis. This includes showing the equations you used and showing your calculations. If a calculation is repetitive, only one sample calculation may be appropriate. Tables of the important calculated quantities should be here as well. What was the result of the experiment? Graphs (well labeled) may be appropriate here. Always refer to figures/tables in text. For example, The schematic of the experimental setup is contained in Figure 1. If you don't remember how to do error analysis, consult the handouts I gave you.

Discussion

Compare your results to a theoretical value if appropriate. Does the result confirm a law of physics? How does the discrepancy between measurement and theory compare to systematic (error due to inaccuracy of equipment, no piece of equipment has perfect accuracy) or random error (taking multiple measurements reduces this)? List sources of error. Human error is not an option here. If you list human error here your will get no credit for this section of the lab report.

Conclusion

The purpose of the experiment should be restated concisely. Was the purpose of the experiment met? If not why? Possibly suggest improvements or enhancements of the experiment. If making a measurement of a particular quantity, requote your result with appropriate error.

A couple more things:
1) Number equations and reference them by number where appropriate in the text.
2) Label figures (graphs), tables with numbers and a title, e.g. Figure 1. Experimental Setup.
3) Include figures and tables in your text. Cut and paste excel plots directly into your document.

Biology Assignment from Professor Lidia Kos, Florida International University

Debate (30% total grade)
The class will be divided into groups of two or three. Two groups will be assigned to a debate day and will have to prepare a short Powerpoint presentation (10–15 minutes) to report to the rest of the class their arguments. One group will collect arguments in favor and the other, against the statement presented for the day. Hardcopies of the presentations will be handed in on the day of the debate. Arguments should be accompanied by references (can be from primary literature, textbook, web, a researcher you know…). At least two papers from the primary literature (preferably not cited in your textbook and published within the last 5 years) should be part of the materials used. All members of the group should be prepared to present. The presenter will be chosen on the day of the presentation by a drawing. The rest of the class will have a 5 minute question period to clarify with the groups their arguments. Each student will then have 15 minutes to write one–two paragraphs stating which group won the debate and justify it based on the arguments presented. These will be turned in at the end of the class. Presentations will be worth 10 points and conclusion paragraphs, 4 points each. Presentations will be graded based on content and organization (not delivery).

Statements to be addressed:
(10/03): Invertebrates preferentially use the cell-autonomous mode of specification.
(10/12): During amphibian gastrulation the ectoderm is induced to become neural tissue.
(10/31): All neural crest cells are initially pluripotent.
(11/14) The heart is formed by two cell lineages.
(11/21): In mammalian sex determination, female is the default sex.
(12/05): Evolution is accomplished through heritable alterations in developmental gene expression patterns.

How to prepare:

1. Read the statement you are going to address carefully. Make sure you understand it.
2. Read the material in the textbook that corresponds to the subject. You might find related information in various chapters or the accompanying websites.
3. For those of you searching for pro or con arguments, use the textbook material as a basis for your own research. I would like you to try to find recent papers (primary literature) supporting your position. However, any source of material is fair game.
4. Put together a short Powerpoint presentation (10–15 minutes) that includes a very brief background of the subject and two or three slides with your arguments (would be good to have figures illustrating the data obtained in the papers). Print the slides and bring me a hardcopy in the day of the debate.
5. During the debate, other members of the class will listen to the presenters and should take notes to help them write the conclusion statement. It would be good to read the related information in the textbook prior to class. Based on the arguments presented by both groups, decide whether you want to support the statement or not. Write a paragraph or two explaining why you reached this conclusion. You should point out which arguments made you decide in favor or against the statement (A sentence saying that the arguments presented by group one were stronger than those presented by group two will not be sufficient). You will have to turn in your conclusion on the day of the debate. If you are absent, you get a 0.

Chemistry Assignment Created by Students from Professor Katherine Kantardjieff Chemistry Class, California State University, Fullerton

Audience analysis of journals and periodicals

1. Go to the library (or surf the net) and identify *five* journals/periodicals in your field.
2. Select three of the five and survey back issues of all three journals for one year.
3. What kinds of papers or articles tend to be solicited or accepted by these journals?
4. What do the journals have in common in terms of subject matter and writing style?

5. Write a short summary of the content of each journal over that year; the summary should consist of supported generalizations derived from your survey.

6. Based on your analysis, write a description of what you believe to be the audience for these journals? Don't say simply "expert" or "general".

7. The Proceedings of the National Academy of Science, USA states in the "Information to Contributors" that "Papers should be written to be understandable to scientists in many disciplines." What would such papers share in common with papers written for a select scientific audience?

7.2: Writing to Learn – Expectations for Writing in the Natural Sciences

Reread the natural science writing assignments above and underline places in the assignments that focus on each professor's expectations and criteria for writing. Individually or in small groups, discuss the assignments and come up with a list of some of the features of writing in the sciences, based on the evidence you found in these three assignments. As you reread and discuss the assignments, think of some of the features of college writing situations we discussed in Part I: purpose, audience, persona, genre, and conventions.

7.3: Learn by Doing – Analyzing Natural Science Assignments

Now that you've practiced analyzing the natural science writing assignments in the previous section, take a closer look at writing in the sciences at your college. Collect two writing assignments from lower-division natural science courses (non-major or general education courses). These two assignments can be from the same course or from different courses. You can collect these assignments from a course you're taking, by requesting them from science professors at your college, or by surfing your college's Web site (e.g. you could go to the search engine on your college's Web site and enter different key terms such as "lab report" or "biology" and "writing assignments"). Once you've collected the assignments, write a 1–2 page rhetorical analysis of the assignments in which you explore some of the following questions:

1. What purposes are students asked to write for? What thinking strategies are required (summarizing, evaluating, synthesizing, arguing)?

2. Does the assignment ask for a recognizable science genre? What are the conventions of the genre?

3. Who is the audience for the writing?

4. What kind of persona is expected?

Examples of Writing in the Natural Sciences

Now that you've analyzed some science writing assignments, you're ready to gain a better sense of science writing by giving a close reading to some sample science texts. The examples of science writing provided below are from three common science genres. The first piece of writing is a scientific abstract, which is a summary of a scientific experiment or report. Abstracts are often found at the beginning of articles in science journals, and they help other scientists reading the journal to have an overall sense of the purpose, methods, and results of the experiment. The second piece of writing is an excerpt from a popular science book aimed at audiences who are interested in science but not experts on the topic. Many scientists report their research in books and articles that are aimed at nonexpert audiences who are interested in science but don't have the experience and expertise to understand formal scientific research reports. The final example of science writing is from a student lab report. We'll talk more about lab reports as an example of a common science genre in the next section of this chapter.

Abstract from the Journal, *Current Biology* (Pruetz and Bertolani, 2007: 412)

Although tool use is known to occur in species ranging from naked mole rats to owls, chimpanzees are the most accomplished tool users. The modification and use of tools during hunting, however, is still considered to be a uniquely human trait among primates. Here, we report the first account of habitual tool use during vertebrate hunting by nonhumans. At the Fongoli site in Senegal, we observed ten different chimpanzees use tools to hunt prosimian prey in 22 bouts. This includes immature chimpanzees and females, members of age-sex classes not normally characterized by extensive hunting behavior. Chimpanzees made 26 different tools, and we were able to recover and analyze 12 of these. Tool construction entailed up to five steps, including trimming the tool tip to a point. Tools were used in the manner of a spear, rather than a probe or rousing tool. This new information on chimpanzee tool use has important implications for the evolution of tool use and construction for hunting in the earliest hominids, especially given our observations that females and immature chimpanzees exhibited this behavior more frequently than adult males.

Excerpt from the Popular Science Book, *A Brief History of Time: From the Big Bang to Black Holes*, by Stephen Hawking (Hawking, 1988: 123)

At the big bang itself, the universe is thought to have had zero size, and so to have been infinitely hot. But as the universe expanded, the temperature of the radiation decreased. One second after the big bang, it would have fallen to about ten thousand million degrees. This is about a thousand times the temperature at the center of the sun, but temperatures as high as this are reached in H-bomb explosions. At this time the universe would have contained mostly photons, electrons, and neutrons (extremely light particles that are affected only by the weak force and gravity) and their antiparticles, together with some protons and neutrons. As the universe continued to expand and the temperature to drop, the rate at which electron/antielectron pairs were being produced in collisions would have fallen below the rate at which they were being destroyed by annihilation. So most of the electrons and antielectrons would have annihilated each other to produce more photons, leaving only a few electrons left over. The neutrinos and antineutrinos, however, would not have annihilated with each other, because these particles interact with themselves and with other particles only very weakly. So they should still be around today. If we could observe them, it would provide a good test of this picture of a very hot early stage of the universe. Unfortunately, their energies nowadays would be too low for us to observe them directly. However, if neutrinos are not massless, but have a small mass of their own, as suggested by an unconfirmed Russian experiment performed in 1981, we might be able to detect them indirectly: they could be a form of "dark matter," like that mentioned earlier, with sufficient gravitational attraction to stop the expansion of the universe and cause it to collapse again.

Excerpt from "Active Ion Transport across Frog Epithelium," a Lab Report Written by Avani Desai for a Science Course at Northwestern University (Desai, 2006: 10)

One of the main goals of this experiment was to determine if active transportation occurs across the frog skin. In part 1 of the lab, it was proved that active transport did indeed occur. Because the concentrations and the solutions on both sides of the skin were the same, there was no electrochemical gradient and therefore no passive transport would have occurred. Yet there was still movement across the skin because there was indeed a transtissue potential. This amount of flow across that membrane could be determined using the short-circuit current. This current indirectly represents the magnitude of the ions flowing across skin; directly, it measures the amount of charge flow needed to counteract the charge flow already occurring in the system. Because there was no passive transport, this flow could only be due to the active transport of the ions. The next aim was to determine if ions other than Na^+ were passing across the skin. The NFR solution was used to measure Na^+ transport. When a high concentration of Li^+ was substituted in, there was a drop in V_{tt} and I_{sc}, in both the group's data and average of the entire class' data (see Table 3 for class data). This indicates that less Li^+ moved across the skin compared to the Na^+. Li^+ has the same charge, but it is smaller in size compared to

Na$^+$. Thus, tt is similar enough to Na$^+$ and small enough that it can pass through Na$^+$ channels, but it cannot bind to the Na$^+$ binding site on the pump. This provides evidence for the pump being specific to Na$^+$ conductance. Furthermore, since K$^+$ is bigger than Na$^+$, it will clog the Na$^+$ channels, as well as the pumps. Fittingly, V_{tt} and I_{sc} decreased by a very large amount, showing even more that it is only Na$^+$ that is being actively transported. Although our individual group's V_{tt} dropped in accordance with the entire class' data, the I_{sc} did not really decrease. In fact, it was higher than that of Li$^+$. The reason for this is that the ammeter was not working well at all. It was not possible to increase the amplitude until V_{tt} reached zero and then take a reading. Thus, in order to take measurements, the knob had to be turned to a maximum and then the ammeter would be turned on. The current would start out high then quickly decrease and the measurement at $V_{tt} = 0$ had to be taken as fast as possible; the point at which $V_{tt} = 0$ could not be held. This undoubtedly led to many errors in all of the short-circuit current data.

7.4: Writing to Learn – Features of Writing in the Natural Sciences

The purpose of this Writing to Learn activity is for you to look closely at the previous examples of science writing and think about important features of writing in the sciences. Reread the three examples of science writing and individually or in small groups come up with a list of features of science writing based on what you've read. With each feature, include a specific example or two from the texts. For example, if you find that one aspect of science writing is being concise, find examples of concise sentences. Be prepared to talk about these features of writing in the sciences as a class.

Exploring Genre in the Natural Sciences: The Lab Report

7.5: Writing to Learn – Reviewing the Concept of *Genre*

Before you read about a common natural science genre – the lab report – review the concept of *genre*. Go back to Chapter 2 and reread the section that discusses genre. Make a list of the concepts and features that define *genre*. Be prepared to list these concepts and features as a class.

Writing might not be the first thing that comes to mind when you think of the natural sciences. You might be surprised how often scientists write to explain their theories and the results of their experiments to fellow scientists and to the general public. You'd probably also be surprised by how many genres of science writing there are: scientific abstracts, experimental reports, poster presentations, popular science books, grant proposals, reviews of scientific literature, field notes, and lab reports. In this section of Chapter 7, rather than try to discuss every type of science genre you might encounter in natural science courses, we'll focus on one common science genre: the lab report. By looking closely at the lab report, you can learn a lot about writing and thinking like a scientist.

Remember that genres are typical responses to rhetorical situations that occur again and again. In the case of the lab report, the rhetorical situation is scientists using the scientific method of forming a hypothesis and then testing it through an experiment. The genre of the lab report evolved over time as a way for scientists to report the results of their experiments in clear and organized ways to other scientists. The discourse community of scientists found that lab reports would be most useful if they had an introduction that describes the hypothesis and background for the experiment, a section on the research methods used, a section that reports the results of the study, a discussion section that explores the significance of the results, and often a conclusion summarizing the results of the experiment and any other key points of the research. This organization is more than simply a template scientists use to plug in information. It's a way to put the scientific method into action and a form that all scientists around the world can follow to communicate their research methods and the results of their experiments clearly to other scientists. If your lab report is well written, other scientists should be able to understand how you conducted your experiment and why you got the results you did. They should also be able to replicate your experiment in their own labs.

Let's review the lab report assignment that was included at the beginning of Chapter 1, a physics lab report assignment from Professor Al Cordes of Clinton Community College:

> Think of a lab report as a document that reports new findings to people that are not necessarily familiar with the concepts with which you are experimenting. It should be written as though you are reporting the results of a new scientific study. Each report should have the following sections:
>
> (1) **Introduction** This section should be a description of the background information that is critical to the experiment, including an explanation as to why the experiment

is significant and a statement of the hypothesis to be tested.

(2) **Methods and Materials** This section should include a detailed description of how the data was collected, and describe dependent and independent variables where applicable.

(3) **Results** Here you should present tables and graphs of data neatly labeled. Calculations are also included in this section. They should be clear and well-organized.

(4) **Discussion/Conclusion** Here you explain and interpret your results. Answer the question: what do these results show? Patterns and trends should be identified and you should conclude as to whether your results support or refute your hypothesis. Also in this section, describe sources of error and how they impacted your results.

Sample Lab Report

Now that you've reviewed a lab report assignment, let's take a close look at a lab report written for an ecology course at North Carolina State University.

The Optimal Foraging Theory: Food Selection in Beavers Based on Tree Species, Size, and Distance (North Carolina State University, 2004)

Abstract. The theory of optimal foraging and its relation to central foraging was examined by using the beaver as a model. Beaver food choice was examined by noting the species of woody vegetation, status (chewed vs. not-chewed), distance from the water, and circumference of trees near a beaver pond in North Carolina. Beavers avoided certain species of trees and preferred trees that were close to the water. No preference for tree circumference was noted. These data suggest that beaver food choice concurs with the optimal foraging theory.

Introduction

In this lab, we explore the theory of optimal foraging and the theory of central place foraging using beavers as the model animal. Foraging refers to the mammalian behavior associated with searching for food. The optimal foraging theory assumes that animals feed in a way that maximizes their net rate of energy intake per unit time (Pyke et al. 1977). An animal may either maximize its daily energy intake (energy maximizer) or minimize the time spent feeding (time minimizer) in order to meet minimum requirements. Herbivores commonly behave as energy maximizers (Belovsky 1986) and accomplish this maximizing behavior by choosing food that is of high quality and has low-search and low-handling time (Pyke et al. 1977).

The central place theory is used to describe animals that collect food and store it in a fixed location in their home range, the central place (Jenkins 1980). The factors associated with the optimal foraging theory also apply to the central place theory. The central place theory predicts that retrieval costs increase linearly with distance of the resource from the central place (Rockwood and Hubbell 1987). Central place feeders are very selective when choosing food that is far from the central place since they have to spend time and energy hauling it back to the storage site (Schoener 1979).

The main objective of this lab was to determine beaver (<u>Castor</u> <u>canadensis</u>) food selection based on tree species, size, and distance. Since beavers are energy maximizers (Jenkins 1980, Belovsky 1984) and central place feeders (McGinley and Whitam 1985), they make an excellent test animal for the optimal foraging theory. Beavers eat several kinds of herbaceous plants as well as the leaves, twigs, and bark of most species of woody plants that grow near water (Jenkins and Busher 1979). By examining the trees that are chewed or not-chewed in the beavers' home range, an accurate assessment of food preferences among tree species may be gained (Jenkins 1975). The purpose of this lab was to learn about the optimal foraging theory. We wanted to know if beavers put the optimal foraging theory into action when selecting food.

We hypothesized that the beavers in this study will choose trees that are small in circumference and closest to the water. Since the energy yield of tree species may vary significantly, we also hypothesized that beavers will show a preference for some species of trees over others regardless of circumference size or distance from the central area. The optimal foraging theory and central place theory lead us to predict that beavers, like most herbivores, will maximize their net rate of energy intake per unit time. In order to maximize energy, beavers will choose trees that are closest to their central place (the water) and require the least retrieval cost. Since beavers are trying to maximize energy, we hypothesized that they will tend to select some species of trees over others on the basis of nutritional value.

Methods

This study was conducted at Yates Mill Pond, a research area owned by the North Carolina State University, on October 25th, 1996. Our research area was located along the edge of the pond and was approximately 100 m in length and 28 m in width. There was no beaver activity observed beyond this width. The circumference, the species, status (chewed or not-chewed), and distance from the water were recorded for each tree in the study area. Due to the large number of trees sampled, the work was evenly divided among four groups of students working in quadrants. Each group contributed to the overall data collected.

We conducted a chi-squared test to analyze the data with respect to beaver selection of certain tree species. We conducted t-tests to determine (1) if avoided trees were significantly farther from the water than selected trees, and (2) if chewed trees were significantly larger or smaller than not chewed trees. Mean tree distance from the water and mean tree circumference were also recorded.

Results

Overall, beavers showed a preference for certain species of trees, and their preference was based on distance from the central place. Measurements taken at the study site show that beavers avoided oaks and musclewood (Fig. 1) and show a significant food preference (x^2=447.26, d.f.=9, P<.05). No avoidance or particular preference was observed for the other tree species. The mean distance of 8.42 m away from the water for not-chewed trees was significantly greater than the mean distance of 6.13 m for chewed trees (t=3.49, d.f.=268, P<.05) (Fig. 2). The tree species that were avoided were not significantly farther from the water (t=.4277, d.f.=268, P>.05) than selected trees. For the selected tree species, no significant difference in circumference was found between trees that were not chewed (mean=16.03 cm) and chewed (mean=12.80 cm) (t=1.52, d.f.=268, P>.05) (Fig. 3).

Discussion

Although beavers are described as generalized herbivores, the finding in this study related to species selection suggests that beavers are selective in their food choice. This finding agrees with our hypothesis that beavers are likely to show a preference for certain tree species. Although beaver selection of certain species of trees may be related to the nutritional value, additional information is needed to determine why beavers select some tree species over others. Other studies suggested that beavers avoid trees that have chemical defenses that make the tree unpalatable to beavers (Muller-Schawarze et al. 1994). These studies also suggested that beavers prefer trees with soft wood, which could possibly explain the observed avoidance of musclewood and oak in our study.

The result that chewed trees were closer to the water accounts for the time and energy spent gathering and hauling. This is in accordance with the optimal foraging theory and agrees with our hypothesis that beavers will choose trees that are close to the water. As distance from the water increases, a tree's net energy yield decreases because food that is farther away is more likely to increase search and retrieval time. This finding is similar to Belovsky's finding of an inverse relationship between distance from the water and percentage of plants cut.

The lack of any observed difference in mean circumference between chewed and not chewed trees does not agree with our hypothesis that beavers will prefer smaller trees to larger ones. Our hypothesis was based on the idea that branches from smaller trees will require less energy to cut and haul than those from larger trees. Our finding is in accordance with other studies (Schoener 1979), which have suggested that the value of all trees should decrease with distance from the water but that beavers would benefit from choosing large branches from large trees at all distances. This would explain why there was no significant difference in circumference between chewed and not-chewed trees.

This lab gave us the opportunity to observe how a specific mammal selects foods that maximize energy gains in accordance with the optimal foraging theory. Although beavers adhere to the optimal foraging theory, without additional information on relative nutritional value of tree species and the time and energy costs of cutting certain tree species, no optimal diet predictions may be made. Other information is also needed about predatory risk and its role in food selection. Also, due to the large number of students taking samples in the field, there may have been errors which may have affected the accuracy and precision of our measurements. In order to corroborate our findings, we suggest that this study be repeated by others.

Conclusion

The purpose of this lab was to learn about the optimal foraging theory by measuring tree selection in beavers. We now know that the optimal foraging theory allows us to predict food-seeking behavior in beavers with respect to distance from their central place and, to a certain extent, to variations in tree species. We also learned that foraging behaviors and food selection is not always straightforward. For instance, beavers selected large branches at any distance from the water even though cutting large branches may increase energy requirements. There seems to be a fine line between energy intake and energy expenditure in beavers that is not so easily predicted by any given theory.

Literature Cited

Belovsky, G.E. 1984. Summer diet optimization by beaver. The American Midland Naturalist. 111: 209–222.

Belovsky, G.E. 1986. Optimal foraging and community structure: implications for a guild of generalist grassland herbivores. Oecologia. 70: 35–52.

Jenkins, S.H. 1975. Food selection by beavers: a multidimensional contingency table analysis. Oecologia. 21: 157–173.

Jenkins, S.H. 1980. A size–distance relation in food selection by beavers. Ecology. 61: 740–746.

Jenkins, S.H., and P.E. Busher. 1979. Castor canadensis. Mammalian Species. 120: 1–8.

McGinly, M.A., and T.G. Whitham. 1985. Central place foraging by beavers (*Castor Canadensis*): a test of foraging predictions and the impact of selective feeding on the growth form of cottonwoods (*Populus fremontii*). Oecologia. 66: 558–562.

Muller-Schwarze, B., A. Schulte, L. Sun, A. Muller-Schhwarze, and C. Muller-Schwarze. 1994. Red Maple (*Acer rubrum*) inhibits feeding behavior by beaver (*Castor canadensis*). Journal of Chemical Ecology. 20: 2021–2033.

Pyke, G.H., H.R. Pulliman, E.L. Charnov. 1977. Optimal foraging. The Quarterly Review of Biology. 52: 137–154.

Rockwood, L.L., and S.P. Hubbell. 1987. Host-plant selection, diet diversity, and optimal foraging in a tropical leaf-cutting ant. Oecologia. 74: 55–61.

Schoener, T.W. 1979. Generality of the size–distance relation in models of optimal feeding. The American Naturalist. 114: 902–912.

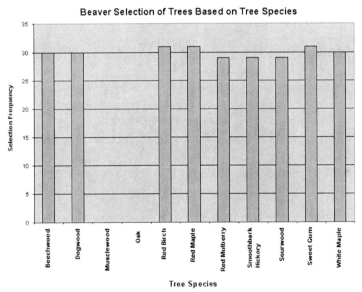

Figure 1.

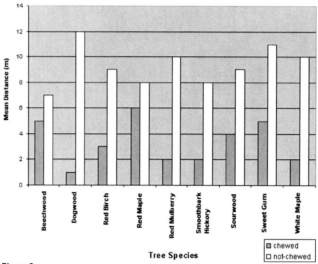

Figure 2.

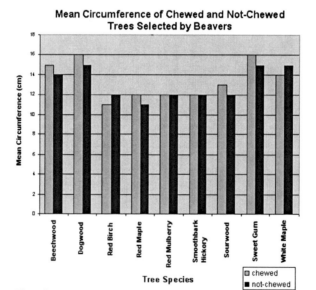

Figure 3.

7.6: Writing to Learn – Analyzing a Lab Report

The purpose of this Writing to Learn activity is to help you understand the genre of the lab report by looking closely at the lab report, "The Optimal Foraging Theory," and discussing it in small groups and as a class. First, reread the lab report. As you read, think about the features of the genre of the lab report and underline any sentences that illustrate these features. Think about aspects of genre like purpose, audience, conventions, and persona. Discuss these features of the lab report in small groups and come up with a list of five features of the genre of the lab report with examples from "The Optimal Foraging Theory" that illustrate these features. Be prepared to discuss what you've found as a class.

Expanding the Conventions of Science Writing: A Student Gets Creative

7.7: Writing to Learn – Breaking with the Conventions of Scientific Writing

The purpose of this Writing to Learn activity is for you to think about ways that students can sometimes break with the conventions of science writing we've been discussing in this chapter. Reread Katrina Outland's article, "The Blob that Attacked Waikiki: The Box Jellyfish Invasion of Hawaii," from Chapter 6. Discuss the ways that Outland's article breaks with some of the conventions of science writing we've been discussing in this chapter.

It's true that most science writing follows the conventions we discussed in the sample passages and the sample lab report in this chapter, but there are some science genres and rhetorical situations that allow you to be a little more creative and to break with the usual conventions of the discourse community of scientists. An example of this is Katrina Outland's article, "The Blob that Attacked Waikiki: The Box Jellyfish Invasion of Hawaii" (Outland, 2008), from Chapter 6. Katrina published this article in *The Journal of Young Investigators*, a journal of undergraduate science writing. *JYI* is run by students and has an audience of students and the general public. The articles in *JYI* are not aimed at scientists who are experts in the area, but at undergraduate students and a general audience of nonexperts. This kind of rhetorical situation allowed Katrina to be creative in her approach to science writing, since she knew she was trying to interest an audience of non-scientists in her topic. Right from the start, Katrina was trying to find creative ways to draw her readers in. The title of her article plays on horror movies ("The Blob that Attacked Waikiki"), and the first sentence of her article sounds like the opening of a book by the horror writer Stephen King: "They come ten days after the full moon, swarming to shore, nearly invisible and wielding poison-loaded tentacles." Katrina's headings are much more playful and informal than the usual headings you would see in a scientific paper: for example, her heading, "Oww! I've been stung!"

Katrina's article shows that sometimes scientists don't follow conventions such as using an objective tone, passive voice, or a standard format. It all depends on the rhetorical situation. If you were writing the lab report for chemistry professor Al Cordes that we looked at in the beginning of this section, you would want to follow the conventions of science writing and the genre of the lab report so your experiment and results would be clear to your professor and to other scientists. If your professor asks you to create a poster explaining evolution for middle school students, you'd probably want to avoid being too formal in your writing and try to find creative ways to appeal to your audience, just as Katrina Outland did in "The Blob that Attacked Waikiki."

Reading in the Natural Sciences

Here's what Professor Jan Pechenik, a biology professor at Tufts University, has to say about reading in the sciences:

> Reading a scientific paper is unlike reading a work of fiction or even a text-book. The primary scientific literature must be read slowly, thoughtfully, and patiently, and a single paper must usually be reread several times before it can be thoroughly understood; don't become discouraged after only one or two readings. (Pechenik, 2007: 28)

Because the natural science reading you'll be doing in college will be challenging, it's going to be important for you to use the kinds of active reading strategies we talked about in Chapter 4. An example of one of these strategies, annotating, is provided below. It is an annotation of the excerpt from Stephen Hawking's *A Brief History of Time* from earlier in this chapter. Take a look at the annotated excerpt and the explanation that follows it of the annotating strategy one student took.

Sample Annotation of a Science Text

At the big bang itself, the universe is thought to have had zero size, and so to have been infinitely hot. But as the universe expanded, the temperature of the radiation decreased. One second after the big bang, it would have fallen to about ten thousand million degrees. This is about a thousand times the temperature at the center of the sun, but temperatures as high as this are reached in H-bomb explosions. At this time the universe would have contained mostly photons, electrons, and neutrons (extremely light particles that are affected only by the weak force and gravity) and their antiparticles, together with some protons and neutrons. As the universe continued to expand and the temperature to drop, the rate at which electron/antielectron pairs were being produced in collisions would have fallen below the rate at which they were being destroyed by annihilation. So most of the electrons and antielectrons would have annihilated with each other to produce more photons, leaving only a few electrons left over. The neutrinos and antineutrinos, however, would not have annihilated each other, because these particles interact with themselves and with other particles only very weakly. So they should still be around today. If we could observe them, it would provide a good test of this picture of a very hot early stage of the universe. Unfortunately, their energies nowadays would be too low for us to observe them directly. However, if neutrinos are not massless, but have a small mass of their own, as suggested by an unconfirmed Russian experiment performed in 1981, we might be able to detect them indirectly: they could be a form of "dark matter," like that mentioned earlier, with sufficient gravitational attraction to stop the expansion of the universe and cause it to collapse again.

Look up photons, electrons, and neutrons

What's an antielectron and anitnuetrino?

How soon could the universe collapse again?!?

When the student began reading this excerpt, he realized right away that this would be difficult reading for him and he would need to read it more than once. The student didn't know a lot about the "big bang" before he read this excerpt, so even though he tried to think back to what he already knew about it, he realized that much of what he was about to read would be completely new information. So the student's strategy was to read the excerpt once and not worry about trying to comprehend everything Hawking wrote, and then to read it again with a pencil in hand to try to get a better understanding. On his second reading, the student underlined what he thought were the key ideas. He knew if he only read this excerpt once and tried to underline the key ideas as he was reading, he probably would have just underlined everything! So he decided to annotate the excerpt on his second reading. This student knew that in science writing, ideas tend to be presented in a logical order; and since he could tell from the first few sentences that the focus of this paragraph would be what happened during the big bang, when he began reading, he was predicting that Hawking would write this paragraph in a cause/effect style – the causes and effects of the big bang. Predicting the structure of the passage helped the student decide what the key ideas were. In the margins he wrote notes to himself and questions for the professor. There were concepts in the excerpt he wasn't familiar with and needed to look up later (e.g. he needed a better idea of what photons, neutrons, and electrons were).

Sample Natural Sciences Reading

7.8: Learn by Doing – Reading Science Texts

The purpose of this Learn by Doing activity is for you to practice reading a science text and practice using one of the active reading strategies we discussed in Chapter 4, annotating. You'll practice annotating the book chapter, "Carnivore Group Living: Comparative Trends" by John L. Gittleman. The chapter is from a scholarly book, *Carnivore Behavior, Ecology, and Evolution*, published by Cornell University Press and aimed at an audience of scientists. First, read the chapter quickly, skimming through it. Then reread the chapter with a pen or pencil in hand and annotate it. You might underline key ideas, circle key words or concepts you don't understand, or write questions or comments in the margins. Once you've reread and annotated the chapter, form small groups and trade textbooks with your peers. Take a look at your peers' annotating strategies and compare them to yours. As a group, come up with a list of annotating strategies that the group thought were effective.

Excerpt from "Carnivore Group Living: Comparative Trends" by John L.
Gittleman (Gittleman, 1989: 183-187)

In contrast to some other mammalian orders, members of the Carnivora do not
commonly live in groups: only about 10-13% of all species aggregate at some
period outside of the breeding season (Bekoff et al. 1984; Gittleman 1984). Because
most carnivores reside in dense habitats and are solitary, dangerous, and nocturnal,
little information existed on their social behavior until recently. Now, more comprehensive and comparative data are available to examine functional explanations of
interspecific variation in grouping patterns across carnivores (for previous qualitative comparisons, see Ewer 1973; Kleiman and Eisenberg 1973; Kruuk 1975; Bertram
1979; Macdonald 1983). In this chapter I briefly review selected hypotheses for the
evolution and maintenance of grouping in carnivores, focusing on those that are
broadly applicable across the order and are testable from the available comparative
data. I then analyze quantitative measures of interspecific variation in social behavior with respect to differences in morphology, physiology, and ecology. The
analysis differs from previous cross-species comparisons of carnivore social ecology
(Ewer 1973; Kleiman and Eisenberg 1973; Kruk 1975; Bertram 1979; Macdonald and
Moehlman 1982; Macdonald 1983; Beckoff et al. 1984; Kruuk and Macdonald 1985)
by being more quantitative, by accounting for morphological and metabolic constraints, and by deriving general trends across the order as a whole rather than in
particular taxonomic families.

To analyze carnivore social behavior, one must first classify functional aspects of
grouping in terms of what general behaviors are being performed. At least four
types of grouping may be distinguished: population groups — individuals sharing
a common home range area; feeding groups — individuals utilizing the same food
resource at a given time; foraging groups — individuals banding together while
searching for food and hunting; and breeding groups — individuals forming a
reproductive unit. Population, feeding, and foraging group sizes are similar, at least
with regard to the number of adult individuals in the group, for most carnivores.
However, for species that remain in groups outside of the breeding season, different individuals are included in various activities. For example, banded mongooses
(*Mungos mungo*) live in packs of approximately 16 individuals that forage on
invertebrates independently of other pack members (Rood 1975, 1986), whereas
dwarf mongooses (*Helogale parvula*) live in multi-male packs of up to 24 individuals,
in which about four adults are reproductively active (Rood 1978, 1980, 1983). In the
case of the African lion (*Panthera leo*), approximately eight individuals live in a
pride encompassing the same home range area, but only three members of the
pride hunt for the entire group (Schaller 1972; Betram 1979). Perhaps the most
extreme example of a division of labor within a group is provided by the spotted
hyenas (*Crocuta crocuta*); in the Ngrorongoro Crater as many as 55 individuals make

up a clan that divides into hunting groups of about seven adults and feeding groups of roughly 19 individuals (Kruuk 1972; see also Mills, this volume). Thus, from these examples, it is clear that functional explanations of group living must distinguish each form of grouping (see also Kleiman and Brady 1978; Van Orsdol et al. 1985).

Many functional explanations have been suggested for grouping in eutherian mammals (for reviews, see Alexander 1974; Wilson 1975; Bertram 1978; Eisenberg 1981; Harvey and Greene 1981; Pulliam and Caraco 1984; Clark and Mangel 1986). Those pertaining to carnivores fall into two categories: anti-predator defense and exploitation of food.

Hypotheses for the Evolution of Group Living

Anti-Predator Defense

Carnivores that compete with other species for food or sometimes serve as food may benefit from group vigilance, whereby encroachers are detected more effectively. Among dwarf mongooses subordinate males are found on the periphery of the pack, where they keep lookout for threatening predators (Rasa 1977, 1986); further, groups with few vigilant guards are preyed upon more frequently (Rasa 1986). Grouping may also help minimize a predator's effect on the group: if by clustering together the members of a group cause a predator to catch only one individual while the rest are able to escape, then gregariousness may evolve (Hamilton 1971). Banded mongoose packs respond to raptors or terrestrial predators by immediately aggregating into a tight bunch, approaching the predator collectively (Rood 1975), and "with mouths pointed in all directions, giving the appearance of one large organism defending itself" (Kruk 1975).

Group defense is expected to be more common in smaller species that are not able individually to ward off larger species (Ewer 1973; Kruuk 1975; Rood 1986). Also, species living in open habitats (e.g., grassland plains) are more vulnerable to predators (or competitors) and therefore more likely to form groups (Lamprecht 1981; Rood 1986). Many of these general associations of size and ecology with group living are also found in primates (Crook 1970; Clutton-Brock and Harvey 1977), ungulates (Jarman 1974; Jarman and Jarman 1979), sciurids (Hoogland 1981), and marsupials (Kaufman 1974; Lee and Cockburn 1985).

Exploitation of Food

In general, group living may be advantageous for locating food resources (Ward and Zahavi 1973), improving chances of finding and catching prey (Schaller 1972; Kruuk 1975), increasing the diversity and size of prey (Kruk 1972; 1975; Schaller 1972; Caraco and Wolf 1975), and competing successfully for food (Lamprecht 1978; 1981). Not all of these factors have been considered for carnivores, mainly because

of the methodological difficulties in carrying out detailed field experiments necessary for teasing apart hypotheses (see Beckoff et al. 1984).

In the search for food it is obvious that many pairs of eyes (or ears) are better
than one. Yet, it is difficult actually to test whether, once food is located, information is being passed on among members of a group. Only a few experimental
studies (e.g., Menzel 1971; Krebs et al. 1972) have shown that individuals forage
more successfully by learning from one another; nevertheless, descriptive studies
show that contact calls by smaller carnivores (e.g., dwarf mongoose; slender mongoose, *Herpestes sanguineus*; white-tailed mongoose, *Ichneumia albicauda*) foraging in
groups for invertebrates may communicate the location of new food resources
(Ewer 1973; Kingdon 1977).

Whether they find new food resources, predators hunting in groups may be
more successful at taking down prey. For example, Schaller (1972) found African
lions had a higher success rate in capturing Thomson's gazelle (*Gazella thomsini*),
zebra (*Equus burchelli*), and wildebeest (*Connochaetus taurinus*) when two or more
lionesses hunted together (see Caraco and Wolf 1975; Van Orsdol 1984). More
extensive data, since collected by Bertram (1975, 1976, 1979) and Packer and Pusey
(1982, 1983a, 1983b), and recently analyzed by Packer (1986), indicate that group
hunting lions may not increase hunting success; data are not conclusive on either
the average biomass of kills made by groups of different sizes or the hunting rates
of different sized groups. The African lion story is a classic case of the paradox
wherein the more information we have, the less we seem to know. Nevertheless,
other carnivores do tend to support the association of groupings with hunting success: Wyman (1967) observed that golden jackals (*Canis aureus*) and black-backed
jackals (*C. mesomelas*) were successful at catching Thomson's gazelle fawns only
when hunting in pairs. And for spotted hyenas hunting wildebeest, 15% of 74
attempts were successful when a single hyena pursued a calf in contrast to 74% of
34 attempts when two or more hyenas attacked (Kruuk 1972). Even though within
species variation of hunting methods seem to indicate benefits from grouping, it is
difficult to compare hunting success rates across species because: (1) definitions of
hunting attempt vary among observers (Scaller 1972; Bertram 1979), (2) hunting
success may depend on hunger level or hunting technique (e.g., ambush versus
cursorial hunting: Van Orsdol 1984; Van Valkenburgh 1985; Taylor, this volume)
and not grouping, and (3) various ecological constraints such as vegetation, habitat
density, or time of day are confounding factors (Bertram 1979; Van Orsdol 1984).

The most common explanation for grouping in larger predators is that concerted
effort permits a wider selection of prey in terms of amount, diversity, and size.
Schaller (1972) and Bertram (1979) observed that African lions living in groups frequently hunted adult buffalos (*Syncerus caffer*) whereas single lions rarely even
attempted an attack at buffalo. However, as Packer (1986) cautions, even though
grouping lions take down and prefer larger prey than solitaries, this does not prove

that lion sociality evolved as a consequence of the advantages of cooperative hunt-ing: cooperative hunting may only be an adaption to group living, rather than the evolutionary force resulting in group living (see Alexander 1974). Nevertheless, cooperative hunting is certainly an important benefit of grouping, and similar accounts of coordinated hunting have been reported for the African hunting dog (*Lycanos pictus*) (Estes and Goddard 1967; Malcolm and van Lawick 1975; Frame et al. 1979; Malcolm 1979), golden jackal (Lamprecht 1978), gray wolf (*Canis lupus*) (Mech 1966, 1970), coyote (*C. latrans*) (Beckoff 1978; Bekoff and Wells 1978; Bowen 1981; Wells and Beckoff 1982), spotted hyena (Kruuk, 1972, 1975; Mills, this volume), Indian dhole (*Cuon alpines*) (Davidar 1975; Johnsingh 1982), and cheetah (*Acinonyx jubatus*) (Caro and Collins 1986; Ashwood and Gittleman, 1989).

There are a number of carnivores that do not fit these generalizations (see also Packer 1986). Among larger species the mountain lion (*Puma concolor*), leopard (*Panthera pardus*), jaguar (*P. onca*), and tiger (*P. tigris*) exploit larger prey than them-selves while hunting solitarily. In the case of some of the smaller Mustelidae (especially species of *Mustela*) individuals regularly kill prey of larger size than themselves (King, this volume). Even so, these examples do not deny the fact that group living is an important benefit, either direct or indirect, for catching large prey.

Finally, group living may carry advantages in defending kills or other food resources from neighboring predators (or other groups). For many carnivores, particularly medium-sized species, protecting kills is difficult; black-backed jackals in the Serengeti lose up to 30% of their Thomson gazelle and hare kills to spotted hyenas (Lamprecht 1978, 1981); spotted hyenas and African lions frequently scav-enge from each other (Kruk 1972); and, both hyenas and lions steal kills from cheetahs, leopards, and African hunting dogs (Estes and Godard 1967; Kruk 1972; Schaller 1972; Bertram 1979; Frame et al. 1979; Packer 1986). In each case, species feeding in groups will usually stand their ground against a scavenger or competitor and will retreat only when feeding individually or in pairs. The exception is that smaller species such as the African hunting dog may give way to a considerably larger species (such as the African lion or the spotted hyena) even when feeding in a group (see Frame at al. 1979).

An inherent difficulty in assessing the importance of competition or defense of kills for the evolution of grouping in carnivores is that there are many other beha-viors that reduce losses in competitive situations. Carnivores will (1) make kills inaccessible to competitors (e.g., leopards hide carcasses in trees), (2) reduce exploi-tation time by fast feeding or group feeding, or (3) cache food (Macdonald 1976). Furthermore, the advantages of group living mentioned above (increased hunting success, prey size, and prey diversity) potentially are associated with a confounding variable, body size. Both population group size and prey size frequently increase with body mass (Clutton-Brock and Harevy 1977, 1983; Gittleman 1985a). All of these variables may be closely linked because they are influenced by similar energetic constraints (see McNab 1980, this volume). Therefore, size-related effects must be considered in searching for comparative trends in the functions of carnivore grouping.

Researching in the Natural Sciences

Scientists establish fact by working with empirical evidence – in other words, evidence that is both observable and verifiable. Experiments must therefore be carefully crafted, conducted, and reported, so that their results can be verified by other scientists. Only after an experiment has been verified and re-verified will its results be considered true.

—Professor Karen Gocsik, Writing Program, Dartmouth College
(Gocsik, 2004)

To do justice to your complex subject, don't just borrow ideas from sources and stitch them together. Of course, like any scientist, you will build in what other people have thought. But show that you are doing your own thinking – seek out opportunities to comment on your sources.

—Professors Kenneth Meiklejohn and Margaret Procter, Institute for the History and Philosophy of Science and Technology, University of Toronto
(Meiklejohn and Procter, 2009)

Reports should usually include a narrative text that describes and explains the information presented. Use the results section to explain the purpose of every figure, scheme, equation and table. Published research results never include "orphan" data, that is, information that is not explained or put into context by the written text.

—Oregon State's *Writing Guide for Chemistry* (Oregon State University, 2001)

7.9: Writing to Learn – Thinking about Scientific Inquiry

The purpose of this Writing to Learn activity is for you to think about what you already know about scientific inquiry before you read about it in this section. Individually or in small groups, make a list of the ways that scientific inquiry is different than inquiry in the arts and humanities or the social sciences. Then make another list of what counts as evidence for good research in the sciences. Be prepared to discuss your lists with the class as a whole.

The Nature of Inquiry and Research in the Natural Sciences

In Chapter 5, we talked about college research as inquiry: asking open-ended questions and exploring these questions in conversation with other scholars. Every discipline defines *inquiry* in different ways. The kinds of questions that are asked and the way researchers try to find answers to the questions will be different for every college course you take. To think about what inquiry and research means in the natural sciences, let's go back to the reading, "Carnivore Group Living: Comparative Trends." When you think about scientific inquiry and research in the studies discussed in the book chapter on carnivore group living, you might notice a few patterns that can help you to understand what inquiry means in the natural sciences.

- **Scientific inquiry involves hypothesis-testing.**

The research that is the subject of Gittleman's chapter on carnivore group living focuses on hypotheses scientists have explored regarding "the evolution and maintenance of grouping in carnivores." Through observation of carnivore behavior, scientists began to speculate about why carnivores formed groups. Was it to defend against predators? Was it for the exploitation of food? Gittleman and other scientists tested these open-ended questions through direct and structured observation of carnivore behavior and through an analysis of the scholarly literature on the subject.

- **Scientific inquiry is systematic and involves testing and experimentation.**

The scientists that Gittleman cites in his study all conducted research on carnivore group behaviors through systematic and structured observations and analysis. Gittleman makes a point in the introduction to the chapter to emphasize that he is focusing on hypotheses that are "testable" using "comparative data." Later in the chapter, in a section not included in the excerpt above, Gittleman uses quantitative data to closely analyze carnivore group behavior.

- **Scientific inquiry involves exploring the research of other scientists.**

You probably noticed how frequently Gittleman cites the work of other scientists, and how he discusses his own arguments in relation to the work of other scientists. In this chapter Gittleman proves to readers that he is aware of the research that has been done in the area he is discussing, and that he is familiar with the most influential researchers (those names that occur again and again in his chapter). Gittleman also shows that he is aware of what has been missing up until this point in the literature, and he shows how his research "differs from previous cross-species comparisons of carnivore social ecology...by being more quantitative, by accounting for morphological and metabolic constraints, and by deriving general trends across the order as a whole rather than in particular taxonomic families." In order to be trusted by fellow researchers, scientists need to show that they have done their homework and have carefully analyzed the research on their topic. This involves frequent citing and a clear and concise description of the results of previous research.

What Counts as Evidence in the Natural Sciences?

To help you think about what counts as evidence for good research in the sciences, let's go back to the lab report we looked at earlier in this chapter. "The Optimal Foraging Theory" provides a good example of the kinds of evidence that are accepted as reliable and persuasive in the discourse community of the natural sciences. When you read the lab report, you might have noticed some types of evidence that are common in science research, as described below.

- **Descriptions of Experiments and Observations**

    The authors of "The Optimal Foraging Theory" present evidence about the value of their experiment and the accuracy of the results by describing the experiment concisely and precisely. The authors present the experiment in a logical order and describe the reasons for the results that they observed. The writing style is formal, precise, and concise. The authors try to describe the experiment as accurately as possible, and they don't reflect on personal experiences (except for their experiences conducting the experiment). The writing goes right to the point and the authors don't use any figurative language such as metaphors or similes.

- **Data Reported in Tables, Graphs, and Charts**

    The authors report the results of their experiment in bar graphs. The purpose of these graphs is to summarize the data and make comparisons. Organizing the data in graphs helps make the results of the experiment clearer to both the writer and the reader. Tables, graphs, and charts are common types of evidence in natural science writing, especially since much science writing involves reporting the results of experiments.

- **Research from Other Scientists**

    The authors of "The Optimal Foraging Theory" cite other scientists as they define key terms and describe the subject of their research. They also place the results of their study in the context of previous studies of beavers' foraging habits in the discussion section of their report. In many science genres it's a common expectation that you will cite other studies that are similar to your own or discuss the connection between your research question and the work of other scientists in the discussion section, a literature review section, or both. Citing research from other scientists shows readers that you're familiar with the discourse community that has explored the research question you're asking, and citing research helps persuade readers that you've done your homework.

7.10: Learn by Doing – Investigating Research in the Natural Sciences

Now that you've looked closely at some of the science research in this book, it's time for you to go out and do some investigating of your own. Choose a natural science topic and do a subject or keyword search in your library book collection database. Find a science book that includes research (you might focus on books published by scholarly presses), and browse through the book, focusing on the kind of research that was done. Write a 1–2 page informal paper in which you discuss the kind of inquiry the researcher(s) engaged in, the research methods used, the type of data/evidence presented by the researcher(s), and the way the data was presented. You don't need to read the entire book to discuss the research methods, but you might take a close look at the places in the book where the writer(s) describe(s) research methods.

Natural Science Reference Books and Databases

In Chapter 5, we discussed some general academic databases and reference books. As you take courses in different disciplines, you'll need to be aware of more specialized databases and reference books. The following is a list of some reference books and databases for the natural sciences:

Science Dictionaries
The Biographical Dictionary of Scientists (2000) R. Porter and M. Ogilvie (eds.) New York: Oxford University Press.
Chambers Dictionary of Science and Technology (1991) P. Walker. Edinburgh: W. and R. Chambers Ltd.
Dictionary of the History of Science (1981) W. F. Bynum, E. J. Brown, and R. Porter (eds.) London: Macmillan Press.
Hammond Barnhart Dictionary of Science (1986) R. K. Barnhart (ed.) Maplewood, New Jersey: Hammond.

The New Penguin Dictionary of Science (1998) M. J. Clugston. London: Penguin Books.

Science Encyclopedias
Biographical Encyclopedia of Scientists (2008) J. Daintith (ed.) Oxford: Taylor and Francis.
Encyclopedia of Physical Science and Technology (2001) R. A. Meyers (ed.) San Diego: Academic Press.
Encyclopedia of World Scientists (2000) E. H. Oakes (ed.) New York: Facts on File.
McGraw-Hill Encyclopedia of Science and Technology (2007) New York: McGraw Hill.

Science Periodical Databases
Biological Abstracts
Chemical Abstracts
ScienceDirect
Wiley InterScience

Citing Sources in the Natural Sciences: CSE Style

In Chapter 5, I mentioned that different disciplines have different conventions for citing sources. In the discourse communities of the sciences, readers will expect you to give credit to the work of scientists whom you refer to in your writing. Scientists build on each other's work to create new knowledge, so it's important to clearly acknowledge information and ideas you're referring to in your writing for science courses. There are different citation systems for different fields of science, but the most common citation style is CSE (Council of Science Editors). By the name alone you can see how discourse communities decide on the conventions of a discipline. The Council of Science Editors has over 1,200 members, and together they help shape the conventions for writing in the sciences. These rules for citing sources may seem to you random at first, but there's a reason that in CSE style you write the author(s) last name(s) and the year whenever you cite an outside source in your paper. In science, the date of the research you cite is usually very important – the most current research is most often the most credible and valuable research. CSE style also has guidelines for formatting your manuscript: setting margins, labeling and placing visuals such as tables and figures, using headings, and other matters.

CSE has two ways of citing sources: the name-year system and the citation-sequence system. In the name-year system, the author of the source is named in the text and in the reference page, which is in alphabetical order. In the citation-sequence system, each source cited is given a number. Every time the source is referred to again, the same number is used as a citation. If you're writing a paper for a science course and you're not sure whether to use the name-year or citation-sequence system, ask your professor. Some science professors – especially in general education science courses – don't require students to use CSE style. For example, the geology professor in the case study at the end of this chapter asks students to use APA style. Since APA style, like CSE style, emphasizes the date of the publication, some science professors ask students to use APA style since it may be more familiar to them. It's important to ask your science professors which citation style they want you to use.

In-text Citations in CSE Style

When scientists use the research of other scientists in their writing, they're very careful to give the author (or authors) and date of the research they cite. It's important that you give credit to your sources whenever you refer to them in your paper, whether you're citing people's data or referring to their ideas or arguments.

One way that scientists integrate information and ideas from other researchers is by quoting them directly. In the CSE name-year system, whenever you have a quote from an author in your paper, make sure that you give your readers the author's name and the date of publication of the source you retrieved the quote from. The author's last name and publication date should be in parentheses at the end of the quote. Here's an example:

> The director of the National Science Foundation argues that "the theory of intelligent design cannot be taught in a science course if it cannot withstand the scrutiny of the scientific method: if it cannot be tested, how can it be taught?" (Munoz, 2005).

The name and date in parentheses is always placed outside the quotation marks, and the period of the whole sentence is placed after the reference given in parentheses. If there are more than two authors, use et al. ("Munoz et al. argue…").

If you're using the CSE citation-sequence style, you use a number in superscript format to cite the source, and then give the full citation on the reference page. Here's how the previous passage would look in the citation-sequence system:

> The director of the National Science Foundation argues that "the theory of intelligent design cannot be taught in a science course if it cannot withstand the scrutiny of the scientific method: if it cannot be tested, how can it be taught?"[1]

In addition to direct quotes from secondary sources, often science writers will integrate facts, data, and statistics. Sometimes you'll quote this data directly, but more often you'll paraphrase the information. For example, let's say you want to cite the following information from an article by Anita Burnell:

> The success rates for cloning are low: the sheep Dolly was the single success of 276 tries. In reproductive cloning in general, over 90% of attempts fail to produce a viable offspring. Besides the low success rate, cloning can also result in animals with poor health. For example, one third of cloned calves have died young.

Although you could put this entire passage in quotes and cite it word-for-word in your paper, since the information is just a series of statistics, it would be more effective to summarize the information in your own words and cite the source. Here's an example in the author-date system:

> Geneticist Anita Burnell presents evidence for the lack of success of cloning at this early stage in the research. Burnell (2005) cites the example of Dolly the sheep, who was the single successful clone of 276 tries. This statistic isn't surprising, considering that, according to Burnell, 90% of reproductive clones don't result in "a viable offspring." Burnell also points out that there are health concerns associated with cloning, as a significant proportion of cloned calves do not make it to adulthood.

Preparing a CSE Style Reference Page

The CSE in-text citations in the author-date system lets your reader know exactly where in your paper you're referring to information and ideas from an outside source, who the authors of the sources are, and when the sources were published. But if other scientists want to check on the reliability of your sources and if they want to find some of those sources to use in their own research, the in-text citation doesn't give them enough information. This is why it's important to include a reference page that gives detailed publication information for every work you cite in the text of your paper. For the conventions of a CSE reference page, go to the reference area of your library and consult the *CSE Style Manual* or visit the following Web sites:

CSE Resource Web Sites

University of North Carolina Library
(http://www.lib.unc.edu/instruct/citations/cse/)

University Wisconsin-Madison Writing Center
(http://www.wisc.edu/writing/Handbook/DocCBE.html)

CSE Style Paper Format
Following are basic guidelines for formatting your paper in CSE style.

- Use a standard 12-point font: Courier, Times, or Bookman.
- Include an unnumbered title page with the title centered and, a few lines below the title, write your name, the course number and title, the professor's name, and the date.
- Use 1" margins except for the upper right-hand corner, which should include a short version of your title and page number on each page. The page after the title page should be numbered page 2.
- For quotations of more than 40 words, indent each line of the quote (using block format) five spaces from the left margin. Do not indent from the right margin.
- Double-space throughout, including the abstract and references.
- Common CSE headings include *Introduction*, *Methods and Materials*, *Results*, and *Discussion*.
- If your professor asks for an abstract, it should appear on its own numbered page, titled *Abstract*, and placed right after the title page.
- Place tables, charts, graphs, and other visuals close to the place you refer to them in the text. Label each visual *Table* or *Figure* and number them consecutively (*Figure 1*, *Figure 2*, and so on).
- Place the reference page after the body of the paper but before the appendices.
- Appendices should be placed at the end of the paper. Number and title each appendix (e.g. *Appendix 1: List of Species*)

Student Writing Case Study: Geology

Alfredo Cadenas as a Sophomore at California State University, Sacramento

In this section of Chapter 7, we're going to look closely at a student writing in a natural sciences course. The student writer, Alfredo Cadenas, was at the time a sophomore at California State University, Sacramento, a large state college in Northern California. The natural science course that Alfredo is writing for in this case study is Geology 5: Geology of Mexico. Geology of Mexico is a general education course in the Geology Department. In many general education courses there is a single, extended writing project that makes up a portion of students' final grades in the course, and this is the case with Geology of Mexico. Although Alfredo had to do some writing for homework assignments and in-class labs, the big writing project for the course was a research paper about the geology of Mexico. In this case study, we'll focus on Alfredo's writing and researching process for his geology of Mexico research paper. Let's start this natural sciences case study by looking at the course description that Alfredo's professor handed out:

Geology 5 – Geology of Mexico

General Information
The objective of this course is to provide an understanding of earth materials and geologic processes through study of the geology of Mexico. This course is a combined lecture/lab course and class meetings will consist of some combination of

lecture and lab activities. There are no prerequisites for this course. GEOL 5 fulfils General Education areas B1 and B3.

Catalog Description

Introduction to Geology through examination of aspects of the geology of Mexico. Emphasizes problem-based approach to learning geology and the process of scientific investigation. Topics include a wide range of geological concepts including plate tectonic setting of Mexico, living with volcanoes, the Mexican volcanic belt, the Mexico city earthquake, issues of water supply, flooding and atmospheric pollution in Mexico City, the Chicxulub crater and geologic time, ore deposits of Mexico.

Expected Learning Outcomes

After taking this course you should have an understanding of:

1. How to apply the scientific method to the examination of geologic processes in Mexico
2. Identify common minerals and rocks of the Earth's crust and interpret them in terms of how they formed
3. Explain the relationship between geologic features of Mexico in the context of plate tectonics
4. Understand the effect of geology on the cultural development of Mexico and predict the consequences of future events.
5. Evaluate the potential impact of land-use decisions with respect to geological hazards

Required Text

Hamblin and Christiansen, 2001, *Earth's Dynamic Systems.* (Tenth Edition)
It is important that you read the assigned sections *before* coming to class and again, more carefully after class. Additional reading assignments will be given in class.

WebCT

Online material for this course, such as homework assignments, lecture slides and supplemental reading material will be available through WebCT. You can login to WebCT at http://online.csus.edu. In order to access the course website <u>you will need a saclink account</u>. If you do not have one you can get one by going to https://www.saclink.csus.edu/saclink/, clicking on register and following the instructions.

Grades and Grading

Your final grade will be based upon the following grading scheme:

Homework assignments and lab activities	30%
Term project	10%
Midterm exams	40%
Comprehensive final exam	20%

Homework Assignments

Short written and/or online exercises will be set during class. The format for homework assignments will be discussed as they are assigned. You are expected to do all of the homework assignments even if you miss class. Completed homework assignments must be turned in at the beginning of class, on the day they are due. Late homework will not be accepted.

Lab Activities

The lab component of this course is designed to reinforce concepts covered during lecture by providing an opportunity to explore certain concepts deeper and to learn skills important in the study of geology. All lab activities should be completed during class time. Labs will be due at the beginning of the next class meeting. Late labs will not be accepted.

Term Project

During the semester you are expected to complete a research paper on some aspect of the Geology of Mexico. Requirements for paper length and format and suggestions for research topics will be given in class during the second week of the semester.

Exams

There will be three midterm exams during the semester. The dates of these exams are shown on the class schedule. Any changes to these dates will be announced in class and on the class web page. Exams will consist of multiple choice and short answer questions and will cover material since the last exam. Exams will include material covered in lecture and lab activities. In some cases exam questions will cover practical skills learned in lab. Your lowest exam grade will be dropped. No make-up exams will be given. The final exam is required and will be a comprehensive exam, covering material from the whole class.

Grade assignment

Letter grades will be based on a scale no more severe than the following:

A	90–100%
B	80–89%
C	70–79%
D	60–69%
F	Below 60%

Plus and minus grades will also be given

Attendance and Class Rules

- Regular attendance is required for you to do well in this class. If you miss a lab I will expect you to make it up on your own time. Lab materials such as maps, rocks and minerals will only be available during scheduled class times.
- Please try to arrive on time. If you are late, please enter quietly to minimize disruption to the class.
- If you need to leave class early (i.e. for an appointment), please let me know beforehand.
- Please turn your cell phones **OFF** while in class. If you are expecting an important call that you have to answer, please inform me before the beginning of class and leave your phone on silent mode.

7.11: Writing to Learn – Comparing First-Year Writing and Geology

The purpose of this Writing to Learn activity is for you to think about the differences between this geology class syllabus and the syllabus from the first-year writing class that we looked at in Chapter 1. Individually or in small groups, compare the two syllabi and make a list of the ways that thinking, writing, and researching processes are described differently in the geology class syllabus than they are in the syllabus for the first-year writing class.

Learning the scientific method is a key point in Alfredo's geology class syllabus, and in our interview Alfredo's professor emphasized that writing is one of the main ways her students learn how to think about science: "In all classes, I view writing as having two main purposes. The first is to encourage each student to learn about one topic at a deeper level than we have explored in class. The second is to provide an opportunity for students to learn more about the scientific writing style and to practice their writing skills." Alfredo's professor emphasizes writing in her classes because writing is so important to scientists. She says:

> In my discipline, writing is extremely important. The best research scientists don't just do cutting-edge research, they know how to convey their results clearly to a broader audience. Professional geologists are expected to not only conduct field work but to write reports on their findings. These reports must be completed on time and be readable. When training our students to be geologists it is our responsibility to teach them not only the skills they will need in their chosen field but the confidence and ability to write up their findings.

In order to help her students learn to write like scientists, Alfredo's professor has students write in a common science genre: a scientific research report. Luckily for Alfredo, his professor gave him some guidelines for scientific writing along with the description of the term paper. The description of the term paper and the guidelines for scientific writing are given below.

Geology of Mexico, Term Paper

During the semester you will research a topic associated with the Geology of Mexico and write a 4–6 page paper on it. I expect this paper to be written in APA style (see http://library.csus.edu/guides/blackmer/APAstyle.htm for help with this). You must use at least one refereed article or book (other than your text book) as well as any web resources.

Your paper should include the following sections: introduction, main body of text (broken into sections if need be) and conclusion. A first draft of your paper will be due at the beginning of week 11 (April 9th). The final paper will be due on Monday May 7th.

Below is a list of suggested research topics. These are just suggestions and you may choose your own topic if you like. On Monday, February 26th we will be visiting the library where a librarian will show you how to locate journal articles and books on your subject. I expect you to have chosen a general subject before this visit so that you can use the time to find your references. You will be expected to find two potential articles during that visit.

<u>Suggested topics:</u>
Oil reserves in the Gulf of Mexico (location, geology, size, etc)
Volcanoes (pick a volcano and do a detailed study of it – location, eruptive history, what kind of volcano, what kind of rocks, hazards etc)
Fossils/dinosaurs in Mexico (e.g. mammoth fossils found in the Valley of Mexico)
Gold, silver or copper in Mexico (location, geology, size, mining history etc)
The K-T impact (evidence for meteor impact, discovery of the Chixulub crater etc)
Earthquakes (pick an earthquake and discuss it – when, where, why it occurred, damage from the earthquake etc)
The geology of a specific region (e.g. Mexico City)
Geology and ancient civilizations (how geology influenced rise/fall of ancient cities, geologic evidence for early inhabitants of Mexico)

Scientific Writing – Guidelines for writing your report

Your reports should be between 4 and 6 pages in length. The final paper may be single-spaced but your first draft must be double-spaced so that I have room for making comments. Any diagrams used should be placed within the text with an appropriate figure caption. Use a smaller size and bold type-face for the figure captions to distinguish them from the rest of the text. Be sure to refer to your figures within the text, thus sending the reader to look at them. As geology is a very visual science I expect each paper to contain at least one figure.

Scientific writing is a little different to other types of composition. Science writing is generally very to-the-point. You should include the facts and not refer to yourself. (e.g. you should not start you paper "I have chosen to write about..."). Whenever you use a technical term for the first time you should define it for the reader.

Structure of report:
A good rule in scientific writing is that you explain what it is you are going to say, then say it, then tell us what you just said. In other words, the report should have an introduction, the main body of text (this can be subdivided) and a summary. Below I describe each of the sections that your report should contain.

<u>Introduction</u> – this is where you introduce the theme of your paper and explain the relevance of the topic. If the geologic process that you are describing affects human activity or is affected by human activity, outline that here. It is in this section that you get the interest of your reader so if you want to be "creative" in your writing, here's where you get to do it.

<u>Main body of text</u> – this is the most important part of your report. Outline all the

issues that you mean to discuss before writing it and make sure that it will flow well. Dividing this part of your paper into sections, each with its own heading will help you to keep your writing organized. This is commonly done in scientific writing to convey complex information to the reader.

Summary – this section outlines all the main points of your report. It's where you tell the reader what it was that you just told them. It should be very concise and sum up in just a couple of paragraphs.

Referencing sources:
I'd like you to use a specific reference system. Rather than using footnotes, scientific papers generally have a reference list at the end. When you state a fact that comes from the reference, refer to the author and the year in the text. Look carefully at how articles are cited in the references that you use.

For references to articles:

- Author, A. N., 2004, Title of Paper, *Name of Journal*, volume of journal, pages.
  e.g: Leeman, W. P., Lewis, J. F. and Evarts, R. C., 2004. Petrologic constraints on the thermal structure of the Cascade arc, *Journal of Volcanology and Geothermal Research*, 140, 67–105

If it is a book that you have referenced:

- Author, A. N., 2004., *Title of Book*, city, publisher, number of pages.
  e.g: Plummer, C. C., McGeary, D. and Carlson, D. H., 1996, *Physical Geology*, *10th ed*, McGraw-Hill, pp 580.

For referencing online sources: Within the text, try to give the author and date if possible. If not, give a shortened version of the web site (e.g the home page). Put the full u.r.l. in the reference list. Remember, online material is not always peer reviewed and so may not be as reliable as a journal or book source.

For more information on this, go to: http://library.csus.edu/guides/blackmer/APAstyle.htm

A word on plagiarism:
Plagiarism is the unacknowledged use of the words or ideas of another. It is quite alright to get your information from outside sources but you may not paraphrase or copy sections of the text without correctly referencing the author. If you must include a section verbatim, make sure you enclose it in quotation marks. If you state a fact that comes directly from one of your sources (not general knowledge, but a

fact) be sure to reference the source of that fact. I do not accept plagiarized work and if I find evidence of it in a paper I will give a zero grade for the report.

When writing about a subject that you are only just learning about, there's a fine line between using the information you have found through research and abusing it. My main advice is: "when in doubt, quote your source." It's better to overuse referencing than to underuse it.

If often helps to outline your paper before you write it. This allows you to put your thoughts in order and think about what it is you want to say. Here is an example outline for a paper on gold deposits in California:

Introduction
Importance of gold in California history
Value of gold mined over time
Importance of understanding how gold deposits are formed in order to find new deposits

Location of gold deposits in California
Two main types of deposit: placer and vein (describe each)
Include a map of gold deposits in California
Describe the different type of rocks they are found in (placer in old stream deposits, vein in veins running through igneous and metamorphic rocks of the Sierra Nevada)

Hydrothermal Gold
General description of hydrothermal veins and how they form
Brief description of the formation of the mother lode

Placer Gold
Brief description of how it forms
Brief description of how the placer deposits in California formed
Connection between placer gold and lode gold in California

Summary
Summarize main points and describe how this information could be used to help look for more gold in California or a similar location.

References

7.12: Writing to Learn – Rhetorical Features of Writing in the Natural Sciences

Reread the scientific research report assignment and the guidelines for scientific writing above and write for five minutes about the ways the assignment and the guidelines connect with the rhetorical features of writing in the sciences that we've been discussing in this chapter. Think about methods of inquiry, purpose, audience, and conventions.

Alfredo's professor provided her students with some suggested topics in the assignment description, but Alfredo had the freedom to work within those suggestions to find a more specific subject to explore. Alfredo chose to research La Pena de Bernal, a boulder in the Mexican city of Bernal. When I asked Alfredo why he chose this topic, he said, "I chose this topic because I had the opportunity to go and visit that place before, so I found it very interesting to know more about something that I have visited before. I believe that in order to write a good research paper we need to write about something we like and something we find interesting for ourselves."

Alfredo's professor said that one piece of advice about writing processes she has for college students is to always get feedback on a draft of a paper. Her advice is to:

> ask your professor or a friend to read over a first or even second draft of a paper. The best way to improve your writing is to get input. In my experience, making changes in response to a careful review of a draft can increase your grade significantly. Don't be scared of asking a professor to look over an early version of your paper; most are happy to do so if it is handed in early.

To make sure that all of her students get feedback and make significant revisions to their term papers, Alfredo's professor requires that each student turn in a draft to her for feedback well before they turn in the final draft. Alfredo did the best he could on the first draft, but he knew he needed to develop his paper more and he needed some feedback from an outside reader for help. Alfredo said about his rough draft: "I didn't have any ideas what else to write. I just wrote the basic information." To develop his report beyond simply the basic information, Alfredo needed some feedback. Read the rough draft that Alfredo turned in for feedback.

La Pena de Bernal: Rough Draft

When I hear the word Mexico, the first thing that comes to my mind is its traditions and its people. Mexico is a beautiful country full of great traditions, hard working people and a country where good food is also one of their main characteristics. Of course there is a lot more to see and discover in Mexico but something that definitely makes Mexico very special is its beautiful landscapes. From the beautiful beaches of the pacific like Puerto Ballarta and Acapulco's bay to the great Aztec ruins located in the center of the country. And talking about landscapes in Mexico there is a place that it's been known as a "magic place." A place where it feels that time has never gone by. The architecture of the town still remains the influence of the colonial time with its magical churches and of course great food. The town is call Bernal and its located 60 kilometers from the city of Queretaro (Colis) But what makes this "magical place" magical is the Pena de Bernal or Bernal's Boulder, a beautiful rock that is the main attraction of thousands of tourist from all over the world. But how and when was this amazing rock formed? Why in Queretaro? What are the effects of this rock for the Bernal's population? All these questions and many more will be the main focus of this paper hoping to get a better understanding of this magical place called Bernal.

How it was formed?

To begin with, la Pena de Bernal was formed 100 million years ago during the Jurassic period. At that time, the boulder was at least three times higher than what it is today. The pena is made of porfiroid rocks and it is one of the three highest monoliths of the world. Only Spain's Rock of Gibraltar and Rio de Janeiro's Pao de Azucar are taller (Mexico Desconocido). According to scientists, this rock got formed because of a volcanic chimney that when it stopped erupting, all the lava cooled down on top of the volcano. La Pena de Bernal is a great example of an intrusive igneous rock. Intrusive igneous rocks are those rocks formed when magma cools and crystallizes below the surface (Class). The best way to identify an indigenous rock is based on its texture that is mostly grain size. It is also based on its chemical composition meaning what minerals the igneous rock contains. Based on my own theory of what I have learned in my geology class, la Pena de Bernal is composed of mostly felsic minerals, meaning that it comes from feldspar and silica. Those minerals have a clear color and that is why it gives its white color to la Pena de Bernal.

Why in Queretaro?

La Pena was formed in Queretaro because Queretaro is part of the Volcanic Belt territory of Mexico. The state is one of the many states located in the center part of

Mexico. In the east part of Queretaro two main physiographic sections are converged, La Mesa Central and the Sierra Madre Oriental. La Mesa Central crosses the region of Bernal and it has a relief approximately 500 ms developed on marine rocks (Ferrari).

Effects in the habitants of Bernal

Because of this great rock, Bernal is one of the main tourist points of Queretaro and thousands of people from all over the world gather in this magic town to feel and explore the energy of the rock. Now that we understand how this pena formed and why did it form in Queretaro it is important to know how la Pena de Bernal affects the habitants of Bernal. Like I said before Bernal is a very tourist place bringing people from all over the world to see such a wonderful geologic landscape. This rock has influenced the habitants to take advantage of the rock in order to have a better economy. A really large percent of the population works in something related to tourism, hotels, restaurants, entertainment, rentals, cloths gifts to primary source of economic in that town, providing many jobs for the habitants (Mexico Desconocido).

Mexico is full of great people and beautiful magic places like Bernal. As Queretaro has been in the central part of Mexico where the Mexican Volcanic Belt is it shows that many years ago there were volcanoes erupting all over the place making la Pena de Bernal a very interesting and beautiful intrusive rock, making Bernal a favorite town for many tourists and a very good source of economy for Bernal habitants. While I was there couple years ago I did feel the magic of the town and the energy that it feels being close to such an enormous rock.

7.13: Writing to Learn – Practicing Peer Response

Reread the term paper assignment description and the guidelines for scientific writing, and then read Alfredo's rough draft again. If you were responding to this draft, what would you suggest that Alfredo should focus on in revising for his next draft? In what ways does Alfredo's draft meet the professor's expectations for effective science writing?

In her feedback on Alfredo's paper, the professor gave him two kinds of help: advice for expanding on what he'd written, and advice for editing his sentences. Read the professor's response to Alfredo's draft below.

I think you have done a very good job with this so far, especially considering how little information is available. I like that you have divided the paper into sections and your ideas are very well organized. I have a couple of suggestions for things to add that will make this paper a little more complete.

Introduction
Your introduction is great. I have made a few editing suggestions on the paper but you don't need to add anything else to it.

How was it formed?
Define porphyritic (see your textbook)
I think you can add some more interpretation by explaining (briefly) what a volcanic neck is and how it forms. You want to mention that it is an intrusive feature that forms below a volcano and is then exposed by erosion of the overlying volcanic rocks. I really like that you talk about how igneous rocks are classified and then apply what you know to deciding what kind of rock it is. I also like that you mention what kind of rocks the intrusion is intruded into in the next section. That should be moved up to this section. I can help you look at the geologic map of Mexico to determine how old these rocks are.

Why in Queretaro?
This section needs to be expanded. The main thing here is to explain why there is an igneous intrusion here (why there used to be a volcano). To do this you should explain the tectonic setting of the area.

Effects on the inhabitants of Bernal
I really like this section and have no suggestions for things to add.

Summary
You have a nice closing paragraph already. The only thing I'd like to see is a very short summary of what you discovered about how the rock formed (two or three sentences).

When I asked Alfredo about the differences between his rough draft and his final draft, he said that for his final draft he added "a lot more information and more research about new stuff." Alfredo told me that in addition to doing more library research, it took him another three hours of revising and editing to write the final draft. Read Alfredo's final draft, given below.

La Peña de Bernal: Final Draft

Introduction

Mexico is a beautiful country full of great traditions, hard working people, and a country where good food is also one of the main characteristics. Of course there is a lot more to see and discover in Mexico, but something that definitely makes Mexico very special is its beautiful landscapes. From the beautiful beaches of the Pacific like Puerto Vallarta and Acapulco's bay, to the great Aztec ruins located in the center of the country. And talking about landscapes, in Mexico there is a place that's been known as a "magic place." A place where it feels that time has never gone by. The architecture of the town still retains the influence of the colonial time with its magical churches and of course great food. The town is called Bernal and it's located 60 kilometers from the city of Queretaro (Colis, 2007). But what makes this "magical place" magical is the Pena de Bernal or Bernal's Boulder in English, a beautiful rock that is the main attraction of thousands of tourist from all over the world. But how and when was this amazing rock formed? Why in Queretaro? What are the effects of this rock on the Bernal's population? These questions will be the main focus of this paper hoping to get a better understanding of this magical place called Bernal.

How was it formed?

La Pena de Bernal was formed 100 million years ago during the Jurassic period. At that time, the boulder was at least three times higher than it is today. The pena is made of porphyric rocks, meaning that the texture of this rock has some crystals distinctly larger than others. It is one of the three highest monoliths of the world. Only Spain's Rock of Gibraltar and Rio de Janeiro's Pao de Azucar are taller (México Desconocido). According to scientists, this rock formed because of a volcanic neck that when it stopped erupting all the lava cooled down on top of the volcano. A volcanic neck is a cylindrical-shaped land form standing above the surface created by magma solidifying in the event of a volcano. The erosion of the sides of the volcano exposes the neck (Ritter, 2006). Volcanic necks were under the surface 20–30 million years ago. With erosion, the necks are now visible because the surface of the land is much lower now that what it used to be millions of years ago. The Pena de Bernal is a great example of many of these volcanic necks.

La Pena de Bernal is also an intrusive igneous rock. Intrusive igneous rocks are those rocks formed when magma cools and crystallizes below the surface. The best way to identify an igneous rock is based on its texture that is mostly grain size. It is also based on its chemical composition meaning what minerals the igneous rock contains. Based on my own theory of what I have learned in my geology class, la

Pena de Bernal is composed of mostly felsic minerals, meaning that it comes from feldspar and silica. Those minerals have a clear color and that is what gives a white color to la Pena de Bernal.

Why in Queretaro?

La Pena was formed in Queretaro because Queretaro is part of the Mexican Volcanic Belt territory. This is a region of the planet which has the most active volcanoes. In Mexico most of the volcanoes are located in the Trans-Mexican Vocánico (CVTM), which are judged the more important active volcanoes of the country. But there are also many volcanoes in other regions. The Mexican Volcanic Belt is an extent volcanic strip of 900 by 70 kilometers generated by the subduction of the oceanic plates Riviera and Cocos, underneath the Mexican continental crust throughout the Pacific coast. This mountainous chain crosses the Mexican Republic and runs from EW, from the islands of Revillagigedo in the Pacific Ocean, to the region of the Tuxtlas in Veracruz (Ferrari, 1999, p. 303). There are two main igneous regions in Mexico, both related to subduction. The Mexican Volcanic belt runs EW and is related to the current subduction of the Rivera and Cocos plates beneath the North American plate. The Sierra Madre Occidental is composed of older igneous rocks related to an older subduction (the same that formed the Rockies in the U.S.) (Hammersley, 2006).

Effects on the habitants of Bernal

Because of this great rock, Bernal is one of the main tourist points of Queretaro and thousands of people from all over the world gather in this magic town to feel and explore the energy of the rock. Now that we understand how this pena formed and why it formed in Queretaro it is important to know how la Pena de Bernal affects the habitants of Bernal. Like I said before Bernal is a very tourist place bringing people from all over the world to see such a wonderful geologic landscape. This rock has influenced the habitants to take advantage of the rock in order to have a better economy. A really large percent of the population works in something related to tourism, hotels, restaurants, entertainment, rentals, clothes, and gifts which are primary sources of economics in that town, providing many jobs for the habitants (México Desconocido).

Summary

Mexico is full of great people and beautiful, magic places like Bernal. As Queretaro is in the central part of Mexico where the Mexican Volcanic Belt is it shows that many years ago there were volcanoes erupting all over the place, making la Pena de Bernal a very interesting and beautiful intrusive rock. It is amazing to know how the level of the surface changes by the erosion, making the neck of volcanoes visible. Now that I understand and discovered how the pena was formed and what it is made of I would like to discover how many more necks I will be able to see in the future. Over the years Bernal has become a favorite town for many tourists which are a very good source of economy for Bernal's habitants. While I was there a couple years ago I did feel the magic of the town and the energy of being close to such an enormous rock.

References

Colis, Paola, Feb 12 2007. La Pena de Bernal, Rotativo de querétaro. http://rotativo.com.mx/turismo/la_pena_de_bernal/0.11.1121.html

Ferrari, L., Lopez-Martinez, M., Aguirre-Diaz, G. & Carrasco-Nunez, G., 1999. Space-time patterns of Cenozoic arc volcanism in central Mexico: from the Sierra Madre Occidental to the Mexican Volcanic Belt. Geology, 27, 303–306.

Hammersley, L., 2006. Lecture and lab materials. California State University, Sacramento.

México desconocido.com. 2007. http://www.mexicodesconocido.com.

Ritter, M.E., 2006. The physical environment: glossary. http://www.uwsp.edu /geo/faculty/ritter/glossary/glossary_V.html.

When Alfredo's professor evaluated his final draft, she used the rubric shown below. Take a look at the rubric and Alfredo's final score:

Introduction (thesis) ....[1–5] <u>5</u>

    5. The point of the essay is clearly stated in the introduction.
    3. The point of the essay is only indirectly stated in the introduction.
    2. The point of the essay can only be inferred after reading much of the essay.
    1. The point of the essay is unclear.

Introduction (justification) .... [1–5] <u>4</u>

    5. Introduction clearly states importance of subject and provokes interest of reader.
    3. Introduction states importance of subject.
    2. Introduction mentions importance of subject.
    1. Lacks any mention of why the reader should be interested.

Organization .... [1–5] <u>5</u>

    5. Well organized and easy to follow.
    3. Sufficiently well organized to follow the flow.
    2. Not well organized.

1. Unorganized and difficult to follow.

Clarity .... [1–5] <u>4</u>

    5. Conveys author's ideas clearly.
    3. Communicates author's ideas, but with difficulty.
    1. Author's ideas are unclear.

Voice and Audience (scientific style) .... [1–5] <u>4</u>

    5. Uses clear, scientific prose. No "creative writing."
    3. Some "creative" writing and reference to personal feelings.
    1. Frequent use of personal references, poor writing style.

Research and References .... [1–5] <u>4</u>

    5. Uses appropriate sources, properly used and cited.
    3. Insufficient technical sources, citations insufficient or improperly used.
    1. Very inappropriate sources, lack of citation bordering on plagiarism.

Format .... [1–5] <u>5</u>

    5. Meets all page and format requirements, uses appropriate headings.
    3. Does not meet all requirements, needs more and better section headings.
    1. Format requirements ignored, inappropriate formatting.

Grammar, Spelling, Sentence Structure .... [1–5] <u>3</u>

    5. Free of spelling, grammar and structural problems.
    3. Minor errors in grammar, spelling or structure.
    1. Grammar and sentence structure problems make essay difficult to read.

Overall Impression .... [1–10] <u>8</u>
Total .... [10–50] <u>42</u>

Comments:
Very nice paper. I really like the sections you added on volcanic necks and the Mexican volcanic belt — they made your paper much more "scientific." Well done.

7.14: Writing to Learn – Reflecting on Revision

Individually or in small groups, compare Alfredo's rough draft and his final draft, using the rubric above as a guide. What changes did Alfredo make in his final draft? Were his changes effective? If Alfredo had a chance to revise his term paper one more time, what changes could he make to further improve his paper?

As you can see by her rubric, Alfredo's professor gave a lot of thought to designing the term paper project, and she really wants her students to learn to write and research like scientists. In our interview, Alfredo's professor had a lot of good advice for college students who are taking a course (or courses) in the natural sciences, so we'll end this case study with her advice:

1. Recognize that writing is a skill that must be honed by constant practice.

2. There are many different types of writing. Make sure that you understand what is expected of you for a given project. Ask for more clarification if you are not clear.

3. Always start a project early, even if you just do the planning stages. You need time to assimilate the material and consider how to present it to create a well-organized piece of work.

4. Ask your professor or a friend to read over a first or even second draft of a paper. The best way to improve your writing is to get input. In my experience, making changes in response to a careful review of a draft can increase your grade significantly. Don't be scared of asking a professor to look over an early version of your paper, most are happy to do so if it is handed in early.

5. Expect a careful review to take about a week. Do not hand in a draft of a paper a few days before the deadline and ask for a review, your professor may not have time.

6. The most important thing of all is to start your research early. It is easy to put off starting on a research paper until the last minute but finding good sources can be very time consuming.

7. Searching for sources, as with writing, is a skill that comes with practice. At times it can be very frustrating learning how to use the various search engines but it will get easier. In the meantime, talk to a librarian or your professor when you need help.

8. In the sciences, the bulk of the material you need for a term paper is in peer-reviewed journals. You absolutely must learn which article search engines (e.g. GeoRef) are the best for your discipline.

9. Often the best resources for a project are found by reading the bibliographies of the first few articles you find.

Examples of Student Writing in the Natural Sciences

For more examples of student writing in the natural sciences, visit the following online student writing journals:

American Journal of Undergraduate Research, University of Northern Iowa
(http://www.ajur.uni.edu/)

Colombia Undergraduate Science Journal
(http://cusj.columbia.edu/)

JOSHUA: The Journal of Science and Health at the University of Alabama
(http://bama.ua.edu/~joshua/)

The Journal of Undergraduate Sciences, Harvard University Science Center
(http://www.hcs.harvard.edu/~jus/home.html)

The Journal of Young Investigators
(http://www.jyi.org)

The UCLA Undergraduate Science Journal
 (http://www.studentgroups.ucla.edu/usj/)

Review of Key Ideas in Chapter 7

- The writing you're assigned in natural science courses will ask you to conduct experiments, integrate research from other scientists, and report the results of your research in genres such as the lab report, the abstract, the literature review, and the scientific research report.
- Writing assignments for natural science courses will often ask you to take on a formal, objective persona and report the results of your research in clear, concise, and precise language. However, there are some types of science writing that break the conventions of a formal persona – for example, science writing for a popular audience.
- Writing is critical for meaning-making in the sciences. Writing about the results of their research is the primary way that scientists communicate new knowledge to other scientists and to public audiences.

- Science genres are not merely templates for organizing your writing. Science genres like the lab report are a reflection of the scientific method of hypothesis-testing, and they've evolved as ways for scientists to communicate effectively and present the results of their research in an organized way.
- Reading assignments in natural science courses are often complex and challenging and will require active reading strategies such as prereading, rereading, and annotating.
- Research and inquiry in the sciences involves testing hypotheses, systematic observation and experimentation, and exploring the research of other scientists.

7.15: Writing to Learn – Reflecting on Writing in the Natural Sciences

Write three things about natural science writing that you learned from reading this chapter, and three questions about writing in natural science classed that you still have.

---

8 Reading, Writing, and Researching in the Social Sciences

Social scientists make it their business to examine behavior – sometimes the behavior of an individual other times the behavior of a system, society, or culture. Social scientists believe that careful observation of behavior will reveal patterns in that behavior, indicating that behaviors aren't random but are in fact driven by certain forces. For the social scientist, behavior is something that might be defined and understood.

—Professor Karen Gocsik, Writing Program, Dartmouth (Gocsik, 2005)

In the process of writing (and re-writing) sociology well, you will improve at thinking sociologically.

—from Writing Within Sociology: A Guide for Undergraduates, Oregon State
University Department of Sociology
(Oregon State University Department of Sociology, 2010)

For me, the distinctive features of writing in sociology are three-fold: explaining complex ideas in terms of social theory, report writing while conducting applied sociology, and writing ethnographies for field work.

—Richard, a sociology major at George Mason University, in the book
Engaged Writers and Dynamic Disciplines
(quoted in Thaiss and Zawacki, 2006: 106)

8.1: Writing to Learn – Social Science Research

Since social scientists study human interactions in groups and look for patterns in human behavior, what kind of research methods do you think they would value the most? What kind(s) of evidence do you think they would use to support their arguments? How do you think these research methods and kinds of evidence differ from research and writing in the natural sciences?

Writing and Critical Thinking in the Social Sciences

Chapter 6 provided an overview of some of the features of reading, writing, and researching in the social sciences. Take another look at this overview to refresh your memory of the way Chapter 6 described writing in the social sciences.

- Social scientists use reading, writing, and researching to explore questions about human interaction.
- Social scientists, like natural scientists, inquire by forming hypotheses, but social scientists' hypotheses focus on human behavior. Social scientists test these hypotheses by designing social or psychological experiments, collecting data through interviews and surveys, and systematically observing human behavior, building on what other social scientists have observed and reported in academic journals and books.

- Social scientists conduct research using quantitative methods (methods that result in numbers and statistics) and qualitative methods (methods focused on observing, describing, and analyzing social behavior, social artifacts, and social institutions).
- Social scientists report the results of their experiments, data collection, and systematic observations in the written genres of case studies, surveys, interviews, ethnographies, and research reports.
- Social scientists build theories of human behavior based on their research, and these theories are constantly being debated by social science discourse communities of writers and researchers.
- Because social scientists study human behavior using a variety of approaches and genres, the level of formality and conventions of social science writing will depend on the writer's purpose, audience, and genre. In general, social scientists tend to value writing that is precise and logically organized and that follows the conventions of whatever social science genre they're writing in.
- Even though social science genres have purposes and conventions that have been agreed upon over time by communities of social scientists, these genres are constantly evolving, and social scientists are always creating new genres and new conventions.

At most institutions, the social sciences include sociology, anthropology, political science, history, psychology, economics, linguistics, social work, and education.

To help introduce you to writing in the social sciences, we'll look at an interview with sociology Professor Todd Migliaccio, who teaches at California State University Sacramento. I asked Professor Migliaccio about reading, writing, and researching expectations in his courses and in the social sciences in general. What he had to say is reported below.

Q: What is the role of writing in the social sciences?
A: The primary way we use writing is to convey ideas, whether it's to students, other social scientists, or the general populace. It's the primary way we share knowledge, findings, and/or information. Social scientists use writing to display connections between theories, challenge theories, or extend theories. It's a primary form of communication, and the best way to locate new findings and discussions in the field.
Q: What is the role of research in the social sciences?
A: Research is about expanding ideas about social concepts and testing them in the empirical world. In the social sciences it's all about data, which we or

someone else has collected, but that you use to test your theory or idea. In the social sciences we're always moving forward and expanding ideas, not just doing the same research again and again. Through the data, we want to be able to make generalizations about a population or at least make claims about the relationship between concepts. One problem we run into with students is that sometimes they think reviewing the literature on a subject is a source of data. Social scientists use a review of prior research on a subject to justify their research – it is not the actual research. The review of past literature helps justify and explain why the data being collected is useful. In their research papers students do a literature review to set up their own research, but then they need to go out and collect data in some form.

Q: Could you define *data* in the social sciences?

A: Data can be anything from statistics to interviews – any information about people or institutions or groups. Data can be broken down into numbers like income and age, or it can be information from an interview about an experience someone has had. Data can be artifacts like CD covers, pictures, television commercials, or magazine covers. We can use anything that is basically "social," because it all reflects the society in which it exists.

Q: What kinds of research and writing assignments do you and professors in your department assign in lower-division general education courses?

A: We generally assign two types of papers. Since students are learning sociology for the first time, a lot of professors rely on journals. In journals students reflect on their experience in relation to class ideas or go out and collect some type of data, and then reflect on the data, as well as the process of collecting the data. A common journal assignment is what is called a breaching experiment, where students break a social norm. Then in a journal they write about their own experiences breaking the norm and what were the reactions by others, and then they connect this to concepts they're talking about in the class. Instead of a journal paper, professors may also assign a brief argumentative paper where students may conduct the same breaching experiment but then use the reactions of people as data to support an argument.

Q: How are reading and writing connected in the social sciences?

A: I think there's a strong relationship between being able to write and being able to read – to see the actual arguments going on in the reading. We emphasize reading not just to understand the ideas in an article but to see how the argument is constructed – getting students to see what is the point-by-point breakdown. In my classes I ask students to answer questions like, "What are the arguments made by the author?" "Do they justify the overall point?" All of this is in the hope that they will better understand not just the article but how to develop their own argument.

Q: Overall, what kinds of thinking are most valued in the social sciences?

A: In all of the social sciences we want you to see beyond what is sitting in front of your face. In sociology, we call it the *sociological imagination*. That means being able to see that there are larger social forces at work beyond your individual issues and problems. We want students to ask the question, "Why?" What is the relationship between your personal history and the history of society? What are the social forces that are creating a social problem? Then it is a matter of students conveying these ideas in their writing, and for us the important thing is that they convey their ideas with a sociological stance – that there are larger social forces that influence our behaviors and experiences. We don't think most people are ever taught to think that way, so it's a primary focus for most of our classes. We want students to think about the social world in a different context.

8.2: Learn by Doing – Interviewing a Social Sciences Professor

Now that you've looked at my interview with a sociology professor, investigate social science writing at your college by conducting your own interview. Contact a professor in a social sciences department at your college and ask if you could interview the professor to ask about his or her expectations for reading, writing, and researching in his or her courses. The first step in this activity is to come up with some interesting interview questions for the social sciences professor about expectations for writing, reading, and researching. You might brainstorm some questions individually, in small groups, or as a class. Once you've set up an interview with a social sciences professor, review the advice in Chapter 5 about conducting interviews. Write a transcript of the interview if you use a recorder, or a summary if you take notes but don't use a recorder. Be prepared to share the results of your interview with your peers in small groups and/or with the class as a whole.

Examples of Writing in the Social Sciences

Now that you've reviewed some features of social science writing and the expectations that social science professors have for student writing, let's take a closer look at social science writing by giving a close reading to some examples from social science texts. The examples of social science writing provided below are from three common social science genres. The first piece of writing is from the literature review section of an article on college students' credit card use published in an economics journal. In a literature review, the writer summarizes, compares, and evaluates the published scholarship on a focused topic. Sometimes a literature review is one section of a research report – the writer reviews the literature on a topic before he or she reports his or her own findings or presents his or her own arguments. Purposes of a literature review are to provide background on the topic, to review what is known about it and what others have written about it, and to build a framework of ideas that can be used to interpret the author's own findings or arguments. In the social sciences, the writer of a literature review might focus on reviewing social theories, quantitative research, qualitative research, or all three. The second piece of writing is an excerpt from a textbook for introductory political science courses, *Introduction to Political Theory*. The final piece of writing is an excerpt from an ethnography, *My Freshman Year: What a Professor Learned by Becoming a Student*, by social scientist Rebekah Nathan. An ethnography is a common social science genre. In an ethnography, the social scientist conducts fieldwork and observes a community, talks with community members, and might even participate as a member of the community (this is called *participant observation*).

Excerpt from the Literature Review Section of "College students' knowledge and use of credit" by Joyce E. Jones (Jones, 2005: 9)

Recent studies of credit knowledge among college students tend to focus on knowledge and understanding of the specifics of the student's credit cards or other debt. For example, Joo, Grable, and Bagwell (2001) found that a significant number of college students in their study knew the Annual Percentage Rate (61.3%), late fee (54.9%), and annual fee (59.5%) for their major credit card. Fewer (39.9%) knew the cash advance fee, however. An exploratory study by Warwick and Mansfield (2000) found only 28.9 percent of students knew the interest rate on their credit card, while more than half knew their credit card limit (57%) and their current credit card balance (52.5%).

A few studies have examined general credit knowledge of college students (or perception of their credit knowledge). Perceived knowledge and understanding about credit card use was examined by Tan (2003), who noted that many of the college students in his study reported "moderate" or "extensive" knowledge (versus "little or none") of the implications of misusing credit cards (90%), how much their debt will ultimately cost (87%), the implications of just making minimum payments (86%), and how to manage their credit card debt (83%). However, knowledge levels were much lower among those students who were having problems handling their debts (24% of the students), defined as those who only paid the minimum each month on their credit cards or who were behind on their payments.

Excerpt from the textbook *Introduction to Political Theory* by John Hoffman and Paul Graham (Hoffman and Graham, 2006: 335–336)

Radical feminism, as indicated from its critiques of other positions, takes the view that feminism ought to deal with the position of women, independently of other ideological commitments. As MacKinnon argues, "feminism is the first theory to emerge from those whose interests it affirms" (Humm, 1992: 119).

Radical feminists argue that women are oppressed because women are women, and men are men. Male domination permeates all aspects of society − from sport to literature, dress to philosophy, entertainment to sexual mores. As Mary Daly argues, "we live in a profoundly anti-female society, a misogynistic 'civilization' in which men collectively victimize women, attacking us as personifications of their own paranoid fears" (Humm, 1992: 168).

This ubiquity of "maleness" extends to the state itself. Weber's view of the state as an institution that claims a monopoly of legitimate force is too limited, in MacKinnon's view, since this monopoly "describes the power of men over women in the home, in the bedroom, on the job, in the street, through social life" (1989: 169). Patriarchy is a comprehensive system of male power and it arises from men. Oppression, as the *Manifesto of the New York Redstockings* in 1969 declared, is total, "affecting every facet of our lives" (Bryson, 1992: 183–4).

Moreover, the radicals argue that women's oppression is the oldest and most basic form of oppression, and whether it arises from socialists who expect women to make tea while men develop political strategy, or it is expressed through black men such as Stokely Carmichael, who see women as having only bodies and not minds, the same point holds: all men oppress women, and all receive psychological, sexual and material benefits from so doing. Germaine Greer argues that her proposition in *The Female Eunuch* (1971) still holds 30 years later − men hate women at least some of the time. Indeed she reckons that in the year 2000 "more men hate more women more bitterly than in 1970" (1999: 14). Greer gives as good as she believes that women get, and argues that "to be male is to be a kind of idiot savant, full of queer obsessions about fetishistic activities and fantasy goals − a freak of nature, fragile, fantastic, bizarre".

Excerpt from *My Freshman Year: What a Professor Learned by Becoming a Student*, by Rebekah Nathan (Nathan, 2005: 50–51)

One of the most interesting community ventures at AnyU came in the form of our second hall meeting in each semester, where we devised our "Community

Living Agreement." Initiated by the RAs, these were to be the local agreements that each wing lived by, the "dos and don'ts" of hall life, fashioned by the residents themselves. The agreement for the first semester was drafted at a "mandatory" hall meeting at which seven people on the wing showed, one of whom left almost immediately because it was her birthday and she was too drunk to pay attention. After pizza, M&Ms, and yet another icebreaker game, the RA introduced our charge of creating a joint compact and handed out cards and pens, asking each person to write down something in the way of a rule or a "don't" that she would like to obtain for the hall. When we'd finished, the RA taped an enormous blank sheet of white paper to the wall, stood next to it with a marker, and said, "Tell me some of your items." Reluctantly and slowly, each person volunteered some rule. "Don't be too loud at night"; "Close the shower curtain so it doesn't flood the little anteroom"; "Don't leave your hair in the drain"; "Keep your door open when you're in your room (unless you're studying/sleeping)"; "Wipe your hair off the shower walls"; "Don't take showers too long if there are people waiting."

There was no real discussion of any of the items. After everyone contributed, the RA took the sheet off the wall and left us to our candy. About one week later a large printed poster appeared on the hall, titled "Community Living Agreement," listing eight items, half of them pertaining to showers and a few to hair.

The same process occurred during the second semester, although shower etiquette had a lower priority. Six items were posted in the hall for our second semester community agreement:

> Keep hair off the shower walls.
> Keep doors open while you're chillin'.
> Sleepovers and parties in the hall are cool.
> Yell "flushing" if there's someone in the shower [because the shower water turned scalding during the flush].
> No writing on the bathroom stall walls [this was the RA's].
> Say "hi" to people to be friendly.

Although the agreement no doubt reflected some important values held by the residents, including sociability, courtesy, and cleanliness, it was the relationship of the individuals to the community agreement that interested me most. There had been no road map for actually creating an agreement, no mechanism for turning individual opinions into a community document. No one, including the RA, was comfortable suggesting that we might modify, prioritize, or remove individuals' suggestions from the list. While the seven students in attendance were considered to "represent" the others, because the latter did not show up to participate, there was no means for making the "agreement" binding on hall residents. As a result, the list remained posted for a semester, but each student on the hall decided whether she would abide by the agreement or not.

I never once heard anyone yell "flushing" in the bathroom, nor did I ever see a "cool sleepover" or public party on the hall. It seemed to me that the same people who kept their doors open prior to the agreement, including me, were the ones who kept their doors open afterward. There was never any follow-up or discussion about whether our agreement was being honored.

Community in the American university is paradoxically a private and an individual decision. As Robert Putnam documents in his history of community in the United States, *Bowling Alone*, the private decision to participate in community life is one that individuals in recent U.S. history are making less and less. From civic and religious life to political participation and informal social connections, there is an increasing individualism in American life that is evident in our universities as well.

In such a historical light, the trends in dormitory living are thought-provoking. The newest dormitories being built across the country are both higher in amenities and lower in density than those of the past. It is no longer considered a viable model of campus life to have a hall full of people sharing a communal bathroom, lounge, and washing machine. The old blueprint of collective living has given way to much more individualized and opulent arrangements. Put in student lingo, individualism "rules."

8.3: Writing to Learn – Features of Writing in the Social Sciences

The purpose of this Writing to Learn activity is for you to look closely at the previous examples of social science writing and think about features of writing in the social sciences. Reread the three examples of social science writing and individually or in small groups come up with a list of features of social science writing based on what you've read. With each feature, include a specific example or two from the texts. For example, if you find that one aspect of social science writing is being concise, find examples of concise sentences. Be prepared to talk about these features of writing in the social sciences as a whole class.

Exploring Genre in the Social Sciences: Ethnography

Most social science genres involve reviewing and evaluating social science research, or observing and analyzing human behavior in social contexts and collecting data about that behavior. In social science courses, professors assign the genres of: literature reviews, book reviews, observation essays, interview papers, case studies, and social science research reports. One social science genre that requires both integrating social science research and theory and doing primary research through observations and interviews is the *ethnography*.

In one of the readings in the previous section, the excerpt from Rebekah Nathan's *My Freshman Year*, you got a glimpse of an ethnography. Nathan, a social scientist, posed as a college student in order to learn about university undergraduate culture. For a year she attended classes, lived in a dorm, observed student behavior, took notes on what she observed, and interviewed students. Then Nathan reported the results of her study in a systematic and organized way. She described the setting for her fieldwork and the reason she was observing this particular culture; she discussed rituals, artifacts, social roles, and social beliefs of the culture she observed; she presented evidence from her observations, experiences, and interviews; and she came to some conclusions about undergraduate life based on her observations.

The genre of the ethnography is social science in action. It's a genre that evolved as a response to a common rhetorical situation in the social sciences: the need to report the results of direct experiences with a culture in a detailed and organized way that relates to the interests of other social scientists. The ethnography is also a genre which has evolved as the way that social scientists create knowledge has changed over time. There's a long tradition of social scientists attempting to be objective and by reporting what they observed as neutral observers of a culture. More recently, the discourse community of social scientists has become skeptical about whether it's possible – or even desirable – to be an objective observer of culture. Many social scientists now argue that it's impossible to study human behavior with the same level of neutrality and objectivity as scientists study other types of natural phenomena. Participant-observer ethnographies like Rebekah Nathan's, in which social science researchers are active participants in the culture they're studying, are becoming more common in the social sciences as more subjective and personal forms of creating knowledge become accepted by the discourse community of social scientists. The ethnography is a good example of how the genres of a discipline are a reflection of the ways of thinking and the ways of making knowledge in that discipline, and how genres change as ways of thinking within the discipline change.

Let's take a look at an ethnography assignment from an Introduction to Anthropology course to see a concrete example of ethnography. The following assignment is from Professor Melissa Johnson of Southwestern University. As you read the assignment, think about the ways it explains the conventions of the genre of the ethnography.

Mini-Ethnographic Research Assignment

This handout should supply you with some general guidelines on your mini-ethnographic research and analysis assignment. This assignment allows you to experience what it is like to do cultural anthropology, learn first-hand about some key ethnographic research methods and critically analyze and reflect on the culture(s) around you.

There are six components to this project: 1) coming up with a fieldsite/topic, 2) finding three academic (peer-reviewed) articles that provide some scholarly context to your topic, and that help you hone your research questions; 3) putting together a mini-research proposal considering the ethical dimensions and dilemmas of your project 4) conducting the research (participant observation and possibly interviews and creating field and interview notes) 5) turning in a progress report mid-way through your work on the project 6) analyzing your data and writing your paper.

Following are some potential suggestions for possible topics and/or ethnographic "fieldsites"; you are more than welcome to come up with alternatives.

Consumption Patterns among some group	What it means to be Latino/a, African-American, Asian, White etc. at SU	Social Patterns at a Popular Cafe or Restaurant	Immigration in Georgetown/Austin	Social Organization and Ritual practice at a Church service
Volunteerism	Bilingualism and Code switching	Patterns of Smoking among SU students	A Bar mitzvah	Social Analysis of a South-western student organization
Social patterns at a bar or nightclub	Social and Cultural Patterns in the Commons	Gender Roles within X community	Courtship and Dating/Inter-racial Dating	
Skateboarders	Vegans, Vegetarians	Thrift Store Shopping	Experiences of Handicapped Students at SU	Migrant Workers
Sorority Life, Fraternity Life	A Wedding or any religious ritual	A Baptism	A Funeral	Analysis of a sports event (basketball games, etc.)

Once you've chosen a topic, do an academic search (EBSCOHost, Academic Search Premier, JSTOR, and/or library books) for literature on your topic (use broad key words to try to identify relevant material). Find a few articles and use them to help develop your research questions: what do you want to find out?; what kinds of data will you need in order to answer your question?

Then put together a research plan (when/where/how will you observe/participate/ interview, etc.). You should plan on visiting your site 3 times (unless you are doing a one-time event, in which case you should supplement with interviews), you may also want to include either formal or informal interviews. Your research plan should be as specific as possible about how you will gather data, who you will talk to, etc.

The proposal you turn into me will include an overall description of your project, your research questions, which briefly incorporate some of the questions or frames you discovered in the scholarly literature you looked at, your plan for gathering data, and citations for the three most relevant academic sources you found. **A first draft of the proposal is due in class on Monday February 12.** If required, you may need to turn in a revised version, responding to my comments on February 19. I will then submit all of the class proposals to the Institutional Review Board (IRB) which will determine if there are any ethical or safety issues regarding human subjects. Once I receive the go-ahead from the IRB, you may begin your research once you have received my approval for your project. The proposal is worth 8% of this assignment (2% each for questions, plan, and citations)

The consideration of the ethics of your research

You will be required to write a one page (250 word) minimum consideration of the ethical dilemmas that your research project proposes, using our class session on ethics in anthropology to help you think through what kinds of issues might arise in your project. **This will be due W Feb 21 in class.** This portion of the assignment is worth 8% of the mini-ethnography assignment.

The Progress Report

You are required to turn in a 'progress report' on your research on W Mar 21 in class. This can be a brief (100–200 words) paragraph describing how you are proceeding with the project. Your progress report is worth 6% of this assignment.

On Ethnographic Analysis

Some of the kinds of questions to think about before, during and after your research are listed below. Not every question will be appropriate for every site, and there may be other questions that are equally or more important that occur to you, and that you should consider.

Are there any culturally defined behaviors for this place/event (things that are ok to do, things that are not ok to do)?

What are people doing?

What are they wearing?

How are they talking?

What are the social dynamics? Is one person in charge, several? Do people's positions of power seem to change?

Are there more than one social group within your site? What differentiates them?

Are there differences in behavior, appearance, speech based on gender? based on race or ethnicity? on social/economic class (if you can tell, and how can you tell)?

What is the physical location you are in? (describe it carefully) How is the space used, how is it socially patterned?

If possible, you should take notes during your participant-observation. If this is too intrusive, write down your observations as soon as you can after you have finished.

In your analysis of your data describe what you observed, and identify any patterns that seem to emerge. Please write a coherent essay, do not simply answer the questions above. What did you learn about the subculture of the people you were observing, what kinds of patterns of behavior/performance could you identify? Avoid ethnocentric evaluations – e.g "people acted weirdly," "the men were sexist" and other similar kinds of statements; instead note exactly what people were doing in non-evaluative/non-judgmental terms, e.g. "most of this group swayed back and forth in unison, hopping to the left frequently"; or "a number of the men insisted on going to the bar to buy a drink for the women they were with, even though the women offered to make this trip." Also avoid attributing a motive to these people, unless they tell you why they are doing what they are doing (and even then, that might not be the full story), e.g. "three of the people I interviewed said that they did not feel part of mainstream society, and they expressed this feeling of exclusion by swaying and hopping to the left" or "two men I talked to said they thought it would be too dangerous for women to travel through the bar to get a drink, they wanted to make sure they protected the women." If you do not interview people, or if only person suggests a motive, you may *suggest* motives – "it seems to be it might be the case that…"

Paper Format

Your paper should begin with an introductory paragraph that tells the reader what you are arguing (ie what your analysis of the ethnographic data you collected showed you), and a very brief description of the when, where and who of your research.

You should then describe how you conducted your ethnographic research in the next one to three paragraphs. Include in this discussion any ethical issues linked to your project, including how you informed people that you were doing research. Your aim here should be to convince the reader that we can trust you, that we can learn something from your observations and analyses.

Following your discussion of methods, you should include a brief (one to two paragraphs) discussion of the three scholarly works you found on your topic; and how they connect to the points you will be making in the paper.

The bulk of your paper should include an ethnographic description of the who, what, when you researched and an analysis of the patterns, meanings, etc. that emerged. In other words, here you elaborate the main points you told us about in your opening paragraph. Make sure your evidence supports your claims, and pay attention to the ways of thinking and analyzing discussed in the first handout for the project.

Finally, you should conclude your paper with a paragraph that re-iterates your main point, and perhaps briefly summarizes/recaps your findings.

Your paper should be no less than 1000 and ideally no more than 1250 words (though it is acceptable to go over if you want to), typed and double spaced, with ample margins. Make sure pages are numbered. Incorporate a discussion of the scholarly literature you used to help identify your research question into your paper, and make sure you include a list of works cited at the end of your paper.

If you wish, you may attach your ethnographic fieldnotes and your interview notes to your paper as well, so that I can better understand your approach and the effort you put into this assignment.

What I will be looking for in your papers:
An excellent paper will include a well thought-out research question, appropriate scholarly articles and a well-designed research plan. The paper will provide a rich description of what you observed including some reflection on your role in the research, as well as thoughtful analysis of the phenomenon/a that you observed. The paper will not include ethnocentric evaluations, nor will the author, without ample evidence, impute motives to what people were doing. The paper will be well-organized and be written with a sparklingly clear style and will have no grammar or spelling mistakes.

8.4: Writing to Learn – The Genre of the Ethnography

Reread Professor Johnson's mini-ethnographic analysis assignment and answer the questions below:

1. What is the purpose of the mini-ethnography?
2. How would you describe the role and persona of the student researcher in the mini-ethnography assignment?
3. How does the mini-ethnography introduce students to the research methods of the social sciences?
4. According to Professor Johnson's assignment, how is the genre of the ethnography organized, and how does that organization connect to ways of thinking and making knowledge in the social sciences?

Sample Ethnography

Now that you've reviewed an ethnography assignment, let's take a close look at a published ethnography. The following excerpt is from an ethnography by the anthropologist Napoleon Chagnon, who lived with and studied the Yanomamö people of Brazil in the 1960s.

Excerpt from *Yanomamö: The Fierce People* by Napoleon Chagnon (Chagnon, 1968: 114–116)

Child–Adult Division. Despite the fact that children of both sexes spend much of their time with their mothers, the boys are treated with more indulgence by their fathers from an early age. Thus, the distinction between male and female status develops early in the socialization process, and the boys are quick to learn their favored position with respect to girls. They are encouraged to be fierce and are rarely punished by their parents for inflicting blows on them or on the hapless girls in the village. This can be seen in one of the scenes in the film A Man Called Bee (Chagnon and Asch, 1974a). Kąobawä, for example, lets Ariwari beat him on the face and head to express his anger and temper, laughing and commenting on his ferocity. Although Ariwari is only about 4 years old, he has already learned that the appropriate response to a flash of anger is to strike someone with his hand or with an object, and it is not uncommon for him to give his father a healthy smack in the face whenever something displeases him. He is frequently goaded into hitting his father by teasing, being rewarded by gleeful cheers of assent from his mother and from the other adults in the household.

When Kạobawä's group travels, Ariwari emulates his father by copying his activities on a child's scale. For example, he erects a temporary hut from small sticks and discarded leaves and plays happily in his own camp. His sisters, however, are pressed into more practical labor and help their mother do useful tasks. Still, the young girls are given some freedom to play at being adults and have their moments of fun with their mothers or other children.

But a girl's childhood ends sooner than a boy's. The game of playing house fades imperceptibly into a constant responsibility to help mother. By the time a girl is 10 years old or so, she has become an economic asset to the mother and spends a great deal of time working. Little boys, by contrast, spend hours playing among themselves and are able to prolong their childhood into their late teens if they so wish. By that time a girl has married, and many even have a child or two.

A girl's transition to womanhood is obvious because of its physiological manifestations. At first menses (yöbömou), Yanomamö girls are confined to their houses and hidden behind a screen of leaves. Their old cotton garments are discarded and replaced by new ones manufactured by their mothers or by older female friends. During this week of confinement, the girl is fed by her relatives; her food must be eaten by means of a stick, as she is not allowed to come into contact with it in any other fashion. She speaks in whispers, and then only to close kin. She must also scratch herself with another set of sticks. The Yanomamö word for menstruation translates literally as "squatting" (roo), and that fairly accurately describes what pubescent females (and adult women) do during menstruation. Yanomamö women do not use the equivalents of tampons or sanitary napkins. They simply remain inactive during menstruation, squatting on their haunches and allowing the menstrual blood to drip on the ground. However, women are menstruating relatively infrequently, for they are pregnant or nursing infants much of their lives. After her puberty confinement, a girl usually takes up residence with her promised husband and begins life as a married woman.

Males, on the other hand, do not have their transition into manhood marked by a ceremony. Nevertheless, one can usually tell when a boy is attempting to enter the world of men. The most conspicuous sign is his anger when others call him by his name. When the adults in the village cease using his personal name, the young man has achieved some sort of masculine adult status. Young men are always very touchy about their names and they, more than anyone else, take quick offense when hearing their names mentioned. The Yanomamö constantly employ teknonymy when a kinship usage is ambiguous. Thus, someone may wish to refer to Kaobawä in a conversation, but the kinship term appropriate to the occasion might not distinguish him from his several brothers. Then, Kaobawä will be referred to as "father of Ariwari." However, when Ariwari gets older he will attempt to put a stop to this in an effort to establish his status as an adult. A young man has been recognized as an adult when people no longer use his name in tecnonymous references. Still, the transition is not abrupt, and it is not marked by a recognizable point in time.

Finally, the children differ from adults in their susceptibility to supernatural hazards. A great deal of Yanomamö sorcery and mythological references to harmful magic focuses on children as the target of malevolence. Yanomamö shamans are constantly sending their spirits (hekura) to enemy villages. There, they secretly attack and devour the vulnerable portion of the children's souls, bringing about sickness and death. These same shamans spend an equal amount of time warding off the dangerous spirits sent by their enemies. Children are vulnerable because their souls are not firmly established within their physical beings and can wander out of the body almost at will. The most common way for a child's soul to escape is to leave by way of the mouth when the child cries. Thus, mothers are quick to hush a bawling baby in order to prevent its soul from escaping. The child's soul can be recovered by sweeping the ground in the vicinity where it most probably escaped, calling for it while sweeping the area with a particular kind of branch. I once helped gather up the soul of a sick child in this fashion, luring it back into the sick baby. One of the contributions I made, in addition to helping with the calling and sweeping, was a dose of medicine for the child's diarrhea. A consequence of this set of attitudes about the vulnerability of children is that much of the village's activity with respect to shamanism and curing is directed toward the children.

8.5: Writing to Learn – Rhetorical Features of Ethnographies

The purpose of this Writing to Learn activity is for you to do a close reading of the two excerpts from ethnographies in this chapter, Rebekah Nathan's *My Freshman Year* and Napoleon Chagnon's *Yanomamö: The Fierce People*, and think about the rhetorical situation of the genre of the ethnography. Individually or in small groups, consider the rhetorical features of the ethnography by looking closely at the two examples and analyzing purpose, audience, text, context, and persona. Be prepared to discuss specific examples from the excerpts which illustrate these different rhetorical features.

8.6: Learn by Doing – Practicing Ethnographic Research

The purpose of this Learn by Doing activity is for you to practice an ethnographic research method in an informal way (without the pressure of having to write for a graded assignment in a social science course). In this activity, you'll practice observing social interaction and analyzing what you've observed. Visit a specific location where people gather or a social event (e.g. a mall, a club, a concert, the grocery store) and observe and take notes about the way people are interacting. Once you've collected "data" from your observations, analyze your data. Did you see any patterns in the way people interacted? Did you note any unusual behavior? In what ways did the social structure of the place or event you observed affect individual behaviors? As you write about your observations, try to mimic the style of the ethnographies you read in this section of Chapter 8.

Reading in the Social Sciences

In Chapter 7, we discussed how reading assignments in the natural sciences are difficult and require active reading strategies, and we looked at a sample annotation of the excerpt from Stephen Hawking's *A Brief History of Time* to model one active reading approach. The readings you're assigned in social science courses will also require active reading strategies. Social science books and articles discuss complex social issues and complex theories of social behavior. When you do your social science reading assignments, you're going to need to annotate, reread, and use techniques like a double-entry journal. Below is the excerpt from the textbook, *Introduction to Political Theory*, by John Hoffman and Paul Graham that we looked at earlier in this chapter. If a student knew that the professor wanted the students in the class to read this chapter of the textbook and write a summary and response journal entry, or that there was going to be a short answer exam on this chapter in which the key terms discussed in the chapter would need to be defined and some responses to the chapter content would need to be given, one useful reading technique would be a double-entry journal. As we discussed in Chapter 4, a double-entry journal is a kind of reading log in which you write the key terms and key arguments of a reading on one side of the journal and your questions and responses on the other side. Reread the excerpt and take a look at the sample double-entry journal provided after the reading.

Sample Double-Entry Journal for a Social Sciences Text

Radical feminism, as indicated from its critiques of other positions, takes the view that feminism ought to deal with the position of women, independently of other ideological commitments. As MacKinnon argues, "feminism is the first theory to emerge from those whose interests it affirms" (Humm, 1992: 119).

Radical feminists argue that women are oppressed because women are women, and men are men. Male domination permeates all aspects of society — from sport to literature, dress to philosophy, entertainment to sexual mores. As Mary Daly argues, "we live in a profoundly anti-female society, a misogynistic 'civilization' in which men collectively victimize women, attacking us as personifications of their own paranoid fears" (Humm, 1992: 168).

This ubiquity of "maleness" extends to the state itself. Weber's view of the state as an institution that claims a monopoly of legitimate force is too limited, in MacKinnon's view, since this monopoly "describes the power of men over women in the home, in the bedroom, on the job, in the street, through social life" (1989: 169). Patriarchy is a comprehensive system of male power and it arises from men. Oppression, as the *Manifesto of the New York Redstockings* in 1969 declared, is total, "affecting every facet of our lives" (Bryson, 1992: 183–4).

Moreover, the radicals argue that women's oppression is the oldest and most basic form of oppression, and whether it arises from socialists who expect women to make tea while men develop political strategy, or it is expressed through black men such as Stokely Carmichael, who see women as having only bodies and not minds, the same point holds: all men oppress women, and all receive psychological, sexual and material benefits from so doing. Germaine Greer argues that her proposition in *The Female Eunuch* (1971) still holds 30 years later — men hate women at least some of the time. Indeed she reckons that in the year 2000 "more men hate more women more bitterly than in 1970" (1999: 14). Greer gives as good as she believes that women get, and argues that "to be male is to be a kind of idiot savant, full of queer obsessions about fetishistic activities and fantasy goals — a freak of nature, fragile, fantastic, bizarre" (1999: 327).

(Hoffman and Graham, 2006: 335–336)

Radical feminism: women are repressed because they're women. Male domination permeates society.	Is this true of <u>all</u> aspects of society? Even aspects where men aren't present?

Patriarchy: comprehensive system of male power and oppression. Radical feminists believe oppression of females is the oldest form of oppression.	We talked about this in my philosophy class, too — look up "patriarchy" in my notes for philosophy.
According to radical feminists "all men hate women." All men get psychological and sexual benefits from oppression of women.	This is a big generalization. Do <u>all</u> radical feminists believe that all men hate women?

In the example of a double-entry journal shown above, a student notes key words (*radical feminism* and *patriarchy*) and questions some of the ideas of radical feminism and what the textbook was saying about radical feminism. If the professor wanted the student to write a response to the chapter, the student could go back to his or her double-entry notebook and find places where he or she did some critical thinking and questioned the text.

8.7: Learn by Doing – Reading a Social Science Text

The purpose of this Learn by Doing activity is to practice reading a social science text and practice using one of the active reading strategies we discussed in Chapter 4, the double-entry journal. You'll practice using a double-entry journal on the excerpt that follows from the book, *Unequal Childhoods: Class, Race, and Family Life*, by Annette Lareau. Lareau observed and interviewed families of various races and socioeconomic backgrounds to understand how race and class affects family life, and especially children. First, read quickly, skimming through the excerpt. Then reread the excerpt and take notes in your double-entry journal as you read (you can write the journal by hand or on a computer if you're in a computer classroom or doing this activity outside of class). Once you've completed your double-entry journal, form small groups and share your journal with your peers. Compare journals and take a look at how your peers' journals are similar to and different from yours. Be prepared to discuss with the class as a whole the strategies your group members used in your double-entry journals.

Sample Social Sciences Reading

Excerpt from *Unequal Childhoods: Class, Race, and Family Life* **by Annette Lareau (Lareau, 2003: 91–97)**

All parents are faced with multiple, daily child-rearing tasks. But, in poor families, the difficulties involved in executing those tasks are much greater than in middle-class families <u>and</u> working-class ones. The additional burden created by poverty is not connected to the competence of individuals (although individuals do vary in their social skills). Rather, it is the result of the uneven distribution of structural resources. Unlike in Western European countries, where all families with dependent children get a monthly stipend, in the United States, financial stability is considered a matter of individual responsibility. Public assistance does not cover the minimum costs of raising children. Moreover, the social resources available to the poor are not simply insufficient; they are also bureaucratic, slow working and stigmatized.

Ms. Brindle is not currently employed, but she has held jobs in the past and seems proud of it (e.g., noting that she had worked at McDonald's, she adds, "I was good at it"). She hopes to return to work once Melmel starts school. In the meantime, the Brindles try to survive on public assistance. Twice a month, Ms. Brindle has to go in person to collect her food stamps and cash stipend. Usually, due to lack of childcare, she takes Melmel with her. However, on this day his older sister Jenna watched him. Going to get food stamps is a chore she "hate[s]." The bus ride is long, the disbursement office is bleak, and, on days when food stamps are released, it is crowded with slow-moving lines of tired women (men are vastly outnumbered) towing young children. The lines form outside the building, before the office opens. The day we go, it takes fifteen minutes of inching forward before we even get inside. Once we have edged into the building, we join around seventy-five people who are waiting in another long line in a small, dusty and dirty room. There are no public restrooms; there are no drinking fountains. We wait another thirty minutes. The cashiers move slowly; they look bored and disinterested. At 9:05, we are done but exhausted by the wait.

> While standing in line Ms. Brindle says, sounding anxious and a bit desperate, "I am out of everything. Milk, eggs, bread." We go to the grocery store immediately after we get the food stamps. Katie's mother buys four boxes of cereal, a loaf of white bread, a gallon of milk, bologna, American cheese, a dozen eggs, and a cake mix and frosting. It is Katie's birthday that day. The cake mix calls for vegetable oil. This is an unusual and added expense. Ms. Brindle looks stressed while she is staring at the glistening plastic bottles of yellow oil. She sighs deeply and says, "I wish food was free."

We then head back home; the entire expedition having taken approximately two hours.

Under conditions where every dollar for food matters, unexpected losses present serious problems. One afternoon when Ms. Brindle returns to the apartment after getting her food stamps (she had gone by herself), she is upset. She thinks she has been shortchanged:

> CiCi sat down at the dining room table. She sighed and took off her coat and put it on the chair next to her. She looked at Jenna and said, "I think they gypped me forty dollars. There were all these people in line shouting to hurry up and I tried to count it, but I couldn't concentrate." CiCi sounded sad.

> She started counting each page in the first [food stamp] booklet and then the second booklet… Katie made a noise — a humming noise (it wasn't loud) — while CiCi was counting. CiCi said in an angry tone, "Be quiet. That's what happened in line. I couldn't concentrate. Everyone was yelling."…CiCi looked at Jenna and said, "They're not supposed to do that. They gave me all these books with low numbers (dollar amounts). They're not supposed to do that. They're supposed to give me high numbers." Katie did not say anything after her mom yelled at her but remained quietly sitting on the couch.

> Jenna, seeking to reassure her mother, says, "Don't worry. You don't have to feed me." Nine-year-old Katie is keenly aware of her family's limited resources. She rejects Jenna's logic, saying, "Well, it's still forty dollars."

Doing laundry, a tedious but straightforward chore in middle class homes, is cumbersome, expensive, and frustrating for Ms. Brindle. She finds it difficult to keep a sufficient supply of quarters available. Banks often refuse to sell rolled coins to noncustomers; she does not have a bank account (using money orders when necessary). The grocery store, which does provide quarters, is a twenty-minute bus ride away. Of much greater significance, however, is the fact that the three washers and two dryers at the apartment complex are routinely out of order:

> CiCi says, "I wish I had a car to drive. I'm almost out of clothes." (She looks at her pile of dirty clothes next to the love seat.) I ask, "Is the washing machine broken?" She replies, "When I first went down, I was freakin' out. I went down and the water was coming out of the washers. Today the washers were still full of water. And I went to the ones up [at a nearby complex]. They were locked, so I think they're messed up too… The heat isn't on [in the laundry room]. It's ridiculous…that's why the pipes broke. It's forty below and stuff."

For Katie, broken washing machines sometimes mean no school. In rare cases when she is completely out of clean clothes, she has to stay at home until the laundry can be done.

Having to rely on public transportation, particularly with young children, also makes life more difficult. Little things like handing the fare to the bus driver can be challenging if you are juggling a toddler, a diaper bag, and packages. Similarly, once on the bus, even seated it can be tiring to hold or watch over young children on long rides. Buses often are late, sometimes don't come, and always are much slower than traveling by car. Finally, taking public transportation can be hazardous. Mothers and children stand out in the heat in summer, in the cold in winter, and in rainstorms many months of the year. Buses travel along busy streets, so as they wait at bus stops, parents must watch children very closely to make certain that they keep away from oncoming traffic. Melmel likes buses; he seems to relish the sensation of movement. And Ms. Brindle sometimes uses bus rides as an opportunity for one-on-one time with her son. For example, while riding to a municipal court session (to contest her eviction notice), she smiles at Melmel and says warmly, "Melmel, I love you!" A ride in a car is always preferable, if it can be arranged. In Ms. Brindle's case this is difficult because her brother's car is sometimes not running and even when it is, her schedule and his are hard to coordinate. The same is true for her mother's car. In addition, child car seats are required by law, but they are expensive, heavy, and difficult to move from car to car. When Melmel rides in his grandmother's car, which has no car seat, she keeps an eye out for the police. If she sees a police officer, she pushes her grandson down below the level of the car windows, trying to hide him from view. She says she feels "like a criminal." She can't afford to be caught: "The ticket is a thousand dollars!"

Much as with transportation, poor families have few choices about where they live. Thus, Katie's family makes do with roaches in their apartment, a poorly maintained building, snow and ice on the steps, chronically broken appliances, and leaky plumbing. So far, though, they have been "lucky" with their neighbors, meaning that no serious threats have materialized in this apartment building. Ms. Brindle's former sister-in-law and close friend, Mary, was not so fortunate. Drug dealers moved into the complex.

Despite its many problems, the Brindles' apartment at least provides the family with an autonomous, private living space. Midway into the observation period, however, even that was threatened. Ms. Brindle began falling behind in her rent payments. When she first moved into the apartment, she had expected to split the $600 monthly fee with Jenna. Jenna became sick and then was diagnosed as HIV positive. She could not contribute her share of the rent, and her mother could not afford it by herself. The waiting list for public housing is years long. Moving in with Katie's grandmother was a possibility, but only as a last resort. The house is already crowded: Ms. Brindle's brothers John (the schizophrenic) and Ryan live there. The Brindle family would have to live in the basement. In addition, the wood-burning stove and kerosene heaters Ms. Brindle's mother uses to heat her house would aggravate Jenna's allergies. But most important, Jenna and Grandmom do not get along. They have had many years of bitter conflicts, including a low point when Jenna was ten and her grandmother called her a "whore."

Stymied and unsure of what to do next, Ms. Brindle waited, first using up her last month's rent, and then hoping to move any day. But as the days dragged on, her landlord decided to begin eviction proceedings. On a cold day in February, Ms. Brindle, Melmel, and a field-worker go to municipal court. After waiting hours, they are finally called to the bench. During the brief interaction, the court official tells Ms. Brindle that she has thirty days to move out. The next week, however, she receives a "failure to appear" notice from the court. According to court records, Ms. Brindle had not appeared, and thus her landlord had the right to lock her out of the apartment immediately. Trying to contact the court is an exercise in frustration:

> CiCi says, "I called that number that they gave me and they kept telling me I had to call back. I got tired of calling back. I asked who was I supposed to talk to. I got tired of calling back. Then I got this notice in the mail and I was mad."

In the meantime, Jenna decides to move to Florida to live with her father, and to avoid the cold northeastern winter. After she gets there, things do not work out as planned. Jenna's father proves to be less helpful than she had expected, other arrangements fall through, her health worsens, and she is briefly hospitalized. Frantic with worry, Ms. Brindle decides to move to Florida when Jenna asks her to come. To get money for a ticket, Ms. Brindle sells her living room and bedroom sets. But, the buyers of the bedroom furniture are late in bringing their payment. The delay is excruciating. Ms. Brindle worries that the deal will fall through, leaving her without the money she needs to finance the trip:

> She says, "I need to get the bedroom set sold. It was supposed to be gone but because of the snow they couldn't come get it. They had the money, but who knows if they have the money now? I need the money to get the tickets and I am supposed to go down to pay for the tickets tomorrow. (Her voice is rising with anxiety.) I am waiting for a fifty-dollar check. That will give me enough for the tickets and then anything extra is money to go down there with."

Ms. Brindle is desperate to go to Florida. Having already lost one child, she is distraught beyond words by Jenna's illness. In the fall, when Jenna was first diagnosed, Ms. Brindle attempted suicide. Depressed and overwhelmed, she swallowed a large number of pills with alcohol (in the apartment, with the three children in other rooms). She was rushed to the hospital, had her stomach pumped, and survived. She is determined to take care of Jenna, but the logistics of getting to Florida overwhelm her. She toys with the possibility of leaving Katie behind until the end of the school year. She begins by suggesting that Katie stay with Grandmom until June, but Katie says, "No, I'll go." Later, Katie even more firmly rejects the idea of living with Aunt Mary while her mother is in Florida:

> CiCi says, "You could stay here." A minute passes by and CiCi says, "You could stay with Mary."
>
> Mary who is walking toward the kitchen at this point says, "Eh-eh. If she stayed with me, I would hit her." Mary looks at Katie and says, "Your mom doesn't hit you cuz she's afraid she'll hurt you. But I would hit you so you stop acting like a brat."
>
> CiCi says under her breath, "That's right." Katie does not say anything.

Aunt Mary volunteers, "I would hit her like my father hit me," and then tells a story of how he beat her so badly she bled, but she altered her behavior thereafter.

> Katie says to CiCi, "You did punch me in the face once." CiCi says, "I slapped your face. Don't exaggerate." Katie says, "I went to school with a black eye."

The afternoon wears on; most of the time, everyone is watching soap operas and <u>Oprah</u>. With her mother and aunt only a few feet away, Katie begins to hit herself. There is no mistaking that they have heard and seen her, but there is no reaction on their part:

> Katie starts hitting her forehead with her fist. She is sitting on the bed and falls backwards as she beats her forehead. She is hitting with her right hand. She continues for about three minutes, which seems to me like a very long time.

Moreover, Melmel begins to mimic her:

> Melmel climbs up on the bed between her and myself and imitates Katie. He does this for about a minute. CiCi and Mary watch without saying anything. Katie says to me, "That's why I was in the hospital." I ask, "Why?" She says, "For hurting myself." I ask, "What did they do to you?" She says, "They locked me up." I ask, "And then what did they do?" Katie says, "They taught me about self-esteem and told me not to hurt myself." I looked over once and CiCi and Mary were watching <u>Oprah</u>.

Clearly, Katie does not want to stay behind, either with her grandmother or her aunt. Knowing her daughter's flair for being dramatic, Ms. Brindle may think that Katie is deliberately exaggerating her feelings and thus ignores her. Perhaps, though, she simply cannot allow herself to acknowledge her youngest daughter's feelings, regardless of their validity. Ms. Brindle has a history of depression, and she seems to be haunted by the death of her first child. She feels she <u>must</u> go to Florida to help Jenna. Leaving Katie in someone else's care would simplify several aspects of the move. (When the move finally happened, Ms. Brindle took both Melmel and Katie with her.)

All of the families in the study — all families everywhere — face problems. Differences arise in terms of the specific kinds and amounts of difficulties, the ways in which individuals' temperaments shape their responses to the challenges they face, and the structural resources available to families. The Brindles had more numerous and deeper psychological problems than other poor families we visited. Many of the other challenges they faced, though, were common among poor families and arose from the same basic dilemma: insufficient resources for getting children through the day and meeting their needs. The sorts of difficulties we observed Ms. Brindle trying to cope with — going to get food stamps, finding working laundry machines, dealing with landlords and problematic neighbors, and sorting out errors on the part of powerful bureaucracies — are all <u>routine</u> problems for families below the poverty level.

These everyday sorts of dilemmas fit the definition of social structural problems: they are created by the way the social structural system is organized. Mixed into these social structural problems are the difficulties that arise from the individual biographies of family members. Thus, in observing real families as they move through their days, what we see are the outcomes of an ongoing <u>interaction</u> between structure and biography. Within the sample of working-class and poor families, the structural problems were the most oppressive ingredient in the structure-biography mixture. Insufficient resources shaped where families lived, what jobs parents held (or didn't hold), how individuals traveled from place to place, and how much and what kind of care parents could provide for young children.

In this context, it is not surprising to find that children's leisure activities are given a lower priority. As the next section shows, however, it is not simply the press of everyday life that prompts poor (and working-class) parents to remain relatively uninvolved in their children's play and not inclined to follow up on children's budding interests in music, art, drama, or sports by enrolling them in organized activities. The sense of an <u>obligation to cultivate</u> their children that is so apparent among middle-class parents is uncommon among their poor and working-class counterparts. Likewise, the sense of being <u>entitled</u> to adult attention that is so prevalent among middle-class children is absent in their poor and working-class peers.

Researching in the Social Sciences

Questions are the starting point for all of the social sciences' knowledge-making practices. As the social sciences have grown and developed, the initial questions that were asked have produced answers and theories that in turn have spawned new questions and refinement of original theories. Thus, previous research affects present research...

—Professor Kristine Hansen, Department of English, Brigham Young University (Hansen, 2003: 14)

Social scientists – whether professors or undergraduates – want to know what others have discovered before they begin investigations of their own.

—Professor Lee Cuba, Department of Sociology, Wellesley College (Cuba, 2002: 69)

The Nature of Inquiry and Research in the Social Sciences

In Chapter 7, we talked about the ways that natural scientists define *inquiry*. There are some similarities between research and inquiry in the natural sciences and research and inquiry in the social sciences. In both the natural sciences and the social sciences, researchers explore open-ended but focused questions in systematic ways. In both the natural sciences and the social sciences, writers are more credible when they cite what previous researchers have said about their subject. Both natural science and social science researchers collect data and closely and carefully observe phenomena. However, natural science and social researchers differ in the kinds of questions they ask, the type of phenomena they study, the kind of data they collect, and the research genres and methods they use. To think about what inquiry and research mean in the social sciences, let's go back to one of the readings from Chapter 6, "The Ubercool Morphology of Internet Gamers: A Linguistic Analysis" (Driscoll, 2002), by Dana Driscoll, a student at the California University of Pennsylvania. When you think about inquiry and research in Dana Driscoll's essay, you might notice a few patterns that can help to understand what inquiry means in the social sciences, as explored below.

- **Inquiry in the social sciences involves exploring open-ended but focused questions about social behavior, relationships, and institutions.**

Driscoll focuses on a specific subculture – Internet Gamers – and a specific aspect of that subculture: their dialect. Unlike natural scientists, social scientists focus on human behavior, and especially humans as they interact in groups. Driscoll's research question focuses on finding out what kind of language Internet Gamers use and how that language functions for social purposes within the subculture. Driscoll has a focused topic and question. She doesn't just ask, "What are Gamers like?" or "How do Gamers interact?"

- **Inquiry in the social sciences is systematic and involves collecting data, making observations, conducting interviews and surveys, and analyzing social artifacts.**

Driscoll's study focuses on analyzing a specific set of data: the transcripts of Internet Gamer chat rooms. Driscoll has a large enough sample size (seventy-five chat room logs collected over six months) to make some generalizations about Gamer dialect. She presents plenty of evidence from these chat room conversations to support her assertions about Gamer dialect. Driscoll uses techniques from the discipline of linguistics to analyze the transcripts.

- **Inquiry in the social sciences involves reviewing the research of other social scientists.**

It's typical for social science genres to have a *literature review* section – and social science professors often assign a literature review as a genre in itself. Driscoll devotes a big chunk of the first part of her essay to reviewing the literature on the subject she's studying. Notice that Driscoll not only reviews what research other linguists and sociologists have already done on Internet Gamer language, but she also points out some of the weaknesses in previous studies. She argues that there haven't been enough studies of Gamers conducted, and that the ones that have been done are dated. In the discourse community of the social sciences, studies that create new knowledge and that address a gap in the current research are more valued than studies that repeat what's already been said and done.

What Counts as Evidence in the Social Sciences?

What counts as evidence in a sociology paper? First and foremost, sociology is an empirical discipline. Empiricism in sociology means basing your conclusions on evidence that is documented and collected with as much rigor as possible. This evidence usually draws upon observed patterns and information from collected cases and experiences, not just from isolated, anecdotal reports.

—University of North Carolina Writing Center (2007)

8.8: Writing to Learn – What Counts as Evidence in the Social Sciences?

The purpose of this Writing to Learn activity is for you to consider what counts as evidence for research in the social sciences by looking at the kinds of evidence found in the readings in this chapter. Skim through the reading passages in this chapter and underline places where the authors provide evidence to support their ideas and arguments. Individually or in small groups, create a list of the kinds of evidence the authors use, and be prepared to discuss specific examples with the class as a whole.

Each type of social science genre uses different kinds of evidence. Some social science genres focus on the use of quantitative evidence, some focus on qualitative evidence, and some include both quantitative and qualitative kinds of evidence. Whether you're writing a case study, a literature review, a research report, or an ethnography, there are certain kinds of evidence that tend to be valued by the discourse communities of social scientists. If you completed Writing to Learn Activity 8.8, you probably found some similarities in the kinds of evidence presented in the excerpts from social science writing in this chapter. Some types of evidence you might have noticed in the readings in this chapter are described below.

Quantitative Data from Primary and Secondary Research
Social scientists are often looking for patterns in social behaviors, and one way to present evidence of a pattern of behavior is to quantify it. Social scientists use statistics, charts, graphs, and other numerical forms of data to support arguments about patterns they see in human interaction. For example, in the excerpt from "College Students' Knowledge and Use of Credit," Joyce Jones reviews surveys of college students that present statistics about how much college students know about credit card use. Statistics from surveys and questionnaires are a common form of evidence in the social sciences. Social scientists are careful to design surveys and questionnaires that are unbiased and that accurately represent the population the researcher is trying to sample. Social scientists are also careful to present statistics accurately and explain statistical evidence clearly to readers. A social scientist who uses poorly designed surveys or who misrepresents statistical results loses credibility as a writer.

Descriptions of Human Interaction that the Researcher Has Observed or Participated in

Social scientists need to be skilled at listening, watching, and reflecting. In genres of social science writing that rely on ethnographic evidence, clear and detailed description is critical as a form of evidence. Socials scientists often present evidence of patterns in human interactions using specific examples from observation. Social scientists are especially interested in events that occur repeatedly in a community, such as rituals and ceremonies. For example, in the excerpt from *Yanomamö: The Fierce People*, anthropologist Napoleon Chagnon focuses on the rituals surrounding a girl's menstruation, and he gives a detailed description of the rituals based on careful observation.

Information from Interviews and Discussions

The strategies for conducting effective interviews that we discussed in Chapter 5 will be helpful to you in your social science courses. Information from formal and informal discussions with members of the group or culture being studied are critical kinds of evidence for social scientists. Statistics are important, and so are the observations of the researcher, but in interviews and discussions research participants can speak for themselves and give first-hand evidence. For example, consider the wealth of evidence that Annette Lareau was able to provide readers by conducting interviews with the family members she observed for her book *Unequal Childhoods*. In her interviews, Lareau asked focused questions about things she observed and was able to obtain information about the motivations and points of view of the family members she studied.

Close Reading and Analysis of Cultural Texts, Artwork, and Rituals

In the excerpt from *My Freshman Year*, Rebekah Nathan uses a communal text – the "Community Living Agreement" of the dorm she lived in for a year – as evidence for her arguments about the nature of community at college campuses. Nathan presents evidence directly from the communal text and reflects on the deeper connections between the Community Living Agreement and her theories of college and community. In social science courses, you might find yourself analyzing government documents, works of literature, advertisements, fashion, music, and other kinds of texts. Anything that reveals something important about a culture and the way humans interact can be useful evidence in the social sciences.

Research from Other Social Scientists

In her essay about credit card usage and college students, Joyce Jones devotes an entire section to reviewing previous studies that were similar to hers. Throughout *My Freshman Year*, Rebekah Nathan discusses theories of community from other sociologists and evidence from prior ethnographies of undergraduate life. There are few genres of social science writing that don't demand at least some conversation with secondary sources. In the social sciences, knowledge is *socially constructed*. Researchers are expected to be familiar with significant studies on the subject they're investigating, and to cite those studies when they report the results of their own research. Your social science professors will want to know how the research you do connects to and builds on previous research. They will also want you to prove to your readers that you're knowledgeable about your subject and that you've carefully researched your topic.

8.9: Learn by Doing – Investigating Research in the Social Sciences

Now that you've looked closely at some of the social science research in this chapter, it's time for you to go out and do some investigating of your own. Use one of the social science databases from the next section of this chapter to find an article in a social science journal. To make this search more interesting to you, think about a social sciences subject that you're interested in exploring, and use that subject for key words when you search the database. Once you've found an article, find the journal in your library (or read it online if you can access the full text from the database) and analyze the article, focusing on the research methods. Write a 1–2 page essay in which you discuss the kind of inquiry the researcher(s) engaged in, the research methods used, the type of data/evidence presented by the researcher(s), and the way the data was presented.

Social Science Reference Books and Databases

In Chapter 5, we discussed some general academic databases and reference books. As you take courses in different academic fields of study, you'll need to be aware of more specialized databases and reference books. Below is a list of some reference books and databases for the social sciences.

Social Science Dictionaries

General
Dictionary of the Social Sciences (2002) C. Calhoun (ed.) New York: Oxford University Press.

Dictionary of Statistics and Methodology: A Nontechnical Guide for the Social Sciences (2005) W. P. Vogt (ed.) Newbury Park, California: Sage

International Encyclopedia of the Social Sciences (1998) D. Sills and R. K. Merton. New York: MacMillan.

A New Dictionary of the Social Sciences (2007) G. Mitchell (ed.) New Brunswick, New Jersey: Aldine Transaction.

Anthropology

Dictionary of Anthropology (1987) C. Seymour-Smith. New York: Palgrave MacMillan.

The Dictionary of Global Culture (1996) K. A. Appiah. New York: Knopf.

Economics

A Dictionary of Economics (2010) J. Black (ed.) Oxford: Oxford University Press.

The McGraw-Hill Dictionary of Modern Economics (1983) D. Greenwald. New York: McGraw-Hill.

The MIT Dictionary of Modern Economics (1992) D. Pearce (ed.) Cambridge, Massachusetts: MIT Press.

The Penguin Dictionary of Economics (2003) G. Bannak et al. (eds.) London: Penguin.

Routledge Dictionary of Economics (2002) D. Rutherford (ed.) London: Routledge.

History

A Dictionary of American History (1997) T. Purvis (ed.) Somerset, New Jersey: Wiley-Blackwell.

Dictionary of Concepts in History (1986) H. Ritter. Santa Barbara, California: Greenwood Press.

A Dictionary of Contemporary World History (2004) J. Palmowski. Oxford: Oxford University Press.

Political Science

The Blackwell Dictionary of Political Science (1999) F. Bealey. Somerset, New Jersey: Wiley-Blackwell.

Dictionary of Geopolitics (1993) J. O'Loughlin (ed.) Santa Barbara, California: Greenwood Press.

The Dictionary of Twentieth Century World Politics (1993) J. Shafritz, P. Williams, and R. Calinger (eds.) New York: Henry Holt.

Psychology

Dictionary of Psychology (1999) J. P. Chaplin. St. Louis: San Val.

The International Dictionary of Psychology (1989) S. Sutherland. New York: Continuum.

Longman Dictionary of Psychology and Psychiatry (1983) R. M. Goldenson (ed.) London: Longman Group U.K.

Sociology

The Blackwell Dictionary of Sociology (2000) A. Johnson (ed.) Somerset, New Jersey: Wiley-Blackwell.

The Concise Oxford Dictionary of Sociology (1994) G. Marshall and D. L. Barthel (eds.) Oxford: Oxford University Press.

A Critical Dictionary of Sociology (1989) R. Boudon and F. Bourricaid (eds.) London: Routledge.

Social Science Encyclopedias

General

International Encyclopedia of the Social and Behavioural Sciences (2001) N. Smelser and P. Baltes (eds.) Oxford: Pergamon.

International Encyclopedia of the Social Sciences (1998) D. L. Sills and K. Merton (eds.) New York: MacMillan.

The Social Sciences Encyclopedia (1989) A. Kuper and J. Kuper (eds.) London: Routledge.

Anthropology

Companion Encyclopedia of Anthropology (2007) T. Ingold (ed.) New York: Taylor and Francis.

Encyclopedia of World Cultures (1991) D. Levinson (ed.) New York: MacMillan.

Economics

Encyclopedia of American Economic History (1980) G. Porter. New York: Charles Scribner's Sons.

The McGraw-Hill Encyclopedia of Economics (1993) D. Greenwald (ed.) New York: McGraw-Hill.

History

Encyclopedia of American History (1996) R. B. Morris. New York: Collins Reference.

Encyclopedia of World History (2001) P. N. Stearns (ed.) New York Houghton Mifflin Harcourt.

Oxford Companion to United States History (2001) P. S. Boyer (ed.) Oxford: Oxford University Press.

Political Science
The Blackwell Encyclopedia of Political Science (1991) V. Bogdaner (ed.) Somerset, New Jersey: Wiley-Blackwell.
Encyclopedia of Government and Politics (2003) M. Hawkesworth and M. Kogan (eds.) London: Routledge
*The Oxford Companion to Politics of the World (*2001) J. Krieger (ed.) Oxford: Oxford University Press.

Psychology
Baker Encyclopedia of Psychology and Counseling (1989) D. G. Brenner (ed.) Ada, Michigan: Baker Academic.
Concise Encyclopedia of Psychology (1998) R. J. Corsini and A. J. Auerbach (eds.) Somerset, New Jersey: Wiley.
Encyclopedia of Psychology (2000) A. Kazdin (ed.) Oxford: Oxford University Press.

Sociology
Blackwell Encyclopedia of Sociology (2007) G. Ritzer (ed.) Somerset, New Jersey: Wiley-Blackwell.
Encyclopedia of Sociology (2000) E. Borgatta and R. Montgomery (eds.) New York: Holiday House.

Social Science Periodical Databases
Anthropological Index Online
EconLit
ERIC
PsycINFO
Social Sciences Citation Index
Social Sciences Full Text
Sociological Abstracts

Citing Sources in the Social Sciences: APA Style

Some subdisciplines of the social sciences will have their own style for citing sources, but most social science fields use APA (American Psychological Association) style. APA style is outlined in the *APA Publication Manual*, which should be available at the reference section of your college's library and perhaps on the library's Web site as well. Like CSE style in the natural sciences, APA style emphasizes the author (or authors) and date of the research. Just as with CSE style and the Council of Science Editors, there's a discourse community that created (and now updates) APA style – the American Psychological Association, which has 150,000 members. Even though the conventions for APA style grew out of the discipline of psychology, other social sciences such as sociology, anthropology, linguistics, political science, and economics often use APA style. In addition to rules about citing and referencing sources, the APA style manual has guidelines for language use (avoiding sexist and biased language), formatting, and using visuals such as charts and graphs.

In-text Citations in APA Style
Social science writers are expected to cite the current and most respected research on their subject. Citing prior studies gives you credibility as a social scientist, and shows your readers that you're knowledgeable about your topic. In APA style, whenever you quote or paraphrase a source, you need to give the author, year, and page number. Here's a hypothetical example:

> McGuire (2005) argues that "the slippery slope of nuclear proliferation, with each side building bigger and deadlier weapons of mass destruction, leads us ever faster to our own destruction" (p. 32).

Note that since you introduced the author (McGuire (2005) argues...), you don't need to include the author's last name in the parentheses at the end of the sentence. If you include the year and the name of the author in the sentence (McGuire (2005) argues...) you only need to cite the page number in the parentheses at the end of the sentence. The parentheses are always placed outside the quotation marks, and the period is placed after the parentheses as this is the end of the entire sentence that includes the quotation and reference. If there are more than two authors, use et al. after the first mention of the source, e.g. (McGuire et al., 2005, p. 32). The first time you mention the source, you must list all of the authors in the in-text reference, e.g. (McGuire, Arroyo, & Kucinick, 2005, p. 32). Typically, you should only quote authors directly when you're trying to capture an author's distinctive style, tone, or argument. Avoid overquoting and turning your essay into a collage of quotes from secondary sources.

When you're citing facts and statistics from a secondary source, it's usually best to summarize the information in your own words. Let's say you want to cite the following information from a hypothetical article by Townsend:

> The number of hours Americans work annually has dropped from about 2,700 at

the beginning of the century to about 1,800 today; average life expectancy has gone up about 45 years to 80.

Although you could put this entire passage in quotes and cite it word for word in your essay, since the information is just a series of statistics, it would be more effective to summarize the information in your own words and cite the source. For example:

> Social scientists argue that American life has vastly improved over the last hundred years. Townsend (2003, p. 59) points out that Americans work 1,800 hours annually today, compared to 2,700 hours at the beginning of the 20th century, and life expectancy has increased to 80 years old.

Preparing an APA Style Reference Page

For details about how to cite different types of source in APA style and how to prepare an APA-style References page, visit the reference area of your library and consult the *APA Publication Manual* or visit the following Web sites:

APA Resource Web Sites

Purdue Online Writing Lab
(http://owl.english.purdue.edu/owl/resource/560/01/)

University of North Carolina Library
(http://www.lib.unc.edu/instruct/citations/apa/)

University Wisconsin-Madison Writing Center
(http://www.wisc.edu/writing/Handbook/DocAPA.html)

APA Style Paper Format

Following are basic guidelines for formatting your paper in APA style.

- Use a standard 12-point font: Courier, Times, or Bookman.
- Include a title page with the title centered and, a few lines below the title, write your name, the course number and title, the professor's name, and the date. Number the title page.
- Use 1" margins except for the upper right-hand corner, which should include a short version of your title and page number on each page.
- For quotations of more than 40 words, indent each line of the quote (using block format) five spaces from the left margin. Do not indent from the right margin.

- Double-space throughout, including the abstract, footnotes, and references.
- Primary headings should be centered and all key words in the heading should be capitalized. Secondary headings should be italicized and flush against the left-hand margin.
- If your professor asks for an abstract, it should appear on its own numbered page, entitled "Abstract," and placed right after the title page.
- Place tables, charts, graphs, and other visuals close to the place you refer to them in the text. Label each visual "Table" or "Figure" and number them consecutively (Figure 1, Figure 2, and so on).
- Place the reference page after the body of the paper (or the after the footnotes, if included) but before the appendices.
- Appendices should be placed at the end of the paper. Number and title each appendix using Roman numerals (for example, Appendix II: Interview Questions)

Student Writing Case Study: Sociology

Bethany Coston as a senior sociology major

In Chapter 1 we looked at a case study of a student in a first-year writing course, and in Chapter 7 we looked at a case study of a sophomore writing in a general education geology course. Now we're going to look at a student writing in an upper-division course in her major. At the time I conducted this case study,

Bethany Coston was a senior at a small liberal arts college in Michigan (her college will remain anonymous because one of her papers is a study of intimate violence at her school). The social science course that Bethany is writing for is A&S 360: Intimate Violence. Intimate Violence is a course for sociology majors, so this case study will give you a sense of writing in the social sciences and give you an idea of what writing in the major is like. As you look at the assignments in Intimate Violence and read Bethany's papers, remember that this isn't a general education course for first-year and sophomore students, and the writing and researching is very much *discipline-specific*. Many upper-division courses in the major have intensive writing requirements. Bethany's professor asked students to write ten informal reflection papers, a collaborative class research project, and a presentation based on original research. If you compare the syllabus for Intimate Violence with the syllabus for Geology of Mexico from Chapter 7, you'll see how the expectations for reading, writing, and researching in the major are much greater than the expectations for general education courses:

A&S 360: INTIMATE VIOLENCE

Course Description:

This course examines violence between intimates, primarily (but not solely) within the United States. Intimate violence is a broad term that covers a range of interpersonal relationships (kids, parents, spouses, partners, acquaintances, siblings, etc.) as well as various forms of abuse (emotional, physical, neglect, sexual assault/rape, etc.). Intimate violence is traced socio-historically covering theoretical, methodological, empirical, legal, and applied issues and debates within the field. Only in the last few decades have issues of intimate violence become a public concern. Previously, violence amongst family members was considered a 'private' or 'domestic' matter. Today, various forms of intimate violence, such as child or partner abuse, are considered to be social problems (i.e., a 'public' concern). We will examine why this transformation from private to public took place, as well as address how widespread intimate violence is in our society. Among other things, we will attempt to pinpoint the incidence and prevalence of intimate violence, and, in the process, identify causes and solutions.

Contentious debates in the field are driven largely by theoretical differences as to the causes of intimate violence. These debates weigh the relative merits of positions taken by family sociologists ("General Systems/Family Violence Theory,"), feminists (violence as a gendered phenomenon), psychologists ("Intergenerational Transmission Theory"), and other social scientists ("Resource Theory," subcultural theories, etc.). We will explore these perspectives, examining their usefulness for explaining the behaviors of perpetrators and victims/survivors. Violence is gendered and we will thus analyze how important gendered socialization and structural gender inequality are in shaping individual's violent behavior and to what degree this influences various forms of violence (e.g., heterosexual rape vs. same-sex partner violence). This will be conducted as a seminar, where students will be expected to actively guide the direction of the course.

General Requirements: Daily class participation; intensive reading & writing, original research

Objectives:

- Learn, explore, apply, and critically evaluate basic intimate violence concepts, theories, and research methods
- Analyze connections between individuals' experiences with violence and societal patterns and social forces
- Conduct original sociological research, analyze your data, and write up and present your findings to the class

Required Readings:

> Straus, Murray A. 2001. *Beating the Devil Out of Them: Corporal Punishment in American Children*. Transaction Publishers.
> Sipe, Beth and Evelyn J. Hall. 1996. *I Am Not Your Victim: Anatomy of Domestic Violence*. Thousand Oaks, California: Sage Publications. Coursepack. Available through the Anthropology & Sociology department.

Course Requirements:

1. <u>Careful and thorough reading</u> of all assigned materials *prior* to class discussion
2. Regular <u>attendance **AND** (*!!!*) participation</u> in class (20% of your grade)
3. <u>Lead a Class Discussion</u> (in groups of TWO): You and your partner will lead one class during the semester, *meeting with me in advance* to discuss how you will organize the class (lecture, discussion, group activity, video, etc.; handout and further information in class). **Select Partners & Dates by February 1** (10%)
4. <u>Ten reflection papers</u> (handout and further information in class) (30%)
5. <u>Contributions to the course research project</u> (To be discussed further in class) (10%)
6. A <u>final paper and presentation</u> based on original research (handout and

further information in class); Drafts due NO LATER THAN one week prior to presentation. **Presentation Dates: April 23, April 25, April 30, May 2;** (30%)

Grading Scale:

A...4.0 (92 and above) — represents work outstanding in quality
A–...3.7 (90–91)
B+...3.3 (87–89)
B...3.0 (82–86) — work which is more than satisfactory.
B–...2.7 (80–81)
C+...2.3 (77–79)
C...2.0 (72–76) — fulfills all of the basic requirements for the course.
C–...1.7 (70–71)
D+...1.3 (67–69)
D...1.0 (60–66) — below the 2.0 level in quantity and quality.
F... 0.0 (59 or below) — unsatisfactory in either quantity or quality

Course Policies:

I have many goals for myself and my students every time I teach (and I hope you always set goals for yourself and the course). One of my goals is increasing *communication*, both with students and among students. I understand that some of you may find yourselves unable to attend lecture one day, however it is your responsibility to obtain the notes from your peers as well as find out about any important announcements. Please do not hesitate to talk to me if you feel as though you are falling behind.

Although I will often guide lecture/discussion, you will quickly learn that I expect and promote *active learning*. By this I mean that you will engage the issues and material in class rather than listening to me talk for three hours each week. I promise to use different forms of media, provide group exercises, and generally guide discussions that you will simply have to participate in because you will be unable to contain your thoughts. In turn, **by the first class meeting of each week I expect you to have read all of the assigned material for that week**. Attendance will help you understand the material. Participation will help me understand how well you understand the material.

Let me know *in advance* if you will be unable to turn in an assignment on time or if you will be absent on the day of an exam. **Late papers** will only be accepted under _extreme_ circumstances, and grade reductions will follow accordingly.

It is of utmost importance that we **respect** each other as well as our various viewpoints, even if they challenge your beliefs, values, knowledge, or way of life. This is a place of higher education, where we will take advantage of the opportunity to further educate ourselves and each other. You will often find yourself in disagreement with peers, readings, videos, or my lecture — good! All information you encounter _should_ be critically assessed, however it is important that we all raise our concerns in a way that promotes (rather than shuts down) further discussion. Further, you will be expected to support your arguments intelligently.

Turn in **hardcopies** of all assigned work (_no email attachments_!!!!!!).

I strongly encourage you to submit **rough drafts** and meet with me to discuss/ improve your papers. **Final papers** should be proofread.

You are required to turn in work that falls within a reasonable range of the assigned **page limits** (e.g., a 4 page paper could go plus or minus half a page). This is to ensure fairness and consistency, as much longer papers give the authors the advantage of additional analysis.

If you require **special accommodations** for learning disabilities, please notify me within the first three weeks of classes so that we can arrange accordingly.

Academic dishonesty will not be tolerated in any form (i.e. cheating, plagiarism, etc.). If you are unsure about whether your actions fall under these guidelines, please do not hesitate to speak with me.

8.10: Writing to Learn – Social Science Syllabus Analysis

The purpose of this Writing to Learn activity is to have you think about the ways that the syllabus for Intimate Violence connects to the discussions of writing and researching in the social sciences in this chapter. Reread the syllabus and write about the ways that it reflects the ways of thinking and researching and the expectations for writing that are important in the social sciences.

If this Intimate Violence class seems a little intimidating to you, keep in mind that this is a class for sociology majors. When you start taking classes in your major, you'll go through a transition period when you'll probably struggle a bit with reading, writing, and researching in your chosen field. Your general education classes help introduce you to the expectations for different disciplines, but you'll still find that it will take a lot of practice and feedback for you to go from an apprentice writer in your major to an experienced writer like Bethany, who's a senior. When I interviewed Bethany's professor, I asked him about the way his expectations for writing and researching differ in general education classes and classes for sociology majors like Intimate Violence. He pointed out that the prerequisites for Intimate Violence include Introduction to Sociology and a class that focuses on social science research methods. Here's what Bethany's professor had to say about his expectations for writing in general education classes and in upper-division classes in the major like Intimate Violence:

> The writing load exceeds those of all of my general education courses, but more importantly the quality of writing must be better. In particular, reflection papers must go well beyond summarizing readings. Students must demonstrate an ability to critically evaluate an article's theoretical perspective(s), methods, and findings, and connect the articles to other research as well as "real world" events (in their lives, the media). Final research papers mirror those of a journal article. Students must utilize multiple theories, incorporate relevant material from inside and outside of the course, conduct original research, report findings, and discuss the findings in the context of their theories and literature. Though I use similar assignments in some general education courses, students in lower division courses work in groups. Students in Intimate Violence do not have research or writing partners, and again, the quality and quantity standards are much higher.

In terms of quantity, Bethany's professor asked students to write frequently in both short reflection papers and a more extensive research article. The goal of the reflection papers is for students to think critically about the articles assigned for class discussion. Bethany's professor gave the students the information sheet below describing the reflection papers.

Reflection Papers Information Sheet (A&S 360 – Intimate Violence)

Over the course of the semester you will write ten (10) Reflection Papers worth thirty percent (30%) of your grade. You may turn in one reflection paper for ANY unique topic that we are covering for the day/week. NOTE: It is up to you to make sure you submit no less than ten over the course of the semester. Additional reflection papers are welcome, and only your ten best papers will count towards your grade.

What are Reflection Papers???

Reflection Papers for this class are simply **1–1½ page typed, SINGLE space (standard font size/format) responses to and discussions/critiques of readings**. You should respond to (SOME, NOT ALL OF) the material we are covering on the syllabus the week the paper is due, however as we get further along in the semester you are encouraged to revisit and tie in earlier issues to current debates (as any good sociologist would!). Obviously with the limited space you have you are not required to discuss everything we cover. PLEASE — NO SUMMARIES; **be reflective and critical and demonstrate some original thought**.

What Writing Style Should I Be Using???

In short, any style that you'd like. Unlike your other papers for the course, reflection papers do not have to be formal (though they can be if that is what you choose). Previously, students have written these as an ongoing journal, a letter to a family member or friend, a formal critique, an editorial for a newspaper, and so forth — choose whatever style you'll enjoy the most.

Why Reflection Papers???

This is a seminar-style course. The course will only be as good as class discussion, so having you read, think deeply about, and regularly write your critical thoughts on the readings will prepare you for intelligent participation in class discussion.

How are Reflection Papers Graded???

Each R.P. will be worth 3% of your overall grade. The highest score — full credit — is reserved for those students demonstrating an ability to offer **original, critical analysis**. I will solicit the authors of outstanding reflection papers to see if they will volunteer to post their papers (anonymously) on our Web site.

Are You Going to Write Reflection Papers???

Yes I am! I will write an R.P. occasionally and post it on the course website. If you are interested in posting your reflection papers (anonymously) I strongly encourage you to email them to me and I will post them on the website as well. Looking at my samples as well as those of your peers should help you when writing later papers, and I expect that you will look at the website weekly to read newly posted papers.

You probably noticed that in the reflection papers Bethany's professor emphasizes critical thinking and original ideas. Most college professors want you to join in the conversation and add your own ideas, instead of merely summarizing what others have said. In academic writing being original doesn't mean you have to come up with an idea that no one's ever thought of before on a subject that no one's ever written about before. This reflection paper assignment asks students to first read what someone has already said about a subject and then add something from their own perspective to the conversation. This is exactly what Bethany does in her reflection papers. What follows is an example of one her reflection papers.

The Things I Never Knew About Corporal Punishment

I'm not sure how to say this, so I guess I should just come out and admit it: I love the show "Supernanny." No, it's definitely not my guiltiest pleasure, but it does rank among the most embarrassing favorite shows. Deep down inside, I think that it's probably weird and wrong to document the very most private moments of a parent(s) daily lives and how they discipline their child/children; but on the flip side, I love watching that British nanny come over and turn things around, almost like magic. This show was also my first exposure to the idea of discipline without physical punishment. I was spanked as a child, but only for doing very inappropriate things; however, watching this show made me realize that I probably a) wanted more attention from my parents, or b) was definitely too young to know any better! The most interesting thing for me to realize, though, was that there are other ways to teach children right from wrong without beating it into or out of them. In fact, it would seem that even the most disagreeable children succumb to authority if it's consistent, serious, and nonnegotiable. However, for one reason or another, parents often and frequently use spanking, slapping, or other forms of physical punishment as their only means of "controlling," or modifying, behavior.

This is a somewhat scary fact, according to Straus; and I'm starting to agree. This agreement is not without reservation, but regardless, I was shocked by all of the data collected about the effects of corporal punishment. For example, while it is always difficult to truly know the validity and applicability of statistics, the fact remains that Straus conducted research and in his research pool (be it interview, CTS, etc), he found that not only are adolescents who were hit by parents more likely to be depressed, but they are also more likely to have thoughts about killing themselves. Not only that, but tendencies towards violence and crime were also higher, in general. This is somewhat odd to me, because as a child of hitting, slapping, and severe spanking (belts, metal objects, etc), I don't consider myself any of the above things. Yet, in the very moment that I just wrote that, I realized I did suffer from anxiety disorders and severe self-esteem issues (which could be a spurious correlation, however), and I do have a rather "feisty" disposition — I like to slap/hit when someone makes fun of me, in an "aw, shucks" kind of way, and I do yell a lot instead of talking things through rationally. Obviously, all of these things could be caused by innumerable other variables, but the prospect of it makes for an interesting examination into how we discipline our children, which is exactly what Straus is trying to say/do.

However, what is almost more disturbing to me than the effects is the fact that there is more physical punishment and physical abuse occurring than we have statistics for, and there is a very fine line between punishment and abuse. This gray area is what scares me. How hard does a parent have to hit for it to cause injury? How often does a parent have to spank for it to be abuse? These issues are not only hard to define, but are also still a culturally private (and somewhat acceptable) practice. Even though most parents would never say they abuse their children, the situations of harsh or severe punishment would tell a different story. Not only that, but sometimes, for the very inexperienced or stressed parents — among other factors, physical punishment can turn into physical abuse. And as Straus pointed out before, among the many causes of depression, suicide, violence, and crime, this punishment and abuse is one convincing catalyst.

I am very interested to see what Straus has to say about sex and violence, and if he can offer any alternatives to skeptics. I am not a skeptic, however, because I have seen Supernanny do it, so I know it's possible. I kind of just wish everyone would watch Supernanny; everyone could learn a thing or two about children and parenting from that woman. Then again, we could all learn something from Straus, too; but who am I kidding, people don't read books anymore...

8.11: Writing to Learn – Reflecting on Social Science Conventions

In what ways does Bethany's reflection paper break with some of the conventions of writing in the social sciences that we discussed in this chapter? In what ways does Bethany's reflection paper reflect the ways of thinking in the social sciences?

Bethany's professor assigns the reflection papers as a way for students to explore sociological theories and research in a personal and informal way, but he also wants students to learn to report on the results of their own research in more formal sociology genres like the kind of research articles you might find in a sociology journal. Bethany's professor told me that "final research papers mirror those of a journal article." The final research paper and presentation in Intimate Violence is typical of the kind of extensive research and writing you're likely to encounter when you begin taking classes in your major.

Final Paper and Presentation (A&S 360 — *INTIMATE VIOLENCE*)

Pending IRB [Institutional Research Board, DM] approval, your final assignment will revolve around the campus survey we will be conducting as part of the class.

Upon completion of data entry, each student will receive a copy of the data set. Students should begin thinking about what specific variables they want to focus on for the final paper, consult with me to make sure their topics are unique, and then begin data analysis.

Given the pre-requisites for this course, students will be expected to conduct bi-variate data analysis at a minimum, and possibly multivariate analysis for those students who have received training in SPSS. We will discuss data analysis more in class after Spring Break. There are thorough literatures for all of the issues covered in our survey, so locating resources for your literature review should not be a problem.

I will allow some students to conduct their own research on topics not addressed in our survey, so that we cover a variety of intimate violence issues during the last part of the course (student presentations). IF YOU WILL BE CONDUCTING YOUR OWN RESEARCH, please see the next two paragraphs for key information... (if you are using survey data, turn to page two)

RESEARCH METHODS: **If you do not use our survey data, you must conduct some other form of original research.** You can do _interviews_ with relevant volunteers (see me if you want to do this), pass out _surveys_ (see me), do _content analysis_ (examine relevant current/historical documents first-hand; see me), or _do some observation_ (e.g., attend a court case; see me). You must obtain approval from me PRIOR TO CONDUCTING YOUR RESEARCH. **Failure to obtain approval for your research method prior to conducting your research will result in a failing grade for the entire assignment.**

Sample Topic Ideas for students NOT using the class survey
As we shall cover in class, intimate violence is a broad field covering many forms of violence. You should select a broader topic and then narrow it down as you think about what research you will be conducting and what you find in the literature. If your general topic is _Child Sexual Abuse_, examples of narrow topics within this field would be: _Identifying Risk Markers for Adult Perpetrators of Child Sexual Abuse_; or, _Women as Perpetrators or Co-victims of Child Sexual Abuse?_

*Your paper should include theory from the broad field and subfield as well as an analysis of your narrow topic.

**You can select whatever narrow topic interests you, however a few ideas are ('Your General Topic' and...): Theoretical or methodological debates (e.g., the Conflict Tactics Scales), interesting and/or counterintuitive empirical findings, perpetrators or victims/survivors, legal issues, not-for-profit organizations trying to eradicate intimate violence, specific programs for perpetrators or victims, long-term effects on victims/survivors, etc.

THINGS TO DO FOR EVERYONE:

1.   Pick *specific* research topic and presentation/due date by March 5th: You must meet with me and receive approval for both your topic and presentation date so that the projects are unique, so I can confirm they are appropriate for the course (neither too narrow nor broad), and so I can evenly distribute presentations. Your grade will be reduced by 20 points (out of 100) if you fail to meet with me.

2.   Presentation Date Options: **April 23, April 25, April 30, May 2**

3.   **Write your paper and put together a 15 minute presentation**: Rough drafts are welcome in advance (let's meet during office hours so we can discuss the paper).

4.   **Give Presentation/Submit Paper:** Paper is due during day of presentation, or, for those presenting the last week of class, your paper is due: **Friday, April 27**

CLASS PRESENTATION: You will provide a 15 minute informative and entertaining summary of your paper, followed by a 5 minute Q&A period. Along with your peers, I will be asking questions of all presenters to see how well you know the material. Multimedia access will be available on all three presentation dates. PRACTICE YOUR PRESENTATION AND MAKE SURE IT DOES NOT EXCEED 15 MINUTES!!!

1)   We must be efficient (but not rushed) with our presentations, so I'm requiring you to bring in a cd, flashdrive, etc. if you need to use the laptop/projector. DO NOT plan on logging into the network and retrieving your files, as this is a waste of class time.

2)   DO NOT RELY ON TECHNOLOGY — Bring hardcopies of all electronic files on the day you present (note: this is a good policy for the rest of your life!!!)

PAPER: The paper must be thirteen to fifteen (13–15) pages in length, typed, double-space, Times New Roman 12 point font, one inch margins, no cover page. You must use no less than seven (7) **outside academic** sources as well as class readings (can use other sources in addition; e.g., internet, newspapers, etc., but they must be *in addition to* seven academic sources). A 'References' page should be included at the end with full citation information (i.e., author, title, year, publisher, city, etc.). For examples of how to cite chapters, books, and journal articles properly, look at the 'References' pages after each article in the course reader. Additional information about organizing and writing your paper will be provided in class.

GRADES: You will receive a grade for the composite of your paper, presentation, and fielding of questions during your presentation. Twenty percent of your final class grade will be based on the paper and ten percent of your final class grade will come from your presentation and fielding of questions (for a total assignment value of 30% of your final grade).

8.12: Learn by Doing – Analyzing a Social Science Research Article

The purpose of this Learn by Doing activity is to get a first-hand look at the type of sociology research article Bethany was asked to write by finding an example in a sociology journal. Find an article that reports the results of sociological research on date rape by searching one of the sociology databases listed in this chapter (Social Sciences Citation Index, Social Sciences Full Text, or Sociological Abstracts) using the keyword term "date rape." You might be able to access the full text of the article online, or you might need to find the article by locating the journal in your college's library. Once you've located a social science research article focused on date rape, skim through it and create a list of some of the rhetorical features of the genre of the sociological research article. You can think about the following questions to help you make your list:

- Who seems to be the audience (or audiences) for the article?
- How is the article structured?
- How would you describe the author's persona?
- What kind of thinking strategies does the author use (summarizing, defining, synthesizing, arguing)?
- How would you describe the author's research methods?
- What kinds of evidence does the author use to support his or her points?
- What are the citation conventions?

Bethany reported that her writing process for her research article was much different from her writing process for the reaction papers. Here's what she said about her writing process for the research article:

The writing process itself for this final paper differed greatly from that of the reaction papers. Reaction papers tend to be much less formal; I use "I" more, I speak directly to the professor, and I worry less about grammar and cohesiveness. As it is, literally, a "reaction" to something, these papers are just thoughts on a page. However, for the final paper I begin with an outline. I title all of my necessary sections, I–VI, or however many sections I need: Introduction, Theory and Literature (can be and is often broken into multiple sections), Methods and Data, Findings, Discussion, Conclusion, Policy Implications, and Future Research. Some of these final sections can be grouped into the Conclusion section, depending on the length and depth of the paper. I then put any journal articles, book sections, or miscellaneous information underneath the appropriate sections, also in outline form. Then, one by one, I elaborate on the articles and information, tying them in to the section and the paper as a whole. Normally I have a research topic, both general and specific, and an end goal in mind. I make sure that every statement I make not only makes sense, but ties back into these things. I usually start with the literature and theory section, because that provides me with information for the rest of the sections, and also tends to open up doors of thought I may not have previously considered.

Bethany said that one of the biggest pieces of advice she has for college students as they move into courses in their major and are given extensive research paper assignments is to write more than one draft. Bethany's advice is to "please, please, please (!) give yourself enough time to write multiple drafts of your papers. Although in the beginning, it may feel as though this takes more time, it will save you from those dreaded all-nighters, and those even more dreaded bad grades." Bethany's professor had similar advice for his students about writing as a process: "My basic advice is writing is a process. No one writes well their first draft, and they need to get other eyes on their work (whether that's peers, the writing center, or myself)."

Bethany also had a lot to say about her researching process, and a lot of good advice about researching. Here's what she told me about researching:

In general, the key is: the more time you spend on research, the less time you spend writing. This is because you won't have to stay up all night, every night, pulling things out of nowhere (if you know what I mean) to get to the page length minimum. But, seriously, research is the single most important aspect of your college career. To start, it's not easy to find legitimate sources. Note here: *Wikipedia* is not a legitimate source. I usually start the process by using *Google Scholar* to determine what articles and authors have been cited the most. This gives me a good basis when furthering the research. The next step is to search online databases and journals. Your school's online library, accessible through their home page Web site, normally gives you access to a variety of journals and databases offering full-text articles in .pdf form. These online journals and databases can be searched just like Google, using author name, keyword, year of publication, etc. You won't be able to find a non-legitimate source using these resources. The final step is searching through your library's book database. A good place to start is to look up general keywords in the database (i.e. *violence, gender, women and sport,* etc.). Then, when you have the call numbers for 5–10 books, you can go browse the sections they're in. Usually the sections will contain other books of interest to your research. Another good source, which you should always utilize, is your professors. They are likely to have a plethora of books and an extensive internal rolodex of journal articles that they either own or remember from their undergraduate and graduate careers.

In determining which sources are good and which aren't, there are some key rules to follow. The first thing to look at is where you found the source. I don't recommend ever using Web sites as sources, unless they are a governmental agency, social movement organization (realizing these are somewhat biased), or verifiable Web sites. You want to be able to clearly cite the author, publisher or company endorsing the information, and date it was written or published. In general, personal Web sites, blogs, and *Wikipedia* are not good sources of information. Once you've cut out all non-legitimate sources, you'll want to look at date of publication. While some information, including theories, may still be applicable and useful, you'll generally want to include a lot of recent and up-to-date information as well. Additionally, one helpful tip is to be very careful about how often you have to cite. While it is important to always cite information that isn't common knowledge, or anything that is taken directly from others' works, you also want to be able to put almost everything you say into your own words. Unique thoughts backed up by previous research are more influential then verbatim recitation of that previous research.

Bethany did a lot of researching, drafting, and revising before she came up with the draft of her research article that she decided to show the professor to get some feedback. In his response to her draft, Bethany's professor said that the strength of her paper was that it "closely mirrors that of an academic journal" and that Bethany did a good job of making clear what issues she will be focusing on, what other scholars have said, and what she found in her own research. Bethany's professor also told her that "it appears as if you've already written several drafts of the paper before submitting it for feedback." Bethany's professor suggested that as she revised for the final draft, she should work on evaluating the theories she applies in her research and "explicitly assess the merits of each theory," and she should "be more cautious interpreting her results" as she considered the significance of her data. Bethany's professor also suggested that she work on creating "smoother transitions between paragraphs and sections to make the read less choppy." Bethany considered her professor's feedback and continued to draft and revise her paper. Her final draft that follows here reflects the hard work she put it into researching and revising.

Dating Violence and Fraternity Men: The Problem with Perpetuating Patriarchy by Bethany Zoston

Introduction

Rape in fraternity, athletic, and group settings has been studied by researchers in the past, but this research seems limited. Mainly, the research available has looked at group setting set in terms of fraternity rape, and therefore gang-rape. While gang-rape is an important aspect of violence in the culture of fraternities, and the socialization of masculinity, it is also essential to look at the connection between fraternity membership and sexual assault and rape within intimate partner relationships. An examination of the risk factors in dating relationships with a focus on fraternity membership is essential, because if the risk factors that lead to gang-rape perpetrated by fraternity men are the same factors that lead to dating violence, prevention and intervention are needed at all institutional levels — especially if, and it seems likely from the research, dating violence is more prevalent than gang-rape.

Kantor and Jasinski (1998) outlined some of the risk factors for partner violence, including male dominance, and the social norms of control, gender, and intergenerational transmission. They also indicated that there are a series of risk makers, or characteristics, generally associated with an increased likelihood of being aggressive or violent towards a wife, some of which include being working class, excessive alcohol use, low income, and witnessing violence as a child or teen. Likewise, Denise Gamache (1998), examined the issue of violence in the dating context, and inferred that cultural norms for gendered behavior, control and domination, and jealousy all play a part in dating violence.

Peggy Reeves Sanday looked at the prevalence of gang-rape in fraternities, and the culture of masculinity that exists in these "brotherhoods," in her book <u>Fraternity Gang Rape</u>. She writes at length about the sexual ethos that permeates fraternity life, the ideas, norms, and eventually behaviors that lead to sexual assault and rape. Among these ideas are rape myths, such as "she wanted it"; gendered stereotypes, such as masculine prowess; and behavioral norms in relation to generous alcohol consumption and sexuality and sexual partners (Sanday 1990). Moreover, she discusses the bond these fraternity "brothers" have with one another, and the power of the group to influence behavior and belief, mainly in avoidance of humiliation. Kimmel addresses this issue as well, stating, "... the animating condition for most American men is a deeply rooted fear of other men" (2004:145).

This idea of the power of the situation is very important in examining violence perpetrated by fraternity men. However, what is most important, and most absent, from the research on college-aged men is the connection between known risk factors in dating relationships and the "new" risk factor: fraternity membership. The purpose of this paper is to explore a somewhat new territory of intimate violence, and examine all of the factors that may lead college-aged men to be violent towards their partners. I hope to study this issue from a gender-based critique; considering that patriarchy, male social power, is bad for both men and women, in that it not only diminishes women's existences, but also reduces men to "objects" of their gender. In doing this, and keeping in mind that social change is slow, I desire to reach a new understanding of intimate violence between dating partners and the effects of fraternity membership on relational aggression.

Background

While many theories exist that look at intimate violence in marriages, very few are directly applicable to intimate relationships outside of marriage and cohabitation, and my research requires theories that can be applied to all relationships. The specific interest is in dating relationships, and applicability to men involved in Greek, social-fraternity life. This distinction is important, because as many have reported, "compared to non-fraternity men, fraternity men have been found to have more traditional attitudes toward women (Schaeffer & Nelson, 1993), a more sexually permissive peer group (Lottes & Kuriloff, 1994), stronger belief in male dominance (Kalof & Cargill, 1991), and greater belief in rape myths..." (Bleeker and Murnen, 2001).

Social Learning Theory

This theory focuses on the processes involved in learning behaviors, values, and ideologies. These processes are differential association, definitions, differential reinforcement, and imitation. Differential association is the process by which one is exposed to, and thereby learns, normative definitions that are favorable or unfavorable to behavior. Definitions are a person's personal attitudes and beliefs, or the meanings that one attaches to a certain behavior. Differential reinforcement is the existence or possibility of anticipated or actual rewards and punishments that are the outcome of certain behaviors. And finally, imitation is the process of engaging in a certain behavior after observation of that behavior (Akers, 2005).

There are two specific issues to be addressed when looking at intimate partner violence in college-aged dating relationships. The first, of particular interest to this research, is the culture of fraternity life. There exists, in many but not all fraternities, a culture of dominance, hierarchy, and violence. This begins very early in the pledge process, with hazing and bullying, and continues through the entirety of Greek life. The fraternity is a "brotherhood," and becomes a new family. This family serves to establish a new social reality and social order for an individual, sometimes superseding all previous internalized attitudes and opinions. The expectations for behavior, in terms of sexuality and alcohol, are quickly learned, and if an individual desires to be accepted and not ridiculed, he will behave in the most favorable, and expected, way.

The second issue regarding social learning theory is that of imitation, particularly when encountering the theory of intergenerational transmission. Intergenerational transmission is the idea that violence is passed down from one generation to the next, particularly when sons see their fathers abuse their mothers — or are the victims of the abuse — and then go on to be violent themselves. However, I believe that it is more appropriate to look at intergenerational transmission as a potential factor in violence, not as a theory unto itself. There are many other aspects of social learning that serve to develop a person's social reality, norms, behaviors, and attitudes; imitation occurs as a result of not only witnessing violence, but also by having definitions for behavior that are inclusive of such violence.

Exchange theory
This theory extends upon the idea of rewards and punishments brought about from social learning theory. Gelles wrote that, in concordance with exchange theory, violence and abuse were used when the rewards were higher than the costs (Gelles 1993). This is one very popular way to examine intimate violence, as the cultural realities of non-intervention, low reporting rates, and lack of enforcement tend to decrease the "costs" associated with violence.

However, in particular regards to dating relationships, I will use exchange theory as did Sedikides et al. (1994), who focus is on the rules and expectations that regulate the giving and receiving of benefits within relationships. For example, they examined gender differences in desired benefits and perceived costs in dating partnerships. The benefits outlined in the article include assistance with everyday tasks, emotional and material support, intimacy, and social alliance, among others; perceived costs of being in a relationship include ineffective help, invasion of privacy, criticism, fear of abandonment, and loss of individuality (Sedikides et al., 1994). In terms of fraternity life, benefits may include social status, male peer acknowledgement, and/or (reinforcement) of sexuality and masculinity.

However, while the study touches on the subject of fighting and violence briefly, I believe an extension is needed in the research. Making the step from a lack of received benefits in a relationship, or a response to certain relational costs, to violence, is not very difficult when also examining certain gender-based, social issues. Additionally, perpetuation of masculine and feminine norms, respectively, lead to many of the relational differences noted in the study; and these differences can, as shown, lead to conflict. If the social exchange between two partners is unequal, it is most likely due to their gendered socialization.

Feminist Theory

Feminist Theory exists because, as Yllö writes, gender and power must be taken into account when studying and trying to understand intimate partner violence (1993: 47). The main premise of the theory is that a patriarchal society has led to continued male dominance, and this power has infiltrated every individual's sense of identity, men and women alike. It does not matter what we think or do — from our opinions on love and relationships to our ambition and independence — everything that we as humans do is gendered.

Because our identities are rooted in our socialization, and because male power and control has defined certain expectations for both men and women, we, as gendered human beings, end up performing these expectations. West and Zimmerman remarked on this behavior as "doing gender," and there is an appropriate and inappropriate way to *do* gender (1987). In America, the rigid stereotypes for men have called for independence, bravery, and a lack of emotion; for women, the feminine straightjacket has produced, in images and in the minds of real women, a sense of insecurity, shyness, and codependence. These socially constructed characteristics are the expectations for gender; and because sex is so intrinsically linked to gender, they perpetuate and maintain male power within society.

Yllö wrote about the "Power and Control Wheel" in her research, which is a model that was developed to link all forms of violence and coercive control. She refers to them as control tactics, and together, they paint a picture of relational and intimate violence that develops from domination (1993: 54–55). It is not psychology, or simple relational conflict, but male power that leads to yelling, hitting, and even rape between partners. Hyde's "Gender Similarities Hypothesis" supports this argument, as it states that research shows men and women are more similar than different psychologically (2005: 581). Therefore, if violence were gender neutral, not only would both men and women perpetrate on the same frequency — which is not factual, but that violence as a result of psychological problems would be equally to blame for both men and women perpetrators. However, violence seems to be less about sex differences, and much more about gender.

This dichotomy between that which is "male" and that which is "female" only serves to make our society blame different factors for men's violence, when the truth to the situation is that patriarchy maintains male power within society and relationships. The simple fact is that men perpetrate the majority of violence in America, and an overwhelming majority of intimate partner violence around the world. If intimate partner violence is to be fully understood, a feminist paradigm must be incorporated into the theoretical discussion. Whether it is a matter of social learning, personal gain, control, or a combination of all three, male power and masculinity cannot be ignored or denied.

Hypotheses

This research examines many aspects of abuse, assault, and rape among college students at X College. Of specific interest are issues regarding patriarchal opinions and beliefs, and the perpetration of violence, among men. I focus on Greek men, specifically. My hypotheses are: 1) Greek men on X College's campus will have more patriarchal opinions than non-Greek men; 2) Greek men will be more likely to have committed acts of abuse than non-Greek men; 3) Patriarchal opinions will correlate positively with committed acts of abuse among the non-Greek male population; and 4) Patriarchal opinions and committed acts of abuse will correlate more strongly within the Greek male population than in the non-Greek population.

Methods

Sample

In the original survey, there were 486 student participants from X College. Of these, 103 were first-year students, 151 were sophomores, 122 were juniors, and 110 were seniors (also included were fifth year returning seniors). There were 187 male and 295 female surveyed. Half of the respondents were either Natural Sciences & Mathematics majors or Social Science majors, although there were also Humanities, Fine Arts, and Applied majors, and those who were Undecided. In the sample, 265 respondents were non-Greek, and 217 were Greek.

Given the focus of my research, however, I limited the sample to include only the males, and for a majority of the data analysis I looked at only Greek males. Because I looked at specific questions in my analysis, I had to drop some respondents due to blank answers. After certain respondents were dropped, I was left with a non-Greek male sample size of 95, and a Greek male sample size of 79.

Variables

Dependent variables. The central dependent variable in this analysis concerns abuse against dating partners and boyfriends/girlfriends. This abuse was measured in terms of verbal abuse, forced sexual acts, physical abuse, and sexual assault. The following questions were analyzed in this research (Yes/No responses; Choices of at X College? A student? Away from X College?): Have you ever touched someone sexually without their consent (code=utouch)? Have you ever tried but failed to perform (or failed to force someone else to perform) a sexual act against their will (code=utried)? Have you ever performed or forced someone to perform a sexual act against their will (code=uforce)? In addition to these questions, I also examined answers to the questions (circled if applicable): Have you ever verbally abused a girlfriend/boyfriend or someone you're dating (code=uverbgb, uverbdt)? Have you ever used physical violence against a girlfriend/boyfriend or someone you're dating (code=uphysgb, uphysdt)?

Another dependent variable was patriarchal attitudes or beliefs. In order to analyze and measure patriarchal attitudes or beliefs, I examined answers to the following statements: Most women want men to be in charge (code=incharge); Problems between couples should remain private (code=private); A woman should never pay for dinner on a first date with a man (code=womanpay); Part of being a man is being ready to use violence (code=menready); If I could do it without getting caught, I'd force someone to have sex (code=forcesex). These questions required Likert-scale responses of 1–4, 1 being Strongly Agree and 4 being Strongly Disagree.

Independent variables. The main independent variables in this research were sex and Greek affiliation. It was my belief that male sex would influence both strength of patriarchal beliefs and frequency of perpetrated abuse. Moreover, I hypothesized that Greek males would have even stronger patriarchal beliefs, and to commit more acts of abuse, than non-Greek males. Another independent variable was patriarchal attitudes or beliefs. I hypothesized that patriarchal attitudes or beliefs would correlate with perpetrated abuse. Pearson's correlations were used to examine the relationship between these variables.

Findings

Hypothesis 1: *Greek men on X College's campus will have more patriarchal opinions than non-Greek men.*

There were not considerable differences between Greek men and non-Greek men on the subject of patriarchal opinions (Table 1). On average, the Greek males tended more towards agreeing than non-Greek males, but were still mostly split between Agree and Disagree for the questions about men being in charge, troubles between couples remaining private, and women paying for dinner on first dates. The Greek males also disagreed less strongly on the issues of being a man means being ready to use violence, and forcing someone to have sex if they wouldn't get caught; however, overall, all men disagreed with these questions. All men, Greek and non-Greek alike, disagreed very strongly with the issue of forcing someone to have sex, with the means being 3.89 and 3.9, respectfully.

Table 1 shows the relationship between Greek affiliation and patriarchal opinions.

	Incharge	private	womenpay	menready	forcesex
Greek Males	2.69	2.24	2.24	3.38	3.89
Non-Greek Males	3	2	2.49	3.48	3.9

Hypothesis 2: *Greek men will be more likely to have committed acts of abuse than non-Greek men.*

This hypothesis had the most support (Table 2). While non-Greek men committed almost no acts of forced sexual contact or physical abuse, Greek men committed an average of 2.4 acts in these categories. Even more startling is that these acts were committed against fellow students, and at X College, more than away from X College; whereas non-Greek males committed only 2 failed forcible sexual acts away from X College, and 1 act of physical violence against a girlfriend/boyfriend.

Verbal abuse was highest among both groups, with 9 acts being committed against girlfriends/boyfriends, and 4 acts against someone the respondent was dating, for non-Greek males. For Greek males, the numbers were startlingly higher. These men committed 17 acts of verbal abuse against girlfriends/boyfriends, and 4 acts against someone they were dating.

Table 2 shows the relationship between Greek affiliation and self-reported acts of abuse.

	Greek Males	Non-Greek Males
utouchxcollege	4	0
utouchstudent	5	0
utouchaway	3	0
utriedxcollege	2	0
utriedstudent	2	0
utriedaway	2	2
uforcexcollege	2	0
uforcestudent	1	0
uforceaway	1	0
uverbgb	17	9
uverbdt	4	4
uphysgb	0	1
uphysdt	2	0

Hypothesis 3: *Patriarchal opinions would correlate positively with committed acts of abuse among the non-Greek male population.*

This data was the least expected (Table 3). Because of the relatively non-existent numbers reported for acts of sexual contact and verbal abuse, there were no possible correlations for a majority of the answers. That being said, there were two weak negative correlations. The first was between opinions on women wanting men to be in charge, and trying (but failing) to force someone to perform a sexual act away from X College. This means that the more the respondent agreed with the statement "most women want men to be in charge," the more likely they were to have tried to force someone to perform a sexual act against their will, away from X College. Since there were only two respondents who answered "Yes" to trying to force someone away from X College to perform a sexual act this correlation is more related to the fact that most respondents answered "No," regardless of their patriarchal opinions; and that the two respondents who answered "Yes" have a greater tendency towards traditional gender-role belief.

The second weak negative correlation was between the issue of forcing someone to have sex, and verbally abusing a dating partner. In this case, the more a respondent agreed with the statement "If I could do it without getting caught, I would force someone to have sex," the more likely they were to verbally abuse someone they were dating.

Another weak positive correlation was made between the issue of women paying for dinner on a first date, and verbally abusing a boyfriend/girlfriend. This shows that the more a respondent disagreed with the statement, "A women should never pay for dinner on a first date with a man," the more likely they were to have verbally abused their girlfriend. This is an interesting discovery, as one would think the opposite would be true. However, it would seem that there is potential for male respondents to think it is O.K. for women to pay for dinner on a first date, but still have tendencies towards abuse. This is an interesting notion, as the premise may not, necessarily, be gender-role behavior but monetary costs. The college-aged student is not particularly wealthy, and as Sedikides et al. (1994) pointed out in their research, a very big "cost" associated with intimate dating relationships is monetary sacrifice.

Table 3 shows the correlation between patriarchal opinions and self-reported acts of abuse among the non- Greek male population.

	incharge	private	womenpay	menready	forcesex
utouchxcollege	ALL NO	ALL NO	ALL NO	ALL NO	ALL NO
utouchstudent	ALL NO	ALL NO	ALL NO	ALL NO	ALL NO
utouchaway	ALL NO	ALL NO	ALL NO	ALL NO	ALL NO
utriedxcollege	ALL NO	ALL NO	ALL NO	ALL NO	ALL NO
utriedstudent	ALL NO	ALL NO	ALL NO	ALL NO	ALL NO
utriedaway	-0.2	0.06	0.01	-0.1	0.05
uforcexcollege	ALL NO	ALL NO	ALL NO	ALL NO	ALL NO
uforcestudent	ALL NO	ALL NO	ALL NO	ALL NO	ALL NO
uforceaway	ALL NO	ALL NO	ALL NO	ALL NO	ALL NO
uverbgb	0.1	0.1	0.2	-0	0
uverbdt	-0.1	0.08	0.01	-0.1	-0.2
uphysgb	ALL NO	ALL NO	ALL NO	ALL NO	ALL NO
uphysdt	ALL NO	ALL NO	ALL NO	ALL NO	ALL NO

Hypothesis 4. *Patriarchal opinions and committed acts of abuse will correlate more strongly within the Greek male population than the non-Greek population.*

This hypothesis was weakly supported (Table 4). Given the higher numbers reported within the male Greek population, and given their tendency towards slightly more patriarchal beliefs, the correlations here were much stronger. In particular, the issues of men being ready to use violence, and that of forcing sex, provided some of the strongest data.

For instance, there was a weak negative correlation between men being ready to use violence and forcing someone at X College to perform a sexual act against their will. This means that the more respondents agreed with the statement "Part of being a man is being ready to use violence," the more likely they were to have forced someone at X College to perform a sexual act.

Another weak negative correlation occurred between the issue of forcing someone to have sex, and actually forcing someone to have sex at X College. Here, the more respondents agreed with the statement "If I could do it without getting caught, I'd force someone to have sex," the more likely they are to have actually forced someone at X College to perform a sexual act against their will.

Lastly, there was a moderate negative correlation between the issue of forcing someone to have sex and using physical violence against a dating partner. In this instance, the more a respondent agreed with the statement "If I could do it without getting caught, I'd force someone to have sex," the more likely they were to have used physical violence against a dating partner.

Table 4 shows the correlation between patriarchal opinions and perpetrated acts of abuse among the Greek male population.

	incharge	private	Womenpay	menready	forcesex
utouchxcollege	0.095	0.004	0.057	0.115	-0.081
utouchstudent	0.107	-0.014	-0.009	0.0086	-0.058
utouchaway	-0.093	-0.069	0.205	-0.187	-0.28
utriedxcollege	-0.04	-0.056	-0.11	-0.08	0.046
utriedstudent	-0.04	-0.06	-0.11	-0.08	0.047
utriedaway	0.066	0.062	0.04	0.027	0.046
uforcexcollege	-0.146	-0.056	0.116	-0.294	-0.367
uforcestudent	0.05	0.13	-0.03	-0.06	0.03
uforceaway	0.047	0.127	-0.025	-0.056	0.033
uverbgb	0	-0	0	0	0
uverbdt	0.17	0.089	0.11	0.038	-0.081
uphysgb	ALL NO	ALL NO	ALL NO	ALL NO	ALL NO
uphysdt	-0.14	-0.056	0.27	-0.187	-0.574

Discussion

These results provide a small insight into the potential issues of fraternity involvement and sexual, physical, and verbal abuse in intimate relationships. While the correlations were very weak among most variables, and only one was moderate, any correlation with such a small sample size — and the inherent problems in underreporting that arise therefrom — can, and should, be taken seriously. The problems with dating and relational abuse at X College are not unique; and the attitudes and opinions of the men are not very different from what has previously been reported.

It would seem that the culture of masculinity is the biggest risk factor for dating violence. The perpetuation of masculine "norms" in fraternity life, such as reducing women with derogatory names, and then forcing this practice into the reality of the brotherhood, and the appropriation of alcohol as a "social aide," or social stimulant, only serves to maintain the norms and expectations for behavior that were previously learned through socialization. Particularly, alcohol as a risk factor for dating violence becomes even more dangerous when use is in relation to the fraternity setting. Fraternities tend to run the social scene at many colleges around the United States (Sanday 1993), and the binge-drinking and late-night parties put both men and women at risk for violence, assault, and rape. Moreover, the risks are no lower for those in dating relationships, as compared to those who will experience stranger or acquaintance rape, because of the social circumstances encountered at a fraternity or with fraternity men.

While the questions about patriarchy and gender roles received a mixed bag of answers, settling somewhere in between agree and disagree, it would appear that the social reality of gender and control influence behavior, even in the absence of self-reported patriarchal beliefs. This reality of male power and machismo masculinity is supported in the case study of the Alpha Beta Fraternity done by Rhoads in 1995. He reported that even though Alpha Beta Fraternity was self-proclaimed as "progressive," the context of male domination, female passivity, and strong perceptions of appropriate gender behavior existed and ruled fraternity life there. Stair-diving to prove masculine prowess and fearlessness, verbal — somewhat subconscious — blaming of women in rape cases, and rampant alcohol use drove the social and private lives of the men in the chapter (Rhoads, 1995).

However, it would be myopic to argue that the socio-cultural influences of patriarchy, and the process of social learning, are the only factors that influence dating violence. It would also be easy to say dating violence only occurs within relationships with a male, Greek partner, but this is just not true. As many have argued, patriarchy does not affect all men equally (Smith and White, 2001). There are also personality characteristics which seem to influence tendencies and levels of violence among the male population. Some of these include: emotional dependence, insecurity, low empathy, poor communication and social skills, narcissism, and anxiety or depression (Kantor and Jasinski, 1998). Yet, in the study conducted within this paper, it would appear that using personality characteristics such as these as a "reason" for violence and abuse does not fully make sense. It is not particularly easy to understand how members of a fraternity, a "brotherhood" with eternal bonds and ties to friendship and family, would create depressed, insecure, or non-empathetic human beings. What is easier to examine, however, is how fraternity life can lead to narcissism, with increased social status and the continuing drive to maintain and increase this status, and potentially anxiety, which is related to the fear of humiliation. Constantly having to prove and perpetuate masculinity can be tiring, and if doing gender in this way is "fake" or an act, then it becomes a struggle to maintain the façade and a Russian roulette of sorts, wondering when someone will figure out who the real person is.

What remains interesting, however, is that while it would appear statistically impossible to have such low rates of violence and abuse occurring, many of the Greek men did report using coercive, controlling, and abusive tactics. We know that underreporting occurs in both female and male populations who are victimized, but it must be understood that self-reporting violence and abuse is not something that most people willingly do. Given the methods for collecting the data, this self-reporting seems high. However, it is important to always remember that these rates are much higher in reality.

Conclusion

This is a limited study. While the survey produced close to 500 respondents, the nature of my focus limited the possible participants. The low sample and the subject of the survey all lead to low reporting, and therefore low correlations. However, the effects of Greek membership on dating violence need to be studied much more extensively before any results of mine, with a terribly small sample, have the capability to disprove implications of violence among this population.

Moreover, because this was cross-sectional data, there's no way to examine what causes the prevalence of, or lack of, patriarchal beliefs. It is a chicken-and-egg question of what comes first, the patriarchal beliefs that cause a tendency towards participation in all-male groups, or the all-male groups causing a tendency towards patriarchal beliefs? I would argue that both of these are contributing factors to dating violence. For some men, joining an all-male fraternity changes and alters their opinions and attitudes towards masculinity, women, and reality. They learn new social norms and become "different" people than they were before. However, for a majority of men, the patriarchal attitudes and opinions already existed; and for many more, the desire to join a "brotherhood" is brought on by our patriarchal society's socialization of masculinity.

Future research should focus on longitudinal effects of fraternity membership, looking at how much opinion changes from freshman year to senior year; or even beginning in high school and following men through their college years. This would help to see if joining an all-male fraternity influenced their patriarchal beliefs and their masculinity, or if their tendency towards masculine behavior is what leads them to join in the first place. A longitudinal study would also be helpful in measuring strengths and weaknesses of beliefs and actions. For example, did one's traditional beliefs get stronger after joining, or did they stay the same as they had been before?

Additionally, more research in general should be done looking at dating violence among the Greek population. I believe that being Greek is a "super" risk factor when it comes to dating violence. The issues of personality, gender/patriarchy, and alcohol all come to a head in the fraternity culture. A focus on gang-rape is an important and critical issue for our society today, but the issues of dating and intimate violence among this population are vastly underrepresented in past and current research.

In terms of policy implications, it would seem that educational programs are just not working. Whatever approach is currently being taken, students are not getting the message. At the collegiate level, educational programs should be focused on the good, not the bad. Instead of teaching a gendered view of violence, where all men are/have the capability to be perpetrators, and women are relatively passive victims, focus on ending violence. Unity among the male and female populations, with regard to educating others about intimate partner violence, and supporting those who have been affected — both male and female — will serve to bring eradicating IPV to the forefront; the new battle is between society and violence.

It is also important to keep in mind that education needs to start at a much younger age for this type of programming to be effective. Likewise, a social atmosphere of acceptance and support at the collegiate level is necessary if violence in dating relationships at this level is to end. Administrations and teachers, at all levels, should help promote academic "safe zones," and groups on campuses which foster support and encouragement for issues of violence and abuse should be considered bigger resources to campuses and promoted as such.

In the end, it seems that the most influential dynamic in the perpetration of violence is society itself. I'll conclude with a quote, which I believe summarizes the extent of the dating violence problem occurring all over the United States today. It is important to remember that while a gendered view of violence presupposes male perpetration and female victimization, the reality of the situation is that men do perpetrate most acts, and most of those are against women. The importance of further research and stricter sanctions, and my passion for an end to intimate partner violence, is quoted in Smith and White's longitudinal study on violence against young women in dating relationships, "The greatest risk factor is being female" (2001:5).

References

Akers, Ronald L. (2005). Social Learning Theory. *Boundaries: Readings in Deviance, Crime, and Criminal Justice.* Boston, MA: Pearson Custom Publishing.

Bleecker and Murnen. (2005). Fraternity membership, the display of sexually degrading sexual images of women, and rape myth acceptance. *Sex Roles, 53,* 487–493.

Gamache, Denise. (1991). Domination and Control: The Social Context of Dating Violence. *Dating Violence: Young Women in Danger,* ed. By Barrie Levy, M.S.W. Seattle, WA: Seal Press.

Gelles, Richard J. (1993). Through a Sociological Lens: Social Structure and Family Violence. *Current Controversies on Family Violence,* ed. By Richard J. Gelles and Donileen R. Loseke. Newbury Park, CA: Sage Publications.

Hyde, Janet Shibley. (2005). The Gender Similarities Hypothesis. *American Psychologist, 60(6),* 581–592.

Kantor and Jasinski. (1998). Dynamics and Risk Factors in Partner Violence. *Partner Violence,* ed. By Jana L. Jasinski and Linda M. Williams. Thousand Oaks, CA: Sage Publications.

Kimmel, Michael S. (2004). Men, Masculinity, and the Rape Culture. *Transforming a Rape Culture*, ed. By Emilie Buchwald, Pamela R. Fletcher, and Martha Roth. Minnesota: Milkweed Editions.

Rhoads, Robert A. (1995). Whales Tales, Dog Piles, and Beer Goggles: An Ethnographic Case Study of Fraternity Life. *Anthropology and Education Quarterly, 26(3),* 306–323.

Sanday, Peggy Reeves. (1990). *Fraternity Gang Rape: Sex, Brotherhood, and Privilege on Campus.* New York: New York University Press.

Sedikides, Oliver, and Campbell. (1994). Perceived benefits and costs of romantic relationships for women and men: Implications for exchange theory. *Personal Relationships, 1,* 5–21.

Smith and White. National Criminal Justice Reference Service. (2001). Developmental Antecedents of Violence Against Women: A longitudinal Perspective. U.S. Department of Justice, Document #187775.

West and Zimmerman. (1987). Doing Gender. *Gender & Society, 1(2),* 125–151.

Yllö, Kersti A. (1993). Through a Feminist Lens: Gender, Power, and Violence. *Current Controversies on Family Violence*, ed. By Richard J. Gelles and Donileen R. Loseke. Newbury Park, CA: Sage Publications.

8.13: Writing to Learn – Social Science Research Article Conventions

Reread Bethany's research article and make a list of the ways that it conforms with the conventions of writing and researching in the social sciences that we've been discussing in this chapter. Also note any ways in which it departs from those conventions. Be prepared to share your list in small groups and to report what the groups found to the class as a whole.

The writing that Bethany was assigned in the Intimate Violence course may seem intimidating to you now if you're a first-year or second-year student, but keep in mind that Bethany is a senior and she's writing for an upper-division sociology class in the major. Remember that Bethany took a general education class that introduced her to the discipline of sociology, and she also took a class in her major that introduced her to sociology research methods. This case study of Bethany is included in *Exploring College Writing* to show you an example of a student writing in the social sciences, but it's also an example of the ways that writing in the major is usually more extensive and complex than writing in a general education class. The more classes with intensive writing you take before you enter your major, the better prepared you'll be for the challenging writing and researching which professors in your major field will assign.

Examples of Student Writing in the Social Sciences

For more examples of student writing in the social sciences, visit the following online student writing journals:

UCLA Undergraduate Psychology Journal
(http://www.studentgroups.ucla.edu/upj/)

The Undergraduate Journal of Psychology, UNC Charlotte
(http://www.psych.uncc.edu/Journal.htm)

Undergraduate Journal of Social Sciences, West Point
(http://www.dean.usma.edu/sosh/ujss/)

Undergraduate Research Journal for the Human Sciences
(http://www.kon.org/urc/urc_research_journal.html#)

Review of Key Ideas in Chapter 8

- The writing you're assigned in social science courses will ask you to observe social interactions, collect data to support your claims, conduct interviews and surveys, integrate research and theories from other social scientists, and report the results of your research in genres such as the ethnography, the case study, and the social sciences research report.
- Writing is critical for meaning-making in the social sciences. Writing about the results of their research is the primary way that social scientists communicate new knowledge to other social scientists and to public audiences.
- Social science genres are not just templates for organizing your writing. Social science genres like ethnography are a reflection of social science research methods, and they've evolved as ways for social scientists to communicate effectively and present the results of their research in an organized way.
- Reading assignments in social science courses are challenging and often discuss complex theories of social behavior and institutions, and they will

require active reading strategies such as prereading, rereading, annotating, double-entry journals, and others.

- Research and inquiry in the social sciences involves exploring questions about social interaction, systematically observing and collecting data about social behavior and institutions, and exploring the research of other social scientists.

8.14: Writing to Learn – The Features of Social Science Writing and Researching

Now that we've looked closely at writing in the social sciences, create a bulleted list of the features of social science writing and researching like I did at the beginning of the chapter, but use your own words. If you've already taken or you are currently taking a class in the social sciences, does this list match with your professor's expectations for writing and researching?

---

9 Reading, Writing, and Researching in the Arts and Humanities

Students of the humanities need to write well because their disciplines, whether art history, literature, or languages, exist to promote understanding of the arts and their relations to other human endeavors. That understanding is gained primarily and shared primarily through words.

—Professors David Paxman and Dianna Black, Department of English, Brigham Young University (Paxman and Black, 2003: xi)

We write about art to clarify and to account for our responses to works that interest, excite, or frustrate us. When writing a paper we not only look at what is in front of us, but what is within.

—from *A Guide to Writing about Art*
(University of Iowa Writing Center, 2009)

Why write about a work of art? For these reasons at least: first, because writing about a work of art leads us to read, observe, or listen to it more attentively, to notice characteristics about it we might overlook in a more casual reading, looking, or hearing. Second, because writing about works of art stimulates us to think about them. Putting words on paper provokes thought, gets our mind into gear. Third, we may wish to clarify our *feeling* about a work of art, as well as our *thinking*.

—Professor Robert DiYanni, English Department, Pace University
(DiYanni, 2004: 19)

In some disciplines such as literary criticism, texts not only communicate, they are unabashed celebrations of language. Vivid metaphors, dramatic sentences, and self-conscious phrasing distinguish these works from writing in other disciplines where words are chosen to make language appear to be a transparent medium for expressing ideas.

—Professors Patricia Linton, Robert Madigan, and Susan Johnson, Psychology
Department, University of Alaska, Anchorage
(Linton, Madigan, and Johnson, 1994: 67)

9.1: Writing to Learn – Differences between Writing in the Humanities and the Sciences

Reread the quotes at the beginning of this chapter and write about the differences between writing in the arts and humanities and writing in the social and natural sciences that are reflected in the quotes. Be prepared to discuss what you've written with the class as a whole.

Writing and Critical Thinking in the Arts and Humanities

In Chapter 6, you were presented with an overview of some of the features of reading, writing, and researching in the arts and humanities. Take another look at this overview to refresh your memory of the way writing in the arts and humanities was described:

- Arts and humanities scholars use reading, writing, and researching to explore questions about the meaning and value of human experiences and artistic creations.
- Arts and humanities scholars make arguments and support their arguments by using the application of theories, close readings of texts and other artifacts, and discussions of personal experiences. When arts and humanities scholars make arguments and develop theories, they build on the conversation of academic discourse communities taking place in scholarly journals and books.
- Arts and humanities scholars publish their arguments in a variety of written genres such as reviews, critical analysis papers, interviews, creative writing, and scholarly books.
- Because arts and humanities scholars focus on exploring ideas and arguments rather than conducting systematic experiments, arts and humanities genres tend to be less prescriptive than scientific genres in terms of language and form. Because the theories and arguments expressed by arts and humanities scholars are often personal and subjective, a personal voice and engaging style is often valued in arts and humanities writing.

At most colleges, arts and humanities disciplines include English, theatre, dance, music, art, philosophy, religious studies, classics, women's studies, foreign languages and literatures, communication studies, and journalism.

Writing in a Philosophy Department: Oregon State University

Now that you've reread the overview of writing in the arts and humanities, let's look at a concrete example of writing in the arts and humanities. The Philosophy Department at Oregon State University places a lot of importance on writing – they even created their own writing guide for philosophy students. In this section of Chapter 9, we'll look at excerpts from the Oregon State Philosophy Department's student writing guide, *Welcome to Writing Philosophy Papers: A Student's*

Guide. We'll also look at some writing assignments from two professors in the department, William Uzgalis and David Arnold.

First, let's take a look at the Philosophy Department's student writing guide. It's clear from the guide that writing is very important in philosophy:

> Writing is the principal means of communication among philosophers. If you want to demonstrate your understanding to a professor...if you want to convince someone that your position is the correct one...if you want to relate an abstract idea to your own experience, chances are that you will need to do so in writing. (Oregon State University Department of Philosophy, 1997)

Notice that the guide doesn't focus on using writing only to summarize someone else's ideas, or writing as simply correct grammar and mechanics. The focus of writing in philosophy is communicating to other philosophers and convincing your readers of the value of your argument. The writing guide also talks about the basic thinking and writing skills that students will need in their philosophy classes:

> Basic skills in writing philosophy:
> 1. identifying a philosophical problem;
> 2. organizing ideas;
> 3. defining concepts;
> 4. analyzing arguments;
> 5. comparing and contrasting;
> 6. giving examples;
> 7. applying theory to practice; and,
> 8. testing hypotheses.

The first item on this list is solving a philosophical problem. Here's how the writing guide defines problem-solving in philosophy:

> Philosophy is a problem solving enterprise. Part of what one learns in becoming a philosopher is to find problems and then to use all the skills at one's disposal to solve them. A philosophy paper without a problem is very much like a body without a head, or perhaps a more accurate metaphor would be a body without DNA — that is a body whose organizing principle is missing. So, what is a problem, and particularly a philosophical problem? One answer is that a problem is a question not easily answered. If I ask you "What time is it?" — there is a question which is usually easily answered. You look at your watch and give me the answer. If we start wondering what justice or beauty is, or if we have free will, we may find that these questions are not at all easy to answer. (Oregon State University Department of Philosophy, 1997)

Solving difficult philosophical problems is a focus of one of Professor William

Uzgalis' philosophy courses at Oregon State, PHIL 302: History of Western Philosophy from 1492–1776. In his syllabus, Professor Uzgalis gives students this advice about writing papers in his course:

> Your paper should be organized around a problem, philosophical or interpretative, and some claim you are making and arguing for which is connected to the solution of that problem. What you say should be relevant to and support your claim. When you present your view, consider what might plausibly be said against it and respond to this. When you criticize someone else's view, consider how that person might reply to your objections.

Exploring intellectual problems, making and supporting claims, and considering different points of view are thinking and writing skills that are common in the arts and humanities, not just in philosophy.

Following is an example of one of Professor Uzgalis' writing assignments.

Free Will and Determinism

A problem which is discussed by many philosophers of this period and subsequently is the problem of free will and determinism. The rise of Newtonian science, for example, led to the belief that the natural world is a deterministic system. But the pressures of determinism can clearly be seen as early as Descartes and Hobbes. What about free will then? Descartes, Locke, Hume, Holbach and others have discussions of this issue. Probably it would be best to pick one such author and ask:
(a) Is Holbach's (or Hobbes) system of determinism consistent or plausible?
(b) Is Hume or Kant's solution to the problem of free-will and determinism satisfactory?
(c) How does accepting determinism affect one's views about the problem of evil? Jonathan Edwards or possibly Anthony Collins would be good candidates for research here.
A good short account of determinism by a contemporary hard determinist is Richard Taylor's chapters on hard determinism and fatalism in his book Metaphysics, Prentice Hall. Hume's position can be found in the Inquiry Concerning Human Understanding and Treatise on Human Nature. Leibniz is of particular interest in regard to this question. I would start with the MacDonald's book Leibniz. An American philosopher who was influenced by Locke and others is Jonathan Edwards, a New England Calvinist preacher. A contemporary treatment of this problem is found in Daniel Dennett's book Elbow Room — Dennett is a defender of free will.

In this assignment, Professor Uzgalis is asking students to read some complex works of philosophy. In his syllabus, he warns students that the course readings won't be easy:

> Often encountering a philosophy text for the first time is difficult. You may well know little about the author, the book may be written in a language of a bygone age, the problems unfamiliar. These difficulties beset the first reader of even beautifully written philosophical works.

Many of the readings you're assigned in arts and humanities courses will discuss issues or artists that you're not familiar with. Even when you're reading about issues you are familiar with, or reading a novel or poem you've read before, you'll be challenged to think about these issues and works of art in new ways. Don't be frustrated if you're having trouble understanding what you're reading. As Professor Uzgalis says, even "beautifully written" prose can be challenging when you're being presented with new ideas. The active reading strategies discussed in Chapter 4 can help you with difficult texts like the kind Professor Uzgalis assigns.

Professor David Arnold's goals for his writing assignments in PHIL 160: Quests for Meaning: World Religions are similar to Professor Uzgalis's goals for writing in his assignments. Professor Arnold outlines his teaching philosophy and methods in his syllabus:

> Students will look at the values, history, beliefs, practices, and drawbacks of the world's great religions. The methods will include posted lecture notes, Blackboard discussions, writing, reading of texts, visiting a worship site, engaging in current news events, hopefully listening to believers of different spiritual traditions. The material of this class invites each person to analyze from her or his own experience of encounter with those of other religious traditions. It may surprise you to hear that we shall be as much about the asking of the right questions as about the possibility of satisfactory answers. The heart of the course: to develop an empathy and understanding for religious traditions similar to and different from the student's. Students will need to listen critically, ask questions, evaluate their own thinking and that of others. Films and images from eastern and western traditions will be made available throughout the term (the films are listed on the syllabus below). The course is so designed that the texts will profoundly inform discussion, so read each slowly and well.

Just like Professor Uzgalis, Professor Arnold wants students to ask questions and critically evaluate ideas. In addition to class discussions, writing is a primary way students explore questions and think critically in Professor Arnold's course. One type of writing assignment Professor Arnold assigns is weekly electronic discussion board posts. Here's how Professor Arnold describes the discussion board posts on his syllabus:

> For this class, guiding questions (you'll see them listed each week on the syllabus below) for each week's readings will initiate discussion. All students will commit to thoughtful reflection of the assigned readings, the initial questions, and the issues raised by one another in discussion of the week's material.

Weekly electronic discussion board posts or journal entries in a notebook are common assignments in arts and humanities courses. Like Professor Arnold's discussion board posts, most journals ask you to reflect, explore, and respond. Typically, journal assignments are less formal than more extended assignments such as critical analysis essays or research papers.

In the social sciences, a common assignment is an observation paper, in which you're asked to observe human interaction and analyze it based on social theories. In the arts and humanities, observation papers are also common. Arts and humanities observation essays usually focus less on the way people are interacting and more on evaluating the aesthetic value or deeper meanings of what you're observing. Here's an observation paper assignment from Professor Arnold's philosophy course:

> One Worship site visit, due on Monday of Week 9. If you choose this option, you will write a 2-3 page evaluative paper on the site visited. It will include your observations of the sacred space, the nature of the worship experience (which senses were quickened — was there incense, chanting, silence, stained glass, etc.), and your critical appraisal of the event, in light of our course. That is, how can one understand the ways this worship experience is meaningful for the participants? You will evaluate these observations in three sections, guided by the three divisions of Porterfield's book: "Practice," "Experience," "Community." Zero points will be awarded if this format is not adopted. The goal is to use Porterfield as a "lens" through which one may understand active worship. Typed, double-spaced, 12 point pitch, with your name and the course on the upper left-hand corner of the first page. Attach any image of a bulletin, pamphlet, etc. from the worship event after the last page. (Prior students have even included a photo image of the religious site, but you needn't.)

Notice that Professor Arnold asks students to evaluate and analyze a worship site through the lens of a philosopher, Porterfield. It's common for arts and humanities scholars to analyze a text, event, or work of art by applying another scholar's theory.

The writing assigned in the Philosophy Department at the University of Oregon is representative of the kind of writing and thinking you'll encounter in arts and humanities courses. Now that we've looked at some writing assignments, let's look at some examples of student and professional writing in the arts and humanities.

Examples of Writing in the Arts and Humanities

We'll take a closer look at writing in the arts and humanities by giving a close reading to some examples from arts and humanities texts. The first piece of writing is from a textbook for music courses, *The Cambridge Companion to Blues and Gospel Music*. The second piece of writing is from a biography of the painter Pablo Picasso, *Life of Picasso*, by John Richardson. The third piece of writing is from a student philosophy essay, "Is Language a Requirement for Thought?" by Marissa Curran, a student at Washington University in St. Louis. Marissa's essay was published in *Ex Nihilo*, an undergraduate philosophy journal published by the University of Texas at Austin. In her essay, Marissa analyzes the philosopher Donald Davidson's claim that language is a requirement for thought.

Excerpt from *The Cambridge Companion to Blues and Gospel Music* (Moore, 2003: 2)

It is impossible to date the origin of the blues with any precision, although its roots in the music which West African slaves would have brought with them to the Americas have always been assumed. There are accounts of calls and field hollers back into the nineteenth century. Working individually in the fields in comparative quiet, such calls had practical use (to ease the drudgery of repetitive actions, or to call instructions to animals) but they would also sometimes become communal expressions, as when one field hand picked up the call from another, and so on. These workers were politically segregated. The hopes which had arisen in the wake of the 1875 Civil Rights Act, which gave blacks equal treatment in terms of access to accommodation, places of entertainment, and public transport, were dashed on its repeal in 1883. Segregation became more rigidly enforced to the extent that in 1896 the U.S. Supreme Court validated new segregationist laws (the "Jim Crow" system) enacted in southern legislatures (and which received national government sanction in 1913). These were extreme. The economic depression of the 1880s and 1890s hit African Americans hardest, as they were increasingly barred from any form of economic competition with whites. And, as the blues became identified as a recognizable genre (singers like the stylistically eclectic Henry Thomas and Charley Patton, born in the 1870s and 1880s, are usually cited as among the first "blues" singers), someone like Patton was treated as racially "black" even though he had long, wavy hair and a comparatively light skin. The repertoire of most of these singers extended far wider than just the blues — folksongs, dances, worksongs, even minstrel songs on occasion. The term "blues," however, has attained such currency that it has come to symbolize the entire repertoire.

Many of these early singers were travelers. A disproportionate number were blind or otherwise disabled (music being one of the few sources of income for such individuals), carrying their songs from community to community by railroad, by steamboats, by wagon and even by foot. As travelers, it was vital that their means of earning were portable — hence the widespread adoption of the guitar as an accompanying instrument. (The guitar had played a role in both nascent jazz bands, for example that of Buddy Bolden in the late 1890s, and the early string bands.) Blues thus settled down in the years prior to their first recordings as an acoustic form, in which the singer accompanies him-(or less often her-) self on the guitar, particularly for various social events (dances, picnics etc.). This form has been identified by various names: country blues or rural blues (recognizing its original location) or downhome blues (a term more favored by players themselves). Geographical location is also important: there are recognizable stylistic differences between singers emanating from Texas, from Mississippi, from Alabama or from Georgia.

Excerpt from *A Life of Picasso* by John Richardson (Richardson, 1991: 228–229)

Three successive self-portraits provide insight into the artist's diminishing peace of mind over the seven months he spent in Paris on this trip. Compared with the one painted immediately after his arrival in June, the one painted just before he left at the end of the year demonstrates how rapidly and deeply his view of himself as well as the world had changed. The images are as different as masks of the comic and tragic muse. The first self-portrait…is a brilliantly theatrical — one might say operatic — performance. Suitably enough, it ended up in the collection of Hugo von Hofmannsthal (bought in 1913 with his first royalties from Rosenkavalier). Picasso portrays himself with all the panache of a society painter of the belle époque — elegantly mustachioed and arrogantly assured in his bouffant white smock and vermillion lavalière. As a self-portrait, it is a consummate bravura painting; it is also a masquerade. This is the first time Picasso capitalizes on his amazing eyes: the area of white above and below the pupil is no exaggeration. The charismatic miranda fuerte and the defiant inscription, "Yo Picasso" ("I, Picasso"), dare us to question his right to be the new messiah of art. To bolster the authority of the image, Picasso has had recourse to a great old master, Nicolas Poussin: one to whom he will return more than once in future years. He has glanced back at that artist's self portrait in the Louvre. ("Picasso does not redo Poussin. He is Poussin in 1901."[51]) "Yo Picasso" also looks forward: to fauvism. Years later Picasso boasted that his green shadow anticipated the green stripe down the forehead and nose in Matisse's famous fauve portrait of his wife...

The second of the three self-portrait paintings, done a month or two later, is also self-dramatizing, also inscribed with an empathetic "Yo." But in its black gloom, this baleful, Munch-like image — evidently done by lamplight — is in total contrast to its meretricious predecessor. The expressionistic fervor and intensity is very close to that of the Casagemas death heads, and can be attributed to the same source: van Gogh. Thanks partly to van Gogh, the eager boy wonder of the Vollard show has all of a sudden turned into a visionary old beyond his years, whose burning gaze defies the world with ferocious Nietzchean authority.

Excerpt from "Is Language a Requirement for Thought?" by Marissa Curran, a Student at Washington University in St. Louis (Curran, 2006: 99–100)

Davidson says that "neither language nor thinking can be fully explained in terms of the other."[21] I want to disagree, and will go on now to argue that thought can be explained without a dependence on language (or, more precisely, without dependence on a complex language like ours). The study of autism provides evidence in support of my claim, since it is widely believed that autistic persons think in terms of pictures. The speech function is the exact function that is either impaired or entirely lacking in autistic children and adults.[22] Is Davidson willing to argue that they cannot think? He is forced to either argue this or risk inconsistency in his position, neither of which is an attractive option. I claim that the thoughts of those who suffer from autism simply do not come to them in the form of words and phrases, but in pictures, feelings and sensations. Let's turn to those who are able to shed light on autistic and animal minds.

Temple Grandin, a leading figure in the on-going study of autism and the mental capabilities of animals, believes that philosophers like Davidson who maintain that language is necessary for thought are "totally ridiculous."[23] Grandin is herself autistic, and has worked with dogs, cats, and horses for many years. She suggests that there are multiple similarities between people with her disease and these higher animals. She says neither autistic people nor animals think in language, and gives an example of the way her own mind works: "If you said to me 'teakettle,' pictures of teakettles would start coming into my head...animals also think in smells and sounds. They can think in touches. It's sensory-based thinking rather than language based. They can take smell pictures and sound pictures and associate them together into categories to form...concepts."[24]

9.2: Writing to Learn – Features of Writing in the Arts and Humanities

The purpose of this Writing to Learn activity is to look closely at the previous passages and think about important features of writing in the arts and humanities. Reread the three examples of arts and humanities writing, and then individually or in small groups come up with a list of features of arts and humanities writing based on what you've read. For each feature, include a specific example or two from the texts. For example, if you find that one aspect of writing in the arts and humanities is complex sentence constructions, find examples of complex sentences. Be prepared to talk about these features of writing in the arts and humanities as a class.

Exploring Genre in the Arts and Humanities: The Performance Review

You'll encounter a wide variety of genres in your arts and humanities courses. Some genres, such as reading response journals and critical essays, will ask you to closely read a text (or performance or a work of art) and analyze, evaluate, and respond to the text. Other genres, such as summaries and annotated bibliographies, will ask you to concisely state the main ideas of a text. There are many arts and humanities genres that ask you to both summarize and evaluate a scholarly text, performance, or work of art. You're probably already familiar with the genre of the review and subgenres of the review such as the book review, the film review, the concert review, and the theatre review.

In this section of Chapter 9, we'll take a close look at the genre of the performance review. You're already familiar with many types of performance reviews, like movie reviews in your local newspaper or reviews of concerts in magazines such as *Rolling Stone* or *Vibe*. The genre of the performance review asks a writer to use thinking skills that are common in many arts and humanities genres: close reading (in this case *reading* a performance), summarizing main ideas (or the plot, in the case of performance of a play), giving a personal response and evaluation, and supporting your judgments with evidence and well-developed points. Arts and humanities writers review performances in order to give audiences of other scholars as well as the general public an evaluation of a performance. For example, a theatre critic reviewing a play for the *New Yorker* magazine wants to give readers of the *New Yorker* a sense of what the play is about and who the characters are; to evaluate the strengths and weaknesses of the script, the acting, and the production; and to help readers decide if they should go to see the play. The same theatre critic reviewing the same play for the academic journal, *Theatre Journal*, might evaluate the production and the acting in the context of how they connect to or expand on a specific tradition or philosophy of theatre and acting. This same writer publishing in *Theatre Journal* may be less interested in whether or not readers should see the play and more interested in analyzing the play and the performance for the benefit of other theatre scholars. The length of the performance review, the persona the writer of the review takes on, and the structure of the review will depend on the rhetorical situation: the purpose and audience. Usually, when arts and humanities professors assign performance reviews, they want you to experience a performance, show that you've understood it, and then show that you have the tools to evaluate the performance and make educated judgments. Making *educated* judgments might mean referring to aspects of performance discussed in class, presented in lectures by the professor, or mentioned in the readings for the course. Let's take a look at some performance review assignments from arts and humanities courses.

Examples of Performance Review Assignments

Theatre Review Assignment from Professor Steve Gilliam, Trinity University

You are to submit a two page theatre review for either one of the two Trinity productions for this semester. For form and style, we invite you to read reviews from any large city newspaper. The New York Times is probably best known for its theatre reviews. However, LA, Chicago, Seattle, etc., all have newspapers which cover the arts and theatre in specific. You will note by reading these articles that they are organized in similar ways. Part of your assignment is to discover the art of writing a theatre review. Out of town newspapers are available in the Library in the Periodical Section or over the internet.

You will note that a theatre review is not a summary of the story, or plot of the play. It is not a paper discussing the meaning of the play (although some of this may be useful). Rather, a review discusses the production. Your review must comment on the performances (not every cast member) as the newspaper articles demonstrate. Also, you are to comment on at least two production elements (scenery, costumes, sound, lights). You may attend dress rehearsals and the previews if you would like to have a better understanding of the show. Regardless, you are to react to one of the public performances. You should state which show you attended in the review as every performance is different.

Film Review Assignment from Professor Jyotsna Kapur, Southern Illinois University, Carbondale

Write a 3–4 page film review/critique of <u>Syriana</u> (Stephen Gaghan, 2005) in which you comment on and evaluate the film and discuss its relevance to our historical moment. Discuss if you found the film powerful and worth seeing and give reasons for your judgment. Do not plagiarize, be generous and give credit to others. Writing pointers:

- Clearly indicate your judgment of the film's quality. However, avoid an opinionated thumbs up/thumbs down approach that uses a film's "entertainment" value as the only criterion. Be aware of personal preferences and point them out. Use the vocabulary you have learnt in this class to write a critical review that shows knowledge of film history and form. A good critic raises the level of media culture — winning audiences for complex and innovative work.
- Brief plot synopsis — characters and conflicts. Don't give away the ending. Follow first time mention of character names with names of the actors in parentheses.
- Mention striking aspects of the film's formal devices — editing, sound, mise-en-scene, cinematography, narration. Acting is often an important criterion.
- Compare the film with others — same director, same theme, contemporary films.
- Brevity: vivid descriptions followed by opinions stated briefly and precisely. Pauline Kael: "Literal-minded in its sex and brutality, Teutonic in its humor, Stanley Kubrick's *A Clockwork Orange* might be the work of a strict and exacting German professor who set out to make a porno-violent sci-fi Comedy."

Dance Review Assignment from Professor Artemis Preeshl, Loyola University New Orleans

Attend a live dance concert and write a review. Address each question specifically. Your observations should reflect how the performance affected you. Subordinate your opinions and judgments to your observations of actual events on stage. A good dance review evokes a visual image of the concert. The reader should feel as if he or she viewed the performance. It is paramount that you vividly describe the movements. Discuss how the dancers moved and the dynamics with which the movements were performed. Use everyday language as if writing for a newspaper. Answer the following questions:

- Title of the dance(s), the choreographer(s). Highlight the exceptional performers including their roles and names. Describe how they moved and why it was special.
- What was the theme or concept that unified the choreography? Identify any aspect of the performance that detracted from the theme or concept.
- How well did the dancers control their technique? Were their movements fluid, efficient and dynamic?
- Which styles of dance were presented? Describe how the dancers' movements influenced the style of the dance(s).
- How did the dynamic elements of time, space and energy contrast or cohere within the dance(s)? Were the architectural lines of the dancers' bodies well-defined? Was the spatial intent of the choreographer clear?
- As an ensemble, how well did the dancers work together to embody the concept or theme of the piece(s)?
- Did the dancers' performance and the choreography compliment and accent the music?
- Discuss the impact of the cultural aspects of the dance(s) including costumes, music and style of movement.
- How did the production elements (lighting and costume, set and sound) enhance or detract from the mood or tone of the piece(s)?
- Which images resonate or stand out? How did the images evoke emotions such as disturbance or humor?
- Support your ideas by describing actions, movement, designs in space and relationships.

9.3: Writing to Learn – The Genre of the Performance Review

The purpose of this Writing to Learn activity is to help you understand the genre of the performance review by looking closely at the three review assignments above and then discussing them in small groups and as a class. First, reread the three performance review assignments. As you read, think about the features of the genre of the performance review and underline any key sentences in the assignments that illustrate these features. Think about aspects of genre such as purpose, audience, conventions, and persona. Discuss these features of the performance review in small groups and come up with a list of ten important features of performance reviews. Be prepared to discuss what you've found as a whole class.

Sample Film Review

Now that you've looked at some performance review assignments, let's take a close look at an example of a published review. Below is a film review of Quentin Tarantino's *Pulp Fiction* from *Cineaste*, a quarterly magazine of the art and politics of films. According to *Cineaste's* Writer's Guidelines, their target audience is "sophisticated about art and politics."

Pulp Friction: Two Shots at Quentin Tarantino's *Pulp Fiction*
By Pat Dowell and John Fried (Dowell and Fried, 1995: 4–5)

Quentin Tarantino, the genius of the moment embraced by so many who would never vote Republican, is the hip version of the angry white guy who does. Tarantino's manifestation of the phenomenon is not so crude, except facetiously so, but there is a reflexive form of machismo evident in the two films he has directed, Reservoir Dogs and Pulp Fiction. In both, of course, the prime tool is a gun, and the standard operating procedure is force. Both films are widely admired as the ultimate tough-guy movies, unflinching in their portrayal of graphic violence — but with a sense of humor and pop-culture erudition. And both are instances of the pop culture trend of the decade — they are hermetically sealed and running for cover from any kind of contact with the real world. It is a trend best exemplified by Forrest Gump, the desperately optimistic version of the formula; Reservoir Dogs and Pulp Fiction are the most artful examples yet of the obverse, cynical form of the phenomenon.

Tarantino's stylish presentation of violence has been the predictable subject of greatest controversy in the mainstream press. He unabashedly loves the stuff, and presents himself in an off-screen image that might be termed geek macho, a blend of seen-it-all posturing and avid fanzine enthusiasm. He reportedly carries the wallet Jules flashes in Pulp Fiction — the one emblazoned with the words "bad mother-fucker" — which he has shown to reporters. Yet he conspicuously indulges in a nerdy obsession, collecting memorabilia from old television series. The men in his movies are a teenaged video clerk's fantasy of cool dudes, just as another generation of American men — a generation often termed "quiet" and noted for its penchant for gray flannel — found an adolescent fantasy of guns and sex in tough guy Mike Hammer. Mickey Spillane's detective was the hero of the American movie that seems to be the most thoroughgoing inspiration for Pulp Fiction: the sublime Kiss Me Deadly, directed by Robert Aldrich in 1955. From this movie comes Pulp Fiction's McGuffin, the mysterious briefcase (whose contents are a subject for so much speculation in the Tarantino areas of the Internet). The shot of Vincent and the others opening the briefcase, its unseen contents lighting each curious, awestruck face, is a direct quote from Aldrich's Cold-War film noir, which was a stylish vortex around a "box with atomic power."

Such references make it clear that Tarantino is a professional as well as an amateur collector. His movies are the perfect post-modern phenomenon, a pastiche. So much so, that <u>Film Threat</u> magazine has accused him of stealing <u>Reservoir Dogs</u> from a Hong Kong director, practically shot for shot. Certainly there are similarities enough for Tarantino to acknowledge his homage to Pingo Lam's <u>City on Fire</u>, but he is, rightly I think, oblivious to charges of plagiarism as mostly irrelevant. Jean-Luc Godard, whom Tarantino admires enough to name his production company A Band Apart (Anglicizing a 1964 Godard title, <u>Bande a part</u>), is also a quoter, for instance. Godard is further alluded to in <u>Pulp Fiction</u> in the look Tarantino gives Uma Thurman, who is coiffed and made up to resemble Godard's erstwhile star and lover, Anna Karina.

But Godard borrowed with a difference — to comment, to satirize, to discredit, to examine, to open other possibilities. Tarantino borrows to create cultural culdesacs, places of intellectual safety and anesthesia. And his thrust is basically conservative — he is first and foremost an ingenious curator displaying his collection of cultural trivia. The published screenplay of <u>Pulp Fiction</u> often provides directions in terms of other movies (for the first scene, according to the published screenplay, the lines are to be said "in rapid-pace <u>His Girl Friday</u> fashion"), and he is taking American movies back to basics just as surely as the Republicans are returning the nation to the values of the decade in which <u>Kiss Me Deadly</u> was produced.

For all its interrupted storylines and O. Henry surprises, <u>Pulp Fiction</u> is self-consciously conventional in content, just as Tarantino is a proud partaker of the mass-media fiction world of the pulp magazines, a genre of strict narrative conventions. The boxer whose honor won't permit him to throw the fight, the gangster's moll with a wandering eye, the camaraderie of professional killers — these are all subjects so hoary as to be clichés.

In using them as a starting point, <u>Pulp Fiction</u> rejuvenates the fundamentals of American moviemaking, the kiss-kiss bang-bang first principles (with an emphasis on the "masculine" side, the bang-bang), by pumping the old storylines up with an intricate web of quotations from the communal media world of television, movies, and, in perhaps Tarantino's most significant addition, the universal experience of being a consumer. One of the most famous exchanges in the movie is the conversation between Jules and Vincent about McDonalds in Paris. "Royale with Cheese" has made it into the language far enough to become an allusion in other media; I recently heard a television newscaster use it in a story about foreign food, without attribution to the movie, simply as a commonly understood joke. Similarly, in <u>Reservoir Dogs</u>, one of the script's earliest dialog set-pieces is a jokey round-robin on the eternal consumer problem of tipping. Tarantino is definitely distinctive as a writer in his attention to the quotidian details of commerce.

Yet only in this most superficial way does <u>Pulp Fiction</u> traffic with everyday reality. In general the tone of Tarantino's work is a rejection of anything resembling the "real" world. Sure, there are scenes in coffee shops "like Denny's," as the script denotes, and in old cars and suburban tract homes, but the movie exists only in the terms of other movies, and is not, as collagists like Godard might construct, an undermining of those terms. In fact, the perfection of its escapism places it squarely in the most traditional and the most contemporary wave of Hollywood movie-making. In that respect, the two most talked-about movies of 1994, Forrest Gump and Pulp Fiction, are not so different as advertised. Their narrative structures certainly diverge, but their sensibilities are the two sides of a single coin.

Just as much as Forrest Gump, Pulp Fiction rejects the notion of engagement with the reality available to most Americans. Forrest succeeds because he's too dumb to take it seriously, while Pulp Fiction's various protagonists succeed and fail on a relatively random basis that has little to do with their actions. Most of what they do doesn't make a difference in their destinies (since life is like a box of chocolates). A pothole or a trip to the bathroom at the wrong moment means life or death (more than once for Vincent Vega), or a kid's bad aim with a handgun becomes a miracle for Jules. So many movies now are daydreams about people surviving or succeeding because they don't connect with the world around them — the sitcom refugees of The Brady Bunch, the low-watt Forrest Gump, the insulated Nell. Pulp Fiction is a more sophisticated rendering of the spirit of helplessness and resignation that animates those films to imagine a solution. The answer Tarantino offers is to stop worrying and learn to love it. Let the new Stanley Kramers (as Tarantino has called Oliver Stone) worry about the meaning and effect of it all.

The I-don't-care sensibility (precisely anticipated as the coming zeitgeist twenty years ago by Robert Altman's Nashville, which ended with a chorus of "It don't bother me") is another aspect of the post-modern sensibility. Pulp Fiction wears this mantle very effectively, projecting a stance of having passed beyond tacky social problems like racism. Race is the least discussed aspect of this movie, despite the fact that Tarantino draws his allusions not only from his favorite white and Asian filmmakers but also from the black action heroes of the Seventies, from whom Jules gets his hairstyle. Pulp Fiction fancies itself postracist, and in it Affirmative Action is officially superannuated, as marked by the salt-and-pepper casting of the two lead enforcers, Vincent and Jules, who work for a black man. Note also the sub-liminal casting of a black woman as the bossy wife that Jimmie, played by Tarantino himself, fears will return home angry to find "a dead nigger" splattered all over her well-kept house.

Several writers (J. Hoberman first, I think) have noted already that Tarantino has given himself a role in which he gets to throw the word "nigger" around, and, I might add, "dead nigger" at that. Strangely racist as that may seem, this personal appropriation for the director represents, I think, the wannabe posturing of a hip white guy, an insiderish declaration of swaggering brotherhood that certainly throws a different light on the rape of Marsellus, the "blackest" and "baddest" of the movie's black men. Tarantino deals out fear and punishment to black men simultaneously in constructing the figure of Marsellus, who threw a man out a window for massaging his (white) wife's feet, and who is himself subjected to the most humiliating of sexual attentions, rape (by a white racist), only to be rescued by the (white) man he was trying to kill.

There is in Pulp Fiction not only the spectacle of racism, in that incident in which neo-Nazi sadists display their obsession and are killed, but also a kind of post-civil-rights bravado as well, I think — the same kind of attitude manifesting itself in discussions in Newt's Congress, where eager young turks of the Republican Party proclaim that Affirmative Action is no longer needed as a remedy for "past" injustices. The assumption is that America has learned the lesson of civil rights. This is essentially an evolutionary adaptation of white racism, going undercover socially and psychologically in the name of free enterprise and a perverted notion of equal opportunity, and it manifested itself in the way the distributors of Pulp Fiction dealt with the expected Oscar nominations for the film's cast.

Miramax expected that the members of the Academy of Motion Picture Arts and Sciences would be confused about who belonged in what category. So the distributor sent a helpful letter to AMPAS members explaining that John Travolta was an actor in a leading role and Samuel L. Jackson was an actor in a supporting role. The understandable confusion would result from the fact that the two play partners, each with big solo scenes and with comparable screen time. Miramax clarified the situation by explaining that Travolta's Vincent appeared in more episodes and wove the stories together. The distributor's motive was to promote one of the actors out of the supporting category so that either might have a chance at winning something, instead of canceling each other out. But clearly the white guy has a better chance at a leading-role prize and the black guy at supporting role, it goes without saying, since that's the way America still assigns the relative importance of the races. Racial politics played a subtle role in this little off-screen vignette, providing an ironic contradiction to the assumptions on which the movie's displays of racial interaction are based.

The movie's attitudes toward gender follow a similar pattern of displaying stereotypes under the guise of postfeminist sensibility, with the added innovation of Tarantino's gift for sharp dialog and quotidian allusions. Tarantino makes movies a pleasure to listen to again, even though his characters don't have anything to say. The dialog has the sound of an improvisation — actors bullshitting — but the staging and editing are classic genre stuff, with forced perspective, sensational angles, and dramatic use of shadow and color.

The structure of Pulp Fiction is not so new as it looks. It should be familiar to any television watcher, for it is our psychological accommodations to TV's dramatic shape that Tarantino exploits for his narrative surprises. Every day Americans are quite at home with stories that come to a rest, divided into segments to be interrupted by other stories and then resume. The interruptions are called commercials and increasingly they are commercials for other stories both on television and in the movies. Channel surfing also segments the stories we watch. In Pulp Fiction Tarantino starts episodes and lets them come to what feel like commercial breaks. The setup scene of Honeybunny and Pumpkin in the coffee shop planning their robbery is exactly like the tease that opens most television shows before the first commercial; audiences don't expect it in a movie and so don't frame it as such, but, after surfing in and out of other episodes, Tarantino eventually returns to it.

Pulp Fiction not only incorporates the structure of watching television (and does so brilliantly) but it reproduces the everyday experience of living in a fragmented society, in which each of us must stitch together a coherent narrative out of the bombardment of information and drama that is our daily passage through a market culture.

Quentin Tarantino is not the first poet of the consumer age, but he may be the first who has given himself so completely to it. Nothing but the ephemeral products of the marketplace seems to inspire him, and he seems only to exist in the shards he has collected for his private amusement. At the heart of his films is the exhilaration of watching a gifted fetishist arrange the useless objects of his obsession; it's like looking into the abyss and longing to fall into the restful emptiness. He is the distillation of Hollywood's eternal pledge that "It's only a movie," and a fitting hero for the centennial of commercial cinema.

9.4: Writing to Learn – Applying Genre Knowledge

The purpose of this Writing to Learn activity is to apply some of what you've been learning about the genre of the performance review to the film review of *Pulp Fiction*. Reread the review of *Pulp Fiction* and answer the five questions below:

1. How much of the review is summary of the plot of the movie?
2. What aspects of the film does the reviewer evaluate?
3. What connections and comparisons does the reviewer make between *Pulp Fiction* and other films?
4. How would you describe the persona the reviewer takes on? How does the purpose and audience of the review affect the persona of the reviewer?

9.5: Learn by Doing – Writing a Movie Review

The purpose of this Learn by Doing activity is to practice writing in the genre of the performance review. Choose a movie you've seen recently and write a 1–2 page review of the movie. Consider your peers in your course as the primary audience – as you evaluate the movie, think about whether or not you would recommend that your classmates go to see it. As you write the movie review, think about the features of the genre of the performance review that we've been discussing in this chapter. Your professor might ask you to share the review in small groups or make copies for other class members.

9.6: Writing to Learn – Reflecting on Your Reading Processes

The purpose of this Writing to Learn is for you to reflect on your reading processes with a text from the arts and humanities. Think back to the last time you were asked to read a story, novel, poem, or play for a course (high school or college). Write about how your process for reading a work of fiction differs from your process for reading a nonfiction book. Do your reading processes for novels and stories differ when you read them by choice, as opposed to reading a novel or story for a school assignment?

Reading in the Arts and Humanities

When I was an undergraduate at the University of Florida, I read very different kinds of texts for each arts and humanities course I took. In my sophomore year, I read novels for my American literature course, attended performances of plays for my theatre course, read (and reread multiple times) difficult and dense essays about the philosophy of science in an introduction to philosophy course, and analyzed paintings in an art survey course. Even though I probably didn't realize it at the time, I was using different reading strategies for each type of text I read. When I read novels, I concentrated on the writer's voice and style, the way the plot developed, and how the writer described characters, and I underlined places in the text where I noticed important plot points or character descriptions. When I analyzed paintings, I kept a notebook and did some freewriting about what I saw in the paintings and how I reacted to them. When I read the philosophy essays, I struggled just to understand the main arguments each philosopher was making, so

I created a basic outline of the main arguments of each of the essays we read. At the time, I didn't know that professors had a word for what I was doing when I was outlining the philosophy essays: I was creating a "text map." In Chapter 4, we discussed text maps and I gave you an example of a text map. If I was asked to write a summary of a difficult reading, one strategy would be to write a text map. Read the excerpt below from the essay, "Self-Reliance," by Ralph Waldo Emerson. If a philosophy or literature professor asked me to summarize the essay, I might create a text map like the one that follows the essay.

Excerpt from "Self-Reliance" by Ralph Waldo Emerson (Emerson, 1841)

These are the voices which we hear in solitude, but they grow faint and inaudible as we enter into the world. Society everywhere is in conspiracy against the manhood of every one of its members. Society is a joint-stock company, in which the members agree, for the better securing of his bread to each shareholder, to surrender the liberty and culture of the eater. The virtue in most requests is conformity. Self-reliance is its aversion. It loves not realities and creators, but names and customs.

Whoso would be a man, must be a nonconformist. He who would gather immortal palms must not be hindered by the name of goodness, but must explore if it be goodness. Nothing is at last sacred but the integrity of your own mind. Absolve you to yourself, and you shall have the suffrage of the world. I remember an answer which when quite young I was prompted to make to a valued adviser who was wont to importune me with the dear old doctrines of the church. On my saying, "What have I to do with the sacredness of traditions, if I live wholly from within?" my friend suggested, — "But these impulses may be from below, not from above." I replied, "They do not seem to me to be such; but if I am the Devil's child, I will live then from the Devil." No law can be sacred to me but that of my nature. Good and bad are but names very readily transferable to that or this; the only right is what is after my constitution; the only wrong what is against it. A man is to carry himself in the presence of all opposition as if every thing were titular and ephemeral but he. I am ashamed to think how easily we capitulate to badges and names, to large societies and dead institutions. Every decent and well-spoken individual affects and sways me more than is right. I ought to go upright and vital, and speak the rude truth in all ways. If malice and vanity wear the coat of philanthropy, shall that pass? If an angry bigot assumes this bountiful cause of Abolition, and comes to me with his last news from Barbadoes, why should I not say to him, "Go love thy infant; love thy wood-chopper; be good-natured and modest; have that grace; and never varnish your hard, uncharitable ambition with this incredible tenderness for black folk a thousand miles off. Thy love afar is spite at home." Rough and graceless would be such greeting, but truth is handsomer than the affectation of love.

Your goodness must have some edge to it, — else it is none. The doctrine of hatred must be preached, as the counteraction of the doctrine of love, when that pules and whines. I shun father and mother and wife and brother when my genius calls me. I would write on the lintels of the door-post, <u>Whim</u>. I hope it is somewhat better than whim at last, but we cannot spend the day in explanation. Expect me not to show cause why I seek or why I exclude company. Then again, do not tell me, as a good man did to-day, of my obligation to put all poor men in good situations. Are they my poor? I tell thee thou foolish philanthropist that I grudge the dollar, the dime, the cent, I give to such men as do not belong to me and to whom I do not belong. There is a class of persons to whom by all spiritual affinity I am bought and sold; for them I will go to prison if need be; but your miscellaneous popular charities; the education at college of fools; the building of meeting-houses to the vain end to which many now stand; alms to sots, and the thousand-fold Relief Societies; — though I confess with shame I sometimes succumb and give the dollar, it is a wicked dollar which by and by I shall have the manhood to withhold.

Virtues are, in the popular estimate, rather the exception than the rule. There is the man and his virtues. Men do what is called a good action, as some piece of courage or charity, much as they would pay a fine in expiation of daily non-appearance on parade. Their works are done as an apology or extenuation of their living in the world, — as invalids and the insane pay a high board. Their virtues are penances. I do not wish to expiate, but to live. My life is for itself and not for a spectacle. I much prefer that it should be of a lower strain, so it be genuine and equal, than that it should be glittering and unsteady. I wish it to be sound and sweet, and not to need diet and bleeding. I ask primary evidence that you are a man, and refuse this appeal from the man to his actions. I know that for myself it makes no difference whether I do or forbear those actions which are reckoned excellent. I cannot consent to pay for a privilege where I have intrinsic right. Few and mean as my gifts may be, I actually am, and do not need for my own assurance or the assurance of my fellows any secondary testimony.

What I must do is all that concerns me, not what the people think. This rule, equally arduous in actual and in intellectual life, may serve for the whole distinction between greatness and meanness. It is the harder because you will always find those who think they know what is your duty better than you know it. It is easy in the world to live after the world's opinion; it is easy in solitude to live after our own; but the great man is he who in the midst of the crowd keeps with perfect sweetness the independence of solitude.

If I needed to summarize the main ideas of this excerpt, I might create a text map of each paragraph:

Paragraph 1:
People in society surrender liberty and culture.
Society wants people to conform.
Society is against self-reliance.

Paragraph 2:
Being a real person = being a nonconformist.
Your own nature and integrity is more sacred than religious traditions.
What's "good" and "right" is what's right for you.

Paragraph 3:
Don't give in to society's demands out of penance.
Act in a genuine way and don't look for the assurances of other people to
decide how you act.

Paragraph 4:
Don't worry about what other people think of you.
Don't live by how other people tell you to live.

When I began to read the Emerson excerpt, the first thing I did was try to remember my previous experiences reading Emerson's essays. I remembered reading a few of his essays in high school, and I remember that I thought his ideas were interesting but that I had a difficult time understanding him at times because his sentences were long and complex. So when I began reading this excerpt from "Self-Reliance," I was ready for some long and complex sentences that I would need to reread. As I began reading, I realized that Emerson's style reminded me of a preacher. He would focus on a theme and then repeat his point in different ways. So rather than trying to find a central idea in each sentence, I began to focus on the first time Emerson introduced an idea, and not worry about all of the different ways he restates his main points. In my text map, I tried to put Emerson's main ideas in my own words so I could understand them better. When it was time to write my summary, I might go back and find a few lines from the essay to include in my summary to capture the tone of Emerson's argument. As I read I was tempted to respond to Emerson. I started to question whether or not it was really a good idea to always be a nonconformist, and whether it was true that what was right for an individual was always the right thing to do. But since I knew I was going to have to write a summary of Emerson's essay and not a response, I didn't include any of my responses in my text map.

9.7: Learn by Doing – Reading Arts and Humanities Texts

The purpose of this Learn by Doing activity is to practice reading an arts and humanities text and using one of the active reading strategies we discussed in Chapter 4 – the text map. You'll practice creating a text map for the excerpt that follows from the film textbook, *The Art of Watching Films*. As you read the excerpt, create a text map by jotting down the main ideas and central arguments in your own words. Once you've completed your text map, form small groups and share your text map with your peers. Be prepared to discuss with the class as a whole what your group saw as the main ideas and arguments, and whether or not your group disagreed about which ideas and arguments were most important.

Excerpt from *The Art of Watching Films* by Joseph Boggs and Dennis Petrie (Boggs and Petrie, 1999: 483–484)

No art form exists in a vacuum. The more popular an art is, and the wider its appeal to all segments of the population, the more closely it is tied to the social values, mores, and institutions of its audience. As both an extremely popular medium and an industry involving great financial risk and profit potential, the American film naturally must be responsive to social and economic pressures.

So film is not an independent entity but an integrated part of the social fabric, for its very survival depends on maintaining and continuing its popularity. To achieve real popularity, a movie must, first, be believable. Its actions must take place in an environment that has credibility, and its story must reflect the common truths of the society in which it is made. This is not to say that a film must reflect reality as the way things actually are within the society. The truth it portrays may mirror people's hopes, dreams, fears, and inner needs. When real life does not fulfill these needs, people are primed to respond sympathetically to an artistic expression of them in film.

Film does not create <u>new</u> truths for society. It cannot reshape a society that is not ready for change. But this fact does not mean that film is not a powerful instrument for social change. The motion picture's power as a social force comes from its ability to pick up, amplify, and spread to society as a whole currents that already exist among segments of the population. Film also speeds popular acceptance of social change. The dramatically powerful presentation of new ways of thinking and behaving on screens twenty feet high in thousands of movie theatres across the country gives those new ways a significant seal of approval.

It is because of film's potential for legitimizing new standards of behavior — and for inspiring imitation of that behavior, especially by young members of its audience — that most systems of censorship or control have originated. In fact, the way systems of censorship develop usually follows a pattern that goes something like this. A traumatic event disrupts the stability of the social structure (some past examples: World War I, the Depression, World War II, the Vietnam War, the women's movement, the sexual revolution, the drug revolution, the civil rights movement). This event causes a significant shift in moral values and codes of behavior within certain segments of the population. Such changes create pressure for the entertainment media to reflect the truth of the new attitudes and standards of behavior. But a conservative element within the society vigorously resists the changes and demands that films be controlled or censored to prevent the spread of shocking behavior and ensure that movies reflect the truths of society as the conservative element believes they <u>should be</u>. Most censorship within the film industry reflects an uneasy compromise between advocates of change and supporters of the status quo.

Researching in the Arts and Humanities

The research paper gives you the opportunity to think seriously about some issue or question of interest to you in relation to the texts of the course. It is a quest for knowledge through your own thought as well as through consulting the work of others.

—University of Kansas Humanities Writing Guide
(Humanities and Western Civilization Program, 2010)

Research should be done with an open and discriminating mind. A good writer is willing to be redirected down new paths and, if necessary, to change a position.

—Professor Timothy Corrigan, English Department, University of
Pennsylvania (Corrigan, 2004: 129)

As the idea of discourse communities must make clear, writing is one important part of a conversation about ideas that matter in a field. Research papers are one way teachers ask you to join that conversation; you are expected to read pub-lished scholars and then build from their ideas and arguments to develop and define your own.

—Professors Mashey Bernstein and George Yatchisin, Writing Program and
Education Graduate School, University of California, Santa Barbara
(Bernstein and Yatchisin, 2001: 21)

9.8: Writing to Learn – Your Experiences with Arts and Humanities Research

The purpose of this Writing to Learn activity is to start you thinking about your own experiences researching in arts and humanities courses before you read more about research in this next section. Think back to a research paper you've written for a course in the arts and humanities (high school or college) and write about your research process, what kinds of primary and secondary sources you used, the types of thinking skills required (arguing, summarizing, evaluating, etc.), and the persona you took on in your paper.

The Nature of Inquiry and Research in the Arts and Humanities

One way to gain a concrete idea of what inquiry and research means in the arts and humanities is to analyze some actual research paper assignments from arts and humanities courses. The three research paper assignments below are all from college arts and humanities courses. As you read them, think about the way each professor defines research and inquiry in the assignments.

Research Paper Assignment from Professor Phillip Jenkins, a Religious Studies Professor at Pennsylvania State University

I offer one OPTIONAL suggestion for the research paper in this class. I want you to go to the Palmer Museum of Art and choose either one or two art objects, which might be paintings, sculptures, coins, masks, and so on. The only restriction is that the object must be religious in nature, or have a religious theme (or what you can convince me is a religious theme). There is a huge range of potential choices here, including Hindu, African and Chinese items, as well as Jewish and Christian. Just to take one example, the rooms containing European art of the sixteenth through the eighteenth centuries have a lot that might be of interest (One tip: choose something complex or detailed enough to give you enough to write on, i.e. don't choose just a coin portraying a Star of David, or a simple crucifix.)

I am placing no restrictions on the objects that can be used, but would strongly encourage you to explore the Asian and African items in addition to the more familiar Judeo-Christian areas. You must tell me the object you have chosen before writing the paper, and I must approve your choice. There is no reason why two or more people should not choose the same item. Cooperate by all means, but remember that this is not meant to be a collaborative project, and people will be marked on their own individual work.

I then want you to write a paper on the object(s) based on the following questions. Some may be more or less appropriate in any given case, but your paper should at least touch on ALL the following:

1. Describe the object. Who made it, when and where, and how do we know?
2. What is its religious content? With what religious tradition is the object associated? Explain the object to someone who has no idea whatever of the religion in question. How far is it possible to understand the object without a knowledge of the religious context?
3. Did the object serve a religious function? If so, what? Was the object worshiped in its own right; was it meant to assist in meditation; did it have a ceremonial use; or what. Briefly, what was (is) its function? Do the ideas belong more to "high" or popular religious culture? Who paid for the object and why?
4. Does the object tell a story, and if so, what? Can we identify the source of the story in some text or sacred writing? How does the object treat the original source?
5. In this course, we will be discussing a lot of religious themes and ideas (eg sacrifice, pilgrimage, sanctity) as well as religious dimensions of issues like violence and sexuality. Which, if any, of these are relevant to understanding the object in question? How far are the ideas present here common to other religious traditions, or are they peculiar to the source in question?
6. How does the artist explore and/or build upon distinctly religious ideas? How does the artistic treatment support or detract from the religious content? Does the artistic treatment draw on secular traditions (that might be a tough question, but see if you can find out)?
7. What do you think about the ethical or religious dilemmas involved in keeping a holy object in a museum and displaying it like this? Is this a troubling situation? Would it trouble a person who belonged to the religious faith in question?

8. IF you choose two objects, compare and contrast their religious meanings. If you pursue this course, the different objects must derive from two different religious traditions.

Research Essay Assignment from Professor Holly Hassel, a Women's Studies Professor at the University of Wisconsin

Drawing upon your choice of **three selections** from <u>Women: Images and Realities</u> from the introduction, or any in part 1 (p. 8–40), and **two outside sources** (books or articles, <u>not</u> internet sites), you should write a short essay of 3–4 pages that answers the question "What is women's studies?" This essay should take the form of an argumentative synthesis in which you make connections between your five texts to arrive at a definition of the field that is satisfying to you. Your essay should provide a brief summary of each document upon which you rely, a discussion of the connections, comparisons, commonalities, and contrasts between the perspectives, and take your own position within a clear, well-written thesis statement.

Your essay may want to consider several ideas and terms:

Patriarchy	**Sexism**	**Gender studies**	**Feminism**	**Women's movement**
Liberation	**Oppression**	**Sex**	**Gender**	**Canon**

And many others! But these are some to get you started thinking.

Before getting started with your writing, you should review the online readings about evaluating sources and locating credible research. If you have trouble, contact me or the lurking librarian, so we can direct you to appropriate sources, search databases, and resources.

The paper should be, typed or word-processed, double-spaced, with one-inch margins. Use 10 or 12 point Times New Roman or Arial font. Be sure to use correct MLA documentation style including a works cited page.

Evaluation: This paper will be evaluated on several criteria:

- **Clear thesis statement:** the paper has a main point indicating the writer's rhetorical stance on the topic.
- **Coherence:** how well do your supporting points relate to your thesis statement? How well does the piece use transitions between ideas to convey a sense of unity?

- **Development:** how fully does the project develop its points? Does it respond to the reader's needs completely?
- **Synthesis:** how well has the writer made connections between the various sources and definitions? Does the writer demonstrate a clear understanding of the subject matter? Has the writer answered the question?
- **Organization:** does the paper have a clear structure and sense of organization? Are points ordered logically and effectively?
- **Documentation:** Does the project follow all guidelines for MLA style, including works cited page, parenthetical documentation, citation of sources?
- **Mechanics and Grammar:** Does the paper follow standard conventions for English grammar and punctuation. Does the paper use each appropriately, effectively, and correctly?

Scholarly Paper Assignment from Professor Ed Reber, a Humanities Professor at Dixie State College of Utah

The paper is designed for you to demonstrate that you can read, understand, synthesize, and express clearly some of the philosophical, literary, scientific, and/or cultural ideas that have been important in Western culture. The paper should be written in the general form of a letter to one of the authors in our text book, telling that author of the ways in which their ideas, philosophies, and deeds have influenced our western civilization and perhaps have influenced you in your personal world view. This assignment is not intended for you to give a mere chronology or biography of the person's life; rather, you must show that you understand the historical impact of the person's ideas, inventions or influence. **You should show in your essay that you have done research beyond the readings in our text to gain in-depth knowledge of the person to whom you write.**

It is important for you to cite material that you have studied. Both **in the text of the essays themselves**, and in a Works Cited at the end of the essay, you should let your reader know the sources of your information. (There is a guide sheet in Appendix 5 for you to follow.) In doing your research, encyclopedias may be a good place to begin, **but your research should show some familiarity with original writings from the author and some good analyses from more scholarly texts. Papers will be graded on the quality of the research, organization, correct use of standard written English, correct MLA citations, and creativity.**

9.9: Writing to Learn – Analyzing Arts and Humanities Research Assignments

Reread the three research paper assignments above and, individually or in small groups, create a list of the features of research and inquiry in the arts and humanities, based on the evidence of the assignments. For each feature, find a specific example from one of the assignments. Be prepared to discuss your features of arts and humanities research and inquiry with the class.

In most of your arts and humanities courses, the types of research and inquiry you do will be very different from research and inquiry in the natural and social sciences. Rather than conducting experiments or systematic observations of natural phenomena or human interactions, in arts and humanities courses your research is more likely to consist of closely analyzing books, works of art, or performances. Rather than looking for patterns in data and reporting those patterns in charts and graphs, in arts and humanities courses it's more likely your professors will ask you to look for patterns of ideas in essays, books, novels, or plays. Rarely in your arts and humanities research writing will you be asked to take on the *neutral* and *objective* persona of much scientific research. Inquiry in the arts and humanities is usually more *personal* and *subjective* than inquiry in the sciences, although you will often be asked to engage with previous scholarship on your subject so you can speak as an informed member of the discourse community of experts on your topic.

9.10: Writing to Learn – Analyzing a Student Research Paper

The purpose of this Writing to Learn activity is to get a sense of the nature of inquiry and research in the arts and humanities by looking at a concrete example of humanities research. Read "Blurred by Our Cultural Lens: Issues with Oral Literature and the American School System," a research paper by Stephanie LeBlanc, a student at James Madison University, which you can find at the end of Chapter 6. Write about the ways that LeBlanc practices inquiry and research. What kinds of arguments does she make, and how does she use research to explore and support her arguments? For what purposes does she use secondary sources? What kinds of thinking skills does she apply in her research (summarizing, synthesizing, evaluating, and so on)? Be prepared to talk about your analysis of LeBlanc's essay with the class.

If you completed Writing to Learn Activity 9.10, you looked carefully at Stephanie LeBlanc's research paper, "Blurred by Our Cultural Lens: Issues with Oral Literature and the American School System," from Chapter 6. When you think about inquiry and research in LeBlanc's essay, you might notice a few patterns that can help you understand what inquiry means in the arts and humanities.

- **Inquiry in the arts and humanities involves asking open-ended but focused questions about scholarly texts, works of art, and performances.**

LeBlanc's research paper focuses on questions about how oral literature is defined and taught in schools. There is no right or wrong answer to these questions, and they are especially interesting questions to explore because readers may not even be aware of this problem. To help her explore these questions, LeBlanc reflects on the Native American oral tradition.

- **Inquiry in the arts and humanities involves a close and careful analysis of scholarly texts, works of art, and performances, and consideration of social and historical forces that help shape texts.**

In order to develop and support her arguments, LeBlanc cites scholarly books and articles written by folklorists who have written about her topic. LeBlanc also refers to the Native American oral tradition and places this tradition in a historical context. LeBlanc is interested in the social and historical forces that have shaped our attitudes towards oral literature. It's common for scholars in the arts and humanities to discuss the ways that historical and social forces shape texts and works of art, and also to talk about what texts and works of art tell us about history and society.

- **Inquiry in the arts and humanities involves exploring what other scholars have said about the scholarly text, work of art, or subject you're investigating and integrating the ideas of other scholars into your discussion.**

LeBlanc's ideas and arguments shape her essay, but she also considers the work of other scholars. For example, LeBlanc cites the scholar, Gerald Haslam, who provides strong support for LeBlanc's arguments about the value of oral literature. LeBlanc also critiques what other scholars have said about her topic. Although she uses the ideas of the scholar William Murphy to support her arguments, LeBlanc also critiques Murphy's description of oral literature as "primitive." Sometimes you'll integrate the ideas of other scholars to help support your analysis of a text, and sometimes you'll cite other scholars to show the ways that you are disagreeing with their interpretations. You want to show your readers that you're familiar with what the discourse community of arts and humanities scholars has already written about your topic. At the same time, you don't want to lose track of your own ideas and responses to a text. Notice that LeBlanc integrates research from the scholars who have commented on oral literature, but she doesn't let the voices of other scholars dominate and take over her paper.

9.11: Writing to Learn – What Counts as Evidence in the Arts and Humanities?

The purpose of this Writing to Learn activity is to consider what counts as evidence for research writing in the arts and humanities by looking at the kinds of evidence found in the readings in this chapter. Skim through all of the reading passages in this chapter and underline places where the authors provide evidence to support their claims and arguments. Individually or in small groups, create a list of the kinds of evidence the authors use. Be prepared to discuss specific examples with the class as a whole.

What Counts as Evidence in the Arts and Humanities?

If you completed Writing to Learn activity 9.11, you were able to find in the readings for this chapter some common types of evidence that authors use. Some of the types of evidence you might have noticed are described below.

- **Specific examples from scholarly texts, works of art, and performances**

In his biography of Picasso, John Richardson closely analyzes Picasso's paintings to provide evidence for his assertions about Picasso's life and personality. In the excerpt in this chapter, Richardson shows how Picasso's mood had changed in Paris by doing a close reading of two of Picasso's self-portraits and comparing features of the paintings such as Picasso's use of color, his expressions in the portraits, and the way Picasso painted his eyes. In the arts and humanities, giving examples often means being detailed and descriptive. Notice how Richardson uses descriptive language to convince us that the two self-portraits reflect very different moods in Picasso. His persona is not at all detached or neutral like a scientist writing a lab report. In the book that I took the excerpt from, Richardson includes photographs of the paintings. It's common in research in arts and humanities to include visuals such as pictures of art work in your research papers.

- **Information and examples from the wider cultural context of the scholarly text, work of art, or performance**

In Pat Dowell and John Fried's review of *Pulp Fiction*, the writers place Tarantino's film in a cultural and historical context in order to support their evaluations of the film. They discuss cultural icons that connect to *Pulp Fiction*, such as Mike Hammer, previous films that Tarantino makes reference to, another director who is similar to Tarantino (Godard), and current politics (the Republican Party). Just as in research in the social sciences, arts and humanities researchers frequently use evidence from the wider culture and from human history to support their assertions about a text.

- **Well-developed and coherent personal arguments, ideas, and experiences**

Often writing assignments in arts and humanities courses will ask you to focus on your own opinions, arguments, and experiences. Unlike natural scientists, who try to be objective when they conduct experiments, and social scientists, who try to collect enough data to make generalizations about human behavior, the disciplines of the arts and humanities tend to value personal arguments and experiences. This doesn't mean that you can argue anything you want about any text or work of art and expect your readers to be persuaded by your arguments. Personal arguments need to be coherent, well-developed, and supported with evidence. Consider, for example, the excerpt from Emerson's essay "Self-Reliance." Emerson is arguing against commonly accepted ideas about the value of conforming to social expectations, but even though he's saying things that could be considered controversial, he's developing his arguments and not just ranting. He is also carefully choosing relevant personal experiences to use to support his points.

- **Arguments and theories from other arts and humanities scholars**

In her philosophy essay, Marissa Curran sets up her argument by showing how she is in disagreement with Donald Davidson's theory of language. Curran quotes Davidson and also summarizes some of his key ideas. Curran also cites Temple Grandin, "a leading figure in the on-going study of autism." Curran then uses Grandin's theories to help support her argument that thought is not dependent upon language. Arts and humanities scholars sometimes dispute or complicate the theories and arguments of other scholars, as Curran does, and sometimes they use the theories and arguments of other scholars to help them better understand a text.

Citing the scholars who have talked about the subject you're focusing on shows your readers that you're engaging with the discourse community in your discipline and that you're staking out your own position within this community.

9.12: Learn by Doing – Analyzing Arts and Humanities Research Paper Assignments

Now that you've looked over the sample arts and humanities research assignments and essays in this chapter, it would be helpful for you to get a better sense of arts and humanities research at your own college. In this Learn by Doing activity, you'll do a little investigating of your own and find and analyze some research paper assignments from the arts and humanities at your college. First, you'll need to form small groups of 3–5. Each group member will be responsible for finding one example of a research paper assignment from an arts and humanities course. You can use a research paper assignment from a course you're currently taking, or you can try to find a research assignment by doing a search on your college's Web site. For example, you can enter the key word "research paper" in your school's search engine, or use key phrases matching specific courses, like Cultural Anthropology or Art History. You can also ask an arts and humanities professor if he or she is willing to share a research assignment – tell the professor that you need to collect a research paper assignment for a course project.

Once everyone in the group has collected a research paper assignment, share the assignments among the group and analyze them. Make a list that answers the following questions:

- What types of inquiry and thinking skills (arguing, synthesizing, evaluating) are asked for in the research papers?
- What counts as evidence in the research papers?
- What kinds of research would you need to do for the assignments (e.g. finding books, searching academic databases, conducting interviews)?

Arts and Humanities Reference Books and Databases

In Chapter 5, we discussed some general academic databases and reference books. As you take general education courses in different fields of study, you'll need to be aware of more specialized databases and reference books. Following is a list of some reference books and databases for the arts and humanities.

Arts and Humanities Dictionaries

Art
Grove Dictionary of Art (2000) J. Turner (ed.) New York: St. Martin's.
McGraw-Hill Dictionary of Art (1969) B. S. Myers (ed.) New York: McGraw-Hill.
The Oxford Dictionary of Art (2004) I. Chilvers (ed.) Oxford: Oxford University Press.

Film
Cinema: A Critical Dictionary (1980) R. Roud. New York: Viking.
The Complete Film Dictionary (1998) I. Konisberg. New York: Penguin
Critical Dictionary of Film and Television Theory (2000) R. Pearson and P. Simpson (eds.) New York: Routledge.
The Film Studies Dictionary (2001) S. Blandford, B. K. Grant, and J. Hillier (eds.) London: Hodder Arnold.

Literature
Dictionary of Literary Biography. Gale. http://www.gale.cengage.com/
A Dictionary of Literary Terms and Literary Theory (1998) J. A. Cuddon. Somerset, New Jersey: Wiley-Blackwell.
A Dictionary of Writers and their Works (2001) M. Cox. Oxford: Oxford University Press.

Music
Harvard Biographical Dictionary of Music (1996) D. Randel (ed.) Cambridge, Massachusetts: Harvard University Press.
The New Grove Dictionary of Music and Musicians (2003) S. Sadie and J. Tyrell (eds.) Oxford: Oxford University Press.
The New Harvard Dictionary of Music (1986) D. Randel (ed.) Cambridge, Massachusetts: Belknap Press.

Philosophy and Religious Studies
Dictionary of Comparative Religion (1978) S. G. Brandon (ed.) New York: Scribner.
The Cambridge Dictionary of Philosophy (1999) R. Audi (ed.) New York: Cambridge University Press.
The Oxford Dictionary of World Religions (1997) J. Bowker (ed.) Oxford: Oxford University Press.
The Penguin Dictionary of Philosophy (1998) T. Mautner (ed.) New York: Penguin.

Theatre and Dance
The Drama Dictionary (1990) T. Hodgson. Lanham, Maryland: New Amsterdam Books.
International Dictionary of Theatre (2002) J. P. Saint (ed.) Chicago: St. James Press.

Arts and Humanities Encyclopedias

Art
The Artists Illustrated Encyclopedia (2001) P. Metzger. Cincinnati: North Light Books.
The Grove Encyclopedia of Materials and Techniques in Art (2008) G. Ward. Oxford: Oxford University Press.

Film
The Film Encyclopedia (1998) E. Katz. New York: Collins Reference.
New York Times Encyclopedia of Film (1992) G. Brown (ed.) New York: Taylor and Francis.

Literature
The Cambridge Guide to Literature in English (1994) I. Ousby (ed.) New York: Cambridge University Press.
Encyclopedia of Literature and Criticism (1993) M. Coyle, P. Garside, M. Kelsall, and J. Peck (eds.) New York: Routledge.
The Oxford Companion to English Literature (2000) M. Drabble (ed.) Oxford: Oxford University Press.
The Oxford Encyclopedia of American Literature (2004) J. Parini (ed.) Oxford: Oxford University Press.

Music
The Encyclopedia of Popular Music (1998) C. Larkin (ed.) New York: Grove's Dictionaries.
The Garland Encyclopedia of World Music (1997–2001) B. Nettl and R. Stone (eds.) New York: Routledge.

Philosophy and Religious Studies
The Encyclopedia of Religion (1993) M. Eliade (ed.) New York: MacMillan Reference Books.

Encyclopedia of Religion and Ethics (2001) J. Hastings (ed.) Boston: Adamant Media Corporation.

The Oxford Companion to Philosophy (1995) T. Honderich (ed.) Oxford: Oxford University Press.

Routledge Encyclopedia of Philosophy (1998) E. Craig (ed.) New York: Routledge.

Stanford Encyclopedia of Philosophy (2009) The Metaphysics Research Lab. http://plato.stanford.edu/contents.html

Theatre and Dance

The Cambridge Guide to Theatre (1995) M. Banham. New York: Cambridge University Press.

McGraw–Hill Encyclopedia of World Drama (1984) S. Hochman. New York: McGraw-Hill.

The Oxford Companion to the Theatre (1983) P. Hartnoll (ed.) Oxford: Oxford University Press.

The Oxford Encyclopedia of Theatre and Performance (2003) D. Kennedy (ed.) Oxford: Oxford University Press.

World Encyclopedia of Contemporary Theatre (1998) D. Rubin. New York: Routledge.

Arts and Humanities Periodical Databases

Art Abstracts

Art Full Text

Arts and Humanities Citation Index

Humanities Abstracts

Humanities Full Text

MLA Bibliography

Music Index

Philosopher's Index

Citing Sources in the Arts and Humanities: MLA Style

Most professors in the arts and humanities will ask you to use MLA (Modern Language Association) style when you cite sources and prepare a Works Cited page. Unlike CSE and APA, MLA style emphasizes the author and not the date of publication. In the sciences, the most recent experiments are usually the most reliable and most frequently cited. However, the author is also cited in CSE style, since the reputation of the scientist is important. In the arts and humanities, there's a greater emphasis on the quality of writing and the expertise of the author.

Science research done in ancient times is hardly of value today, other than of historical interest, but philosophers still discuss the ideas of Plato and Aristotle, and they continue to publish books and articles debating the merits of the arguments of these ancient philosophers. It's understandable, then, that MLA style would emphasize the author and deemphasize the date of publication. In addition to rules about citing and referencing sources, the MLA style manual has guidelines for language use (avoiding sexist and biased language) and formatting.

In-text Citations in MLA Style

If the credibility and expertise of authors is an important part of writing and researching in the arts and humanities, it makes sense that arts and humanities scholars are careful to acknowledge the authors they are in conversation with in their papers. In MLA style, whenever you quote or paraphrase a source, you need to give the author and page number. Here's an example:

> Min argues that "works of art have no inherent meaning. It is the observer who brings meaning to the work, not the work that brings meaning to the observer" (32).

Note that since you introduced the author (Min argues...) you don't need to include the author's last name in the parentheses. The parentheses are placed outside the quotation marks, and the period is placed after the parentheses. If there is more than one author, use et al. (Min et al. 32).

In the previous passage, it made sense to quote Min directly in order to capture the voice and tone of her strong assertion. But if you're integrating facts or statistics from a secondary source, it's better to put the information in your own words and then cite it rather than quoting it directly.

Let's say you want to cite the following information from an article (hypothetical) by Ray Suarez:

> There is ample proof that art museums across the nation are doing better than just treading water. In a 2005 survey of 138 art museums, it was reported that attendance has risen by 24% from 2004 to 2005, and membership has risen by 28%. The museums reported that private funding is mostly stable, with only a slight decrease (down 2%)

Although you could put this entire passage in quotation marks and cite it word-for-word in your essay, since the information is just a series of statistics, it would be more effective to simply summarize the information in your own words and cite the source. For example:

> Art historian Ray Suarez argues that American art museums are doing well. Suarez

points to a 2005 national survey of art museums that reports an increase in attendance (up 24%) and membership (up 28%) from 2004 to 2005, as well as stability in
private funding (59)

Preparing an MLA Style Works Cited Page

For details about how to cite different types of source in MLA and how to prepare
an MLA-style Works Cited page, visit the Web site or reference area of your
library and consult the *MLA Handbook* or visit the following Web sites:

MLA Resource Web Sites

Purdue Online Writing Lab
(http://owl.english.purdue.edu/owl/resource/747/01/)

University of North Carolina Library
(http://www.lib.unc.edu/instruct/citations/mla/)

University Wisconsin-Madison Writing Center
(http://www.wisc.edu/writing/Handbook/DocMLA.html)

MLA Style Paper Format

Following are basic guidelines for formatting your paper in MLA style.

- Use a standard 12-point font: Courier, Times, or Bookman.
- In the upper left-hand corner of page 1, type your name, your professor's
  name, the course number and title, and the date (double-spaced). Double
  space between the heading, title, and body of the paper. The title should be
  centered, but not underlined or put in bold type face.
- Use 1" margins except for the upper right-hand corner, where you should
  include your last name and page number on each page, ½" from the top.
- For quotations of more than 40 words, indent each line of the quote (using
  block format) five spaces from the left margin. Do not indent from the right
  margin.
- Double-space throughout, including the Works Cited page.
- Place figures, tables, or other visuals close to the place you refer to them in
  the text. Label each visual and number them consecutively (Figure 1,
  Figure 2, and so on.).
- Place the Works Cited page after the body of the paper.

Student Writing Case Study: Literature

Antonio Javier as a senior at California State University Sacramento

Antonio Javier was a senior English major at California State University Sacramento at the time this case study was conducted. In this case study of writing in the arts and humanities, we'll look at one of Antonio's papers in ENGL65: Introduction to World Literature in English. ENGL65 is a general education course with a mix of English majors and students from a variety of majors other than English. The syllabus for ENGL65 is given below.

English 65. Introduction to World Literature in English

Course Objectives
To familiarize students with some significant and culturally diverse examples of World Literatures written in English from the colonial and post-colonial eras.
To introduce students to some of the major literary genres and modes employed by these writers in their colonial and post-colonial contexts.
To provide students with the opportunity to examine some recurring themes in world literature written in English.
To help students understand the relevance of past periods and of different cultures to our modern world.
To give students practice in analyzing, discussing, and writing about literature.

Required Texts
Chinua Achebe, *Things Fall Apart*
V.S. Naipaul, *The Mystic Masseur*

Mordecai Richler, *The Apprenticeship of Duddy Kravitz*
Victor Ramraj, *Concert of Voices*
Course Reader

Grade Breakdown
Journal: 15%
Paper 1: 15%
Paper 2: 25%
Exam: 25%
Participation: 20%

Attendance Policy

I will be taking attendance every class. Each student will be permitted 4 absences; after that number, each extra absence will cause your course grade to drop one notch (from a B− to a C+, for example). Why you miss class is your business, and only becomes my business if your absences start to mount up. Of course, if something extremely emotionally taxing or catastrophic happens to you this semester, I will be glad to discuss it with you and will try to make allowances.

Plagiarism and Academic Dishonesty

Taking credit for work that isn't yours is morally wrong and intellectually inexcusable. Any instances of plagiarism on any assignment in this class will be punished with an automatic F in the course and will be reported to Student Affairs. Please also note that handing in the same paper for two classes without notifying your instructors and getting their permission is academic dishonesty, and will earn you the same penalty as plagiarism.

Journals

The journal is a notebook that you will buy and leave with me every class. Instead of pop quizzes, you will spend time at the start of each class writing in your journals. You will answer one impromptu question posed by me, and then write a short general response to my prompt about the assigned reading for that day (or another subject, if you prefer, or if I haven't provided a prompt). The object of this is both for you to demonstrate to me that you have done the assigned reading and to prepare everyone for a fruitful, focused and more inclusive class discussion.

Paper 1

For the first paper (2–3 pages, double-spaced) you will examine one text (poem, story, novel or essay) we have read so far in the class and make an argument about an aspect of it. Your paper must follow a conventional outline (brief introduction, main argument and conclusion) but need not be an attempt to exhaust a given topic. No secondary sources are permitted.

Paper 2

For the second paper (3–4 pages, double-spaced) you will make an argument about a theme or idea that has appeared in at least two novels, stories, essays or poems we have read up to and including the due date. No research or secondary material (critical essays etc.) is required, but you are encouraged to seek out critical material to help you choose and define a topic. Your paper must follow a conventional outline (introduction, main argument and conclusion) but need not be an attempt to exhaust a given topic.

Exam

We will have a 2-hour final exam that will cover material from the entire course. The exam will be open-book, so the emphasis will not be on memorization but rather on your ability to interpret and compare texts. More will be said later. N.B. Please note that anyone who fails the exam cannot pass the class.

Kickoffs

Kickoffs are in-class presentations that should last no more than 5 minutes. They should not concentrate primarily on biographical or background material, but rather draw our attention to a particular point about or passage in the readings for that class. A kickoff should offer an insight about what everyone has read for that day's class; any background information should be very brief, and should be subordinated to the point you are making about the text itself.

Course Goals for English 65

What: To help students become more confident and skilful in writing about literature.

How: I offer detailed feedback on required student papers (both positive and critical) and make myself available to read extra drafts of mid-term papers and rough drafts of final papers. Please do not feel in the least bit awkward about asking for extra help with your writing, especially in the last half of the course when I have seen everyone's work and my reading load drops off considerably. Students of all ages, abilities and experience can and do benefit from having someone look at their rough work or help with revising more polished efforts. You should avail yourself of every opportunity to improve your writing, whether by working with me or with a tutor at the Writing Center in Calaveras Hall. Notwithstanding my emphasis on participation, the dirty little secret of English classes is that nothing is more central in determining your final grade than your writing skills.

What: To help students become more confident and skilful in reading literature.

How: On the assumption that a bored teacher is a bad teacher, I refuse to teach anything that bores me, which means that I generally assign ambitious, complex texts in my classes. I believe that this in itself will help you flex your reading muscles and develop new strategies for interpreting difficult works, but I also try to focus on specific passages and details in class discussions to make these texts more accessible and enjoyable. I also encourage creative student approaches to texts and will try to offer general themes and motifs to look for as you read on your own (though I refuse to tell you in advance what a given text "means," which would defeat the purpose of assigning challenging works). The most important skill for students to develop in reading is what Keats called "negative capability," or the ability to go on in a condition of uncertainty; while one never wants to feel completely lost, language's capacity for conveying multiple (and even contradictory) meanings creates ambiguity that students must learn to tolerate, and even welcome, if they are to develop confidence as readers of literature.

What: To help students develop their ability to discuss literary texts with others.

How: I assign kick-offs and/or in-class presentations and encourage regular and meaningful participation from all students. I also encourage students to address their ideas and remarks to their classmates (and not just me) by assigning respondents for many student presentations and kick-offs as well as organizing goal-driven group work on occasion. I also try to allow students to investigate their ideas in class discussion, firstly by making sure I understand them myself (excuse my occasional slowness on the uptake if I ask you to repeat something or explain it further), and secondly by pursuing their implications as fully as I can by playing the devil's advocate or by extrapolating on your idea to test its limits (once again, please excuse me). There is no such thing as a final resting place for a literary discussion, so the best comments are always only partly true, and there is no such thing as a stupid question.

What: To familiarize students with new and important texts from all over the English-speaking world and invite them to relate the ideas and experiences described in those texts to their own lives.

How: I have chosen a cross-section of male and female writers from many different countries and cultures with regard both for their high literary value and for their intellectual, historical or cultural significance. No one on this syllabus is here to fill out a quota; they are all extremely able and/or influential figures whose work deserves our attention.

9.13: Writing to Learn – Comparing Courses across Disciplines

Compare this syllabus with the syllabi for the case studies of student writing in Chapters 7 and 8. How are the course goals and objectives in this literature course different from the course goals in the social and natural science courses? How are the genres and expectations for the writing assignments different? In what ways do these differences reflect the different conventions for writing and thinking in the social sciences, natural sciences, and arts and humanities that we've been discussing in Chapters 6–9?

Antonio was asked to write two essays for ENGL65, and both essays asked for ways of thinking that are valued in the arts and humanities: making arguments about texts, analyzing a theme across multiple texts, and reading closely and carefully. I asked Antonio's professor how he defines *analysis*, and how he sees his definition of analysis connecting to the ways of thinking in his academic field of literary studies:

> "Analyzing" is basically the process of proving an argument or claim with evidence (i.e. direct quotations and details from a text), using a reasonably coherent, logical flow of ideas, and connecting each subsidiary point back to the main claim. A successful analysis needs breadth as well as internal coherence, though; it should satisfy me that the student has grasped the important aspects of a given text as they relate to his/her argument. If an analysis is coherent but incomplete, then there's a problem. However, I make it clear that even if I disagree with a given "argument" made about a text, I will respect the logic of the analysis that supports it if that analysis is solid and sufficiently broad.
>
> To me, knowledge is made in English studies through the endless process of coming up with arguments about and analyses of important or provocative texts. These arguments and analyses get more sophisticated as a writer progresses, but the process remains the same.

As you can see by this quote from Antonio's professor, analysis and argument are closely linked in the arts and humanities. Both involve looking closely at texts and providing evidence with examples from texts that support the claims made in the analyses and arguments. By completing this paper, Antonio was learning how to write and think like an arts and humanities scholar. He was also learning to read texts like an arts and humanities scholar, and the texts in English 65 were often challenging and complex. Antonio's professor had some good advice for students about reading challenging texts in arts and humanities classes:

> I advise reading with a pen or pencil in hand so they can mark up their texts and come to class with questions about particularly difficult passages. They should also use a dictionary to look up words they don't understand, though few seem to be inclined to do so. I would also recommend reading a text slowly, and more than once... I want to alert them to the fact of a given text's difficulty, and to underline my view that struggling to find meaning (sometimes unsuccessfully) is part of one's humanistic education, and is nothing to be ashamed of.

Since both essay assignments which Antonio was assigned were similar, we'll focus on just one of the essays, paper #2. Here's a reminder of the assignment for paper #2:

Paper 2
For the second paper (3–4 pages, double-spaced) you will make an argument about a theme or idea that has appeared in at least two novels, stories, essays or poems we have read up to and including the due date. No research or secondary material (critical essays etc.) is required, but you are encouraged to seek out critical material to help you choose and define a topic. Your paper must follow a conventional outline (introduction, main argument and conclusion) but need not be an attempt to exhaust a given topic.

To gain a sense of how Antonio thought about the assignment and found a topic to write about, let's hear what he reported about his writing process:

> The very first thing I do when I have a writing assignment similar to the ones [in Introduction to World Literature] is to review the topics (or questions, dependent upon the assignment, of course), and figure which one I am most knowledgeable in based on how much I could think of off the top of my head. This is the easy part. I write down a few notes on a piece of scratch paper, and compile them so that I could come back to them after the second phase in my topic selection. The second phase is assigning a level of difficulty and likelihood of me creating a decent paper for it. This way, I select the most difficult paper to write with the most detail I could possibly put in it. In other words, I select a topic based on three criteria: basic knowledge of the topic, level of difficulty, and amount of detail I can put in it. I feel that the selection of the

topic is the most important part of writing a paper, and would advise new college students to take time in assessing what they are writing on. This way they don't get stuck writing an "impossible" paper and will be able to write the most efficient paper they can.

Before Antonio begins to draft his paper, he thinks about his topic in his head and by jotting notes on a piece of scratch paper. Each student in Antonio's class probably had a different strategy for getting started: jotting down notes as Antonio did, reviewing the course readings, freewriting, talking with the professor or peers about topic ideas, etc. There are many different ways to get started, but the important thing is to find strategies that work for you.

One of Antonio's rough drafts of paper #2 is given below.

> In the beginning of the semester, we read Achebe's "Girls at War" and were treated to a very non-traditional female character that sought to defy even the former identity she adopted early in the story. Even up to now reading literature from different corners of the world, we see much of the same willingness to defy tradition. What is striking is that in each of the last portions of the world that was covered in the latter half of the semester, there are examples of women more than willing to defy their respective tradition. The difference comes in the resulting consequence of each woman's respective defiance. Some are implied, some are threatened and some are experienced all depending on the culture in which each woman inhabits.

> The first example is in Nayantara Sahgal's story, "Martand." In this story, we find the wife of a man named Naresh, who is wise beyond his years. Naresh is a passive, realistic man who has seen and experienced the horrors of rebellion and has succumbed to the comforts of what is familiar. The man counterpart to Naresh is Martand. Opposed to Naresh's beliefs, Martand is a passionate, idealistic Kashmir rebel who wants change in their country. In this story, we are not given much description in Naresh's wife, but we are certainly given the impression that she is allied with Martand's beliefs. Near the end of the story, the author reveals that Naresh's wife has been having an affair with Martand. It is also at this point in time that the author also reveals what happens to people who share in the same points of view as Martand. In the end, Martand is murdered by one of his own assistants. Because of Martand's demise, we are given the impression that if Naresh's wife continued to rebel as Martand did, she would likely share the same fate as him. Through Naresh's wife's defiance, she faces multiple consequences.

> The first consequence Naresh's wife has to face is the consequence of cheating on her husband for Martand. The simple fact that Naresh's wife felt compelled to share Martand's beliefs and opinions attracted her to him even more, and ultimately ends up having to choose between the two men. Near the end of the story, Martand and

Naresh's wife have an argument over whether or not they should tell Naresh about their illicit relationship, but it is not revealed as to whether or not Naresh's wife will actually leave him. The author also does not reveal explicitly whether or not Naresh finds out about the relationship between Martand and his wife. The second consequence Naresh's wife has to face is not explicitly revealed in the story, rather is implied that should Naresh's wife follow the path of Martand, she will eventually share the same demise as he. The very last lines of the story say, "As we clung together I knew we had both changed invisibly beyond recall. Naresh, mourning Martand, had found his faith in goodness again, while I, surely as I breathed, knew that everywhere within hand's reach was evil" (Sahgal). Through these very last lines, the reader can assume that Martand's death has made Naresh's wife aware that her continued defiance and want for change will leave her dead as Martand, and that should she share the same goals as he, she will undoubtedly share the same enemies as he as well.

On the flip side of Martand, we find ourselves with Canada's Margaret Atwood. Atwood, when asked about what is Canadian about Canadian Literature, says, "A lot of Canadian Literature is about life boats. I didn't make up the notion that Canadian Literature is about Survival, but that it certainly emerges as one of the central themes" (Clarkson) In a New York Times article, she notably says, "Survival has preoccupied Canadians for 400 years" (Walz) Though it isn't explicit that Atwood is defying the traditional role of the woman, she most certainly breaks the traditional stereotype that women cannot be recognized for their political views and opinions. In contrast to Naresh's wife, who remains in the background unsure of whether or not she should adopt her husband's way of thinking or Martand's, Atwood has been critically acclaimed for her works most notably *Survival: A Thematic Guide to Canadian Literature*. This success and independence leads her to become a "talented leader of a coterie of Canadian writers" (Walz)

What is surprising about the contrast between Naresh's wife and Atwood is that Atwood openly attacks her country's defeatist personality, while Naresh's wife cannot decide whether or not she wants to follow Martand's footsteps in fear that she too will be ostracized as Martand is. Atwood even questions if her countrymen "have had a will to lose as strong and as pervasive as the Americans' will to win" (Walz) One can conclude that the socio-political consequences of their actions eventually lead both Atwood and Naresh's wife to their ultimate decisions: Atwood with her active voice, wanting to create change, and Naresh's wife with her passiveness and fear of sharing the same demise as Martand.

Take a look at Antonio's final draft, with comments about how he revised the essay:

In the beginning of the semester, we read Achebe's "Girls at War" and were treated to a very non-traditional female character that sought to defy even the former identity she adopted early in the story. Even up to now reading literature from different corners of the world, we see much of the same willingness to defy tradition. What is striking is that in each of the last portions of the world that were covered in the latter half of the semester, there are examples of women more than willing to defy their respective traditions. The difference comes in the resulting consequence of each woman's respective defiance. Though the women we have read about want to break the stereotype of the traditional woman, there are two very different examples of how women act upon their impulse to break their traditional roles. These differences are set by how their cultures can and will react to their willingness to create this change.

The first example is in Nayantara Sahgal's story, "Martand." In this story, we find the wife of a man named Naresh, who is wise beyond his years. Naresh is a passive, realistic man who has seen and experienced the horrors of rebellion and has succumbed to the comforts of what is familiar. The man counterpart to Naresh is Martand. Opposed to Naresh's beliefs, Martand is a passionate, idealistic Kashmir rebel who wants change in their country. In this story, we are not given much description of Naresh's wife, but we are certainly given the impression that she is allied with Martand's beliefs. One cannot exactly blame her however, as when contrasted to Naresh, Martand and his opinions are very passionate, exciting and enticing to a woman of Naresh's wife's position. To have to listen to the defeatist attitude of her husband, anyone can understand how and why Naresh's wife can be easily swayed by Martand's beckoning. Sure enough, near the end of the story,

Antonio added his interpretation of the story, and not just a plot summary.

the author reveals that Naresh's wife has been having an affair with Martand. It is also at this point in time that the author also reveals what happens to people who share in the same points of view as Martand. In the end, Martand is murdered by one of his own assistants. Because of Martand's demise, we are given the impression that if Naresh's wife continued to rebel as Martand did, she would likely share the same fate as him. Through Naresh's wife's defiance, she faces multiple consequences.

The first consequence Naresh's wife has to face is the consequence of cheating on her husband for Martand. The simple fact that Naresh's wife felt compelled to share Martand's beliefs and opinions attracted her to him even more, and ultimately she ends up having to choose between the two men. Near the end of the story, Martand and Naresh's wife have an argument over whether or not they should tell Naresh about their illicit relationship, but it is not revealed as to whether or not Naresh's wife will actually leave him. The author also does not reveal explicitly whether or not Naresh finds out about the relationship between Martand and his wife. The second consequence Naresh's wife has to face is not explicitly revealed in the story, rather is implied that should Naresh's wife follow the path of Martand, she will eventually share the same demise as he. The very last lines of the story say, "As we clung together I knew we had both changed invisibly beyond recall. Naresh, mourning Martand, had found his faith in goodness again, while I, surely as I breathed, knew that everywhere within hand's reach was evil." Through these very last lines, the reader can assume that Martand's death has made Naresh's wife aware that her continued defiance and want for change will leave her dead as Martand, and that should she share the same goals as he, she will undoubtedly share the same enemies as he as well.

On the flip side of Martand, we find ourselves

Antonio added a close reading of the last lines of the story to explain the second consequence Naresh's wife has to face.

with Canada's Margaret Atwood, our second example. Atwood, when asked about what is Canadian about Canadian Literature, says, "A lot of Canadian Literature is about life boats. I didn't make up the notion that Canadian Literature is about Survival, but that it certainly emerges as one of the central themes" (Clarkson) In a New York Times article, she notably says, "Survival has pre-occupied Canadians for 400 years" (Walz) Though it isn't explicit that Atwood is defying the traditional role of the woman, she most certainly breaks the traditional stereotype that women cannot be recognized for their political views and opinions. In contrast to Naresh's wife, who remains in the background unsure of whether or not she should adopt her husband's way of thinking or Martand's, Atwood has been critically acclaimed for her works, most notably *Survival: A Thematic Guide to Canadian Literature.* This success and independence leads her to become a "talented leader of a coterie of Canadian writers" (Walz)

Antonio added a conclusion that synthesizes his interpretations of the two authors.

What is surprising about the contrast between Naresh's wife and Atwood is that Atwood openly attacks her country's defeatist personality, while Naresh's wife cannot decide whether or not she wants to follow Martand's footsteps in fear that she too will be ostracized as Martand is. Atwood even questions if her countrymen "have had a will to lose as strong and as pervasive as the Americans' will to win" (Walz). One can conclude that the socio-political consequences of their actions eventually lead both Atwood and Naresh's wife to their ultimate decisions: Atwood with her active voice, wanting to create change, and Naresh's wife with her passiveness and fear of sharing the same demise as Martand.

There is a saying that "behind every great man, there is a great woman." There are exceptions though, in that sometimes, the woman acts on her own and breaks their traditional roles as support for their men. Both Atwood and Naresh's wife follow this defiance of traditional roles, but both resolve this defiance in completely different manners. This difference comes in the form of the socio-political consequences of what they aim to accomplish. Due to the fact that Naresh's wife's lover Martand ends up murdered for wanting to create change in his war-ridden country, Naresh's wife ends up not acting upon her impulse to create a similar change. Atwood, on the other hand, seeks to break the stereotype not only of her image as a woman, but as a Canadian. Atwood succeeds in getting her message across and is critically acclaimed for it globally.

Works Cited

Clarkson, Adrienne. "Atwood as Canadian literary critic." Margaret Atwood: Queen of CanLit. CBC. 6 Nov. 1972.
Walz, Jay. "Canadian Writers Debate Nationalism." New York Times. 24 Apr. 1973.

9.14: Writing to Learn – Reflecting on Literature Papers

How is Antonio's paper similar to and different from papers you've written for literature classes in high school or college?

Even though this was Antonio's final draft that he turned in to the professor for a grade, no piece of writing is ever truly "finished." Antonio told me that, when I asked him to reflect on his essay months after turning it in, he realized he still could have done more researching and could have written another draft. Antonio said:

I am, however, guilty of not doing enough research to support my paper, as it is thoroughly lacking in my analysis of "Martand." Reflecting upon this, however, I was still able to analyze the story well enough to apply it to the concepts

Atwood is exploring in *Survival*. If I could make any changes to my paper, it would most definitely be to reinforce it more thoroughly with a bit more research.

I hope that after reading the case studies in *Exploring College Writing*, you've come to see that college writing requires extensive processes of drafting and revising, and that these processes are always connected to the genre of what you're writing, the discipline you're writing in, and the context of the professor and the specific course.

Examples of Student Writing in the Arts and Humanities

For more examples of student writing from the arts and humanities, visit the following online student writing journals:

The Allegheny Review
(http://webpub.allegheny.edu/group/review/)

History Matters, Appalachian State University
(http://www.historymatters.appstate.edu)

Illumination: The Undergraduate Journal of Humanities, University of Wisconsin-Madison
(http://illumination.library.wisc.edu/)

Scribendi, University of New Mexico
(http://www.unm.edu/~scribend/)

Rutgers University Undergraduate Philosophy Journal
(http://www.eden.rutgers.edu/~journal/index.html)

Review of Key Ideas in Chapter 9

- The writing you're assigned in arts and humanities courses will ask you to respond to, analyze, synthesize, and evaluate scholarly texts, works of art, and performances in genres such as the review, the critical analysis essay, the personal essay, and the research paper. In arts and humanities courses, you will be asked to observe performances and works of art and to closely and carefully read written and visual texts, as well as give your personal response in conversation with discourse communities of arts and humanities scholars.

- Writing is fundamental to thinking in the arts and humanities. Writing reflections on and evaluations of human experiences and works of art is the primary way that arts and humanities scholars create knowledge and share ideas.

- Arts and humanities genres are not just templates for organizing your writing. Arts and humanities genres like the performance review are a reflection of the way scholars in the arts and humanities observe, respond, and evaluate. Genres are not just formats but ways of thinking.

- Reading assignments in arts and humanities courses are varied and require different reading strategies for different purposes and genres. Close reading is an important strategy in the arts and humanities, and close reading requires rereading and annotating.

- Research and inquiry in the arts and humanities involves exploring questions about the meaning of human experiences, works of art, and written texts. Sometimes inquiry in the arts and humanities will involve only your own personal response, and sometimes you will be asked to join the scholarly conversation and integrate and apply the ideas of other arts and humanities scholars.

9.15: Writing to Learn – Differences between Humanities and Science Writing

Now that you've explored writing in the natural and social sciences and writing in the arts and humanities, let's reflect on the differences between writing in science and writing in the arts and humanities. Write about what you see as the major differences between reading, writing, and researching in the natural and social sciences, on the one hand, and reading, writing, researching in the arts and humanities, on the other hand.

Writing Projects for Part III

Writing Project III.1: Writing Assignments across the Curriculum

Prompt

Collect six writing assignments from professors at your school and write a 1–2 page rhetorical analysis of each assignment. Collect two assignments from a course or courses in the natural sciences, two from the social sciences, and two from the arts and humanities. In your rhetorical analyses, consider purpose, audience, persona, context, and genre. After you've conducted the six rhetorical analyses, write a 2–3 page reflection in which you compare and contrast the expectations and conventions of the different writing assignments and disciplines.

Purpose

The purpose of this analysis of writing assignments is to look closely at the expectations for writing at your school and to compare the way those expectations differ from one discipline to another. Writing assignments are a reflection of a professor's and a discipline's expectations and conventions, so looking closely at writing assignments will give you a window into writing expectations at your institution. This project will also give you some practice in understanding writing assignments.

Audience

The goal of this rhetorical analysis of writing assignments is for you to gain a better understanding of the writing expectations at your institution, so think of yourself as the primary audience for this writing project. Your professor will be reading your analysis and evaluating how carefully and thoughtfully you've read the assignments, so you will also want to make your analysis clear to readers.

Your professor may even ask you to present the results of your analysis to the class as a whole, so it's possible that your peers could become another audience for this project.

Genre

It's common for college professors to ask you to analyze texts: to read texts closely and critically and search for meaningful patterns. Professors will ask you to write these kinds of analysis papers to get you to read carefully and to think deeply about what you're reading. In this project, in addition to practicing analysis, you'll gain a better sense of the genre of the college writing assignment.

Conventions

College analysis essays usually include sample lines or passages from the reading being analyzed as a way to show readers you're looking closely at the text. It would therefore be helpful to include excerpts from the assignments you're analyzing. Integrating information about writing expectations in different disciplines from Chapters 6–9 would also help support and develop your analysis. Usually an analysis essay is organized and systematic. Review the discussion of common college thinking and writing strategies in Chapter 2 to remind yourself what *analysis* means for college writing.

Evaluation Criteria

The most important aspects of this writing project are the depth and quality of your analysis and your comparison in the reflection letter of the assignments and the expectations of the different disciplines. Your analysis will be stronger if you cite specific lines or passages from the assignments. You might also refer to information from Chapters 6–9 to help support your analysis. Your analysis should be organized and clear to the reader.

Writing Project III.2: Interview with a College Professor

Prompt

Interview a college professor about expectations for reading, writing, and researching in a discipline that you're interested in discovering more about (e.g. your potential or actual major subject). Record and transcribe the interview, and then write a 2–3 page reflection on what you learned from the interview. Give a brief presentation to the whole class summarizing your findings.

Purpose

The purpose of this interview project is for you to get information about writing in a discipline directly from a professor in that discipline at your institution. If you choose a discipline that you're interested in, you can get a better sense of the expectations for reading and writing in that field (which may be your future major) Even if you're not sure what you might major in, this interview will give you insight into junior-level and senior-level writing expectations. You might ask questions about the kinds of reading the professor assigns, the person's idea of what good writing is in the major, the kind of research methods used in the discipline, common genres students are asked to write in, and any other aspects of the discipline that are relevant to college work. For advice about conducting interviews, review the section in Chapter 5 on interviewing.

Audience

Your audience for this interview is both yourself and your classmates. Your primary goal is to learn something about reading, writing, and researching expectations in a discipline that you're interested in, but you'll also be telling your peers about what you discovered in a brief presentation. Transcribing the interview will help both you and your professor to see exactly what questions you asked and what the professor said in response to your questions. Reflecting on what you transcribed and summarizing your findings in a presentation to the class will help you explore the most important things you learned in the interview.

Genre

The interview is a common genre in college and beyond. Interviews are especially common in the social sciences, since they are an important research method for qualitative investigations. They are also a key method of obtaining information in journalism and other media studies, and they are increasingly used in nursing, public health, and other allied medical professions. Interviews give researchers a chance to ask focused questions and to hear directly from the people they're studying. One convention of the genre of the interview is the interviewer's responsibility to accurately record and transcribe what the interviewee said. Since an interview report is a direct transcription of someone's words, it's important not to merely write down "the gist" of what someone said, but to make sure you have a person's exact words – including, to the extent that it is feasible, self-corrections and meaningful non-language sounds such as laughs or sighs. A careful researcher can analyze such features along with the interviewee's words in interpreting attitudes and other aspects of meaning. Such features can be put into square brackets, using a hyphen to indicate a brief (1 second or less) break in speech and a series of these to indicate breaks of several seconds.

Evaluation Criteria

Your peers and your professor will be looking for you to design thoughtful, focused questions, to accurately transcribe what the professor has said, and to give a concise summary of your major findings in your presentation. You should show in your reflection that you have carefully read over your transcription and thought about what you learned about reading, writing, and researching in the professor's discipline.

Writing Project III.3: Academic Discourse Community Mini-Ethnography

Prompt

Choose an academic discourse community and use ethnographic methods (observation, interviews, surveys, analysis of documents) to investigate the reading, writing, and researching conventions of the community. The community could be broad (e.g. a department or subdiscipline within a department) or narrow (e.g. a class or a discussion group). In a 5–7 page report, write up the results of your research using the ethnographies you studied in Chapter 8 as a model.

Purpose

In this ethnography project, you'll need to draw on all of the skills you've been practicing: collecting data, analyzing texts closely for their rhetorical features, interviewing and observing individuals and groups, analyzing and synthesizing materials from your research, and reporting the results of your analysis to an audience. This project will involve your most in-depth study of a discourse community, since you'll be analyzing data you've collected using a variety of research methods and sources. Since you're going to do extensive research, choose a discourse community that you're interested in finding more about. You might choose a department that you're thinking of majoring in (e.g. Mechanical and Electrical Engineering or Anthropology), a specific discipline you're interested in (e.g. electrical engineering or cultural anthropology), or a club or discussion group you might join (e.g. the College Democrats or a Women's Studies Discussion Group).

There are a variety of questions you could explore in your academic discourse ethnography:

What kinds of texts does the community value?
What purposes do texts serve in the community?
What kinds of information does the community need?
What information-gathering or research methods are used by the community?
What specialized terms do community members use?
What are some common genres used in the community, and what are the conventions of those genres?
What kinds of personas do writers in the community take on?
How is power/authority distributed in the community?

Audience

For this project, imagine that you're a social scientist reporting the results of your research to an academic audience who are not familiar with the genres and conventions of the discourse community you're investigating. You'll need to provide your audience with sample documents from the discourse community (e.g. assignments, passages from representative texts, and/or excerpts from other written, digital, or visual genres), evidence from observation and interviews, and your own in-depth analysis. Your audience will be looking for your insights into the way the discourse community communicates, and they will expect you to organize your thoughts and report your findings clearly.

Genre

In Chapter 8, we took a close look at the genre of the ethnography, and you might go back to Chapter 6 as well and reread Dana Driscoll's ethnographic analysis of the language of the discourse community of Internet gamers, "The Ubercool Morphology of Internet Gamers: A Linguistic Analysis." You'll notice that Driscoll's study is organized in different sections, which include: an overview of the group being studied, a discussion of her research methods, the results of her analysis, and a discussion of the relevance of those results. In his ethnography about the Yanomamö people, Napoleon Chagnon organizes his analysis by theme. The excerpt from Chagnon's ethnography in Chapter 8 focuses on "Child–Adult Division," and Chagnon also has chapters on warfare, politics, trading, and other themes. In her ethnography of college life, *My Freshman Year*, Rebekah Nathan organizes her book chronologically, beginning with her first encounters with the group she's studying (college students). As you can see by these examples, there are a variety of ways you can organize an ethnography. The important thing is to find a way to organize your results so that your audience will be able to understand your analysis. In some ethnographies, the researcher is just an observer of the community, in some he or she participates to a limited degree, and in some he or she is a full participant. You'll need to decide to what extent you'll participate in the community, perhaps as a full or partial participant or as only an observer. Even if you just observe the discourse community, the expectations of the genre of the ethnography are that the researcher collects data from a variety of sources, such as documents, interviews, surveys, and repeated observation.

Evaluation Criteria

The depth of your research will be an important part of the way readers will evaluate the quality of your results. Readers will expect your observations to be repeated and systematic, and to persuade them of the value of your findings, you'll need to use evidence from a variety of research methods. The way you report the results of your research will also be important. You should present plenty of evidence of the ways the discourse community communicates and an in-depth and organized analysis of that evidence. Your final draft should be clear and free of errors – your audience won't trust your research and analysis if you don't carefully edit in order to communicate clearly to your readers.

References

Adbusters (2009a). Obsession Men. Retrieved on 1 March 2010 from https://www.adbusters.org/gallery/spoofads/fashion.

Adbusters (2009b). Obsession Women. Retrieved on 1 March 2010 from http://adbusters.org/spoofads/fashion/obsession-w/.

American Association of Colleges and Universities (2007) *College Learning for the New Global Century*. Washington, DC: American Association of Colleges and Universities.

Anzaldúa, Gloria (1987) How to tame a wild tongue. *Borderlands/La Frontera: The New Mestiza*. San Francisco: Spinsters/Aunt Lute.

Aristotle (2004) *Rhetoric* (trans. W. Rhys Roberts). Retrieved on 1 March 2010 from http://www.public.iastate.edu/~honeyl/Rhetoric/index.html.

Bacon, Francis (1620) *Novum Organum*. Retrieved on 1 March 2010 from www.books.google.com.

Bartholomae, David (1995) Writing with teachers: A conversation with Peter Elbow. *College Composition and Communication* 46(1): 6–71.

Bauman, Amy (March 2007) What is college-level writing? Moving the conversation forward. *The NCTE Council Chronicle* 16(3): 1–8.

Baure, Jennifer (2003–2004) An assessment of HIV research in the last three years. *Prized Writing*, 31–36.

Bean, John (2001) *Engaging Ideas: The Professor's Guide to Integrating Writing, Critical Thinking, and Active Learning in the Classroom*. San Francisco: Jossey-Bass.

Bernstein, Mashey, and Yatchisin, George (2001) *Writing for the Visual Arts*. Upper Saddle River: Prentice Hall.

Bizzell, Patricia (1992) *Academic Discourse and Critical Consciousness*. Pittsburgh: University of Pittsburgh Press.

Boggs, Joseph, and Petrie, Dennis (1999) *The Art of Watching Films*. Mountain View: Mayfield.

Booth, Wayne C. (2004) *The Rhetoric of Rhetoric: The Quest for Effective Communication*. Malden: Blackwell Books.

Boyer, Ernest (2003) Two essential goals. In Virginia N. Gordon and Thomas L. Minnick (eds.) *Foundations: A Reader for New College Students* 30–32. New York: Thomson.

Brandeis University (2010) Brandeis University Writing Rubric. Retrieved on 1 March 2010 from http://www.brandeis.edu/.

Brooke, Robert, Mirtz, Ruth, and Evans, Rick (1994) *Small Groups in Writing Workshops*. Urbana, Illinois: National Council of Teachers of English.

Budden, Herb, Nicolini, Mary B., Fox, Stephen, and Greene, Stuart (2002) What we talk about when we talk about college writing. In Thomas Thompson (ed.) *Teaching Writing in High School and College: Conversations and Collaborations* 73–93. Urbana, Illinois: NCTE.

Burke, Kenneth (1969) *A Rhetoric of Motives*. Berkeley: University of California Press.

California State University, Sacramento Faculty Senate Reading and Writing Subcommittee (2010) University Writing Rubric. Retrieved on 1 March 2010 from http://www.csus.edu/wac/WAC/Teachers/index.html.

Caroll, Lee Ann (2002) *Rehearsing New Roles*. Carbondale: Southern Illinois University Press.

Chagnon, Napoleon (1968) *Yanomamö: The Fierce People*. New York: Holt, Rinehart and Winston.

Clotfelter, Charles T. (2006) *After Brown: The Rise and Retreat of School Desegregation.* Princeton, New Jersey: Princeton University Press.

Coe, Richard (2002) The new rhetoric of genre: Writing political briefs. In Ann M. Johns (ed.) *Genre in the Classroom: Multiple Perspectives* 197–210. Mahwah, New Jersey: Lawrence Erlbaum.

Colorado School of Mines Writing Center (2010) *Mission Statement*. Retrieved on 1 March 2010 from http://www.mines.edu/academic/lais/wc/mission2.htm.

Conference on College Composition and Communication (1974) CCCC statement on students' right to their own language: Explanation of adoption. *College Composition and Communication* 25(1): 1–18.

Cook, Devan (2006) What goes on in ENC1101. *Our Own Words: A Student's Guide to First-Year Writing*. Retrieved on 1 March 2010 from http://english3.fsu.edu/writing/book/view/31.

Cope, Bill, and Kalantzis, Mary (eds.) (2000) *Multiliteracies: Literacy Learning and the Design of Social Futures.* New York: Routledge.

Corrigan, Timothy (2004) *A Short Guide to Writing about Film*. New York: Pearson/Longman.

Council of Writing Program Administrators (2000) WPA outcomes statement for first-year composition. Retrieved on 1 March 2010 from http://www.wpacouncil.org/positions/outcomes.html.

Council of Writing Program Administrators (2003) *Defining and Avoiding Plagiarism: The WPA Statement on Best Practices*. Retrieved on 1 March 2010 from http://www.wpacouncil.org/node/9.

Cuba, Lee (2002) *A Short Guide to Writing about Social Science*. New York: Longman.

Curran, Marissa (April 2006) Is language a requirement for thought? *Ex Nihilo* 6: 99–100.

Davis, Robert, and Shadle, Mark (2000) Building a mystery: Alternative research writing and the academic art of seeking. *College Composition and Communication* 51(3): 417–446.

Desai, Avani (2006) Active ion transport across frog epithelium. In Judith Ferster (ed.) *Papers across the Curriculum*. Upper Saddle River, New Jersey: Pearson/Prentice Hall.

Devitt, Amy (1993) Generalizing about genre: New conceptions of an old concept. *College Composition and Communication* 44(4): 573–586.

Dickinson College Biology Department (2010) *Writing a Scientific Paper*. Retrieved on 1 March 2010 from http://alpha.dickinson.edu/departments/biol/BioWriting Guide/biogdline.html.

DiYanni, Robert (2004) *Writing about the Humanities*. New York: Pearson/Prentice Hall.

Douglas, William (2003) *Television Families: Is Something Wrong in Suburbia?* Mahwah, New Jersey: Lawrence Erlbaum Associates.

Dowell, Pat, and Fried, John (July 1995) Pulp friction: Two shots at Quentin Tarantino's Pulp Fiction. *Cineaste* 21(3): 4–5.

Driscoll, Dana (2002) The ubercool morphology of internet gamers: A linguistic analysis. *Undergraduate Research Journal for the Human Sciences* 1. Retrieved on 1 March 2010 from http://www.kon.org/urc/driscoll.html.

Dunn, Dana (2004) *A Short Guide to Writing about Psychology*. New York: Pearson.

Elbow, Peter (1976) *Writing without Teachers*. New York: Oxford University Press.

Emerson, Ralph Waldo (1841) Self-reliance. Retrieved on 1 March 2010 from http://www.youmeworks.com/selfreliance.html.

Fox, Tom (1999) *Defending Access: A Critique of Standards in Higher Education*. Portsmouth, New Hampshire: Heinemann: Boynton/Cook.

Freire, Paulo (1986) *Pedagogy of the Oppressed*. New York: Continuum.

Gates, Henry Luis, Jr. (1988) *The Signifying Monkey: A Theory of Afro-American Literary Criticism*. New York: Oxford University Press.

Gearhart, Sally Miller (1979) The womanization of rhetoric. *Women's Studies International Quarterly* 2: 195–201.

Genung, John F. (1899) *Outlines of Rhetoric*. Boston: Ginn and Company.

Georgia State University (2010) Georgia State University Writing Standards. Retrieved on 1 March 2010 from www2.gsu.edu/~wwwgea/Teaching_Resources /pdf/writing_standards.pdf.

Gittleman, John L. (ed.) (1989) Carnivore group living: Comparitive trends. In John L. Gittleman (ed.) *Carnivore Behavior, Ecology, and Evolution* 183–187. Ithaca, New York: Cornell University Press.

Gocsik, Karen (2004) *Writing in the Sciences*. Retrieved on 1 March 2010 from http://www.dartmouth.edu/~writing/materials/student/sciences/write.shtml.

Gocsik, Karen (2005) *Writing in the Social Sciences: General Advice for Non-Majors*. Retrieved on 1 March 2010 from http://www.dartmouth.edu/~writing/materials /student/soc_sciences/write.shtml.

Goldfield, David, Abbott, Carl, DeJohn Anderson, Virginia, Argersinger, JoAnn E., Argersinger, Peter H., Barney, William L., and Weir, Robert M. (2007) *The American Journey*. Englewood Cliffs, New Jersey: Prentice Hall.

Greif, Judith, Hewitt, Walter, and Armstrong, Myrna (1999) Tattooing and body piercing: Body art practices among college students. *Clinical Nursing Research* 8(4): 368–385.

Hamid, Sara (2010) Writing a research paper. *Purdue University Online Writing Lab*. Retrieved on 1 March 2010 from http://owl.english.purdue.edu/workshops /hypertext/ResearchW/.

Hansen, Kristine (2003) *Writing in the Social Sciences*. Boston: Pearson.

Hanson, Elizabeth (2004) *Animal Attractions: Nature on Display in American Zoos*. Princeton, New Jersey: Princeton University Press.

Harris, Joseph (1989) The idea of community in the study of writing. *College Composition and Communication* 40(1): 11–22.

Hawking, Stephen W. (1988) *A Brief History of Time: From the Big Bang to Black Holes*. Toronto: Bantam.

Hoffman, John, and Graham, Paul (2006) *Introduction to Political Theory*. New York: Pearson.

Humanities and Western Civilization Program (2010) *University of Kansas Humanities and Western Civilization Writing Guide*. Retrieved on 1 March 2010 from http://www.hwc.ku.edu/~hwc/pdf/HWCWritingGuide.pdf.

Information Systems and Technology Department, Weber State University (2010) *IST Flow Chart*. Retrieved on 1 March 2010 from http://www.weber.edu/SBE/Flow .html.

Johns, Ann M. (2002) Introduction: Genre in the classroom. In Ann M. Johns (ed.) *Genre in the Classroom: Multiple Perspectives* 3–16. Mahwah, New Jersey: Lawrence Erlbaum Associates.

Jones, Joyce E. (2005) College student's knowledge and use of credit. *AFCPE* 16(2): 9.

Kennedy, George (1991) *Aristotle on Rhetoric: A Theory of Civic Discourse*. New York: Oxford University Press.

Knisely, Karin (2005) *A Student Handbook for Writing in Biology*. Sunderland, Massachusetts: Sinauer.

Lareau, Annette (2003) *Unequal Childhoods: Class, Race, and Family Life*. Berkeley: University of California Press.

LeBlanc, Stephanie (2009) Blurred by our cultural lens: Issues with oral literature and the American school system. *Write On.* Retrieved on 1 March 2010 from http://www.jmu.edu/writeon/2009/winners2009.htm.

Leki, Ilona (1992) *Understanding ESL Writers: A Guide for Teachers* Portsmouth, New Hampshire: Boynton/Cook.

Linton, Patricia, Madigan, Robert, and Johnson, Susan (1994) Introducing students to disciplinary genres: The role of the general composition course. *Language and Learning across the Curriculum* 1(2): 63-78.

Marian College Department of English and Communication (2010) *Beyond Freshman Composition: Making Use of What you Learned in ENG 101.* Retrieved on 1 March 2010 from http://llc.marian.edu/writing_beyond.shtml.

McCarthy, Lucille (1987) A stranger in strange lands: A college student writing across the curriculum. *Research in the Teaching of English* 21(3): 233–262.

McCormick, Kathleen (1994) *The Culture of Reading and the Teaching of English.* Manchester, U.K.: Manchester University Press.

Meiklejohn, Kenneth, and Procter, Margaret (2009) *Writing about Physics (and Other Sciences).* Retrieved on 1 March 2010 from http://www.writing.utoronto.ca/advice /specific-types-of-writing/physics.

Melzer, Dan (2002) What to expect in ENC1102. In Florida State University First-Year Writing Program (ed.) *Our Own Words: A Student's Guide to First-Year Writing.* Retrieved on 1 March 2010 from http://english3.fsu.edu/writing/book /view/32.

Melzer, Dan (2009) Writing assignments across the curriculum: A national study of college writing. *College Composition and Communication* 61(2): 240-261.

Miles, Matt (Spring and Fall 2004) Personal appearance and implications of sexuality. *e-Vision* 5. Retrieved on 1 March 2010 from http://www.jmu.edu/evision /Current%20Issue/Volume%205/Miles%20essay.htm.

Moore, Allan (2003) *The Cambridge Companion to Blues and Gospel Music.* New York: Cambridge University Press.

Nathan, Rebekah (2005) *My Freshman Year: What a Professor Learned by Becoming a Student.* Ithaca, New York: Cornell University Press.

National Council of Teachers of English (2004) *NCTE Beliefs about the Teaching of Writing.* Retrieved on 1 March 2010 from http://www.ncte.org/positions/statements /writingbeliefs.

Nelson, Kimberly (2006) The great conversation (of the dining hall): One student's experience of college-level writing. In Patrick Sullivan and Howard Tinberg (eds.) *What is "College-Level" Writing?* 283–296. Urbana, Illinois: National Council of Teachers of English.

North Carolina State University (2004) The optimal foraging theory: Food selection in beavers based on tree species, size, and distance. Retrieved on 1 March 2010 from http://www.ncsu.edu/labwrite/res/labreport/res-sample-labrep1.html.

Northern Virginia Community College Writing Center (2008) *Homepage.* Retrieved on 1 March 2010 from http://www.mines.edu/academic/lais/wc/mission2.htm. <http://www.nvcc.edu/loudoun/english/writingcenter/.

Ohio State University First-Year Writing Program (2010) *Student's Guide to First-Year Writing*. Retrieved on 1 March 2010 from http://english.osu.edu/programs /firstyearwriting/resources/student/writers_companion/acquainted.cfm.

Oregon State University (2001) *Writing Guide for Chemistry*. Retrieved on 1 March 2010 from http://www.chemistry.oregonstate.edu/writing/WritingGuide2000 .htm#table%20of%20contents.

Oregon State University Department of Philosophy (1997) *Welcome to Writing Philosophy Papers: A Student's Guide*.

Oregon State University Department of Sociology (2010) *Writing within Sociology: A Guide for Undergraduates*. Retrieved on 1 March 2010 from oregonstate.edu/cla /sociology/pdf/socwritingguide1-7.pdf.

Outland, Katrina (2008) The blob that attacked Waikiki: The box jellyfish invasion of Hawaii. *The Journal of Young Investigators* 12. Retrieved on 1 March 2010 from http://www.jyi.org/features/ft.php?id=103.

Paxman, David, and Black, Dianna (2003) *Writing about the Arts and Humanities*. New York: Pearson.

Pechenik, Jan A. (2007) *A Short Guide to Writing about Biology*. New York: Longman.

Perl, Sondra (1979) The composing processes of unskilled college writers. *Research in the Teaching of English* 13(4): 317–335.

Porush, David (1995) *A Short Guide to Writing about Science*. New York: Longman.

Potter, Lisa (2007) Now with 50% less sugar: The transformation of television families from idyllic to realistic. *The Printers Devil*. Retrieved on 1 March 2010 from http://www.asu.edu/clas/english/writingprograms/printersdevil/PD2007.html.

Press, Andrea, and Strathman, Terry (1993) Work, family and social class in television images of women: Prime-time television and the construction of postfeminism. *Women and Language* 16(2): 7–15.

Pruetz, Jill D., and Bertolani, Paco (2007) Savanna chimpanzees, *pan troglodytes verus*, hunt with tools. *Current Biology* 17(5): 412–417.

Purdue University Department of Physics (2008) *The Importance and Purpose of Group Work in Physics 151*. Retrieved on 1 March 2010 from http://www.physics .purdue.edu/academic_programs/courses/phys152/groups.shtml.

Quinones, Layla (2009) *E-Portfolio*. Retrieved on 1 March 2010 from http://www.eportfolio.lagcc.cuny.edu/scholars/doc_fa09/eP_fa09/Layla.Quinones/ about.html.

Rich, Adrienne (1973) Diving into the wreck. *Diving into the Wreck: Poems 1971– 1972*. New York: W. W. Norton & Company.

Richardson, John (1991) *A Life of Picasso: The Early Years, 1881–1906*. New York: Random House.

Rose, Mike (1989) Remedial writing courses: A critique and a proposal. *College English* 45(2): 109–128.

Rubin, Alan (2006) *Disturbing the Solar System: Impacts, Close Encounters, and Coming Attractions.* Princeton, New Jersey: Princeton University Press.

Schilling, Jason (2006) *A Guide to Writing and Undergraduate Research Paper.* Retrieved on 1 March 2010 from http://www.csus.edu/wac/WAC/Students /research_guide.html.

Sleiman, Feras (2006) Review of *Dying to Win: The Strategic Logic of Suicide Terrorism. University of Michigan Journal of Political Science* 2(5): 127–130.

Smitherman, Geneva (1986) *Talkin and Testifyin: The Language of Black America.* Detroit, Michigan: Wayne State University Press.

Sommers, Nancy (1980) Revision strategies of student writers and experienced adult writers. *College Composition and Communication* 31(4): 381–384.

Sternglass, Marilyn (1997) *Time to Know Them: A Longitudinal Study of Writing and Learning at the College Level.* Mahwah, New Jersey: Lawrence Erlbaum.

Sullivan, Patrick (2006) An essential question: What is "college-level writing?" In Patrick Sullivan and Howard Tinberg (eds.) *What is "College-Level" Writing?* 1– 30. Urbana, Illinois: National Council of Teachers of English.

Swales, John (1990) *Genre Analysis: English in Academic and Research Settings.* Cambridge: Cambridge University Press.

Thaiss, Chris, and Myers Zawacki, Terry (2006) *Engaged Writers and Dynamic Disciplines: Research on the Academic Writing Life.* Portsmouth, New Hampshire: Boynton/Cook.

Tolman, Lydia (2004–2005) The rise of Starbucks. In Arizona State University Writing Programs (ed.) *The Printer's Devil 2004–2005.* Retrieved on 1 March 2010 from http://www.asu.edu/clas/english/writingprograms/printersdevil/PD2004- 5.html.

United States Bureau of Justice Statistics (2007) Adult correctional populations, 1980– 2007. Retrieved on 1 March 2010 from http://bjs.ojp.usdoj.gov/.

United States Census Bureau (2000) *Population by Age Group.* Retrieved on 1 March 2010 from http://www.census.gov/.

United States Department of Health and Human Services (2001) *Percentage of High School Students who Reported Sexual Risk Behaviors.* Retrieved on 1 March 2010 from http://www.hhs.gov/.

University of Iowa Writing Center (2009) *A Guide to Writing about Art.* Retrieved on 1 March 2010 from http://www.uiowa.edu/~writingc/writers/handouts/Writing AboutArt.shtml.

University of Miami Writing Center (2010) *Mission Statement.* Retrieved on 1 March 2010 from http://www.as.miami.edu/writingcenter/mission.

University of North Carolina Writing Center (2007) *Sociology.* Retrieved on 1 March 2010 from http://www.unc.edu/depts/wcweb/handouts/sociology.html.

University of Texas Division of Rhetoric and Writing (2010) Skills and strategies. *Student Guide to First-Year Writing*. Retrieved on 1 March 2010 from http://www.utexas.edu/cola/progs/rhetoric/rhe306/student_guide/chapter_7/6/.

Waldo, Mark (2003) *Demythologizing Language Difference in the Academy: Establishing Discipline-Based Writing Programs*. Mahwah, New Jersey: Lawrence Erlbaum.

Walvoord, Barbara (1990) *Helping Students Write Well: A Guide for Teachers in all Disciplines*. New York: Modern Language Association.

Ward, Martha (1996) *A World Full of Women*. Boston: Allyn and Bacon.

Whitesel, Cynthia (2010) *Online Guide to Writing and Research*, University of Maryland University College. Retrieved on 1 March 2010 from http://www.umuc.edu/prog/ugp/ewp_writingcenter/writinggde/chapter1/chapter1-01.shtml.

Wilhoit, Stephen (2002) *The Allyn and Bacon Teaching Assistant's Handbook.* New York: Longman.

Williams, Joseph M., and McEnerney, Lawrence (2008) *Writing in College: A Short Guide to College Writing*, University of Chicago Writing Program. Retrieved on 1 March 2010 from http://writing-program.uchicago.edu/resources/collegewriting/high_school_v_college.htm#_Toc431538571.

Winchell, David (2006) Review: *The Revolution Will Not Be Televised. Res: A Journal of Undergraduate Research and Writing* 3(1): 80–81.

Writing Lab at Purdue (2010) *The Purdue Online Writing Lab.* Retrieved on 1 March 2010 from http://owl.english.purdue.edu/.

Wynn, Tess (2001) *Proposal to Study the Effects of Woody and Herbacious Vegetation on Streambank Erosion*. Retrieved on 1 March 2010 from www.writing.engr.psu.edu/courses/presentations/poster3.pdf.

Yale University (2001) *Writing Prose*. New Haven, Connecticut.

Zinn, Howard (1999) *A People's History of the United States*. New York: HarperCollins.

Author Index

American Association of Colleges and
    Universities 216
Anzaldúa, Gloria 102–103
Aristotle 57

Bartholomae, David 270
Baure, Jennifer 82–83
Bean, John 186
Bernstein, Mashey 458–459
Bizzell, Patricia 271
Black, Diana 434
Boggs, Joseph 457–458
Booth, Wayne 57
Bratt, Melissa 34–53, 91–92
Brooke, Robert 140
Burke, Kenneth 57

Cadenas, Alfredo 349–365
Carroll, Lee Ann 11, 22
Ceideburg, Laura 167
Chagnon, Napoleon 382–384
Coe, Richard 56
Colorado School of Mines Writing Center
    143
Conference on College Composition and
    Communication 93, 97
Cope, Bill 68
Corrigan, Timothy 458
Coston, Bethany 404–432
Council of Writing Program
    Administrators 32–33
Cuba, Lee 394
Curran, Marissa 443

Davis, Robert 217
Desani, Avani 324–325
Devitt, Amy 68
DiYanni, Robert 435

Douglas, William, 81–82
Dowell, Pat 88, 448–452
Driscoll, Dana 84–86, 296–306
Dunn, Dana 186

Emerson, Ralph Waldo 454–455

Fox, Steve 28
Fox, Tom 271
Freire, Paulo 290
Fried, John 88, 448–452

Gates, Henry Luis 100
Gearhart, Sally Miller 57–58
Genung, John 101
Gittleman, John 336–341
Gocsik, Karen 341, 368
Graham, Paul 374, 385–386
Grief, Judith 79–80

Hamid, Sarah 207
Hansen, Christine 147–148, 394
Harris, Joseph 93
Hawking, Stephen 323–324, 334–335
Hesse, Doug 22–23
Hoffman, John 374 385–386

Isako Wong, Sophia 186

Javier, Antonio 473–485
John, Ann 68
Jones, Joyce 373–374

Kalantzis, Mary 68
Kennedy, George 57
Knisely, Karin 317

Laulainen–Schein, Diana 168

LeBlanc, Stephanie 306–312, 463–465
Leki, Ilona 93
Linton, Patricia 435

McCarthy, Lucille 55
McCormick, Kathleen 168
McEnerney, Lawrence 24–26
Meiklejohn, Kenneth 341
Miles, Matt 61–68
Moore, Allen 441–442

Nathan, Rebekah 374–376
National Council of Teachers of English
    168
Nelson, Kimberly 11, 115
Northern Virginia Community College
    Writing Center 143

Oregon State University Department of
    Sociology 369
Outland, Katrina 292–296, 333–334

Paxman, David 434
Pechenik, Jan 334
Perl, Sondra 115
Petrie, Dennis 457–458
Porush, David 316
Potter, Lisa 90–91
Press, Andrea 86
Procter, Margaret 341
Purdue University Department of Physics
    148
Purdue University Online Writing Lab 155

Quinones, Layla 151

Richardson, John 442–443
Rose, Mike 22
Royer, Tina 12
Rubin, Allen 100

Schilling, Jason 208
Shadle, Mark 217
Sleiman, Feras 71–74
Smitherman, Geneva 102–103
Sommers, Nancy 118–119
Strathman, Terry 86
Sullivan, Patrick 16, 21
Swales, John 271

Tinberg, Howard 16, 22
Tolman, Lydia 209–213, 242

University of Iowa Writing Center 435
University of Kansas Humanities and
    Western Civilization Program 458
University of Miami Writing Center 142–
    143
University of Texas Division of Rhetoric
    and Writing 140

Waldo, Mark 98–99, 271
Walvoord, Barbara 270
Ward, Martha 99
Whitesel, Cynthia 23–24
Wilhoit, Stephen 56
Williams, Joseph 24–26
Winchell, David 74–75, 89
Wynn, Tess 152

Zawacki, Terry Meyers 278
Zinn, Howard 171–173

Subject Index

academic reading
    connections to writing 179–181
    features of 174–176
    processes for 182–196
    purposes for 197–201
    visuals in 202–205
academic researching
    conducting interviews and surveys
    239
    evaluating sources 239–241
    expectations for 209–214
    integrating sources 249
    nature of 217–221
    processes for 221–228
academic writing
    common features of 17–18
    composing processes for 117–120
    definitions of 16–17, 21–23
arts and humanities
    citation style for 470–472
    reading in 453–458
    reference books and databases for
    467–470
    researching in 458–467
    student writing case study of 473–
    485
    student writing journals of 485
    writing samples of 306–312, 441–
    452

collaborative writing 147–149
contrastive rhetoric 93–104

disciplines 270–272
discourse community 271–272
document design 150–164

editing 133–136

first-year writing
    case study of 34–53
    definitions of 29–31
    outcomes statement for 32–33
    student writing journals of 53

general education 272–278
genre
    definitions of 68–75
    tips for writing in 76–77

invention 125–128

natural sciences
    citation style for 345–348
    reading in 323–341
    reference books and databases for
    344–345
    researching in 341–344
    student writing case study of 349–
    366
    student writing journals of 366
    writing samples of 292–296, 323–
    332

peer response 139–141
plagiarism 249–254

revision 128–132
rhetoric 57–58
rhetorical situation 58–61
rhetorical strategies 78–92

social sciences
    citation style for 402–404
    reading in 385–393
    reference books and databases for
    398–401

researching in 394–398
student writing case study of 405–432
student writing journals of 432
writing samples of 296–305, 372–384

timed writing 137–138

writing centers 142–145
writing groups 141–142
writing portfolios 145–147